Contemporary Leadership in Sport Organizations

Contemporary Leadership in Sport Organizations

David Scott, EdD
University of New Mexico

HUMAN KINETICS

Library of Congress Cataloging-in-Publication Data

Scott, David, 1956-
  Contemporary leadership in sport organizations / David Scott, EdD.
    pages cm
  Includes bibliographical references and index.
1. Sports administration. 2. Sports--Management. 3. Leadership. I. Title.
  GV713.S33 2014
  796.06'9--dc23

                    2013026763

ISBN-10: 0-7360-9642-6 (print)
ISBN-13: 978-0-7360-9642-3 (print)

The web addresses cited in this text were current as of September, 2013, unless otherwise noted.

Acquisitions Editor: Myles Schrag; **Developmental Editor:** Kevin Matz; **Assistant Editors:** Anne Rumery and Susan Huls; **Copyeditor:** Joyce Sexton; **Indexer:** Andrea Hepner; **Permissions Manager:** Dalene Reeder; **Graphic Designer:** Joe Buck; **Graphic Artist:** Denise Lowry; **Cover Designer:** Keith Blomberg; **Photograph (cover):** Corbis RF/age fotostock; **Art Manager:** Kelly Hendren; **Associate Art Manager:** Alan L. Wilborn; **Illustrations:** © Human Kinetics; **Printer:** Sheridan Books

Printed in the United States of America   10 9 8 7 6 5 4 3 2 1

The paper in this book is certified under a sustainable forestry program.

Human Kinetics
Website: www.HumanKinetics.com

United States: Human Kinetics, P.O. Box 5076, Champaign, IL 61825-5076
800-747-4457
e-mail: humank@hkusa.com

Canada: Human Kinetics, 475 Devonshire Road Unit 100, Windsor, ON N8Y 2L5
800-465-7301 (in Canada only)
e-mail: info@hkcanada.com

Europe: Human Kinetics, 107 Bradford Road, Stanningley, Leeds LS28 6AT, United Kingdom
+44 (0) 113 255 5665
e-mail: hk@hkeurope.com

Australia: Human Kinetics, 57A Price Avenue, Lower Mitcham, South Australia 5062
08 8372 0999
e-mail: info@hkaustralia.com

New Zealand: Human Kinetics, P.O. Box 80, Torrens Park, South Australia 5062
0800 222 062
e-mail: info@hknewzealand.com

E5214

This book is dedicated to the memory of my father,
Albert Clifton Scott (1931–2010),
an avid college football fan, sport enthusiast, Texas Aggie,
and truly authentic and inspiring leader.
You were a mentor, friend, and role model for professionalism,
responsibility, caring, and endless support.
You are deeply missed.

Contents

Preface

The world in which we live is experiencing profound and rapid change. Technological advancements in communications, science, engineering, medicine, and other industries are occurring at a pace beyond imagination. Societies in many parts of the world, as well as organizations and institutions, are becoming increasingly diverse; and significant movement toward globalization is evidenced by increasing compression and integration of economies, social and business interactions, cultures, and ideologies. In this environment, sport organizations at all levels face new and continuing challenges as well as complexities that require leaders to be astute problem solvers, to have exceptional ability to create and implement shared vision, to demonstrate emergent and responsive strategic thinking, and to be extraordinarily adaptable. In addition to all this, many believe that long-term organizational success is ultimately achieved through leadership that is also values oriented, authentic, and often team based.

Challenges and opportunities encountered by leaders within sport organizations are similar in many ways to those for organizations in other industries. However, there are also many aspects of sport organizations, depending on type and level, that present unique and different challenges. Similar to organizations in other industries, all sport organizations involve leading and communicating with people. All function, at some level, within a legal, economic, sociocultural, and political environment. Many also operate directly or indirectly in a global context. Moreover, like leaders in other industries, sport organization leaders around the globe are facing a rapidly changing and increasingly technological society. Most sport organizations now have a direct Internet presence and have employees or athletes who communicate with each other and the general public regularly through e-mails and social networking sites such as Facebook, MySpace, Twitter, LinkedIn, and Flickr.

In contrast to organizations in most other industries, many sport organizations operate within a high-profile and visible public environment with multiple constituents who are keenly interested in and often emotionally attached to the organization. In addition, competitive sport teams and athletes at all levels typically attract significant media attention, spanning from the local newspaper, radio, or television to the national media and major broadcast networks. These aspects of sport organizations create additional challenges for leaders; they must be prepared to deal effectively with issues creating news that can travel around the world almost instantly. Additionally, leaders of sport organizations assume responsibility for addressing challenges that include, but are not limited to, (a) maintaining financial solvency or economic viability in increasingly uncertain circumstances; (b) successfully leading change or being expected to produce significant organizational turnaround in a short time frame; (c) effectively navigating an increasingly litigious sport environment (especially in the United States); (d) addressing issues of diversity including racial and gender equity; (e) dealing with what many believe to be overcommercialization in sport, as well as athlete substance abuse and an overall decline in sportsmanship; and (f) navigating carefully through occurrences of ethical misconduct and occasional criminal behavior of employees or athletes. Throughout this book, many of these issues are illustrated through real and hypothetical examples that potentially affect leadership thought, strategy, and action.

Given this leadership context and the challenges for sport organizations, the purpose of this book is to provide a foundational and contextualized body of information regarding contemporary leadership thought and practice that will inform, assist, and hopefully inspire students and practitioners of sport management. It is important to note that while the majority of the book attempts to focus on the newest findings from research, as well as advice from practicing leaders and expert consultants across several industries, the text also provides foundational and historical information, particularly in chapter 1, that is still germane to leadership in today's world.

Contemporary Leadership for Sport Organizations is intended primarily for upper-level undergraduate as well as graduate students in sport management who are preparing for leadership roles in sport organizations. The book is also designed to be useful for those who are currently sport managers or administrators in sport-related organizations. It is important to note that the text includes numerous citations and references to academic research related to leadership from disciplines including business, sociology, and psychology. References to and summaries of many leadership studies from sport management are also included. This information is intended to be helpful for readers thinking of pursuing research or becoming faculty members interested in the academic study of leadership in sport. Also, specific examples and case studies, as well as "On the Sidelines" stories, "Your Thoughts" boxes, and questions at the end of chapters, are incorporated throughout the book to provide examples and stimulate discussions applicable to a broad range of sport leadership roles across youth, amateur, intercollegiate, professional, and commercial sport organizations.

Throughout, the book addresses question such as, What is meant by "effective" leadership in sport, and What are three "Rs" that relate to effectiveness? Are organizational outcomes such as winning, maximum attendance, and profits the primary indicators of good leadership? What are "competing values" for leaders of complex sport organizations? To what extent is ethical decision making a fundamental leadership responsibility, and what instances and

examples exist of both positive and negative leadership in this regard in sport? What role do leaders play in developing the core values and culture of sport organizations relative to their business practices, employee relationships, and product or service offerings? What are "emotionally intelligent" leaders, and how do they influence people and outcomes in sport organizations? How do leaders more effectively deal with turnaround situations in sport organizations, where expectations for short-term outcomes are typically high and the results are often immediately and publicly scrutinized by fans, boosters, and the media? What leadership behaviors and actions can be most effective in crisis situations that may be faced by sport organization leaders of today? What does it mean to "lead diversity" in a sport organization?

Chapter 1 provides broad introductory and foundational information. The intent is to (a) define and describe leadership, including levels of leadership analysis and both classic and contemporary leadership styles; (b) address how sport organization leaders typically assume both managerial and leadership roles and discuss how these roles both differ and are intertwined; and (c) review the historical foundation and evolution of business leadership theory from the academic literature and give examples of how these theories relate to sport situations and issues. Table summaries of the leadership research conducted over the past few decades specifically in sport management are included.

Chapter 2 is also a foundational chapter for the book, focusing on why and how sport leaders should balance what I believe to be three critical dimensions of leadership: *results, relationships,* and *responsibility,* referred to as the three "Rs" of leadership. This chapter recognizes that achieving success in only one or two of these dimensions leads to an imbalance that ultimately affects leadership outcomes and leader credibility. Certainly, producing results as measured by appropriate criteria relative to the type and level of sport organization is a critical element of leadership. However, equally important is the ability to build and maintain effective relationships as well as to demonstrate ethical, professional, and social responsibility. If performance in any one of these dimensions is inadequate, the foundation for effective leadership is unstable.

Chapters 3 through 9 address what are considered across much of the literature as key elements of contemporary leadership theory and practice. These chapters present historical and foundational leadership and management concepts considered seminal to the domain, but the majority of the information in these chapters concerns research findings, proposed models, and practical examples from sport occurring within the last decade. Chapters 3 and 4 focus primarily on internal elements of personal and organizational leadership, including the concept of emotional intelligence for individuals in leadership roles and the ability to understand, and build an effective organizational culture. Chapter 5 addresses common expectations and challenges for sport organization leaders, including creating a shared vision and understanding the roles and responsibilities of traditional strategic planning versus emergent strategic thinking and adaptation. Chapter 6 presents theories and contemporary thought for helping leaders navigate through and attempt to solve complex problems in organizations through individual, team-based, and "framing" approaches to problem solving.

Chapter 7 addresses three conceptually separate domains of leadership: change, turnaround, and crisis leadership. The section on change leadership applies the most recognized work in the business literature to sport organization leadership. Turnaround leadership is then addressed relative to how sport organization leaders can more effectively deal with situations in which expectations for dramatic and short-term positive outcomes are high and the results are often immediately and publicly scrutinized by fans, boosters, and the media. The last section of the chapter, on crisis leadership, focuses on how crisis situations such as real or potential health threats to employees and athletes, criminal or unethical activity, natural disasters, or terrorism may put a sport organization leader front and center in the public eye and how elements of various contemporary leadership theories and models can be used as tools in these situations.

Chapters 8 and 9 focus on critical areas in modern sport organizations that also require astute and insightful leadership to achieve optimal outcomes. The challenges and opportunities covered in chapter 8 include effectively leading diversity in sport organizations; this comprises understanding the differences between surface-level and deep-level diversity as well as valuing and creating a culture of diversity, developing proactive strategies for diversity management, and improving cultural competence both personally and across a sport organization. Chapter 9 focuses on understanding globalization in sport and its influence on leadership thought and behaviors, as well as the competencies that must be developed for effective global leadership.

Chapter 10 shifts to information intended to assist students in understanding more about the process of leadership learning and development. This chapter includes recent research and practical recommendations on individual self-directed leadership development, mentoring, experiential-based action learning, and new trends in leadership development through technology-based training media. The book concludes with chapter 11, which provides future considerations for leadership and an introduction to the concept of sport organizations as learning organizations. Several brief case studies representative of current and future challenges for sport leaders are included in chapter 11 to provide opportunity to apply many of the concepts presented throughout the book toward potential solutions to these issues.

As you will likely conclude from reading this book, leadership is not an exact science, nor is it purely art. From my perspective, after years of both studying and practicing leadership, it is a careful blend of both. It is also important, relative to the contents of this book, that you think in terms of not only what you know about leadership and its theoretical foundation, but most importantly what you can consistently *apply* or *do* that will determine your effectiveness as a leader now and in the future.

One of the objectives of this book is to help you think intensely and critically about your own leadership knowledge and development and to use this as a resource for dealing with the complex leadership challenges you may face in sport organizations. I also believe that many of the elements within this book are applicable to *anyone* working *at any level* within the sport industry. As suggested by Kouzes and Posner (2007, p. xv), "leadership is everyone's business and the first place to look is within yourself." There are many indications in the literature, as well as in my own organizational experience, that traditional thinking about leadership as emanating only from the top of the organizational hierarchy or primarily from highly charismatic individuals may be giving way to the idea that 21st-century organizations are different from those in the past and require new approaches to leadership. For example, it is increasingly evident in the literature that contemporary organizational leadership is likely to occur through both formal and informal collaborations, team-based problem solving, and the empowerment of individuals so as to maximize intellectual capital at all levels within an organization. If this is indeed the case in modern sport organizations, then the

eBook available at HumanKinetics.com

ability to learn and apply new paradigms of leadership will ultimately become critical to success. Hopefully, this book will move you in that direction.

Presentation Package

The presentation package for *Contemporary Leadership in Sport Organizations* includes over 200 PowerPoint slides of text and artwork from the book that instructors can use for class discussion and demonstration. The slides in the presentation package can be used directly in PowerPoint or printed for transparencies or handouts for distribution to students. Instructors can easily add, modify, and rearrange the order of the slides as well as search for images based on key words.

The presentation package is free to course adopters and available at www.HumanKinetics.com/ContemporaryLeadershipInSportOrganizations.

Acknowledgments

The publication of this book represents an incredible journey of learning, reflection, commitment, and challenge. The process also had its share of apprehension and frustration. Numerous individuals provided support and encouragement that helped bring this effort to a successful conclusion.

I offer my deepest gratitude to my wife, Karen, for the constant encouragement, patience, and support she provided during this project. Without your love, understanding, inspiration, and natural insights to leadership and relationship building, I could not have completed the task. Additionally, I thank you for the many hours you spent listening to ideas, providing input and suggestions, and organizing as well as producing the extensive reference list for the book.

I extend heartfelt appreciation to my immediate and extended family members who expressed interest, excitement, and encouragement along the way. Knowing that each of you was supporting me through the process was a blessing and a motivating force. I also acknowledge and thank a very special circle of neighbors and friends who regularly inquired about my progress. Your interest and support are deeply appreciated.

My colleague and friend Dr. Richard Howell deserves special thanks for helping me capture some of the time needed to complete the project and for providing constant encouragement. I also offer special acknowledgment to my colleagues in the sport administration program at the University of New Mexico. Graduate students Jalen Dominguez, Dan Ballou, and John Nachtegal spent time searching through the literature to provide reference material for several of the chapters.

Finally, although it is impossible for me to acknowledge the countless individuals who contributed to my leadership development over the course of my life and career, I would like to specifically recognize Dr. David Stotlar, leader, researcher, practitioner, and highly respected scholar in the field of sport management. Dave helped me find my way into an academic career in sport management and provided the initial motivation and foundation on which I have developed professionally.

A Leadership Primer

Part I of the book provides introductory and foundational information to leadership. The intent of chapter 1 is to (a) define and describe leadership, including levels of leadership analysis and both classic and contemporary leadership styles; (b) address how sport organization leaders typically assume both managerial and leadership roles and discuss how these roles both differ and are intertwined; and (c) review the historical foundation and evolution of business leadership theory from the academic literature and give examples of how these theories relate to sport situations and issues.

Chapter 2 is also a foundational chapter for the book, focusing on why and how sport leaders should balance what I believe to be three critical dimensions of leadership: *results, relationships,* and *responsibility,* referred to as the three "Rs" of leadership. This chapter recognizes that achieving success in only one or two of these dimensions leads to an imbalance that ultimately affects leadership outcomes and leader credibility. If performance in any one of these dimensions is inadequate, the foundation for effective leadership is unstable.

A Leadership Primer

Learning Objectives

After studying this chapter, participating in the game plan activity, and answering the questions at the end, you will be able to

1. define leadership and describe areas of responsibility for leaders,
2. discuss the concept of management and leadership as mutually exclusive or integrated,
3. explain the levels at which leadership occurs and is analyzed,
4. identify various leadership styles and evaluate these styles in yourself and others,
5. discuss the role of followership relative to leadership,
6. recognize key elements of "effective" leadership that have been historically supported by research,
7. analyze and discuss foundational leadership theories and apply them to current sport organization issues,
8. discuss the up-to-date findings and identify new opportunities for research in sport leadership, and
9. recognize contemporary areas of leadership study and practice.

Self-Assessment

1. From your experiences and observations at this point in your life or career, what do you consider to be absolutely essential to effective leadership?
2. Who and which experiences (positive or negative) have most influenced your thoughts about leadership and how you go about leading others?
3. What do you consider your current strengths and weaknesses as a leader?
4. What is your current knowledge of foundational leadership theories, and to what extent are you familiar with the leadership research in sport?
5. What are the contemporary areas of leadership study that interest you most?

The self-assessment is intended as a springboard for you to embark on your study of leadership for sport organizations. Each chapter in the book begins with a similar assessment related to the chapter topic. As you ponder the questions from a personal viewpoint, many of your ideas, experiences, and opinions about leadership will come to mind. Contemplate your answers to these questions specifically as they apply to your current role in a sport organization or to a role to which you aspire in the future. I recommend that you not only reflect on these questions yourself, but also discuss them with other students or colleagues and carefully consider the differences and similarities in your perspectives. When you reach the end of this chapter, you will be asked to repeat the self-assessment to determine what learning has occurred and what similar or different thoughts you may have as a result of studying the material in the chapter.

The first few sections of this chapter will assist your initial understanding of foundational leadership concepts, including the challenge of specifically defining leadership, the settings in which leadership occurs in sport, and the various levels on which leadership can be analyzed in organizations. You are then introduced to concepts of individual versus shared process in leadership, the importance of followership, and classic as well as contemporary leadership styles that are recognized in the literature. Key elements of effective leadership are then presented, with descriptions of each along with references to the supporting academic research.

The chapter then focuses on historical leadership theory and research to help readers understand the evolution of leadership theory over the last century. This section is designed to summarize the primary theoretical foundations of leadership and to help readers develop insights into how these theories may be used as tools and resources for evaluating and addressing current sport organization leadership issues. A summary of sport-related leadership research over the last few decades reviews studies related to three primary categories or domains: (1) leadership styles and behaviors of managers or administrators in noncoaching roles, (2) leadership in coaching, and (3)

leadership and its relationship with organizational culture in sport organizations. Opportunities and recommendations for expanding research in these areas are included, as well as discussion of the need to develop future sport leadership research aligned with the contemporary topics presented in this book. Chapter 1 concludes with an introduction to contemporary leadership thought and recognition of the various issues of modern leadership study and practice addressed throughout the book.

Defining Leadership

Without a full understanding of the multitude of contextual components of each leadership situation in sport organizations, it is difficult to arrive at a single definition that adequately meets all individual, organizational, and cultural perceptions of leadership. Researchers and authors from business, psychology, sociology, economics, the military, and other areas who have studied and practiced leadership for several decades confirm that a single universal definition of leadership is evasive. For example, Bernard Bass, one of the most influential leadership researchers of the last few decades, noted that "there are almost as many definitions of leadership as there are persons who have attempted to define the concept" (Bass, 1990, p. 11). More recently, Warren Bennis, regarded as a national leadership authority, advised that "we must remember that the subject [leadership] is vast, amorphous, slippery, and, above all, desperately important" (Bennis, 2007, p. 2).

Given these challenges in arriving at a universal definition, there are still many perspectives and interpretations of leadership that yield commonalities for a conceptual starting point in defining the term. Well-known leadership expert and author John Gardner defines leadership as "the process of persuasion or example by which an individual (or team) induces a group to pursue objectives held by the leader or shared by the leaders and their followers" (Gardner, 1990, p. 1). Also, many definitions of leadership in the literature recognize that leaders *influence* others. The ability of a leader to influence others may originate from many sources, including his personal charisma, knowledge, skills, experience, or positional role in an organization. Northouse (2010) defines leadership plainly as a "process whereby an individual influences a group of individuals to achieve a common goal" (p. 2). Northouse also suggests that "defining leadership as a *process* means that it is not a trait or characteristic that resides in the leader, but rather a transactional event that occurs between the leader and the followers" (p. 2).

Perhaps the most compelling international research to support defining leadership simply as the ability to influence others was the original GLOBE leadership research project, in which 54 researchers from 38 different countries reached consensus and defined leadership as "the ability of an individual to influence, motivate and enable others to contribute toward the effectiveness and success of the organizations of which they are members" (House, Javidan, and Dorfman, 2001, p. 494).

In sport, it is generally easy to recognize the influence that coaches, general managers, CEOs, owners, and so on have in their organizations. However, it is critically important to note that even if an individual is influential in a leadership role, there are a multitude of contextual factors that may prevent or minimize the leader's effectiveness in achieving desired or expected organizational outcomes.

Other common perspectives regarding responsibilities of leadership that go beyond the definition "ability to influence others" are also important and are presented here for consideration and deliberation (see the following sidebar). As you read through the statements, think about how these areas of responsibility and perspectives of leadership may apply in the sport organization where you currently work, compete, or desire to be employed in the future.

Settings for Leadership in Sport Organizations

Reflecting on the various settings or contexts in which organizations across all industries operate, Hackman (2010) recently suggested that understanding context, specifically as it influences leadership in organizations, can be very challenging. Using examples of leadership across a variety of organizations including a Boy Scout troop, a professional string quartet, and a senior corporate leadership team, Hackman questioned whether leadership can operate in the same way and "even *mean* the same thing across these contexts" (p. 111). When considering this relative to sport organizations, it is obvious that there are a plethora of settings and contexts for leadership within the sport industry. While it is important to remember that individuals at any level can demonstrate aspects of leadership, sport organizations offer a wide variety of formal leadership and managerial opportunities. Positions typically associated with leadership exist for owners, general managers, athletic directors, coaches, program directors, marketing or sales executives, and other personnel (event, facilities, and media communications) spanning numerous professional, amateur, and commercial settings as listed in table 1.1.

Responsibilities of Leadership

Ethical and Moral Responsibility

- Leaders must be morally and ethically responsible.
- Leaders exert influence in ways that move individuals toward attainment of mutually agreed upon and values-based goals.

Visioning, Aligning, Inspiring

- Leaders invoke a vision of the future and lead change in that direction.

- Leaders align people with a vision and inspire them to overcome obstacles in order to reach the desired future (Kotter, 1996).

Results, Purpose, and Meaning

- Leaders have the capacity to produce desired and quantifiable outcomes.
- Leaders infuse purpose and meaning into the lives of individuals and into the organizational experience (Podolny, Khurana, and Besharov, 2010).

Table 1.1 Examples of Organizational Settings for Leadership Opportunities in Sports

Competition sports	Recreational and health-based activities	Governance and administration	Commercial or corporate
Major professional sport teams	Intramural and recreational sports	Professional sport federations	Broadcast and media organizations
Intercollegiate athletics	Commercial and community fitness	National and International Olympic Committees	Sporting goods manufacturers
National and international sport federations	Amateur sport clubs	Sport commissions and league offices	Sporting goods retailers
Interscholastic athletics	N/A	High school activity associations	Research and development
Motor sports	N/A	N/A	N/A
Equine sports and rodeo	N/A	N/A	N/A
Action, adventure, and extreme sports	N/A	N/A	N/A
Disability sports	N/A	N/A	N/A
Youth sport leagues	N/A	N/A	N/A

Management and Leadership: Mutually Exclusive or Integrated?

It is often argued that management and leadership exist independently of each other. Some believe that individuals are cut out to be either a manager or a leader and will not be effective in the role for which they are not well suited. Many academicians, leadership consultants, and practitioners support the argument that leadership is something distinctly different from management. For example, Nienaber (2010) suggested that individuals at upper levels in the hierarchy are more involved in tasks relating to the survival and growth of an organization and are more likely to be perceived in leadership roles. On the other hand, individuals in the lower ranks of the organization are typically involved in tasks relating to operational issues, such as creating and maintaining an optimal working environment.

However, many scholars and practitioners now argue that, in reality, it is impossible to completely separate the two constructs and that an integrated or managerial–leadership approach is more aligned with the role requirements of managers in modern organizations (Kent, 2005; Mintzberg, 2009; Murray, 2010; Nienaber, 2010; Yukl, 2009). Supporting this argu-

ment, management expert Henry Mintzberg (2009), in his book *Managing*, straightforwardly questions the distinction often made between management and leadership. He suggests that while the two can be separated conceptually, they cannot easily be separated in practice and questions what the distinction really means in the everyday life of organizations. Certainly most, if not all, individuals working in sport management are hired into roles that require competencies in and applications of both management and leadership. According to Yukl and Lepsinger (2004), a common misconception is that leadership and management are two separate and mutually exclusive processes; however, they are complementary processes and can be performed by the same person.

Table 1.2 presents examples of descriptions and identifiers for what are often considered across the literature in multiple fields to be differences between management and leadership.

When reviewing table 1.2, it is important to recognize that people in higher-level managerial roles typically have characteristics and perform tasks that involve elements in all the boxes. As suggested by Murray (2010, p. 10), "The challenge for the modern manager—and the reason why being a modern manager has become such a challenge—is that you must do *all the above.*"

Many people in the sport industry illuminate why it is difficult to disaggregate management

Table 1.2 Management and Leadership as Behavior and Process

	Management	Leadership
Traits, behaviors, and perspectives	Task and process oriented, structured, efficiency minded, organized, commonsense, detail oriented, transactional	Inspirational, relationship oriented, visionary, risk taking, decisive, humble, courageous, unselfish, caring, constant, flexible, transformational
Tasks and processes	Planning, organizing, budgeting, staffing, supervising, coordinating, controlling, monitoring, delegating, negotiating, allocating, evaluating	Initiating change, motivating, coaching, teaching, influencing; envisioning goals, affirming values, serving as symbol

Based on information from Gardner 1990.

from leadership. For example, Rinus Michels, recognized by the FIFA (Fédération Internationale de Football Association) in 1999 as coach of the century, won the European Cup with teams from three different countries and was recognized both as a strong disciplinarian and as a master innovator of modern football (soccer). Lesa France Kennedy, CEO of the International Speedway Corporation, was named the Most Powerful Woman in Sports by *Forbes* magazine in 2009. Kennedy is often described as a visionary who is very influential and is also able to build the relationships needed to solve problems in the NASCAR organization. From the pages of history, Branch Rickey, former general manager of the Brooklyn Dodgers who signed Jackie Robinson to a contract in 1945, was credited with the vision and risk-taking actions that resulted in racial integration of African American athletes into major league sport in the United States. In addition are thousands of individuals throughout the world in executive, administrative, or coaching roles in sport whose work has resulted in outstanding personal and organizational achievement. In most if not all of these cases, it is a combination of experience, knowledge, skills, personality, and the optimization of situational factors associated with both management and leadership that has contributed to their personal effectiveness and the success of their organizations.

Levels of Analysis in Leadership

According to Yammarino, Dansereau, and Kennedy (2001), "although there are literally hundreds of definitions and thousands of empirical studies of leadership" (p. 153),

there are ultimately four perspectives through which leadership is examined—person, dyad, group, and collective. These levels of leadership interaction occur in all organizations; each is identified and described here:

- Person level: Leaders differ in their personal beliefs, styles, and practices. There are no universal standard approaches or formulas that guarantee success.
- Dyads (leader-member exchange) level: Each leader has a unique interpersonal relationship with each follower that results in an exchange whereby the leader provides support for the self-worth of the follower in return for satisfying levels of follower performance (Yammarino, et al., 2001).
- Group or team level: Involves the relationship between the leader and a specific group or set of followers in an organization. This level reflects the leader's capacity for flexibility, empowerment, and the extent to which innovation and creativity is fostered at the group or team level.
- Collective level: Characterized by leadership as it relates to the overall organizational vision, mission, and the extent to which decisions are centralized in an organization. Common problems at this level include lack of clear vision and strategic direction.

Additional Frameworks for Understanding Leadership

One should take into consideration several additional perspectives on leadership when beginning to study foundational components of leadership. The following subsections offer general insights into three areas of consideration relative to (a) leadership as an individual role or responsibility versus its practice as a shared responsibility among organizational members, (b) the relationship between leadership and followership, and (c) descriptions of leadership styles.

Individual Role Versus Shared Process

From a business perspective, Yukl (2009) pointed out that there are two, often conflicting perspectives about how leadership is viewed both in theory and in practice. First, Yukl recognizes that leadership is often considered a *specialized role* in which a person with primary responsibility in a group or organization is acknowledged as the "leader" and other members are considered "followers." For example, in sport organizations, we often think of leadership as emanating from one individual (e.g., the commissioner of a professional sport league, the athletic director, the head coach) or perhaps from a small core group of upper-level front office managers or top assistant coaches. Secondly, Yukl points out that leadership can also be viewed as a *shared influence process* in which the distinction between leaders and followers is less clear, and that many members of a social system may exhibit leadership and can be influential with others at various times. In sport organizations, we often think of this as occurring within athletic or work teams in which leadership may move back and forth among individuals based on their experience, expertise, or skill. It may also emerge among a group as the result of various situational factors.

Leadership and Followership

The relationship between leadership and followership has been a component of leadership study for many years and is acknowledged by numerous researchers (e.g., Burns, 1979; Hollander, 1992; Kellerman, 2008; Kouzes and Posner, 2007; Northouse, 2010; Rost, 1993). As stated by Kouzes and Posner (2007, p. 24), "leadership is a relationship between those who aspire to lead and those who choose to follow." As this statement suggests, *choosing to follow* means that an individual or group is not required or coerced to do so. Reinforcing this idea, Warren Bennis (2007, p. 3) stated that "leadership only exists with the consensus of followers."

Kouzes and Posner point out that in the leader–follower relationship, "fear and distrust will never, ever produce anything of lasting value" but that "a relationship characterized by mutual respect and confidence will overcome the greatest adversities and leave a legacy of significance" (p. 24). Kouzes and Posner's research of over 25 years included surveys of more than 75,000 people around the world about the seven qualities they looked for in a leader they would be willing to follow. A majority of the respondents identified the following four attributes: (1) honest, (2) forward-looking, (3) inspiring, and (4) competent. Fortunately, in sport organizations, many leaders at all levels have demonstrated and continue to demonstrate these attributes consistently throughout their careers.

Regarding the power of followers in the leader–follower relationship, there has recently been increasing evidence of the extent to which followers can affect leader behaviors and action. For example, Kellerman (2008) proposed the idea that followers are increasingly gaining power and influence and that those in leadership positions must acknowledge this or risk seeing their power positions questioned or revoked. The social pressure in Egypt that resulted in the resignation of President Hosni Mubarek in 2011 is direct evidence of the power of followership.

In sport, key strategic constituents or followers (e.g., players, fans, boosters) have the capacity to exert powerful influence on sport organization leaders. Thus, sport organization leaders must acknowledge the reality of dealing with small or large groups of followers who are united in a cause that may not be aligned with the leader's visions or goals. It is important for leaders to think carefully in advance about how to address such situations and prepare to act thoughtfully, consistently, and fairly in order to most effectively navigate these situations. Refer to "On the Sidelines" for an example of this issue in intercollegiate sport.

Leadership Styles

Candidates for a leadership position are commonly asked to describe their leadership style.

On the Sidelines

In 2011, at the University of California at Los Angeles (UCLA), the initial hiring of a defensive coordinator for the football program was rescinded the following day amid strong speculation that UCLA fans and boosters used social media such as blogs, wikis, Facebook, and Twitter to unleash a massive campaign against the hire, thereby putting pressure on the athletic department to change its decision. While this was likely not the only reason for officials to change their hiring decision, it points out how quickly and powerfully a contingent of followers can mobilize and put external pressure on leaders of sport organizations.

Based on information in Sports by Brooks (2011, February 8). UCLA Fan Sites Killed Defensive Coordinator Hire [Web log post]. Retrieved from www.sportsbybrooks.com/ucla-fan-sites-kill-asst-football-coach-hire-29478.

While they often give answers that point to their preferred approach using terms like "consultative," "friendly," "open-door," "engaging," "goal-oriented," and "take-charge," specific classic and contemporary typologies of leadership styles have been developed over the years. In their typology, Lewin, Lippitt, and White (1939) included what were regarded for many years, and still are by some even today, the three classic styles of leadership.

1. **Authoritarian:** Described as a "command and control" approach with a clear separation between leader and "subordinates." Leaders typically make decisions without group input.
2. **Participative:** Participation and involvement in decision making are encouraged. Considered empowering to team members but often less efficient than the authoritative approach.
3. **Laissez-faire:** Considered a delegative or "stand back and watch" approach. Little or no direction is actually provided by the individual in the leadership role.

While this typology remained the primary conceptualization of leadership style for many decades, Goleman (2000) more recently identified six contemporary leadership styles (see table 1.3). Goleman pointed out that the *best leaders are skilled at several of these styles* and are able to switch among them based on the style that is best suited for a particular situation. According to Goleman (2000, p. 11),

Table 1.3 Six Leadership Styles

Style	Description
Coercive	Demands immediate compliance from followers. Decisions are top-down and often undermine followers' motivation and sense of responsibility. Competencies of leader include drive to achieve, initiative, and self-control. Style should be used with caution but works best in turnaround situations or with problem employees. *Style in a phrase: "Do what I tell you."*
Authoritative	Mobilizes people toward a vision. Leader is a change catalyst and demonstrates competencies of both self-confidence and empathy. The style works best when a new vision or clear direction is needed. *Style in a phrase: "Come with me."*
Affiliative	Creates harmony and builds emotional bonds. Leader competencies include empathy, building relationships, and communication. Style works best to heal rifts in a team or to motivate people during stressful circumstances. *Style in a phrase: "People come first."*
Democratic	Forges consensus through participation. Leader competencies include collaboration, team leadership, and communication. Style works best when need is to build buy-in or to get input from employees or followers. *Style in a phrase: "What do you think?"*
Pacesetting	Sets high standards for performance. Leader competencies include conscientiousness, drive to achieve, and initiative. Style works best to get quick results from a highly motivated and competent team. *Style in a phrase: "Do as I do, now."*
Coaching	Develops people for the future. Leader competencies include developing others, empathy, and self-awareness. Style works best to help employees improve performance or develop long-term strengths. *Style in a phrase: "Try this."*

Adapted from Goleman 2000.

"Leaders who have mastered four or more—especially the authoritative, democratic, affiliative and coaching styles—have the best climate and business performance." Additionally, Goleman suggested that the ability to employ these styles and recognize the situations in which they best apply can be learned.

Foundational Elements of Effective Leadership

From the myriad of information sources on leadership available in bookstores and online, it is not easy to determine the elements of truly effective leadership as supported historically by research. However, there are several important research findings and principles in the leadership literature upon which one can begin to construct a foundation for effective leadership. Table 1.4 lists five components of effective leadership along with descriptions of each and the supporting research that has surfaced consistently throughout the general literature on leadership. Read each component and its description and think of instances from sport organization leadership when you have seen these elements in practice.

Historical Leadership Theory and Research

Now that the chapter has provided an introduction to the general concepts of leadership, the purpose of this section is to offer a relatively brief synopsis of the major historical and theoretical foundations of leadership. The rationale for reviewing these theories is twofold: (1) to provide opportunity for a deeper understanding of the study of leadership and how it has evolved over the last century and (2) to allow thoughtful consideration about how many of these theories can still be applied to sport organizations and used as resources and "tools" for addressing current leadership issues. Because of the extensive history of academic research in leadership over the last century, some theories have been excluded, and many are presented in summary tables. This is not because they are unimportant, but because the overall intent of the book is to address more contemporary

Table 1.4   Elements of Effective Leadership

Leadership component	Description	Support from literature
Ability to obtain trust and respect from followers	Associated with values or principle-centered leadership and requires integrity, ethical decision making, and producing results while demonstrating genuine concern for and commitment to the success of followers.	Bennis (1989, 2009), Bennis and Goldsmith (1997), Chatman & Kennedy (2010), Covey (2004, 2006), Rath and Conchie (2008)
Ability to develop shared vision, clarify path, and remove roadblocks	Individually and collectively envisioning future possibilities and aspirations, sharing ideas, and enlisting others in the vision; identifying initial strategies and pathways needed to move effectively toward the desired outcome.	Bennis (1989), House (1971), House and Podsakoff (1994), Kouzes and Posner (2007), Kotter (1996)
Ability to adapt to situations and contingencies	Idea that there is not one best way to lead an organization. Leader decision making and actions are contingent upon interaction of leadership style, characteristics of followers, and numerous other contextual factors. May involve adapting leadership style or behavior to meet the required or preferred leadership needs in the situation.	Chelladurai (1993, 1999), Fiedler (1967), Hersey and Blanchard (1984), Vroom and Yetton (1973), Vroom and Jago (2007)
Ability to motivate and inspire followers	Demonstrating positive emotions, enthusiasm, and optimism. Modeling inspirational behavior, showing individual consideration, and enhancing intrinsic motivation in followers.	Bass and Avolio (1990), Conger (1991), Kotter (1990), Kouzes and Posner (2007)
Ability to achieve results	Recognizing that organizational performance outcomes are essential to overall leader effectiveness. Effective leaders demonstrate positive attributes *and* achieve results.	Drucker (2006), Ulrich, Zenger, and Smallwood (1999)

leadership research and thought. Depending on your level of study or interest in any of the historical theories, you may want to explore the cited references in more detail.

Trait Theory

Think of a coach, a sport organization executive, or other sport administrator whom you consider a great leader. Now, identify the "traits" of the individual that in your opinion most contribute to the person's effectiveness. Did you think of descriptors like "dynamic," "intelligent," or "supportive"? Did you also consider descriptors like "decisive," "motivational," or "problem solver"?

The idea that leaders *inherently* possess certain physical, intellectual, or personality traits that distinguish them from nonleaders was the foundational belief of the trait-based approach to leadership. This approach dominated leadership research from the late 1800s until the mid-1940s and has experienced a resurgence of interest in the last couple of decades. Early trait theorists believed that some individuals are born with the traits that allow them to become great leaders. Thus, early research in this area often presented the widely stated argument that "leaders are born, not made." Also, some of the earliest leadership studies were grounded in what was referred to as the "great man" theory because researchers at the time focused on identifying traits of highly visible leaders in history who were typically male and associated with the aristocracy or political or military leadership. In more recent history, numerous authors (Kirkpatrick and Locke, 1991; Zaccaro, Kemp, and Bader, 2004; Northouse, 2010; Yukl, 2009) have acknowledged that there are many enduring qualities, whether innate or learned, that contribute to leadership potential. These traits include such things as *drive, self-confidence, cognitive ability, conscientiousness, determination, intelligence,* and *integrity.* Northouse (2010) pointed out that one strength of the trait approach is that it has identified desirable traits for leaders that can be used in self-analysis to help supervisors improve their own leadership effectiveness.

It is important to note that although trait theory identifies many of the qualities important to effective leadership, there are also notable criticisms of the trait approach. For example, Northouse (2010) identifies five specific criticisms that are important to consider relative to trait theory:

1. Studies on trait-based leadership over the past century have resulted in an almost endless list of leadership traits.

2. Trait theory does not take into account situational effects (Stogdill, 1948), and individuals with traits effective in one situation may not be effective in another.

3. There is considerable subjectivity in self-help and management books with regard to what are considered crucial leadership traits. Authors often use their subjective experiences as the basis for identifying the critical traits without any strong and reliable research as the foundation.

4. Trait-based research has focused primarily on the identification of traits but has not linked these traits directly with their outcomes relative to such things as productivity or employee satisfaction.

5. The trait approach is challenging for use in leadership training and development because it is difficult to teach or train new psychological traits in individuals.

On the Sidelines

Practical Use of Trait Theory in Sport

On a practical level, the trait approach to leadership can be useful in sport for helping teams and other sport-related organizations identify required or desired traits for a leader (e.g., team captain, coach, organizational administrator) and may be helpful in recruiting or determining those who possess these traits. Additionally, personality and psychological testing in various forms is used by sport psychologists as well as by the National Football League (NFL), National Hockey League (NHL), and National Basketball Association (NBA) in their selection of players for the draft. As pointed out by Northouse (2010), many organizations now use personality assessment instruments to predict how well individuals may fit within their organizations.

Skills Approach to Leadership

In 1955, Robert Katz authored the seminal article, "Skills of an Effective Administrator," in which he proposed that core managerial or leadership skills were not innate traits and characteristics but were rather the kinds of skills that administrators exhibit or "do" in performing their jobs. Katz identified three categories of skills that should be developed in order to improve administrative leadership: (a) technical, (b) human, and (c) conceptual. According to Katz, *technical skills* are those requiring specialized knowledge, analytical skill, and the ability to use methods, processes, procedures, and techniques of a specific discipline. *Human skills* are characterized by the ability to work cooperatively with group members, be aware and sensitive to the needs of others, and build a trusting environment. *Conceptual skills* are those that broadly reflect one's ability to work with ideas, create vision, recognize problems, and develop solutions.

Katz also pointed out that the level of importance of each set of skills was directly correlated with the administrative role or level of a person in the organization. For example, those at the top level of administration in organizations (e.g., CEOs) use more conceptual skills than those at lower levels of leadership (e.g., program managers) whose jobs require more technical skills. In Katz's typology, human skills are equally important across all levels of administration. Figure 1.1 shows Katz's perspective on the relative importance of the three types of skills at lower, middle, and upper management in an organization.

Behavioral Theory

Behavioral leadership theory originated primarily from studies conducted in the 1950s and 1960s at The Ohio State University and the University of Michigan. The Ohio State studies used a questionnaire known as the Leader Behavior Description Questionnaire (LBDQ) originally developed by Hemphill and Coons (1957) and shortened in a revised version by Stogdill (1963). The LBDQ was used in research across numerous organizational settings in different industries, as well as in the military, resulting in the findings that leader

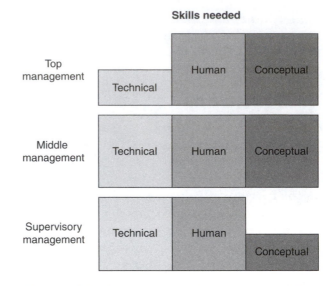

Figure 1.1 Katz's typology of administrative skill.

Republished with permission of Sage Publication, Inc., from *Leadership: Theory and practice*, 5th ed. P.G. Northouse, copyright 2010; permission conveyed through Copyright Clearance Center, Inc.

behavior tends to fall into the two categories of *initiating structure* and *consideration* (Stogdill, 1974). These two behavioral categories are often referred to as "task orientation" and "relationship orientation" (Bass, 1985). These orientations have also been referred to as "production or job centered" and "employee centered" (Blake and Mouton, 1985).

Two Dimensions of Behavioral Theory

- Initiating structure (task orientation)—job centered
    - Emphasizes structure and efficiency in the work environment
    - Ensures well-defined responsibilities
    - Focuses on formalized policy and procedure
    - Prioritizes goal attainment
- Consideration (relationship orientation)—employee centered
    - Demonstrates care and concern for employees
    - Promotes camaraderie
    - Develops and nurtures respect and trust
    - People and their well-being are of utmost importance

The Ohio State studies suggested that these two behavioral dimensions were independent of each other and that a leader could demonstrate behaviors high in one dimension and low in the other, high in both, or low in both. The Michigan studies, also done in the 1950s, initially suggested that structure and consideration were at opposite ends of a continuum; thus leaders who were more structure oriented must be less consideration oriented. A later conceptualization was that leaders could be oriented toward both dimensions at the same time and that the capacity to effectively combine the two is what is needed for effective leadership (Hersey and Blanchard, 1988, 2006; House, 1971).

In more recent research, a meta-analysis conducted by Judge, Piccolo, and Ilies (2004), looking at the relationship between consideration, initiating structure, and leadership outcomes, found that "consideration" was more strongly related to follower satisfaction, motivation, and leader effectiveness. "Initiating structure," on the other hand, was more strongly related to leader job performance and group–organization performance.

Contingency or Situational Leadership Theory

The fundamental premise of contingency and situational approaches to leadership is that certain leadership traits and behaviors are more effective than others *depending on* the circumstances and the context in which they occur. According to this theory, insightful leaders are those who can change or align their leadership behavior and actions to match the situation.

Following up on the behavioral research of the 1950s and 1960s, several researchers in the subsequent decades were instrumental in advancing knowledge and proposing additional questions about the contingent factors or situations that influence or are mediated by leader behaviors. Tables 1.5 through 1.7 outline the

Table 1.5 Fiedler's Contingency Theory

Theory	Foundational proposition	Essential elements and findings
Contingency model	Group performance depends on a proper match between a leader's style of interaction, the situation, and the degree to which the situation gives control and influence to the leader.	In this model: • Leader behaviors occur in two dimensions: *task oriented or relationship oriented.* • Leadership style is not easily changed, so some situations are very unfavorable to a leader with an incompatible style. Thus, improving leader effectiveness requires changing leadership to fit the situation or changing the situation to fit the leader. • A leader can be constrained or supported by his power (control and influence) in the situation.

Based on information from Fiedler 1967.

Table 1.6 Path–Goal Theory

Theory	Foundational proposition	Essential elements and findings
Path–goal theory	Leaders can positively affect performance, satisfaction, motivation, and effort of followers by clarifying paths toward goals, reducing obstacles, and effectively matching leadership style to both follower and environmental characteristics. Effective leaders engage in behaviors that complement the environments and abilities of those they lead in a way that compensates for deficiencies and fosters follower satisfaction and individual and work unit performance (House, 1996).	In this model: • There are four general types of leader behavior: • *Directive leadership* provides clear expectations and guidance and is effective when followers are less experienced. • *Supportive leadership* displays concern for people, enhances their psychological security, and is needed when tasks are highly stressful. • *Participative leadership* encourages followers to contribute to decision making. • *Achievement-oriented* leadership encourages excellence, seeks improvement in performance, and instills confidence in followers' abilities.

Based on information from Evans 1970; House 1971; House and Dessler 1974; House and Mitchell 1974; House 1996.

Table 1.7 Situational Leadership

Theory	Foundational proposition	Essential elements and findings
Situational leadership	Individualistic approach to leadership in which leaders adapt personal levels of task and relationship behavior depending on four levels of follower "readiness." The four levels of readiness are measures of the extent of job maturity (skills and ability) and psychological maturity (willingness and motivation) in followers. Levels of follower readiness: R1—Unable and unwilling or insecure R2—Unable but willing or confident R3—Able but unwilling or insecure R4—Able and willing and confident Leadership styles: HT/LR—High task, low relationship *(telling)* HT/HR—High task, high relationship *(selling)* LT / HR—Low task, high relationship *(participating)* LT/LR—Low task, low relationship *(delegating)*	In this model: • Followers who display R1 characteristics need leadership that is HT/LR (leader provides followers with clear instructions and direct supervision). • Followers who display R2 characteristics need leadership that is HT/HR (leader gradually reduces direct supervision and increases relationship behavior as followers improve skills or confidence). • Followers who display R3 characteristics need leadership that is LT/HR (leader includes the followers as participants, giving them more responsibility, and includes them in decision making). • Followers who display R4 characteristics need leadership that is LT/LR (leader delegates tasks to followers, giving them freedom in decision making and task completion).

Based on information from Hersey and Blanchard 1984; Hersey, Blanchard, and Johnson 2012.

foundational propositions, essential elements, and findings of influential research that established the historical foundation for contingency theory, path–goal theory, and the situational approach to leadership.

One of the more recent contingency theories is the "normative decision model" of Vroom (2003) and Vroom and Jago (2007). This model proposes eight situational contexts and contingencies in which leaders can determine the extent of follower participation (autocratic or democratic decision making) in an organization. The normative decision model is discussed in more detail in chapter 6 in connection with complexity and problem solving in organizations.

An additional contingency theory that should be mentioned in this section is the "multiple linkage model" proposed by Yukl (1981, 2009). The foundational proposition of this model is that the performance of work units is dependent on leadership's ability to identify key intervening variables and correct deficiencies in those variables. Situational variables may include such things as commitment of employees or followers, the ability and role clarification of followers, the level of cooperation and teamwork, the resources available to do the work, and the coordination of work with other parts of the organization.

This model can be especially useful to leaders of sport organizations attempting to analyze the various situational factors that may be preventing success and then developing strategies and actions needed to effectively address those factors.

With specific reference to situational leadership theory and research in sport organizations, Chelladurai (1990) proposed a multidimensional model of leadership effectiveness based on interactions that occur between a leader, members of a group, and situational variables. Chelladurai's model suggests that the effectiveness of a leader is based on a congruence between the leader's *actual* behavior and the behavior perceived to be *preferred* by group members as well as what is *required* relative to the situation. See figure 1.2.

Leader–Member Exchange Theory

Each of the historical leadership theories discussed up to this point focus on the characteristics or behaviors of leaders, those of followers, and contextual or situational factors that influence leader behavior. Another theory, which appeared in the mid-1970s but still has important implications today, is the leader–member exchange theory (LMX).

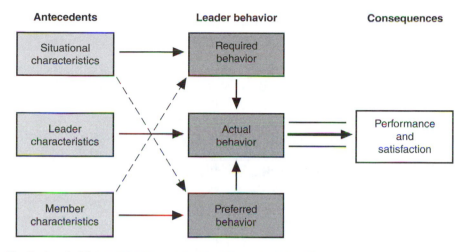

Figure 1.2 Chelladurai's Multidimensional Model of Sport Leadership.

Reprinted, by permission, from P. Chelladurai, 1990, "Leadership in sports: A review," *International Journal of Sport Psychology* 21(4): 328-354.

LMX theory was originally called vertical dyad linkage theory (VDL), in which the theoretical framework focused on the "dyadic" relationship that exists between leaders and individual followers (Dansereau, Graen, and Haga, 1975; Graen, 1976). As research on VDL and LMX theory progressed, it was established that two types of relationships or exchanges take place between leaders and followers:

1. Followers or subordinates who, based on their personalities, perceived competence, work habits, and willingness to take on new or more challenging job responsibilities, become part of an "in-group" in which they experience a high-quality relationship or exchange with the leader.

2. Followers or subordinates who do only what is required of them and do not interact well or involve themselves directly with the leader become part of an "out-group" in which they experience a low-quality relationship or exchange with the leader.

According to LMX theory, followers considered to be in the in-group receive more attention, more responsibility, and greater concern and support than those in the out-group. As research in LMX theory progressed further (Graen and Uhl-Bien, 1995; Liden, Wayne, and Stilwell, 1993; Harter and Evanecky, 2002), it was established that leader–member exchanges associated with high-quality in-group relationships resulted in feelings of mutual trust and respect in relation to the leader as well as more positive outcomes for the followers or subordinates. These outcomes include such things as greater job satisfaction and commitment, positive performance evaluations, and better work assignments. On the other hand, followers or subordinates in the out-group receive less attention and support, are left out of activities and important discussions, have lower negotiation capacity with the leader, and often perform the basic requirements of their job and nothing more. This, of course, can lead to less satisfaction and declining organizational commitment, and can result in higher turnover in these group members. Consequently, Graen and Uhl-Bien (1991) proposed that effective leaders should work to develop high-quality relationships with all followers or subordinates and attempt to make each follower feel like a valued and respected team member.

Charismatic Leadership Theory

The foundational theories for describing and studying charismatic leadership emanated from work by Max Weber (1968), House (1977), and Conger and Kanungo (1987, 1988). Weber originally described charisma as a certain quality of an individual that results in the person's being considered "extraordinary" or "superhuman" or as having "exceptional qualities and powers." According to Weber, these qualities were not found in ordinary people but were regarded as of "divine origin"; and on the basis of these qualities, the individual would be "treated as a leader."

In seminal work on charismatic leadership, House described charismatic leaders as highly self-confident and influential individuals who are often motivational and who elicit willing obedience and emotional attachment from followers. House proposed that charismatic leaders contributed to elevated goals for followers and a feeling that that they would be able to contribute to the overall mission of an organization. Later, House and Howell (1992) proposed that charismatic leaders fall into two categories:

1. Personalized charisma—conceited, nonegalitarian, and exploitive
2. Socialized charisma—collectively oriented, egalitarian, and nonexploitive

House and Howell maintained that modern complex organizations need socialized charismatic leaders who are supportive, sensitive, nurturing, and considerate. These characteristics are very distinguishable from those of personalized charismatic leaders who are power oriented, authoritarian, demanding, dominant, Machiavellian, and narcissistic. This is the side of charismatic leadership that can be negative, dangerous, and ultimately destructive to individuals, organizations, and even nations.

Conger and Kanungo considered charisma in terms of qualities attributed to a leader by her followers. In the "attribution theory" of charismatic leadership, the focus is on followers' perception of a leader's abilities to formulate a vision and to influence others in ways that stimulate them and enhance their belief in the leader. Conger and Kanungo proposed that charismatic leaders are willing to take on higher levels of risk, often use unconventional methods, and may be most recognized and trusted in organizational crisis situations.

According to an important perspective on charismatic leadership introduced by Howell and Avolio (1992), the term charisma is "value neutral." This suggests that the term does not distinguish between that which is ethically or morally good and that which is not. Consequently, according to these authors, charisma can lead people toward "heroic self-sacrifice in the service of a beneficial cause" or toward "blind fanaticism in the service of megalomaniacs and dangerous values" (p. 44). Howell and Avolio identify several distinguishing characteristics of ethical and unethical leadership as listed in table 1.8.

In sport organizations, charismatic leadership is often associated with coaches. For example, when the Pittsburgh Steelers hired Mike Tomlin as the head coach in 2007, he was the second-youngest head coach in the NFL, had not previously been a head coach, had not played in the NFL, and was chosen over at least a dozen other more experienced coaches (Proxmire, 2008). According to Proxmire,

Table 1.8 Ethical and Unethical Charismatic Leadership

Ethical charismatic leadership	Unethical charismatic leadership
Uses power to serve others	Uses power for personal gain or impact
Aligns vision with follower needs and aspirations	Promotes own personal values
Considers and learns from criticism	Censures critical or opposing views
Stimulates followers to think independently	Demands that own decisions be accepted without questioning
Provides open, two-way communication	Provides one-way communication
Coaches, develops, and supports followers	Is insensitive to follower needs
Shares recognition with others	Relies on convenient external moral standards to satisfy self-interests
Relies on internal moral standards to satisfy organizational and societal interests	

Adapted with permission of Academy of Management, *Academy of Management Executive*, "The ethics of charismatic leadership: submission or liberation?" J.M. Howell and B. J. Avolio, 1992, 6(2): 45, 1992; permissions conveyed through Copyright Clearance Center, Inc.

Tomlin was chosen because his "intelligence, presence and charisma convinced the Steelers front office that Mike Tomlin was the person best-suited to succeed Bill Cowher and Chuck Noll . . ." (p. 1). Tomlin went on to lead the Steelers to a Super Bowl victory in 2009.

Full Range Model of Leadership

One of the most influential of the foundational leadership theories is the Full Range Leadership Model (Avolio, 1999). This model developed from many years of foundational research related to transactional and transformational leadership (Burns, 1979; Avolio and Gibbons, 1988; Bass, 1985, 1990; Bass and Avolio, 1989, 1990; Tichy and DeVanna, 1986). The model in its current form consists of nine factors that include inspirational motivation, idealized influence (attributes), idealized influence (behaviors), intellectual stimulation, individualized consideration, contingent reward, active management-by-exception, passive management-by-exception, and the absence of leadership (referred to as laissez-faire). The first eight of these factors are described in the following sidebar.

A final form of leadership not included in figure 1.2 is *laissez-faire*, which has been mentioned previously as a leadership style and defined as the avoidance or absence of leadership (Avolio, 1999). As pointed out by Judge and Piccolo (2004), laissez-faire leaders hesitate to make or avoid making decisions and are often not available when needed.

The Full Range Leadership Model includes all the categories of leadership behavior just listed and recognizes them in two dimensions: (1) the extent to which the leader is passive or active and (2) the extent to which the leadership approach is ineffective or effective. Figure 1.3 illustrates the leader behaviors associated with the full range model and the progression of their effectiveness based on the extent to which the leader is active in using the behavior.

Elements of Transactional and Transformational Leadership

Transactional Leadership

Contingent Reward
- Provides tangible incentives for performance
- Makes clear what can be expected when goals are achieved
- Expresses satisfaction when expectations are met

Management by Exception (Active)
- Actively watches for deviations in or infractions of rules and regulations
- Focuses on mistakes and directing attention of followers to correcting these mistakes

Management by Exception (Passive)
- Waits for things to go wrong before acting
- No interference unless or until serious problems could occur without leader's intervention

Transformational Leadership

Idealized Attributes
- Demonstrates charisma, selflessness, confidence
- Considers moral and ethical consequences of decisions

Idealized Behaviors
- Focuses on sense of mission and organizational values
- Acts in alignment with values

Inspirational Motivation
- Is optimistic and enthusiastic
- Provides excitement and inspires followers

Intellectual Stimulation
- Seeks perspectives of followers
- Helps followers look at problems from new perspectives
- Provides environment for intellectual growth

Individual Consideration
- Treats followers as individuals
- Listens attentively to concerns
- Helps followers develop individual strengths

Based on information in Bass and Avolio 1994.

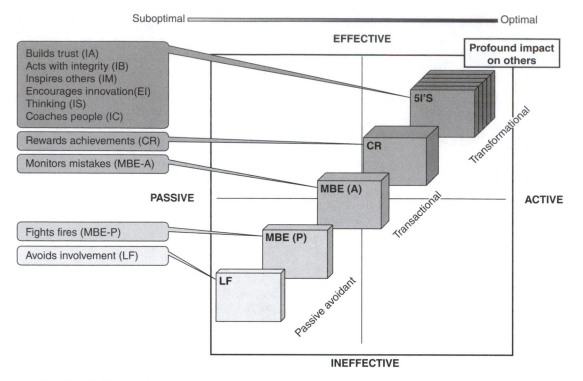

Figure 1.3 The Full Range Leadership Model. Note that the size of each box matters: Its volume represents the exhibited frequency of that style.

Adapted, by permission, from B.M. Bass and B.J. Avolio, 1994, *Improving organizational effectiveness through transformational leadership* (Thousand Oaks, CA: Sage).

In foundational work in this area, Burns (1978) suggested that transactional leadership is common across all types of organizations and involves a transaction whereby leaders exchange something of value (e.g., pay, recognition, praise, special consideration) with individual followers or a group based on their performance or compliance. Burns recognized that the exchange occurs in the absence of an enduring bond or relationship between the two entities. Regarding transformational leadership, Burns proposed that transformational leaders appeal to higher-order needs (e.g., fairness, justice, equality) of followers and seek to unite followers to work toward a common goal or purpose. Transformational leaders also encourage followers to transcend their own self-interest to focus on those of the group or organization.

Previous research in transactional and transformational leadership moving toward the Full Range Leadership Model was carried out by Avolio and Gibbons (1988), Bass (1985, 1990), and Bass and Avolio (1989, 1990). Bass

(1985) approached transformational leadership from the standpoint of how leaders interact with and transform their followers. He proposed that transformational leaders help followers become more aware of the importance and value of their tasks and can get individuals to transcend their own self-interest to focus on team or organizational goals. In order to measure transactional and transformational leadership characteristics, Bass and Avolio (1990) developed the Multifactor Leadership Questionnaire (MLQ), designed to help individuals understand how they perceive themselves as well as how others perceive them in the categories of leadership behavior included in figure 1.3. The MLQ is still widely used today in leadership research around the world as a valid and reliable measure of the full range of leadership approach.

As research progressed in this area, transformational leadership became extensively recognized as the approach necessary for organizational leaders to truly bring about sustainable organizational change. Bass (1985) found that individuals led by transformational leaders have higher aspirations, put forth greater effort, tend to perform beyond expectations, are more satisfied, and have less absence and turnover. Additionally, in a rapidly changing business, technological, political, or economic environment where organizations may be operating with a high degree of uncertainty, transformational leaders can help instill a sense of vision, assist in recognizing and establishing core values for their organizations, and provide support and encouragement to their followers. Also importantly to the model, Bass and Avolio (1993) put forth a fundamental argument that transformational leadership adds to the effect of, or augments, transactional leadership. Although this has not been tested extensively, Avolio (1999) argued that transactional leadership forms the basis for transformational leadership. According to Judge and Piccolo (2004), "without the foundation of transactional leadership, transformational effects may not be possible" (p. 756).

In leadership throughout many previous decades and in many industries, transactional leadership was often the only approach used to move people and organizations forward. However, in modern organizational leadership, research findings support that it is necessary for leaders to carefully consider applying both the transactional and transformational approaches described previously. According to Waldman, Bass, and Yammarino (1990), transformational leadership "augments" transactional leadership rather than replacing it, and elements of both are necessary for individual, group, and organizational leadership.

Foundational Research in Sport Leadership: What We Have Learned

Over the past few decades, sport research on leadership processes and outcomes related to the theories presented in the previous section has increased in the academic literature. Soucie, in a 1994 review of the research on leadership in sport up to that point in time, suggested that the primary focus of published empirical research was in the area of coaching leadership. According to Soucie, the majority of

research studies on managerial leadership in sport organizations, outside of coaching, were doctoral dissertations, with approximately 55 such studies completed between 1969 and 1989.

Since that time, much of the empirical leadership research in sport has included examination of leadership more broadly to cover administrators and executives of sport organizations. It is important to note, however, that the predominant context of sport leadership research in the last several years has been the intercollegiate athletic setting, with some research occurring in recreational settings and relatively few studies in professional sport and interscholastic sport.

The purpose of this section is to review and summarize findings from the foundational sport leadership research since the mid-1990s. Key findings, recommendations, and opportunities for continuing research in this area are included. While many studies in sport indirectly address leadership, the majority of existing empirical research that directly includes leadership as a primary variable is categorized into the following three domains:

1. Leadership style and behaviors (addresses leadership of those in managerial or administrative noncoaching roles)
2. Leadership and coaching (addresses leadership style and behaviors of athletic coaches)
3. Leadership and organizational culture (addresses influence of leadership on culture)

Leadership Style and Behaviors in Sport Organizations

Tables 1.9 and 1.10 summarize key empirical and conceptual research conducted over the last two decades on the leadership styles and behaviors of sport leaders and their influence on various follower or organizational outcomes. Each table also includes future research opportunities and ideas that may be helpful to graduate students (or undergraduates) wanting to conduct research on leadership style and behaviors. Leadership studies associated with trait, behavioral, and management theories

Case Study

Transformation and the Harlem Globetrotters

In 1992, the Harlem Globetrotters were heading down a path in which the product had lost much of its appeal and brand recognition. They were no longer perceived to be stylish or cool and weren't a priority for anyone. When Mannie Jackson took over the organization in August 1993, the Globetrotters had an annual attendance of less than 300,000 and were losing about $1 million on gross revenues of about $9 million. By 2001, the team had attendance of 2 million and had seen $6 million in profit on gross revenues of about $60 million.

To describe the transformation that took place, Jackson recounts that when he took over the organization, he found that people running the company did not respect the players or the product and were indifferent to the customers. In order to save the brand, he put into practice three operating principles that he had used over the course of many years of his work as senior vice president at Honeywell. First, the product would have to be reinvented to become relevant again; second, customers had to be shown that the organization really cared about them; and third, an accountable organization had to be created.

According to Jackson, when he first became interested in buying the organization, he thought that the team had perhaps run its course and made its contribution to the world, but he had a marketing plan that he thought would "make it cool to be identified with the team again." However, the bank owning the team initially rejected his offer and asked him to serve only as an advisor to the team so that it could get maximum value when it was sold.

Jackson met with the team in March 1992 with the intention of letting them know that the team would soon be folding, but as he got into the speech and looked into the eyes of some of the great players from the team's past, he began to tell a different story. He then began to change his vision and started talking about building a competitive team, becoming known for contributions to charity, being good to kids, and rebuilding the organization. According to Jackson, the team got excited and began believing in him. Jackson told the team that saving the Globetrotters had to be a religion, that they would be his disciples and he would be their leader. When he finished speaking, Jackson said that he knew the players were on board and that he became excited, too. His next action was to bring together 12 people he respected, including high-level marketing people from Honeywell, former Globetrotter players, and an arena owner, for a three- and a half-day summit. At this summit, the group started dreaming and asking themselves, What could the Globetrotters be?

What should they be? The group met from morning until midnight each day, and Jackson built a detailed strategic plan from those meetings. Jackson then went back to bankers who owned the team and convinced them to sell him a majority interest in the team.

According to Jackson, reinventing the product involved bringing together the best of the Globetrotters players to compete against first-rate teams all over the world. The Globetrotters played Purdue and then won and lost in a close game to Michigan State, the 2000 NCAA Division I champions. Jackson said, "Games like that make it impossible for people to say that our guys can't hold on their own against top-notch basketball teams" (p. 56). Jackson also indicated that the philosophy was simple. "In each game, we set out to do three things: we're going to show you we can play basketball, we're going to give you an exhibition of basketball feats you've never seen before, and we're going to make you laugh and feel good" (p. 56).

Jackson then went about the task of focusing on customers and building credibility with sponsors and the media. Jackson also found it necessary to make other changes within the organization itself. He indicated that he disrupted the status quo and created a new language around the business. Many of the organization's old-timers had to leave. They couldn't adapt.

As part of the change, Jackson started running the Globetrotters on the basis of a gross profit and break-even analysis. That became the language around the organization: What's the break-even on this event? The company was also divided into business units; staff champions were assigned, and profitability hurdles were set for each one.

Jackson points out that the success of the brand as a business came down to a fundamental point. He expected that people in the organization would sometimes get tired of him, even mad at him, but no one was ever allowed to get mad at the brand. They like what the brand is, and they can define it. Jackson stated, "The brand has taken on a life that's bigger than all of us."

1. What are various indications of transformational leadership seen in the Globetrotter organizational change under Mannie Jackson?

2. What do you think occurred in the original meeting with Jackson and the team that set the stage for the transformation?

3. How do you think the three guiding principles that Jackson used in this transformation could be used to assist in a transformation of your own organization or other sport organizations (at any level)?

Based on information in M. Jackson 2001.

Table 1.9 Key Research Related to Trait and Behavioral Theory in Sport

Theoretical context	Trait and behavioral theories
Leaders studied	Athletic directors, conference commissioners
Key research	*Branch (1990):* Examined NCAA Division I athletic director leader behavior in two dimensions: (1) initiating structure and (2) demonstrating consideration. Branch examined the relationship of these two dimensions to athletic directors' perceived organizational outcomes. *Quarterman (1998):* Assessed perceptions of NCAA Division I, II, and III conference commissioners with regard to demonstration of skills associated with management and those associated with leadership. *Quarterman, Allen, and Becker (2005):* Used the managerial role theory of Mintzberg to examine the importance of interpersonal, decisional, and political or negotiator roles among athletic directors in the National Association of Intercollegiate Athletics (NAIA).
Key findings	From this research, some of the key findings and potential areas for future study are indicated below: Based on findings by Branch (1990), NCAA Division I athletic directors (ADs) were more predisposed to task-oriented and goal-driven behaviors than to behaviors associated with consideration and the development of interpersonal relationships with their staff members. The nature of the roles and responsibilities of conference commissioners across all three levels of NCAA athletics requires that these individuals use skills associated with both management and leadership (Quarterman, 1998). While the interpersonal leadership role of ADs is important to all NAIA ADs, it is ranked higher by private institution ADs than public institution ADs. In public institutions, decisional and negotiator roles are ranked significantly higher (Quarterman, Allen, and Becker, 2005).
Research opportunities and ideas	While trait and behavioral theories of leadership may be considered dated, opportunities exist to better understand the extent to which elements of these older theories are still evident and perhaps useful for appreciating leadership style and its influence on followers and organizational outcomes in sport. These theories may also be useful for gaining insight into the responsibilities and possible role conflicts experienced by sport organization leaders relative to their perceived leadership roles. Significant opportunities exist to conduct future research like this in contexts outside of intercollegiate athletics.

have been combined in table 1.9, as the number of studies in these areas is smaller. Because of the larger volume of studies associated with transactional and transformational leadership theory, table 1.10 is devoted exclusively to this area of research in sport.

Leadership and Coaching

A great deal of leadership research in sport has been conducted in the area of leadership and coaching of athletes. Much of this work was pioneered by Chelladurai and Saleh beginning in the 1980s. Many of these early studies were devoted to the development of models and survey instruments designed to identify styles and approaches to leadership that resulted in various outcomes such as athlete satisfaction, team cohesion, and performance. Key empirical research studies in leadership and coaching, along with opportunities and ideas for future research in this area, are presented in table 1.11.

Leadership and Organizational Culture in Sport

There is considerable support from research both inside and outside of sport for the relationship between leadership and organizational culture. As suggested by Weese, MacLean, and Corlett (1993), successful leaders, including coaches, play a significant role in the development and maintenance of the culture within their teams and organizations. In sport research, this relationship has been studied primarily over the last two decades, with work on leadership and culture in recreational and fitness organizations as well as in intercollegiate and professional sport. See table 1.12 for key research and findings as well as continuing opportunities for research in this area of sport leadership.

Many additional opportunities exist for future research in sport relative to expanding

Table 1.10 Key Research Related to Transactional and Transformational Leadership

Theoretical context	Transactional and transformational theory
Leaders studied	Intercollegiate and interuniversity athletic directors, executive leaders, leaders of international sport organizations
Key research	**Slack and Hinings (1992):** Discussed the change process occurring in Canadian national sport organizations, including the role that transformational leaders play in creating vision and generating commitment to change. **Bourner and Weese (1995):** Explored the relationship between executive leadership in the Canadian Hockey League and organizational effectiveness using the Multifactor Leadership Questionnaire measuring transactional and transformational leadership. **Pruijn and Boucher (1995):** Studied the relationship of transactional and transformational leadership to organizational effectiveness in Dutch national sport organizations. **Doherty and Danylchuk (1996) and Doherty (1997):** Examined transactional and transformational leader behaviors of Canadian interuniversity athletic administrators and the impact of their behaviors on perceived leader effectiveness, commitment, and extra effort of head coaches within their departments. **Yusof (1998):** Examined the relationship between transactional or transformational leadership behavior of NCAA Division III athletic directors and the job satisfaction of their coaches. **London and Boucher (2000):** Explored the relationship between the four elements or factors of transformational leadership and the three types of transactional leadership and athletic program effectiveness in Canadian university athletics. **Kent and Chelladurai (2001):** Used a case study approach in a large university athletic department to examine transformational leadership and its impact on organizational commitment and citizenship behavior among organizational members. **Burton and Peachey (2009), Peachey and Burton (2012):** Studied whether transactional or transformational leadership style in Division III athletic administrators led to more positive perceptions of outcomes and whether male or female sex of the leader influenced the perception of those leaders.
Key findings	• Transformational leadership is considered a key factor in the organizational change process (Slack and Hinings, 1992). • Several of the studies in the area reported positive relationships between transformational leadership and organizational outcomes, including job satisfaction and extra effort (Burton and Peachey, 2009; Doherty and Danylchuk, 1996; Yusof, 1998); other studies did not provide general support that transformational leadership is significantly influential on outcomes (Bourner and Weese, 1995; Pruijn and Boucher, 1995). • Younger interuniversity athletic administrators and female administrators exhibit transformational leadership characteristics more often than older administrators and male administrators (Doherty, 1997). • Transformational leadership was found to have a greater effect on organizational commitment in one case study of a large university athletic department, while leader–member exchange was more influential on organizational citizenship (Kent and Chelladurai (2001).
Research opportunities and ideas	While transformational leadership has become generally accepted as an effective style of leadership for improving organizational outcomes, including employee or follower satisfaction, there still exist many opportunities for research in this area. One area of opportunity is research examining various contextual situations and the extent to which these situations influence or can be influenced by transformational leaders. This research could provide insights into how the four constructs of transformational leadership (idealized influence, inspiration, intellectual stimulation, and individualized consideration) collectively or individually might be applied to various contexts and problems in sport organizations.

Table 1.11 Key Research on Athletic Coaching and Leadership

Theoretical context	Coaching and leadership
Leaders studied	Athletic coaches at all levels including international teams
Key research	**Chelladurai and Saleh (1980):** Developed the Leadership Scale for Sports identifying five factors of coaching leadership behavior: training and instruction, democratic behavior, autocratic behavior, social support, and positive feedback. The scale was slightly revised by Zhang (1994). **Chelladurai (1984):** Examined relationships of the discrepancy between preferred and perceived leadership to athlete satisfaction among sports differentiated by task variability, task dependence, or both. **Pratt and Eitzen (1989):** Assessed the effects of coaching leadership style (authoritarianism, rigor, and intolerance for subordination) on the outcomes of winning in athletic teams. **Riemer and Chelladurai (1995):** Investigated differences in football team personnel with regard to preferred and perceived leadership along with satisfaction with leadership using a multidimensional model and the Leadership Scale for Sports. **Sullivan and Kent (2003):** Examined the relationship of coaching efficacy to leadership style in intercollegiate coaches in the United States. **Beam, Serwatka, and Wilson (2004):** Examined differences in athlete preferred leader behavior for coaches based on gender, competition level, task dependence, and task variability in samples of NCAA Division I and II athletic teams. **Aoyagi, Cox, and McGuire (2008):** Studied the construct of organizational citizenship in sport teams as it relates to leadership, team cohesion, and athlete satisfaction. **Rieke, Hammermeister, and Chase (2008):** Examined the relationships between servant leadership characteristics of coaches and their influence on mental skills, motivation, satisfaction, and performance of high school athletes **Heydarinejad and Adman (2010):** Studied the relationship between coaching leadership styles and team cohesion in the Iranian university football league. **Sullivan and coauthors (2012):** Examined the relationship of coaching context and level of coaching education to coaching efficacy and perceived leadership behaviors in youth sports.
Key findings	• In general, male athletes prefer more autocratic and directive coaches who also demonstrate social support, while female athletes tend to prefer coaches who demonstrate more situational consideration and training and instruction behaviors. Also, independent-sport athletes (e.g., track and field) tend to prefer coaches who are democratic, offer positive feedback, give situational consideration, and provide social support (Beam, Sewatka, and Wilson, 2004; Pratt and Eitzen, 1989). • High school basketball players in one region of the United States preferred servant leadership style to more traditional styles of coaching (Rieke, Hammermeister, and Chase (2008). • Leadership and team cohesion continue to be supported through research as primary contributors to team effectiveness (Aoyagi, Cox, and McGuire, 2008). • Coaching education is found to affect coaching efficacy, and coaching efficacy predicts perceived leadership behaviors of training and instruction, positive feedback, social support, and situational considerations in youth sport (Sullivan et al., 2012).
Research opportunities and ideas	The study of coaching and leadership continues to be addressed primarily in the domains of sport psychology and sport sociology. Little research to date has examined coaching leadership from a perspective of organizational and strategic factors including practice management, game strategy, turnaround process, crisis leadership, and other components of the leadership responsibilities of coaches. Also, research is needed in this area to examine the effects of various situational contexts and factors on leadership decisions and problem solving in coaching. For example, how does the diversity of team members influence coaching leadership based on differences among team members or differences between team members and coach (e.g., racial, cultural, gender)?

Table 1.12 Key Research on Leadership and Sport Organizational Culture

Theoretical context	Leadership and organizational culture
Leaders studied	Recreation and fitness program directors, intercollegiate athletic directors, professional sport owners and general managers
Key research	**Weese (1995, 1996), Wallace and Weese (1995):** Examined relationships in transformational leadership, organizational culture, and measures of organizational effectiveness among campus recreation directors and YMCA directors in Canada. **Scott (1999):** Examined leadership behaviors of intercollegiate athletic directors in top-performing athletic departments relative to their influence on organizational climate and culture in four frames (structural, human resource, political, and symbolic). **Kent and Weese (2000):** Analyzed differences in perceptions of organizational members within a provincial recreation center with regard to leadership, organizational culture, and organizational effectiveness. **MacIntosh and Doherty (2005):** Examined both leader intentions and employee perceptions of organizational culture, along with the existence of subcultures and the influence of subculture on staff member intent to leave the organization and on organizational performance. **Frontiera (2010):** Examined organizational culture change attributed to top leaders (owners or general managers) across selected teams in the NBA, MLB, and NFL.
Key findings	• Leaders of recreation programs who demonstrate high transformational leadership direct programs with stronger organizational cultures and demonstrate more customer-oriented cultures than leaders with low transformational leadership styles (Weese, 1995). Job satisfaction of employees was not found to be different between those led by high transformational leaders and low transformational leaders in YMCA organizations (Wallace and Weese, 1995). • Four frames that describe leadership and organizational climate (structural, human resource, political, and symbolic) were all found to be descriptive of athletic departments across NCAA Division I, II, and III and NAIA institutions. In several athletic departments, evidence of widely shared agreement among head coaches suggests that some athletic directors are strongly influencing the culture of these organizations in one or more of the four frames (Scott, 1999). • In Canadian Provincial Sport Organizations (PSOs), no relationships were found between either transformational or transactional leadership behaviors and the organizational effectiveness of effective PSOs and ineffective PSOs. However, organizational culture-building activities in these organizations were found to be significantly stronger among effective PSOs than ineffective PSOs, supporting beliefs that organizational culture is linked positively to organizational effectiveness (Kent and Weese, 2000). • Quantitative and qualitative study of a large private fitness corporation showed that a significant culture gap existed between the values espoused by leaders of the corporation and employee perceptions of those values. Additionally, subcultures were found to exist in the organization at the head office and club levels. Strong subcultures in the organization were associated with employee retention, and organizational culture was more directly influential on employees than on the performance of the organization (MacIntosh and Doherty, 2005). • In an analysis of culture change in professional sport, five common themes of leadership were identified as contributing to the change process. These themes included (a) identifying symptoms of a dysfunctional culture, (b) leaders' creation of a new "my way," (c) expectations for athletes and staff to "walk the talk," (d) embedding the new culture throughout the organization, and (e) a change in perspective that results in "our way" of doing things (Frontiera, 2010).
Research opportunities and ideas	While it has been established through research in sport management that leadership is a factor that influences the creation, management, and transmission of culture in an organization, there continue to be many opportunities for research in this area. As suggested by MacIntosh and Doherty, future research could try to uncover values that exist within an organization but were not "intended" by leaders. Addressing how these values come into existence in various sport contexts and how they are communicated and supported may provide new insights into the influence of subcultures or other means of culture transmission in an organization. Research could also be conducted in sport to examine the influence of an existing culture on new leaders coming into an organization and the extent to which it can be changed or appropriately managed.

on or refining the research questions outlined in the tables. Also, there is tremendous potential for expanding leadership research in sport relative to the contemporary theories and practices introduced in the following section and covered throughout the remainder of the book.

Contemporary Leadership Thought

Having presented a historical and foundational synopsis of leadership theories, models, and related sport research, the chapter now introduces the most current issues and thought relative to modern leadership theory and practice. Many of the areas mentioned in this section have also been identified as important in relation to the teaching of leadership in sport management (Weese and Beard, 2012). Each of the remaining chapters of the book includes elements and examples of this contemporary thought that can aid current and future sport organization leaders in being responsive and adaptive to a changing world.

The study of leadership today must align with a world experiencing rapid change; global interconnection; diversity in the workforce and ideas; and high-speed technological advancements in all areas of communication, science, and industrial development. Patrick Lencioni (2012) has recently proposed that effective leadership must be team based and points out that "leaders who choose to operate as a real team willingly accept the work and sacrifices that are necessary for any group that wants to reap the benefits of true teamwork" (p. 21). Lencioni asserts that building trust and cohesiveness is paramount to an effective leadership team. Using an important analogy, he argues that modern leadership teams must operate like basketball teams, with members who play together on the court and are mutually dependent and interactive. Lencioni (p. 77) additionally provides six critical questions that must be answered by organizational leadership teams. The answers to these questions must also be effectively communicated and consistently and repeatedly clarified throughout an organization. These are the questions:

- Why do we exist?
- How do we behave?
- What do we do?
- How will we succeed?
- What is most important right now?
- Who must do what?

These simple and straightforward questions serve as an excellent guide for current and prospective leaders of modern sport organizations in establishing clarity of purpose that can direct change and decision making into the future.

Lencioni also asserts that organizations today must be *both smart and healthy*. The "smart" side of the equation encompasses what Lencioni refers to as the decision sciences and includes the classical domains of strategy, marketing, finance, and technology. On the "healthy" side, Lencioni suggests that an organization is healthy when it is "whole" and embodies "minimal politics, minimal confusion, high morale, high productivity and low turnover" (p. 6). Several of the subsequent chapters in this textbook, beginning specifically with chapter 2, address elements of what I suggest can produce more healthy organizations in sport.

Another area of contemporary leadership involves the continuing study and practice of emotional intelligence and its role in effective leadership. As pointed out by Weese and Beard (2012), study in this area is expanding to include neuroscience and research measuring brain patterns *of* leaders and as a response of followers *to* leaders. This area, along with the primary research and recommendations for practice, is addressed in more detail in chapter 3.

Modern leadership thought is also shifting from traditional strategic planning to shared visioning, emergent strategic thinking, and organizational responsiveness. The rapidly changing environments in which organizations operate today make it difficult to develop the traditional deliberate and static strategic long-range plans with unchanging goals and strategies. Chapter 5 addresses this concept and the need for sport leaders to recognize and assume responsibility for guiding modern visioning and strategic thinking.

Modern organizations are also experiencing more complexity and need for adaptability and change. The need for this flexibility is created not only by the political, social, and economic environments in which organizations now operate, but also by the growing diversity of people and ideas within organizations as well as internationalization and globalization across many industries. Organizations also operate within a world with increasing potential for crisis ranging from financial collapse to terrorism and natural disaster. This environment requires leaders of contemporary sport organizations to develop and practice conceptual and problem-solving skills oriented toward modern solutions while maintaining effective relationships among strategic constituents and followers. These areas are addressed in more detail in chapters 6, 7, 8, and 9. Finally, and most importantly, leaders of modern sport organizations must demonstrate an effective balance among producing results; building relationships; inspiring people; and displaying consistent professional, ethical, and social responsibility. These areas form the foundation and focus of the next chapter.

Summary

This foundational chapter begins by presenting definitions, perspectives, and general responsibilities in relation to leadership. Examples of many of the broad categories and types of organizational settings in which sport leadership occurs are included, along with information on the four common levels of analysis in leadership (person, dyad, group or team, collective).

Recognition of leadership as both an individual and shared process, as well as the role of followership in the leader–follower relationship, is also discussed, with examples of how followers or strategic constituents in sport can exert powerful influence on leaders of sport organizations. A brief review of classic and modern leadership styles, along with foundational elements of what constitutes "effective" leadership as supported by leadership research, is included.

The chapter then focuses on the historical foundation of leadership theory by summarizing the evolutionary progress of leadership studies beginning with trait theory and progressing through the skills approach, behavioral theory, contingency or situational theory, the leader–member exchange model, charismatic leadership, and the full range model of transactional and transformational leadership. This summary of foundational theories is followed by a comprehensive review of the academic research on sport leadership that has been conducted in sport management since the early 1990s. Key findings of these studies are included, along with related research opportunities and ideas for sport leadership research in the future. The chapter concludes with an introduction to contemporary leadership thought and practice, which provides initial insights into the various areas of focus for the rest of the book.

Final Self-Assessment

Having read and reflected on the content of this chapter, now consider your responses to the self-assessment questions presented at the beginning of the chapter. Have your perspectives changed, or do you have any new insights or additional questions regarding your understanding of leadership?

1. From your experiences and observations at this point in your life or career, what do you consider to be absolutely essential to effective leadership?

2. Who and which experiences (positive or negative) have most influenced your thoughts about leadership and how you go about leading others?

3. What do you consider your current strengths and weaknesses as a leader?

4. What is your current knowledge of foundational leadership theories, and to what extent are you familiar with the leadership research in sport?

5. What are the contemporary areas of leadership study that interest you most?

Game Plan Activity

With a partner or in a small group, analyze and evaluate the historical theories of leadership presented in chapter 1. Using in-class or online discussion or both, come up with an example of how each theory applies in a sport organization context. Discuss with your partner or group the connections you find between theory and practice in this example. After completing this activity, choose a current sport organization issue from any of the sport media (e.g., daily newspaper, television news or sports broadcast, online sports media) and create ideas for how one or more of the theories presented in this chapter might be the basis for an intervention or solution.

Questions to Consider

1. Are there additional ways in which you think leadership can be defined beyond what is presented in this chapter?

2. Given the information in table 1.4 on elements of truly effective leadership as supported by research, what examples or experiences can you identify that demonstrate how these elements were used in a sport organization? Whom do you consider the most effective leader you have interacted with personally? How has this individual influenced your thoughts and behaviors?

3. What is your perspective on the role and responsibility of followers in a leader–follower relationship?

4. What leadership theories presented in this chapter do you think may be most applicable to the sport organization to which you currently belong or that you aspire to be part of in the future?

5. Review the studies of leadership that have been conducted over the last few decades in sport. What areas interest you most? What additional or new research questions do you have that you might like to explore in a research study?

6. What specific issues or problems should sport organization leaders be prepared to address in today's rapidly changing, complex, diverse, and competitive society?

Recommended Readings

Avolio, B. J. (2010). *Full range leadership development* (2nd ed.). Thousand Oaks, CA: Sage Publications.

Bennis, W. (2009). *On becoming a leader.* New York: Basic Books.

Hersey, P., Blanchard, K. H., & Johnson, D. E. (2012). *Management of organizational behavior* (10th ed.). Upper Saddle River, NJ: Prentice Hall.

Kouzes, J. M., and Posner, B. Z. (2007). *The leadership challenge* (4th ed.). San Francisco: Jossey-Bass.

2

Results, Relationships, and Responsibility

Learning Objectives

After reading and reflecting on the concepts and examples in this chapter, you will be able to

1. identify and explain what results oriented–leaders do,
2. explain how leaders foster effective interpersonal and group relationships and more effectively deal with interpersonal conflict,
3. define and describe professionalism and explain professional responsibility for a sport leader,
4. explain ethical leadership and its role in sport organizations, and
5. appraise your own personal philosophy and standards of professional responsibility.

Self-Assessment

1. What do you currently consider to be the most important accomplishment or outcome of leadership?
2. How do you now (or how would you in the future) go about effectively building relationships and managing interpersonal conflict in a sport organization?
3. What does professionalism mean to you in your role as a sport leader?
4. What do you consider the core values and ethical principles by which a sport organization should operate?

In the multifaceted role of a sport organization leader, you may at times find yourself overwhelmed with tasks and responsibilities far beyond what you expected to encounter. People you are leading will look to you for vision, strategic direction, personal guidance, assurance, solutions to complex problems, support, care, and individual attention—and the list goes on. Depending on the type and level of sport organization you are leading, you may have direct or indirect interactions on a regular basis with board members, superiors, employees, customers, athletes, media, fans, community groups, shareholders, volunteers, and other stakeholders. In all of this, you and the individuals and groups you are leading will be charged with such tasks as delivering products and services and generating outcomes that meet high, and in some cases even unrealistic, expectations. In most cases, you as the leader will ultimately be held accountable for the outcomes even if some variables are outside of your immediate control.

With the aim of assisting with your preparation for this leadership role, chapter 2 approaches the challenge of leading sport organizations by framing or categorizing it into three distinct but integrated dimensions: (1) results, (2) relationships, and (3) responsibilities. Too often in organizations, leaders are effective in one or two dimensions but not in all three. The argument in this chapter is that leaders of modern sport organizations must effectively address all of these dimensions. The chapter explores these three dimensions of leadership, provides examples, poses questions, and offers recommendations for how leaders of sport organizations can strive to balance these challenges as well as attempt to maximize performance in all three dimensions.

The chapter begins with the dimension of *results* and discusses the importance of results or positive outcomes to overall effective leadership. Results, of course, are relative to the type, level, and mission of a sport organization. However, the demand from key stakeholders for winning programs, state-of-the art facilities, or innovative and high-quality products and equipment is perhaps nowhere more prevalent than in the sport industry. Those in leadership roles in sport organizations must recognize and be prepared for a strong expectation among internal and external constituents that they will produce and be accountable for desired outcomes.

The chapter then explores the dimension of *relationships* as a cornerstone of leadership for sport organizations. As pointed out in chapter 1, leader–follower relationships occur at the dyad level (one-to-one level), the group or team level, and the collective organizational level. Developing trusting relationships with all stakeholders, communicating with difficult people, and communicating through challenging and even crisis situations are all critical to the role of a sport organization leader.

Finally, the chapter addresses the dimension of *responsibility* as the other cornerstone of leadership for sport organizations. While leaders of all organizations have a professional and ethical responsibility that is both required and expected of their roles, many sport organizations are under close scrutiny by local or national supporters and the media at all times. Scandals, occurrences of misconduct, unlawfulness, and unethical behavior can destroy the reputation and careers of athletes, coaches, and sport organization leaders. This section focuses on the role of professionalism and ethical leadership, as well as the responsibilities that sport leaders have to their stakeholders.

Results

Achieving results is a critical component of the three "Rs" of leadership addressed in this chapter. As an example of how negative results or outcomes can affect leadership in sport organizations, one can look to the enormous number of head coaching changes that occur across major college and professional sport teams each year. This turnover is an indication of the high demand for fielding not only competitive teams, but teams that compete directly for champion-

> *Leaders do much more than demonstrate attributes. Effective leaders get results.*
>
> Ulrich, Zenger, and Smallwood (1999, p. 1)

In management research, organizational "results" are often measured in two dimensions: (1) organizational performance and (2) organizational effectiveness. The following definitions were suggested by Richard and colleagues (2009, p. 722).

Organizational Performance...

encompasses three specific areas of firm outcomes: (a) financial performance (profits, return on assets, return on investment, etc.); (b) product market performance (sales, market share, etc.); and (c) shareholder return (total shareholder return, economic value added, etc.).

Organizational Effectiveness . . .

is broader and captures organizational performance plus the plethora of internal performance outcomes normally associated with more efficient or effective operations and other external measures that relate to considerations that are broader than those simply associated with economic valuation (either by shareholders, managers, or customers), such as corporate social responsibility.

ships or at least postseason play. Often it is not only the coaches, but also administrators, general managers, and owners who come under fire from external constituents for not meeting expectations of winning. In addition, leaders of sporting equipment, footwear, and athletic apparel companies are pressed with the challenges of delivering products that consistently meet customer expectations, increase sales, and boost shareholder value, all in an increasingly global marketplace. Failing to deliver desired results in these companies can also lead to dissatisfaction with leaders and often brings about changes in leadership at top, middle management, and supervisory levels of the organization.

Both of these constructs are considered important measures of organizational outcomes; and research across business, education, and sport management has generally shown that leadership, to varying degrees, is a factor that either directly or indirectly influ-

ences these outcomes. In alignment with these definitions, a high level of *organizational performance* in sport would be associated with tangible and directly comparable outcomes such as championships, overall winning percentage, financial profits, market share, and perceived or real return on investment for shareholders, sponsors, and boosters. From a perspective of financial results, the following professional sport franchises were listed by *Forbes* in 2010 as the top 10 most valuable sport franchises in the world (see sidebar).

An example of a results-based award in intercollegiate sport in the United States—one that acknowledges organizational performance in terms of winning championships across multiple sports—is the Learfield Sports Directors' Cup. Learfield Sports, in partnership with NACDA (National Association of Collegiate Directors of Athletics), uses a point system that awards points for championships won by both men's and women's sports in each NCAA and

Top 10 Most Valuable Sport Franchises

1. Manchester United Football Club, soccer ($1.83 billion)
2. Dallas Cowboys, football ($1.65 billion)
3. New York Yankees, baseball ($1.60 billion)
4. Washington Redskins, football ($1.55 billion)
5. New England Patriots, football ($1.36 billion)
6. Real Madrid Football Club, soccer ($1.32 billion)
7. New York Giants, football ($1.18 billion)
8. Arsenal Football Club, soccer ($1.18 billion)
9. New York Jets, football ($1.17 billion)
10. Houston Texans, football ($1.15 billion)

From Forbes.com, 2010, *The world's most valuable sports teams.*

NAIA athletic department across the nation. The institutions accumulating the most points in each division receive the award (Glosier, 2011). Stanford University recently won the Division I Directors' Cup for the 17th straight year since 1994.

The other measure of results as already defined, *organizational effectiveness*, goes beyond the purely outcome measures in the preceding examples and additionally includes such measures as job satisfaction of employees, athlete satisfaction, organizational citizenship, and organizational commitment. In addition, measures of an organization's social involvement and service to the community are often considered a part of overall organizational effectiveness. While these measures of effectiveness may contribute directly or indirectly to overall outcomes and are vital to the long-term success of an organization, they are often less well publicized and may even be considered secondary in importance by some external stakeholders. However, the dimensions of organizational effectiveness must be addressed by leaders of sport organizations and are covered in more detail in the later sections "Relationships" and "Responsibility."

A reality of competitive sport across the world, although argued by many to be a source of deviant behavior and cheating, is an expectation on the part of many stakeholders to win. Winning, rightly or wrongly, is considered the top measure of results; it attracts more interest from fans, sponsors, and the media and is typically related to increases in revenue from multiple sources and overall improved financial outcomes for a sport organization. As pointed out at the beginning of this section, failure to win a championship or to be extremely competitive within a relatively short time frame often generates dissatisfaction among key stakeholders that results in loss of support or a demand for changes in leadership. While this can and does, in some cases, drive a sport organization toward a "win-at-all costs" mentality, it is ultimately the role of leaders to enforce responsibility-based leadership (discussed later in this chapter) in order to effectively contain the often overpowering emphasis on winning as the only measure of performance.

While championships and financial performance are key factors in competitive sport organizations, a recreational sport organization is likely to consider measuring its results from a broader perspective. These organizations might view such measures as participation rates, customer satisfaction, and various objective or subjective measures of community outreach as primary indicators of performance.

Recommendations for Achieving Results

We know from years of research across several domains that leadership is only one of many variables that directly or indirectly contribute to the results an organization produces. It may be the primary contributor in some situations and contexts; in others, it is difficult to attribute the outcomes directly to the actions or inactions of those in leadership roles. However, as proposed by Ulrich, Zenger, and Smallwood (1999) in their book *Results-Based Leadership*, there are questions that leaders should address and recommendations for leaders to follow to increase the likelihood that they will have a direct influence on organizational performance and results. Ulrich and coauthors point out that executives tend to think of leadership only relative to the attributes of a good leader (communicates well, empowers others, has integrity, energy, and so on) but tend not to think of results or the importance of attributes and actions to results. These recommendations are included in this chapter as a starting point for sport administrators to consider carefully when focusing on the results component of the three Rs.

Ulrich and colleagues (1999) identify three questions that leaders should carefully consider when taking a results-based approach:

1. What results do you need to achieve? (This helps the leader identify expectations and zero in on strategies.)

2. On a scale of 1 to 100, how able are you to produce those results today? (This assists leaders in examining readiness and abilities to achieve the objectives.)

3. What must you learn and do to make these results happen? (This helps leaders recognize the character, knowledge, and behaviors they must pursue to achieve the desired results.)

The authors recommend that after answering these questions, leaders take the following actions:

- Begin with an absolute focus on results

- Take complete and personal responsibility for your group's results.

- Clearly and specifically communicate expectations and targets to the people in your group.

- Determine what you need to do personally to improve your results.

- Use results as the litmus test for continuing or implementing leadership practice.

- Engage in developmental activities and opportunities that will help you produce better results.

- Know and use every group member's capabilities to the fullest and provide everyone with appropriate developmental opportunities.

- Experiment and innovate in every realm under your influence, looking constantly for new ways to improve performance.

- Measure the right standards and increase the rigor with which you measure them.

- Constantly take action; results won't improve without it.

- Increase the pace or tempo of your group.

- Seek feedback from others in the organization about ways you and your group can improve your outcomes.

- Ensure that your subordinates and colleagues perceive that your motivation for being a leader is the achievement of positive results, not personal or political gain.

- Model the methods and strive for the results you want your group to use and attain.

Leadership is a relationship between those who aspire to lead and those who choose to follow. It's the quality of this relationship that matters most when we're engaged in getting extraordinary things done. A leader-constituent relationship that's characterized by fear and distrust will never, ever produce anything of lasting value. A relationship characterized by mutual respect and confidence will overcome the greatest adversities and leave a legacy of significance (Kouzes and Posner, 2007, p. 24).

Your Thoughts

Choose a sport organization that you are familiar with or aspire to be a part of in the future. Review each of Ulrich and colleagues' points and answer the following questions:

1. What would you choose as the five most critical of these points for achieving results?

2. Which do you think would be the most difficult of these recommendations to implement?

3. How, as a leader, would you go about putting these recommendations into practice?

Sport Research Related to Leadership and Results

In sport research, several studies have measured leadership and its relationship to various dimensions of organizational effectiveness (Kent and Chelladurai, 2001; Kent and Weese, 2000; London and Boucher, 2000; Prujin and Boucher, 1995; Snyder, 1990). However, very few studies, some of them doctoral dissertations, have focused specifically on the relationship between leadership and organizational performance as defined previously. In a relatively recent study, Smart and Wolfe (2003) examined the contribution of leadership and human resources to success in professional baseball and found that player resources (e.g., offense, defense, batting averages) contributed primarily to winning percentage while leadership contributed very minimally. According to the authors, a possible limitation of this research was that the leadership construct was limited to the manager; they recommended that future researchers examine the leadership role of assistant coaches, corporate leadership, or both. Considerably more research is needed in this area to establish the leadership and contextual factors that contribute specifically to performance outcomes.

Relationships

The relationship aspect of leadership is a critical cornerstone of the three elements of leadership. Leaders whose organization produces extraordinary results are still not likely to be effective in the long term unless they attend to the demand for high-quality and trusting relationships. The following sections address various dimensions and present recommendations regarding interpersonal relations, building trust, and dealing with difficult people.

Interpersonal Relations and Communication

Sport organization leaders interact with individuals on a daily basis. These interactions may occur internally as a part of formal work meetings, in individual consultations and employee evaluations, or in informal conversations. Also most, if not all, sport organization leaders must interact with numerous external stakeholders both in one-to-one situations and as a part of larger group events. In all instances, these interactions demand that leaders be highly cognizant of interpersonal relationship skills. In addition, to make things even more challenging, sport leaders are often communicating in the presence of news media personnel, in crisis situations, or immediately after glorious victories or agonizing defeats. In all of these cases, a leader's verbal statements as well as nonverbal communications have the potential to be read, viewed, or heard by any number of people from a small crowd to a worldwide audience. Additionally, situations can develop that have ethical, moral, or legal implications and involve the need for careful and thoughtful interpersonal communications. Consequently, knowledge, experience, and practice in developing relationships are critical for leaders in sport organizations.

Several leadership theories presented in chapter 1 can be applied to the relationship-building role of leaders. One application would be the need to focus on relationship-oriented behaviors and the transformational leadership element *individual consideration*, especially in situations in which followers have the skills needed to perform but lack confidence or experience. As examples, a sport management undergraduate student entering into a new event management internship, a new graduate just beginning a marketing and promotions role, or a young athlete making his first start in competition could all benefit from a leader who is supportive and communicative, who is a teacher, and who demonstrates true caring about the individual and the individual's needs. This idea is supported by Maak and Pless (2006), who argue that leaders assume the role of coaches in cases in which relationship skills are critical to facilitate development, enable learning, and support individuals and teams in achieving objectives.

Another example on a broader scale is in the area of youth and amateur sports, where participation (over performance) is often considered a source of positive individual and social growth, camaraderie, and team building. If managed carefully, this environment can provide excellent opportunities for relationship building and leadership development in participants. At the core of truly developmental and quality youth sport is the need for leaders of these programs to foster and facilitate consistent and effective relationships among participants, parents, coaches, and administrators.

One of the best (and still applicable) set of recommendations for improving interpersonal skills is in Dale Carnegie's classic book, *How to Win Friends and Influence People* (1936). A fundamental idea in this book is that one can improve relationships with others by simply helping people feel important and appreciated. The key points of Carnegie's recommendations are:

- don't criticize, condemn, or complain
- become genuinely interested in other people
- be a good listener
- give honest, sincere appreciation
- smile
- talk about the other person's interests
- make clear how your ideas benefit the other person

- remember a person's name
- sincerely make others feel important

Building Trust

The ability to generate and sustain trust is a critical factor in leading people (Bennis and Goldsmith, 2003). Rath and Conchie (2008), in their book *Strengths-Based Leadership*, noted the results of research in which more than 10,000 followers were asked about the most important things that leaders contributed to their lives. The four top answers were trust, compassion, stability, and hope. Following up on these four basic needs, Rath and Conchie suggested in a *Gallup Management Journal* interview (2009) that leaders must be aware of how their emotional reactions can affect followers. As Conchie stated, "Trust also speaks to behavioral predictability. It's hard to trust a volatile leader in times of change" (p. 1).

There are numerous examples each year of individuals in sport leadership roles who through certain behaviors and actions have lost the trust of followers and stakeholders. In many cases, the trust was undermined as the result of one incident, a bad decision, or a lapse of judgment. Often the loss of trust is the result of a leader's lack of professional, moral, or ethical behavior, which is addressed in more detail in the next section. What is known is that trust takes time and effort to build but can be completely destroyed or lost in a moment. Additionally, professional careers, job positions, and respect of peers, friends, and family are at stake. This point alone should be enough to make those in leadership roles think carefully about their actions.

Bennis and Goldsmith (2003) identify four "ingredients" for creating trust:

1. **Competence:** Followers must believe that leaders are capable of doing their jobs.
2. **Congruity:** Associated with integrity. What a leader says is congruent with what she does.
3. **Constancy:** Followers want leaders who are on their side, who will support and defend them.
4. **Caring:** A leader cares about the lives of followers and cares about the implications of actions and decisions that affect them.

Integrity Check-Up

Use the following checklist to quickly assess the extent of your personal and professional integrity.

Do you:

1. Tell the truth and not stretch, distort, or come in late with it?
2. Live up to your word?
3. Worry about being caught?
4. Worry about what your dad or mom or favorite mentor would think?

Would you:

1. Want your actions to be on the front page of your hometown newspaper?
2. Be pleased and proud if your children or athletes behaved the way you do?
3. Stick with your approach even if it was inconvenient?

Adapted from Benton 2003.

Dealing With Interpersonal Conflict

Conflict is inevitable when individuals, work groups, and teams interact with one another. Everyone has likely experienced situations in which disagreements and differences in goals or expectations among group members resulted in anxiety, anger, and even blatant hostility. Because interpersonal conflict is so common in organizations, the ability to effectively address and manage it is critical for those in leadership roles. Note that this section is not intended to address the macro level of organizational conflict that exists within sport organizations, such as conflicts that lead to professional league lockouts and arbitration.

The role of leadership in addressing complex and structural organizational issues is discussed in more detail in chapter 6. The focus here is on how leaders of sport organizations can more effectively address conflict that arises between individuals or small groups so as to lead to improved relationships.

An important point for sport leaders to remember is that conflict between or among individuals does not typically go away just by avoiding it. While occasional disagreements between employees, coaches, or athletes are sometimes resolved without intervention, in many cases deeper issues such as resentment and incompatible values or personalities do not disappear. The potential negative outcomes that arise from interpersonal conflict include disruptions in the workplace, anger, fear, defensiveness, aggressiveness, and retaliation (Copobianco, Davis, and Kraus, 2004). Thus a more active approach to resolving or managing interpersonal conflict is needed.

Runde and Flanagan (2007) suggest that the "most effective leaders are extraordinarily competent at handling conflict" (p. 115). These authors proposed the concept of the "conflict competent leader," and they provide important insights that can be useful for sport organization leaders when dealing with interpersonal conflict. Runde and Flanagan explain that "conflict competence" requires careful thought and understanding, as well as the ability not to act too quickly (or too slowly) in conflict situations. Leaders must also understand behaviors and approaches of their own that can cause conflict to continue or worsen. According to these authors, there is no simple "script" for leaders to follow when dealing with conflict, and effectiveness often comes from "an array of behaviors, techniques, analysis, timing and attitude" (p. 164). Runde and Flanagan provide suggestions and recommendations that can better enable leaders to deal constructively with interpersonal conflict in their organizations. Table 2.1 presents a summary of their approaches to conflict competent leadership.

Responsibility

This section addresses the fundamental premise that, in addition to producing results and developing positive productive relationships, sport organization leaders have professional, moral, and ethical responsibilities in carrying out their jobs. Sport is an environment, though

---

On the Sidelines

Cultural Considerations in Interpersonal Conflict Resolution

Runde and Flanagan (2007) point out in *Becoming a Conflict Competent Leader* that one must consider cultural differences when dealing with conflict. For example, from a Western viewpoint, for example in North America and Northern Europe, approaches to conflict resolutions are representative of cultures that "value individualism, appreciate openness, directness and goal-oriented solutions" (p. 35). Thus individualistic cultures tend to favor more direct communications when dealing with conflict. However, people in other parts of the world, including Asia, the Middle East, Africa, and Latin America, may approach conflict from a more collectivist view. "In these cultures, maintaining harmony and relationships is considered just as important, or more important, than goal outcomes" (p. 35).

As a sport leader potentially working with employees or athletes from different cultures, how would you go about dealing with conflict between individuals from different cultural perspectives such as those just described? Given the importance of building relationships as a key role of leadership, what would you consider? How would you approach the parties in conflict? How would you acknowledge the cultural differences in your approach?

---

certainly not the only one, in which ethical issues, violations, and scandals make the headlines on almost a daily basis. Many of these issues are presented and discussed in detail in several excellent books, *Ethics in Sport* (Morgan, 2007), *Sports Ethics: An Anthology* (Boxill, 2003), and *Ethics and Morality in Sport Management* (DeSensi and Rosenberg, 2010). These books deal with numerous sport-related social issues including sportsmanship, cheating, rule violations, performance-enhancing drug use, sports and equal opportunity, violence in sport, commercialism, and exploitation. The intent in this section is to highlight and summarize ideas about professional, ethical, and responsibility-based leadership as a cornerstone of the three Rs and to point to its role in helping to deal with the multitude of sociological issues addressed by the literature in this area.

Professionalism

What exactly is meant by professionalism and professional responsibility? What are the traits or behaviors that are associated with professionalism in leadership? Does "professional-

Table 2.1 Conflict Competence for Leaders

Conflict stage	Leadership action
Recognize conflict	Conflict competent leaders should monitor the environment and recognize conflict at an early stage. Addressing conflict before it escalates to higher intensity levels is often the key to an effective solution.
Understand the intensity level of conflict and destructive behaviors	The intensity of conflict ranges from simple differences of opinion and disagreements to discord and polarization that can lead to severe emotional responses and behavior. Understanding and recognizing the various intensity levels of conflict and destructive behaviors can help leaders respond and react in appropriate ways to try to ease the level of conflict.
Foster constructive responses to conflict	• Stay calm and delay initial response to collect thoughts. • Focus on facts. • Demand civility, fairness, and safety among conflicting parties. • Be a teacher and coach: Provide feedback, ask questions, empathize, check for understanding, summarize, offer advice. • Provide learning opportunities for conflicting parties such as assignments and actions that address the issues. • Embrace constructive conflict by demonstrating confidence and inspiring trust and optimism in followers. Have the ability and willingness to look at different angles and perspectives and inspire followers to do so.

Based on information in Runde and Flanagan 2007.

ism" fall under the exacting standards of behavior and performance expected by and for a profession? The answers to these questions are important to responsibility-based leadership in sport. Leaders of sport organizations occupy high-profile positions with a high degree of visibility, even if the organization is small or the setting is a small community. Consequently, lapses in professional behavior often make the news or, at a minimum, spread rapidly through the organization or community network. For these reasons, as well as hopefully to meet one's own personal expectations, attention to professionalism is a critical requirement for a trusted and respected leader. (See the "Professionalism and Employment" sidebar.)

Regarding the questions posed in the preceding paragraph, Stenson (2011), using

Whether one considers sport from a social, personal, political, or economic perspective, it is a relevant human activity that has ethical and moral implications. Individuals who share an interest in sport must ensure that its integrity remains intact and that those in the sport community be treated with respect and dignity. Sport managers, broadly understood, occupy a unique role toward fulfilling this objective because they are important leaders and decision makers, and they set much of the stage for how sport is perceived and actually carried out (DeSensi and Rosenberg, 2003, p. 6).

an applied and practical approach, lists 10 elements that he proposes are necessary for a professional. These are summarized in the "Elements of Professionalism" sidebar.

Ethical Leadership

In the results-oriented world of competition sports, with a pronounced emphasis on "winning" and "winning now," there are many situations in which people in leadership roles find themselves willing to compromise personal integrity and values to produce what internal and external constituents consider the desired result. Consequently, sport, with its many virtues, continues to be plagued by cheating, violations, scandals, and unethical conduct by participants and leaders across all types and levels of sport organizations.

Professionalism and Employment

In 2009, *O&P Business News*, in an article titled "College Graduates Get Failing Grade in Professionalism," reported that a nationwide survey of human resource professionals and business leaders identified five characteristics of professionalism sought by employers of new graduates. These were the five characteristics:

1. Personal interaction skills including courtesy and respect
2. Communication and listening skills
3. A great work ethic, being motivated, and staying on task through completion of a job
4. Professional appearance
5. Self-confidence and awareness

Interestingly, when the participants were asked to rate the presence of "professionalism" in new college graduates at the time, none of the top five traits attained a mean rating of 4, which was defined as "common," on a 5-point scale. How would you rate your professionalism in these five areas?

Elements of Professionalism

- Professionalism goes beyond matters of appearance such as neatness and grooming. It also is not defined by technical skill. Professionalism is, rather, a set of internalized character strengths and values directed toward high-quality service to others through one's work. Real professionals show these inner strengths and attitudes—sound judgment, know-how, business savvy, mature responsibility, problem-solving perseverance, and ingenuity, along with what people call "class."

- Professionals show self-respect in their work. They're conscious that their work reflects their inner character. Their work is, among other things, a statement of their personal commitment to excellence of performance.

- Professionals see their work as service to others. They labor toward the betterment of other people, directly or indirectly: clients, customers, employers, colleagues. Thus they're both *task oriented* and *people oriented*.

- Professionals have an ongoing need to learn and improve, to master traditional approaches and *then* try to improve on them. Professionals respect the experience of others and have high regard for professionalism in other lines of work. They also know how to use the powers of other professionals (lawyers, accountants, consultants) to strengthen their own performance. They seek out sound advice and generally follow it.

- Professionals tend to see problems as challenges and opportunities, not burdensome "hassles" to be avoided. They have a long-term habit of approaching problems confidently and optimistically. They don't let indecision or fear of failure lead to paralysis. They do the best they can with what they have.

- Professionals have a high level of personal responsibility and respect for others' rights. They have a clear sense of the *limits* to their authority and rights of operation. They don't meddle in others' affairs or criticize in areas where they have neither rights nor expertise.

- They make efficient use of resources, especially time. They know how to concentrate mind and will on the tasks before them. They work quickly but not hurriedly. They're careful but not slow.

- They compartmentalize work responsibilities from leisure and personal interests. Work hours are devoted exclusively to job performance, and leisure and personal affairs wait until the job is done. Responsibilities to clients and employers come ahead of self-interested concerns and pleasures.

- Even off the job, professionals demonstrate admirable character: good judgment, good taste, good manners, a respect for quality in general. Their personality shows tasteful self-restraint combined with concern for others and love of life—in a word, "class."

- The character and values of professionalism are built up first in childhood and then strengthened in adulthood through study, training, and work experience. This means that young people, even teenagers, can mark themselves as professionals—earn the respect of all who work with them—during the first few weeks of their first job.

While these behaviors are by no means limited to individuals in the sport industry, clearly they have become commonplace in sport. Nevertheless, there still seems to exist a certain ideal in the general population that sport is, or should be, driven by such core values as fair play, honesty, dedication, overcoming adversity, and teamwork. Failure of sport participants and leaders to demonstrate behaviors aligned with these positive values brings into question their integrity and can undermine the trust of followers and stakeholders. It can also raise concerns in society about the impact that unprofessional and unethical behaviors have on followers and the reputation of an organization.

Ethical leadership and personal integrity have been the subject of numerous studies over the last several years. However, as pointed out by Yukl (2009) despite growing interest in the topic, there is significant disagreement among researchers as to how to appropriately define and assess these two attributes. According to Yukl, ethical leadership typically involves aspects of behavior and motives such as honesty, trustworthiness, and fairness, but also involves attempts to influence the ethical behavior of others. Regarding integrity, Yukl suggests that it is typically defined by the consistency between an individual's espoused values and the person's behavior. However, as he also points out, some argue that integrity more appropriately defined would include behavior consistent with justifiable moral principles and motives involving no intent to harm or exploit followers.

Ethical leadership and integrity are core responsibilities of leaders in sport organizations. Without a doubt, people have high expectations for the performance of sport leaders in their businesses, schools, and communities. Often these expectations, as they relate to achieving the performance outcomes described previously, are very intense and lead to unethical practices on the part of sport leaders. However, while achieving outcomes and results is and always will be critically important in sport, failure to consistently meet expectations of ethical leadership and integrity will ultimately lead to the demise of a sport organization leader.

Tichy and Bennis (2010), both highly regarded leadership experts, say that "great leaders are celebrated for their judgment" (p.

5). These authors argue that good judgment is not a matter of intellect but rather of character and courage. In this sense, character provides a moral compass and lets leaders know what must be done. Courage then ensures that leaders follow through on the decisions they make. According to Tichy and Bennis, without both character and courage, leaders will falter on difficult and important questions.

Servant and Authentic Leadership

Two approaches to leadership that need to be mentioned at this point in relation to responsibility are servant leadership and authentic leadership. Both of these approaches are related to ethical leadership; both have become more prominent in the literature in recent years, and both provide avenues for application and research in sport organization leadership. Servant leadership as originally proposed by Greenleaf (1977) and summarized by Yukl (2010) suggests that serving followers is the primary responsibility of those in leadership roles. Servant leaders pay close attention to follower needs and are empathetic and nurturing. Servant leaders demonstrate integrity, put the needs of others before their own, treat others with respect, encourage personal growth, support fair treatment, and consult with followers regarding decisions that affect them.

Similarly, authentic leadership is characteristic of leaders who have a high level of self-awareness and are also highly supportive of followers. Avolio, Luthans, and Walamba (2004, p. 4) defined authentic leaders as "those who are deeply aware of how they think and behave and are perceived by others as being aware of their own and others' values/moral perspective, knowledge, and strengths; aware of the context in which they operate; and who are confident, hopeful, optimistic, resilient, and of high moral character."

In addition, as Yukl (2010) notes, authentic leaders pursue leadership positions as a means to express values as opposed to meeting a need for status or power. Bill George (2003, p. 18), speaking from years of experience as CEO of a major corporation, asserts that authentic leaders demonstrate five primary characteristics:

1. They understand their purpose.
2. They practice solid values.
3. They lead with the heart.
4. They establish connected relationships.
5. They demonstrate self-discipline.

George (2003) posits that responsible leaders should have character; they should be led by desirable virtues and principles, such as respect, care, honesty, accountability, humility, trust, and active citizenship; and they should practice "introspection." George also notes that being authentic and leading with integrity is possible only if the espoused values and the leadership practice match. When these are in alignment and a leader walks the talk, then the leader is considered legitimate and is trusted by stakeholders.

In this sense, authentic leadership becomes totally different from leadership in the hierarchical structure most familiar to people, and authentic leaders are clearly focused on purpose rather than ego. An important point is that authentic leaders seek to guide their community rather than control it and strive to lead followers by means of authenticity and shared goals.

Currently, servant and authentic leadership research in sport is very limited. A review of the literature in sport revealed that servant leadership has been the primary topic of only one published academic study related to sport leadership and coaching (Rieke, Hammermeister, and Chase, 2008). The researchers, examining 195 high school basketball athletes in the United States, found that athletes who had coaches perceived as servant leaders displayed greater motivation, were more task oriented, were more satisfied, and were mentally tougher and actually performed better than athletes coached by leaders who were not servant oriented. A search for studies specifically focusing on authentic leadership in sport revealed no published empirical research at the time of this writing.

Principle-Centered Leadership

At this point it is worthwhile to refer to the beliefs of the late Dr. Stephen R. Covey as presented in his 1992 book *Principle-Centered Leadership*. In a strong statement about personal responsibility, Covey (1992) wrote, "To value oneself and, at the same time, subordinate oneself to higher purposes and principles is the paradoxical essence of highest humanity and the foundation of effective leadership" (p. 19).

Covey then described what he referred to as "leadership by compass." In his view, principles always point the way, much like compasses, and if read correctly, will prevent one's getting lost or confused by conflicting values. Covey also stated that principles are self-evident and don't shift and change with time or situations. As basic principles that are necessary to move society toward survival and stability, he included fairness, equity, justice, integrity, honesty, and trust. He also suggested that principle-centered leadership must be practiced across four levels:

1. personal,
2. interpersonal,
3. managerial, and
4. organizational.

Unfortunately, we see many examples across society in general, as well as in sport, of regular violations of these principles at one or more of the four levels. Each year in sport we see abundant evidence of rule violations, cover-ups, drug use, and a host of other improprieties that taint public perception and eradicate confidence in leadership. Preventing and overcoming these issues in the future will require that sport leaders assume personal and organizational responsibility and demonstrate a deep, enduring commitment to principle-centered leadership.

Leadership Credibility

The section of this chapter on leadership responsibility would not be complete without reference to the leadership perspectives of James Kouzes and Barry Posner, authors of *The Leadership Challenge* (2007). The authors base their perspective of leadership on more than 25 years of research around the globe—from various countries, cultures, ethnicities, organizations, hierarchies, educational backgrounds, and age groups. Kouzes and Posner (2007, p. 29) report that when people are asked what they are looking for in a leader, these are the four most common answers:

1. Honest
2. Forward looking
3. Competent
4. Inspiring

Three of the four qualities (honesty, competence, and the ability to inspire), according to Kouzes and Posner, are aligned with what research often looks for in leaders relative to perceived trustworthiness, expertise, and dynamism. Individuals who rate highly on these dimensions are considered to have "source credibility," leading to Kouzes and Posner's (2007, p. 37) statement, "Credibility is the foundation of leadership."

Additionally, Kouzes and Posner (2007, 2013), developed a model of leadership over three decades ago that includes what they refer to as the five practices of exemplary leadership. Kouzes and Posner (2013) argue that the model provides an evidence based path for achievement of extraordinary results and that it can turn abstract concepts of leadership into practices and behaviors that can be learned and taught by those willing to accept the leadership challenge.

A summary description of each of the five practices recommended by Kouzes and Posner (2007, 2013) is provided below. Readers are encouraged to pursue more in-depth information on the five practices through additional reading and study of the work of Kouzes and Posner referenced previously.

- **Model the Way.** Leaders help establish principles about how people should be treated, create standards of excellence, and then set examples for others to follow.
- **Inspire a Shared Vision.** Leaders help envision exciting possibilities for the future. They persuade and enlist others to pursue dreams and create an ideal image for the future of an organization.
- **Challenge the Process.** Leaders search for new and innovative ways to improve an organization. They seek opportunities for change from current practices that are not working and are willing to experiment and take risks.
- **Enable Others to Act.** Leaders involve others and create environments of trust, mutual respect, and dignity. They foster collaboration and strengthen others by making them feel more capable and powerful.
- **Encourage the Heart.** Leaders recognize people for their contributions and celebrate their accomplishments. This helps keep hope and determination alive in the organization.

Based on Kouzes and Posner 2007.

On the Sidelines

Responsibility in Intercollegiate Athletics

The following is an interview of Jeremy Foley, athletic director at the University of Florida, conducted by David Jones and posted on usatoday.com (Jones 2011).

FT: *What do you think is the No. 1 thing the SEC should be worried about right now?*

Foley: *I think in this league, like any league in the country, your image, your integrity, that we're doing the right thing. That's a significant issue for intercollegiate athletics right now. There's a perception out there, I read articles every day, 'We're not doing things the right way, we don't have ethics, all we care about is money.' I think we've got to be concerned about that, as a profession, not necessarily (just) as a league . . . I would say that's the biggest thing on our radar.*

FT: *What can you do about that?*

Foley: *Make sure you run your business the right way. We have difficult situations, you deal with them. We all have them or will have them. At the end of the day, I'm also realistic that not everyone is going to buy into it, that what we do there's always going to be an element (that says) all we care about is money, we're not fair, we don't run it right. I could tell you a thousand examples about the good things of intercollegiate athletics does as well. But that being said we've got to make sure we're running athletic programs in an ethical, honest manner and representing all our respective institutions in a first class way . . . . (And) you've got to make sure you are managing your finances in the right way.*

The five practices of Kouzes and Posner summarized here can be very useful to sport organization leaders as a guide for self-evaluation of current practice as well as for future professional development in the areas of leadership behavior and responsibility.

> ### Your Thoughts
>
> Scandals, violations, and unethical practices have been an issue in sport for about as long as sports have been in existence.
>
> - What factors contribute to this, in your opinion?
> - What do you think a leader's responsibility should be relative to these issues?
> - Can leadership training and development be a part of the solution to address these problems? If so, how? If not, why not?

Stakeholder Responsibility

What is the purpose of leadership in a stakeholder society? This question, asked by Maak and Pless (2006), is an important one to consider in relation to managerial leadership in sport organizations. Maak and Pless, using the stakeholder theory approach of Freeman, Wicks, and Parmar (2004), recognize that values are a necessary part of doing business and that leaders should be able to answer two questions: (1) "What is the purpose of the firm?" and (2) "What responsibility does management have to stakeholders?" (p. 102). They point out that leadership research of the past focused primarily on the relationship between leaders and followers *within* an organization. They argue that leadership occurs with stakeholders both within and outside of the organization.

To address the question of what makes a responsible leader, Maak and Pless (2006) proposed a "role model" of responsibility-based leadership that describes the roles a leader should take in leading various internal and external stakeholders. While they did not specifically address stakeholders in a sport context, the requirements of responsible leadership apply well to sport organization leadership. Table 2.2 summarizes the stakeholders and the leader responsibilities as presented by Maak and Pless. Examples of individual or group

Table 2.2 Stakeholders and Leader Responsibility

Stakeholders	Leader responsibility
Employees (athletes and volunteers)	Responsible leaders: • Mobilize people, lead teams, coach and reinforce employees to ethically achieve objectives. • Encourage respectful collaboration, provide humane and safe working conditions. • Provide fair and equal opportunities and labor practices. • Address work–life balance of employees.
Clients and customers (fans, boosters, supporters)	Responsible leaders: • Ensure that products and service meet customer needs and are safe. Take preventive steps to ensure customer well-being.
Business partners (contractual services, sponsors, concessions, security)	Responsible leaders: • Ensure that business partners also apply ethical, environmental, and labor standards. • Ensure that partners are treated respectfully and fairly.
Social and natural environment (impact of stadiums, arenas, and related facilities)	Responsible leaders: • "Address impact of business decisions on social and natural environment" (p. 101). • Encourage and participate in active social engagement for the well-being of the communities they serve.
Shareholders (board members, donors)	Responsible leaders: • Safeguard shareholder investment and ensure adequate return. • Respect shareholder rights and provide regular and transparent communication. • Respect insider knowledge and prevent moral wrongdoing. • Act responsibly and modestly regarding own compensation packages.

stakeholders from sport are listed in parentheses in the left-hand column of the table.

The federal gender equity law, Title IX, designed to ensure fair and equal opportunities for women to participate in high school and collegiate sports, is a prime example of stakeholder responsibility for leaders in these organizations. It is also a source of conflict for many institutions. While Title IX is a federal requirement in the United States and has resulted in large improvements in the total number of women participating in sport, numerous institutions have yet to adequately follow the law. In some cases, women's sport rosters are artificially inflated, or men's sports are eliminated or rosters cut in size to bring the institution into compliance. In other cases, institutions use federal loopholes that allow them to report male practice players as female participants (Thomas, 2011). Leadership aimed at truly meeting the needs of stakeholders (both male and female sport participants) relative to Title IX must address financial, legal, and ethical responsibilities in dealing with this issue.

Another issue related to leadership responsibility to stakeholders in sport is the health and safety of customers and athletes. This represents the direct interaction between leadership and risk management. While there are inherent risks to both participants and spectators in sporting events, people have often been injured or put in harm's way because of the failure of an organization's leadership to adequately address safety concerns, which is a primary responsibility to stakeholders. Concussions and long-term brain damage in football players, several recent deaths and illnesses in athletes resulting from exertional rhabdomyolysis (substantial muscle breakdown and electrolyte imbalance in the bloodstream caused by overexertion), and severe injuries and fatalities in spectators who have fallen from bleachers at ball parks are all prime examples of the need for leadership to assume the professional and ethical responsibility to create and maintain a culture of safety for participants and spectators.

Social Responsibility

Leaders of sport organizations at all levels must also consider how to demonstrate yet another responsibility—social responsibility. This is important both for the outreach and service provided back to the people and communities supporting an organization and as part of a learning experience and leadership development opportunity for organizational members. As an example, a recent summit, Making the Difference: the Sport and Social Responsibility Summit, was held in London in March 2011. The purpose was for sport organization leaders to discuss the relationship between the sport industry and corporate social responsibility. A primary question for the conference was, "How will the relationship between sport, brands, and social projects develop in the years ahead"? The summit included examples from international soccer and the NFL of how sport can work with social projects to ultimately create a positive change in society.

Other programs that demonstrate socially responsible leadership include the NCAA Community and Youth Initiatives, whereby youth receive sport instruction and life guidance from NCAA coaches and athletes; the NFL's Super Bowl XLIV Playbook Workshop Series for Small, Minority and Female Business Owners; and the USOC Champions in Life program, which reaches out to youth with a positive-choice message about staying in school, staying drug free, and avoiding gangs and violence.

At a grassroots level are many examples of existing outreach programs as well as opportunities for leaders of school sport programs and local sport-related businesses to facilitate participation by employees and athletes with local service organizations in food drives, disaster relief, community cleanup events, Habitat for Humanity, and other social outreach efforts.

Summary

This chapter reflects the author's perspective that leadership can be framed in three dimensions: *results*, *relationships*, and *responsibilities*. Leaders are often effective in one or two of these dimensions, but not always in all three.

In sport, producing results is often associated with winning seasons, championships, strong product sales, or shareholder value;

and it is often the failure to meet customer expectations in these areas that leads to high leadership turnover. The chapter defines, discusses, and presents sport-related examples of two common measures of results, organizational performance and organizational effectiveness, that are often linked directly to leadership. The discussion presents three questions that should be strongly considered by leaders, along with recommendations for achieving results, based on the book *Results-Based Leadership* (Ulrich, Zenger, and Smallwood, 2009).

The dimension of leadership and relationship building is then examined, beginning with a focus on interpersonal relations and communication. This dimension is related to elements of many of the theories presented in chapter 1, including behavioral theory and transformational leadership. In addition, the chapter provides fundamental and timeless recommendations for improving relationships as suggested by the Dale Carnegie leadership training program. It includes additional recommendations for creating and maintaining trust, along with ideas and suggestions regarding what it takes to be competent in dealing with interpersonal conflict.

The chapter then focuses on the dimension of responsibility-based leadership with emphasis on professionalism and ethical and principle-centered leadership. It introduces the concepts and theories of servant and authentic leadership with reference to the qualities and behaviors that are necessary in an authentic leader. Effective leadership must be consistent with universally accepted principles of fairness, equity, justice, integrity, honesty, and trust (Covey, 1992); and credibility is a foundational element of effective leadership (Kouzes and Posner, 2007). Five practices of exemplary leaders as recommended by Kouzes and Posner are included to help provide readers with opportunity for self-evaluation and reflection. The chapter concludes with an emphasis on both stakeholder responsibility and social responsibility as obligations of sport organization leaders.

Final Self-Assessment

After having read and reflected on the content in this chapter, consider your responses to the self-assessment questions presented at the beginning of the chapter. Have your perspectives changed, or do you have any new insights or additional questions regarding your understanding of leadership?

1. What do you currently consider to be the most important accomplishment or outcome of leadership?
2. How do you now (or how would you in the future) go about effectively building relationships and managing interpersonal conflict in a sport organization?
3. What does professionalism mean to you in your role as a sport leader?
4. What do you consider the core values and ethical principles by which a sport organization should operate?

Game Plan Activity

Reflect on your leadership experiences to this point. If you have not been in a leadership role, put yourself in the role of a leader you have observed. Using the questions listed, complete a personal audit or rating of your own performance (or that of the leader you have chosen) as to the three Rs discussed in this chapter. Remember that your answers may vary greatly from those of others depending on the sport organization context.

Results

- What are the most important tangible organizational performance outcomes that have occurred under your leadership?

- What stakeholders have benefited from these results? In what ways?
  - How would you rate these results on the following scale?
    (1) Not at all significant
    (2) Fairly significant
    (3) Significant
    (4) Very significant

Relationships

- In what ways have you demonstrated principles of relationship building among those you interact with regularly?
- Who has most benefited from your actions?
- How would you rate your interpersonal relationship-building skills on the following scale?
  (1) Not at all significant
  (2) Fairly significant
  (3) Significant
  (4) Very significant

Responsibility

- In what ways have you demonstrated professionalism and ethical responsibility?
- Who has recognized or acknowledged you for these behaviors and actions?
- How would you rate your performance as a professional and ethical leader on the following scale?
  (1) Not at all significant
  (2) Fairly significant
  (3) Significant
  (4) Very significant

After completing the audit, develop a personal improvement plan that brings any areas needing improvement more in line with both your expectations and those of stakeholders.

Questions to Consider

1. Think of a recent example or find a current issue in the news involving a sport organization, a sport leader, or both. What is at the core of the issue? Does it relate to one of the three dimensions covered in this chapter? What thoughts do you have about how the problem could have been prevented, and what recommendations might you have for a leader for addressing the problem based on information provided in this chapter?

2. Identify a sport leader you respect and assess the extent to which this person demonstrates the five practices of exemplary leadership described in this chapter from Kouzes and Posner (2007, 2013). What are the practices and commitments that stand out about this individual? How would you rate your own practices and behaviors in these areas, and how might you use this information to improve your own professional development as a leader?

3. What are areas of stakeholder responsibility that you think could be improved in the sport organization with which you are most familiar?

4. Develop a list of possible opportunities in your community for sport organizations and sport leaders to become involved and demonstrate social responsibility.

Recommended Readings

DeSensi, J. T., and Rosenberg, D. (2003). *Ethics and morality in sport management* (2nd ed.). Morgantown, WV: Fitness Information Technology.

George, W. W. (2003). *Authentic leadership: Rediscovering the secrets to creating lasting value.* San Francisco: Jossey-Bass.

Rath, T., and Conchie, B. (2008). *Strengths-based leadership.* New York: Gallup Press.

Runde, C. E., and Flanagan, T. A. (2007). *Becoming a conflict competent leader: How you and your organization can manage conflict effectively.* San Francisco: Jossey-Bass.

Tichy, N., and Bennis, W. (2010). Wise judgment: It takes character and courage. *Leadership Excellence,* May, 2.

Ulrich, D., Zenger, J., and Smallwood, N. (1999). *Results based leadership.* Boston: Harvard Business Press.

Contemporary Thought in Leadership Applications for Sport Organizations

Part II, chapters 3 through 9, addresses what are considered across much of the literature key elements of contemporary leadership theory and practice. These chapters present historical and foundational leadership and management concepts considered seminal to the domain, but the majority of the information in these chapters concerns research findings, proposed models, and practical examples from sport occurring within the last decade. Chapters 3 and 4 focus primarily on internal elements of personal and organizational leadership, including the concept of emotional intelligence for individuals in leadership roles and the ability to understand, and build an effective organizational culture. Chapter 5 addresses common expectations and challenges for sport organization leaders, including creating shared vision and understanding the roles and responsibilities of traditional strategic planning versus emergent strategic thinking and adaptation. Chapter 6 presents theories and contemporary thought for helping leaders navigate through and attempt to solve complex problems in organizations through individual, team-based, and "framing" approaches to problem solving.

Chapter 7 addresses three conceptually separate domains of leadership: change, turnaround, and crisis leadership. The section on change leadership applies the most recognized work in the business literature to sport organization leadership. Turnaround leadership is then addressed relative to how sport organization leaders can more effectively deal with situations in which expectations for dramatic and short-term positive outcomes are high and the results are often immediately and publicly scrutinized by fans, boosters, and the media. The last section of the chapter, on crisis leadership, focuses on how crisis situations such as real or potential health threats to employees and athletes, criminal or unethical activity, natural disasters, or terrorism may put a sport organization leader front and center in the public eye and how elements of various contemporary leadership theories and models can be used as tools in these situations.

Chapters 8 and 9 focus on critical areas in modern sport organizations that also require astute and insightful leadership to achieve optimal outcomes. The challenges and opportunities covered in chapter 8 include effectively leading diversity in sport organizations; this comprises understanding the differences between surface-level and deep-level diversity as well as valuing and creating a culture of diversity, developing proactive strategies for diversity management, and improving cultural competence both personally and across a sport organization. Chapter 9 focuses on understanding globalization in sport and its influence on leadership thought and behaviors, as well as the competencies that must be developed for effective global leadership.

Emotional Intelligence and Leadership

Learning Objectives

After reading and reflecting on the concepts and examples in this chapter, you will be able to

1. define and give examples of emotional intelligence (EI) as it relates to sport organization leadership,

2. identify reasons why EI can be important for sport leaders,

3. identify and discuss the history of and major developments in EI research,

4. discuss various methods and potential concerns related to how EI is measured in research,

5. explain the fundamental disagreement among researchers regarding EI and its influence on work or life outcomes,

6. explain Mayer and Salovey's four-branch model of EI, and

7. explain Goleman's four domains of EI and how they might apply in sport organization leadership.

Self-Assessment

1. What is meant by the term "emotional intelligence," and how might it apply to you personally as well as to sport leadership in general?

2. What evidence exists from research regarding EI and its role in producing desired outcomes? What arguments exist to the contrary?

3. What evidence do you see from your personal experience or from observation of sport organizations that the level of an individual leader's EI skills may be a factor related to either positive outcomes or negative behaviors and problems?

4. How would you currently rate your own EI based on challenging situations you have been in and how you have responded to them?

All organizations are made up of humans, and humans are emotional beings. Consequently, many individual and group/team activities elicit feelings among participants that range from boredom, disappointment, and anger, to pure excitement and a sense of tremendous accomplishment. While leaders within organizations often have high levels of intellectual capacity and technical expertise, many of the most challenging problems they must deal with involve responding to and effectively managing the feelings and emotions of organizational members and strategic constituents. According to Mayer and Salovey (1997), reasoning that takes emotions into account is a part of what they refer to as emotional intelligence or EI.

Leaders of sport organizations, as with all organizational leaders, need to recognize the importance of effectively dealing with both their own feelings and emotions and those of the people they interact with and lead. However, in many competitive sport organizations, strong levels of emotion and feelings of attachment not only run internally throughout the organization (e.g., athletes and coaches) but also characterize the fans, boosters, and, in the case of intercollegiate athletics, alumni. Consequently, sport organization leaders may need to be even more adept at reasoning and communicating with their followers and constituents using personal EI traits, behaviors, and strategies.

This chapter explores EI from a foundational research perspective, as well as addressing two models for how EI may be applied relative to leadership practice. The chapter begins with a hypothetical example of how elements of EI can become part of the leadership challenges faced by a sport organization leader. This is followed by foundational information on how EI is defined and why it may be an important area for sport leaders to understand.

The next section of the chapter provides an overview of research in EI, recognizing that there are disagreements among many researchers regarding not only the construct of EI, but also the extent to which it has been validated by empirical research as truly a primary contributing factor to personal or organizational outcomes. It is also acknowledged that research on EI in sport management is very minimal at this time.

The chapter then presents two application models of EI that are widely recognized and that form the foundation for much of the EI training that exists in human resource departments and executive training programs. Examples and potential applications to sport leadership are provided.

Defining Emotional Intelligence

Bar-On (2006) defined EI relative to one's ability to effectively understand oneself and others, relate effectively to other people, and adapt to and cope with one's immediate surroundings. Mayer and Salovey (1997) suggested that "emotional intelligence involves the ability to perceive accurately, appraise and express emotion; the ability to access and/or generate feelings when they facilitate thought; the ability to understand emotion and emotional knowledge; and the ability to regulate emotions to promote emotional and intellectual growth" (p. 10). Mayer and Caruso (2002) later suggested that EI has to do with the capacity to understand and explain emotions as well as to use emotions to enhance thought. Coming from a slightly different perspective, Boyatzis, Goleman, and Rhee (1999) described and defined EI as personal competencies including self-awareness, self-management, social awareness, and social skills that are used at appropriate times and with sufficient frequency to be effective in various situations.

From these definitions, one can gather why EI is recognized by many researchers and practitioners as an important element of one's self-awareness and self-management and also the capacity to understand and relate well to others. While some argument still exists among researchers regarding the conceptualization of EI and its possible overlap with constructs of personality, the application of EI relative to leadership and managing relationships in organizations is of practical significance (see "EI and Sport Leadership" sidebar).

Case Study

Title IX and Booster Clubs

The following hypothetical example of a sport-related situation demonstrates the types of issues a sport organization leader might face that relate to the elements of EI presented in this chapter. Read the situation carefully, and then consider the questions at the end before reading the remainder of the chapter.

Note: This case is modeled on a nonsport example of an EI issue provided by Mayer and Caruso (2002) in an article on understanding and applying EI in business.

Cheryl is a newly hired athletic director at a large suburban high school in the United States. The school where Cheryl now works has a long tradition of success in boys' sports, specifically basketball, but has not seen the same level of success in girls' sports. She also learns early on that the booster club for boys' basketball has a long history of providing outstanding support for that program. In fact, in her first week on the job, the president of the boys' basketball booster club visits her to discuss the club's plans for increasing support for the program—with the specific intent of providing new uniforms and chartered buses for all games more than an hour's driving distance away.

Cheryl has been reviewing the budget and understands that finances are tight in the department. She also knows that part of her platform for getting the job was her experience with improving girls' athletic programs, and that several constituents expect her to show progress in this area soon. Cheryl also knows that as the Office for Civil Rights interprets Title IX, economic hardships are not a justification for discrimination. Moreover, Cheryl realizes that it would be a violation of Title IX to allow the booster club for boys' basketball to provide the benefits they are planning unless she and the district find a way to provide the same or closely similar benefits for the girls' basketball program.

Cheryl recognizes the dilemma. Her administrative situation certainly involves technical and legal components that she can explain (e.g., *why* the school must comply with Title IX and *how* the school district will provide resources to demonstrate that benefits, including services, treatment, and opportunities, are equivalent for male and female participants), but it also has a strong emotional component. In this example, it is assumed that there are strong *feelings*, including resentment, among booster club members as well as many parents and athletes from both boys' and girls' programs regarding the requirements for equity.

This situation presents a challenging administrative leadership problem for Cheryl—the technical and legal elements of the problem are closely intertwined with the emotional aspects of the issue. Cheryl's approach to the problem and ultimate outcomes will require that she have not only a complete understanding of the legal and financial issues, but also an understanding of her own emotions and how to effectively manage the emotions of others.

Your Thoughts

- What does this case study demonstrate about why emotions must be considered in leadership decisions and practices in sport organizations?
- What potential exists to build positive relationships or to create negative relationships in this situation?
- What knowledge regarding EI could be useful in this situation?

Why Is EI Important for Sport Leaders?

As mentioned in the introduction to the chapter and in the case study that follows, sport leaders often operate in an emotional environment, especially in competitive professional, intercollegiate, and amateur sports. They also frequently have a large number of internal and external constituents who are directly or indirectly affected by the decisions they make. Hackman and Wageman (2007) suggest that considerable emotional maturity can be required of effective leaders in dealing with their own personal anxieties as well as the anxiety of others. According to Hackman and Wageman, leaders demonstrating emotional maturity are able to move toward an anxiety-arousing state of affairs rather than moving away from it in order to reduce anxiety.

EI and Sport Leadership

In 2007, in an online article in *USA Today*, Brady drew attention to issues occurring at the time within three major professional sports that had the potential to undermine the credibility of the sports among their fans and supporters. He pointed to three adverse events going on simultaneously that presented significant problems for the leaders of the organizations. Briefly, a National Basketball Association referee was accused of betting on games that he was officiating and later pleaded guilty to the charges. The owner of the Atlanta Falcons, Arthur Blank, was addressing the Michael Vick dogfighting issue; and the Mitchell report on Major League Baseball came out, implicating seven MVPs and 31 all-stars in illegal use of steroids ("Mitchell Report," 2007).

These situations are all examples of instances in which a leader's fundamental understanding of EI can be helpful for navigating challenging issues internal and external to a sport organization.

Your Thoughts

Considering the definitions and descriptions of EI presented in this section, identify one or more people in sport leadership roles that you would classify as an emotionally intelligent leader. Next, what evidence or examples from sport can you provide that, in your opinion, are not representative of high levels of EI?

Another important component of leadership identified by these authors is the ability of leaders with emotional maturity to inhibit impulses, whether these be to immediately try to correct emerging problems or to exploit immediately appearing opportunities. Hackman and Wageman also suggest that leaders with emotional maturity are able to wait for an appropriate time to get involved—that is, wait until they feel that organizational members are more open to an intervention.

Research and EI

The concept of EI has been the focus of considerable research over the last several decades in many academic fields. However, empirical research on EI in sport management is very minimal. A database search of articles from all academic fields revealed one such study, which was a doctoral dissertation on EI competencies of National Collegiate Athletic Association Division I athletic directors and the organizational climate in their departments (Harris, 2001). It should be noted, however, that the concept is not completely new to sport research overall, as some studies from sport psychology have examined the relationship of EI to athlete performance.

It is important to mention here that there is notable disagreement among researchers regarding the constructs of EI and whether or not many of the elements or traits associated with EI actually belong in the domain of personality or IQ studies. Additionally, some researchers argue that many EI studies have methodological issues and that claims of EI as a primary factor in determining real-world success have not been validated (Waterhouse, 2006). However, many others argue that EI has considerable support from empirical research and that it is linked to performance outcomes as well as to work and life success. It is also noteworthy that the concept of EI has become increasingly prevalent over the last several years in human resource departments and executive training programs across many industries.

Because of the large volume of research in the area, it is not possible to cover every aspect of the literature and to present all the research findings. Thus the purpose of the next few sections is to provide an overview of EI and foundational information about EI that may be helpful to readers currently in sport leadership roles or planning to be in sport leadership in the future. Also, the information in this section may offer insights for those who want to pursue academic research on EI in sport management.

History and Development of EI Research

Research broadly addressing the concept that emotions and social intelligence are associated with positive outcomes such as life success goes back as far as the 1920s and 1930s. However, a major milestone in the advancement of knowledge in this area is credited to the initial work of Howard Gardner (1983) in his book *Frames of Mind: The Theory of Multiple Intelligences*. Gardner proposed that multiple factors beyond the "intelligence quotient" (IQ) play a role in individual accomplishment and achievement in life. These factors initially included self-awareness, social awareness, and interpersonal relationships.

As interest in the topic began to grow, Salovey and Mayer (1990) proposed a model of EI that included four factors: (1) perception of emotions, (2) reasoning with emotions, (3) understanding emotions, and (4) managing emotions in oneself and others. More information on this model and its potential application in sport is presented later in the chapter.

Following the work of Salovey and Mayer, the concept of EI hit the mainstream with the bestselling book by Daniel Goleman, *Emotional Intelligence: Why It Can Matter More Than IQ* (1995). Goleman's book offered the perspective that how individuals manage their own emotions as well as their relationships with others could be more important than IQ to life success. Goleman was also the first to specifically focus on EI relative to leadership performance. Since the publication of Goleman's book, additional research has suggested that EI is a positive predictor of leadership (Caruso, Mayer, and Salovey, 2002; Goleman, Boyatzis, and McKee, 2002; Sosik and Megerian, 1999).

How Is EI Measured?

In research, EI is typically measured quantitatively through self-report questionnaires, informant or multirater instruments, ability-based assessment, or some combination of these (Conte, 2005). While numerous tests and instruments claim to measure EI, the Consortium for Research on Emotional Intelligence in Organizations (2012) identifies 10 EI measurement instruments that have been subjected to the most empirical evaluation based on their inclusion in at least five published journal articles or book chapters. The 10 emotional intelligence measurement instruments are listed here:

1. Emotional Competence Inventory (ECI)
2. Emotional Quotient Inventory (EQ-i)
3. Emotional & Social Competence Inventory – University Edition
4. Genos Emotional Intelligence Inventory (Genos EI)
5. Group Emotional Competence (GEC)
6. Mayer-Salovey-Caruso Emotional Intelligence Test (MSCEIT)
7. Schutte Self Report Emotional Intelligence Test (SSEIT)
8. Trait Emotional Intelligence Questionnaire (TEIQue)
9. Wong's Emotional Intelligence Scale (WEIS)
10. Work Group Emotional Intelligence Profile (WEIP)

The consortium website provides an overview of these instruments and can be useful for those interested in learning more details on the potential use of these instruments in organizational and leadership development in a sport setting or for academic research.

Although EI measurement instruments are widely available and are being used both in research and among organizational consultants, Conte (2005) provides an important academic critique that both researchers and practitioners should consider, especially before using these instruments as part of professional development or employment screenings. Table 3.1 lists four common measures of EI along with brief descriptions and issues or concerns noted by Conte.

Conte concludes from his review that researchers using EI measures still have important issues to address, especially with regard to discriminant validity related to scoring and self-reported measures. While Conte determined that most of the EI inventories and surveys are reliable (i.e., that they produce consistent results when administered by different researchers to different people), their ability to discriminate between concepts has not been well established. Discriminant validity is a statistical test that measures the extent to which theoretical concepts considered to be unrelated are actually unrelated (Campbell and Fiske, 1959). As seen in the right-hand

Table 3.1 Description and Critique of Four Measures of EI

Emotional intelligence measure	Description	Concerns and issues
Emotional Competence Inventory (ECI) (Boyatzis, Goleman, and Rhee, 2000)	Measures 20 competencies found within the four clusters of self-awareness, social awareness, self-management, and social skills.	Possible overlap with the Big Five personality traits (openness, conscientiousness, extraversion, agreeableness, and neuroticism). Conte suggests the need for more peer-reviewed empirical studies to better establish discriminant and predictive validity of the measure.
Bar-On Emotional Quotient Inventory (EQ-i) (Bar-On, 2000)	Measures competencies across the five subscales of intrapersonal awareness, interpersonal relationships and social awareness, adaptability, general mood, and stress management.	Conte suggests that the conceptual relationship of each component of the model to EI is not clear. Also, Conte points out that the EQ-i, while demonstrating adequate reliability, is currently lacking in discriminant and predictive validity.
Multifactor Emotional Intelligence Scale (MEIS) and the Mayer-Salovey-Caruso Emotional Intelligence Test (MSCEIT V.2) (Mayer, Salovey, and Caruso, 2002)	The first version (MEIS) and the updated version (MSCEIT) are ability tests designed to measure EI using the four subscales of perception of emotion, integration and assimilation of emotion, knowledge about emotion, and management of emotion.	Conte finds that scoring techniques for these measures use different approaches including target scoring, consensus scoring, and expert scoring, which creates concerns about scientific standards for determining accuracy among consensus and expert scores. Conte also indicates that the MSCEIT V.2 is relatively new in academic studies of EI, so more research is needed to establish its discriminant and predictive validity.

Based on information in Conte 2005, *A review and critique of emotional intelligence measures.*

column of table 3.1, Conte's review suggests that current EI measurement scales are lacking in discriminant validity. Consequently, it can be difficult for researchers to specifically separate the theoretical concepts they are measuring. For example, a research instrument may be designed to measure a person's self-awareness and also to measure the person's self-management—but it may be that in reality, these two concepts cannot be discriminated from each other. This issue can reduce the ability of the researcher to effectively predict the extent to which each of these concepts is contributing separately to an expected outcome, such as leadership performance.

Conte also suggests that ability-based measures look to be a promising direction for EI research and that considerable research with EI models is still needed to determine what factors are truly predictive of job performance and work outcomes. The four measures reviewed by Conte have not, to this point, been used specifically within leadership studies in sport. They represent an area in which more research is needed to contribute to the overall EI research as well as to produce initial findings in sport management.

Trait and Ability EI

Petrides and Furnham (2001), based on several years of research on the constructs of EI, clarify the existence of two constructs: (1) trait EI and (2) ability EI. According to these researchers, trait EI is associated with self-perceptions within the realm of personality, and ability EI is associated with cognitive ability such as perceiving and expressing emotion and regulating emotion within one's self and others.

However, Petrides and Furman point out that the primary distinction between the two constructs is actually based on the methods used to measure each and not on the elements contained within each. These researchers also note problems with the measurement of ability EI because of the difficulty in creating instrument items that one can score using truly objective criteria and that can comprehensively cover the sampling domain relative to the construct. The authors suggest that as a consequence, most of the current instruments that measure ability EI have problems with construct validity (e.g., Mayer-Salovey-Caruso Emotional Intelligence Test).

Petrides (2011) argues that according to trait EI theory, individuals have certain emotion profiles that will be an advantage in some contexts but will not work well in others. Consequently, from Petrides' perspective, "It follows that no 'magic profile of the "emotionally intelligent" individual, who will excel in all aspects of life, exists' (p. 661). Petrides also points out that emotions, along with the elements of self-concept and self-efficacy, are actually domains of personality and that trait EI theory ultimately needs to be integrated into the mainstream taxonomies of personality. In addition, he emphasizes that EI questionnaires should be considered measures of trait EI "only in so far as their results are interpreted through the lens of trait EI theory" (p. 662).

EI and Leadership at the Top

Higgs and Dulewicz (2002) conducted research with board members of organizations in the United Kingdom to further examine claims by Goleman, Boyatzis, and McKee (2002) that EI becomes more important the higher one advances in an organization. In this study, 339 participants from the leadership positions of board chairmen, CEOs, executive directors, and nonexecutive directors were asked to rate their perception of the relevance of 38 competencies to successful overall performance of the organization. Ten of the 38 competencies were closely associated with a conceptual framework of EI: integrity, listening, motivating others, influence and persuasiveness, achievement motivation, resilience, decisiveness and intuitiveness, determination, sensitivity, and energy. Results of the study indicated that participants rated the EI-related competencies overall as more important for board chairmen and CEOs than for executive directors and nonexecutive directors.

Neuroscience and Leadership

While still in relatively early stages of development, research using imaging techniques in the brain has allowed interesting preliminary observations about resonant and emotionally intelligent leadership. Although it is beyond the scope of this section to review the many studies on brain activity relative to emotions

and leadership, preliminary findings strongly suggest that emotionally intelligent and resonant leadership positively affects various parts of the brain in people who are influenced by such leaders.

These results begin to demonstrate how the EI *of* leaders actually underscores the importance of EI *to* leaders. For example, Boyatzis (2011) points to research over the last decade suggesting that individuals infect others around them with specific feelings and that negative feelings have a stronger impact than positive ones. Leaders, by the nature of their position or power, tend to have a greater effect than others on those around them. According to Boyatzis, leaders who can change their internal state of mind from a negative to a more positive and inspirational state have the potential to profoundly affect those whom they influence. Consequently, Boyatzis says, changing one's internal state may be one of the most powerful techniques that can be used by an effective leader.

Boyatzis (2011, 2012) also suggests that, through neuroscience-based research, we are learning that resonant and emotionally intelligent leadership can arouse a part of the brain in followers called the positive emotion attractor (PEA). This allows the positive development of relationships, attitudes, and improved motivation in others, which may emphasize the importance of a leader's relationship orientation as a predecessor to results orientation—although both are important to overall leadership and outcomes as pointed out in chapter 2. As noted at the beginning of this section, this research is still in its developmental stages. As it moves forward, it will continue to be innovative and exciting and will offer profound insights into the neurological components of effective leadership.

Other Recent Developments in EI Research

Business, social, and psychological research in EI is still developing; and although some researchers argue that there is not strong empirical evidence of a link between EI and performance or leadership effectiveness (Antonakis, 2004; Waterhouse, 2006), Cherniss and colleagues (2006) counterargue that considerable evidence from peer-reviewed research supports a link between EI and a variety of organizational outcomes including leadership effectiveness and organizational performance. For example, Rosete and Ciarrochi (2005) assessed 41 senior executives on measures of EI, personality, and cognitive ability and related those measures to leadership effectiveness. Leader effectiveness was measured objectively by a 360-degree assessment from each leader's subordinates and direct manager. Results of the correlational and regression analysis revealed that higher scores in EI were associated with higher leadership effectiveness and that EI was a stronger factor than either personality or IQ in predicting outcomes. However, Van Rooy, Whitman, and Viswesvaran (2010), while recognizing the importance and great potential of EI, suggest that more conceptual clarity is still needed regarding the construct and propose that research in this area "should not be driven by a single measure or test of the construct" (p. 152).

Applying EI in Organizational Leadership

Two of the commonly recognized models of EI in the leadership and organizational development literature are from Mayer and Salovey (1997) and Goleman, Boyatzis, and McKee (2002). Each of these models is described in the following sections, along with examples of how the models may apply in sport settings.

Mayer–Salovey Four-Branch Model of EI

Mayer and Caruso (2002) describe a four-branch model of skills (Mayer and Salovey, 1997) that relate to EI. In the model, the first two components are identified as *perception* and *facilitation* and are classified as "experiential EI" because they involve, "first, the capacity to perceive emotions in others accurately, and, second, the ability to use emotions to enhance how we think" (p. 3). Using an example from experience, Mayer and Salovey

indicate that when leaders perceive concerns and anxieties among their teams, they use their own emotions to motivate a response to those concerns and to facilitate thoughts and actions.

The second two components of the Mayer–Salovey model are identified as *understanding emotions* and *emotional management*. These components are classified as "strategic EI" because they "pertain to calculating and planning with information about emotions" (p. 3). In the model, understanding emotions involves knowing how emotions change and will change the behavior of people over time. The area of emotional management then focuses on how leaders can combine logic and emotions to improve decision making.

Mayer and Caruso (2002) argue that the four-branch model, along with the Mayer-Salovey-Caruso Emotional Intelligence Test (MSCEIT), provides a model of leadership that gets at a leader's underlying skills as well as ways to conceptualize and implement strategic plans that effectively incorporate emotional relationships in the workplace. The authors give an example for an organization that might have a plan encouraging customers to adopt a new product. While this plan would certainly involve technical components (e.g., product quality, cost, and distribution), it would also need to take into consideration emotional aspects of customer feelings about the company. Carrying out such a plan could involve use of the four-branch model as suggested by Mayer and Caruso and presented in table 3.2.

Goleman and EI

Daniel Goleman is a psychologist, researcher, and prolific author who is widely known for his works on EI. His work is widely cited in academic research, applied psychology, and business literature, as well as across the Internet in articles and consulting websites. In 1995, Goleman published *Emotional Intelligence*, which was disseminated in 40 languages and distributed worldwide and which made the *New York Times* bestseller list. That book, along with a follow-up article, "What Makes a Leader?" (1998), argued that traditional characteristics associated with leadership (e.g., vision, determination, IQ, technical skills)

Table 3.2 Four-Branch Model of Mayer and Salovey

Four-branch model component	Example of action
Perception of emotion	Surveying customers to gain better understanding of their feelings regarding the company and the product
Facilitation of emotion	Ensuring that you are in the right frame of mind to take on sensitive or emotional tasks
Understanding emotion	Charting the emotional impact of marketing plans on customers while also being attentive to the emotional and financial bottom lines
Managing emotion	Leading others in ways that encourage the desired emotional reactions to the plan

Based on information in Mayer and Caruso 2002.

are not sufficient for effective leadership and that EI in the forms of self-awareness, self-regulation, motivation, empathy, and social skills are also critical for strong leadership. Goleman (1998) also argues that EI increases with age and maturity, but that it can be learned or improved through training. Using brain research as a foundation, Goleman posits that EI originates in the brain's limbic system; and research shows that learning occurs best through motivation, extended practice, and feedback, and that training programs must include limbic system training to "help people break old behavioral habits and establish new ones" (p. 97).

In a later book, *The Emotionally Intelligent Workplace*, Goleman (2001) recognizes that human abilities involve both mind and heart (or cognition and emotion). He states that while some human abilities are purely cognitive (e.g., IQ or technical expertise), other skills and abilities fall into an affective domain where individuals must integrate feelings and emotion as a part of performance. Goleman also points out that EI is not used as a screening factor that one must clear to enter a profession; thus there is wide range of EI abilities in any given profession. However, he says, once people are in a job, EI becomes a predictor of who succeeds and who is more likely to be promoted to higher levels of management or leadership.

The next two subsections provide an overview of foundational elements of Goleman's perspective on EI. Examples or hypothetical situations from sport are presented, and readers are encouraged to consider applications of Goleman's approach in their own organizations and life situations.

Resonant and Dissonant Leadership

Goleman, Boyatzis, and McKee (2002), in *Primal Leadership*, identify two types of leadership that may be found among leaders in an organization: resonant and dissonant. According to Goleman and his coauthors, resonant leaders are associated with high degrees of EI, are upbeat and enthusiastic, are capable of effectively managing and directing the feelings of a group, and can empathize with the emotions of the people they are leading. This resonance results in a mutual comfort level between leaders and followers. Goleman and colleagues argue that under an emotionally intelligent resonant leader, people are more collaborative and form emotional bonds that allow them to work together and maintain focus even in the midst of change and uncertainty. In a *Harvard Business Review* article, "Leadership That Gets Results," Goleman (2000) refers to Joe Torre, former manager of the New York Yankees, as a prime example of an emotionally intelligent leader who produced extraordinary results. Torre managed the Yankees from 1996 to 2007 and won 10 division titles, six American League pennants, and four World Series.

On the other hand, dissonant leaders demonstrate low levels or even an absence of EI. These leaders, according to Goleman and colleagues, create environments that are toxic, manipulative, and demeaning to followers and that increase stress. Employees in this environment can become defensive, resentful, angry, apathetic, and burned out. Using the term "primal leadership," Goleman and coauthors make the basic argument that emotionally intelligent leaders create resonance as opposed to dissonance among the people and organizations that they lead.

Goleman's Domains of EI

Goleman (2000) identifies four domains of EI and 18 to 20 competencies that exist across the four domains. Two of the domains, *self-awareness* and *self-management*, fall into the area of personal competence, which relates to how leaders manage themselves. The other two domains, *social awareness* and *social skill/relationship management*, fall into the area of social competence, which has to do with how leaders manage their relationships with others.

Goleman, Boyatzis, and McKee (2002) suggest from their work that no leader is always strong in every one of the competencies across all domains, but that the most effective leaders exhibit strengths in at least six competencies. The domains and competencies of EI identified by Goleman and colleagues are presented in the sidebar "Goleman's EI Domains and Competencies," followed by a discussion of how these competencies may apply in sport leadership.

Each of the domains and competencies provides insights that can be helpful for sport organization leaders to review and reflect upon in connection with their abilities in each area. The domain of self-awareness is one in which many sport organization leaders have opportunities to develop and improve. For example,

Goleman's EI Domains and Competencies

Emotional intelligence—the ability to manage ourselves and our relationships effectively—consists of four fundamental capabilities: self-awareness, self-management, social awareness, and social skill. Each capability, in turn, is composed of specific sets of competencies. Below is a list of the capabilities and their corresponding traits.

Self-awareness

- **Emotional self-awareness:** the ability to read and understand your emotions as well as recognize their impact on work performance, relationships, and the like.
- **Accurate self-assessment:** a realistic evaluation of your strengths and limitations.
- **Self-confidence:** A strong and positive sense of self-worth.

Self-management

- **Self-control:** The ability to keep disruptive emotions and impulses under control.
- **Trustworthiness:** A consistent display of honesty and integrity.
- **Conscientiousness:** The ability to manage yourself and your responsibilities.
- **Adaptability:** Skill at adjusting to changing situations and overcoming obstacles.
- **Achievement Orientation:** The drive to meet an internal standard of excellence.
- **Initiative:** A readiness to seize opportunities.

Social awareness

- **Empathy:** Skill at sensing other people's emotions, understanding their perspective, and taking an active interest in their concerns.
- **Organizational awareness:** The ability to read the currents of organizational life, build decision networks, and navigate politics.
- **Service orientation:** The ability to recognize and meet customers' needs.

Social skill

- **Visionary leadership:** The ability to take charge and inspire with a compelling vision.
- **Influence:** The ability to wield a range of persuasive tactics.
- **Developing others:** The propensity to bolster the abilities of others through feedback and guidance.
- **Communication:** Skill at listening and at sending clear, convincing, and well-tuned messages.
- **Change catalyst:** Proficiency in initiating new ideas and leading people in a new direction.
- **Conflict management:** The ability to de-escalate disagreements and orchestrate resolutions.
- **Building tools:** Proficiency at cultivating and maintaining a web of relationships.
- **Teamwork and collaboration:** Competence at promoting cooperation and building teams.

Based on Goleman 2000.

many organizational leaders in sport are male; and while this has not yet been established through formal research, it may be that the ability of some males to read and understand their own emotions and recognize their effects on others is something they are less than comfortable with and may be viewed as a "soft skill" that they are not well designed to put to use. On the positive side, because many sport leaders, male and female, come from highly competitive backgrounds and have been athletes themselves, it may be that the EI attribute of self-confidence is highly developed among leaders of sport organizations.

With regard to the EI domain of self-management and self-control, even though it is highly developed in many top executives, coaches, and athletes, one does not have to look far to see examples in sport that are less than stellar when it comes to decisions and actions. Achievement orientation and initiative appear to be highly developed in most sport organization leaders and high-profile athletes, but self-control, trustworthiness, and conscientiousness are certainly competency areas in which improvements need to be made across all levels of sport. Continuing occurrences of such things as recruiting violations and criminal activity, as well as sociopathic behaviors among athletes, suggest that insufficient EI may play a role in these situations.

Regarding the domains of social awareness and social skill/relationship management, sport leaders are frequently in situations that require proficiency in these areas. Top executives in commercial sport enterprises, professional and intercollegiate executives and coaches, and athletic directors and coaches of high school and youth league teams regularly interact with individuals in whom they must take an active interest. They are also regularly in situations in which they must try to understand the perspectives of others, for example when a team of designers for a new sport product have an idea that may be risky but could prove to be a boon to the business. Also, although this is certainly not unique to sport but is nonetheless important to recognize, almost all sport organization leaders are in highly visible positions that require frequent interaction with internal and external constituents as well as media

representatives. In these roles, the EI competencies of empathy, service orientation, influence, communication, development of others, managing conflict, cultivating relationships, and promoting teamwork and collaboration are critical leadership skills. The game plan activity at the end of this chapter gives you an opportunity to use Goleman's domains and competencies to reflect upon and rate yourself specifically on your EI traits and skills, as well as those of leaders you know.

Summary

This chapter begins with the idea that sport organizations, like all other organizations, are composed of people who have emotions. Working with people through the challenges and issues that arise in an organization calls for leadership that often goes beyond technical expertise, determination, or intellectual skills. In challenging and complex situations, leaders who have a high level of self-awareness and self-management, as well as the ability to understand the emotions of others and effectively manage interpersonal and social relationships, demonstrate what is referred to as emotional intelligence.

The case study at the beginning of the chapter provides an example of how an athletic director could be faced with an issue involving many elements of the EI construct. Using this as a foundation, several definitions of EI are provided along with rationale supporting the importance of EI for those currently in or planning to pursue leadership positions in sport.

Building on the rationale for the importance of EI, an overview of foundational research and academic works on the construct refers to the contributions of Gardner (1983), Salovey and Mayer (1990), and Goleman (1995) as key to the development of EI as an important component of leadership and its wide acceptance by researchers and practitioners. The chapter also discusses arguments among researchers regarding the construct of EI and whether or not it can be conceptually and practically separated from personality. Various ways in which EI is measured, potential issues with the instruments and methodologies, and differences between the constructs of trait EI and ability EI are discussed. Some researchers argue that there remains limited empirical evidence that EI produces the individual and organizational outcomes its proponents claim. Research specifically focusing on EI in sport management is very minimal.

Relative to how EI is applied in organizations, discussion turns to the four-branch model of Mayer and Salovey, identifying a progression by which leaders must first perceive emotions as part of an issue, then determin-ing how to facilitate and understand emotion in themselves and others, and ultimately developing strategies to manage emotions so as to achieve desired outcomes. Finally, the chapter looks at the classic works of Goleman (1995, 1998, 2000) and research by Goleman, Boyatzis, and McKee (2004) to identify and discuss the four primary domains of EI: self-awareness, self-management, social awareness, and social skill/relationship management.

Final Self-Assessment

Now that you have completed reading and reflecting on EI and its possible role in leadership, consider your responses to the self-assessment questions presented at the beginning of the chapter. What do you now feel you know about EI that you may not have known before? What are ways you can use this knowledge to improve your leadership?

1. What is meant by the term "emotional intelligence," and how might it apply to you personally as well as to sport leadership in general?

2. What evidence exists from research regarding EI and its role in producing desired outcomes? What arguments exist to the contrary?

3. What evidence do you see from your personal experience or from observation of sport organizations that the level of an individual leader's EI skills may be a factor related to either positive outcomes or negative behaviors and problems?

4. How would you currently rate your own EI based on challenging situations you have been in and how you have responded to them?

Game Plan Activity

Using the four domains and the EI competencies within each as identified by Goleman in this chapter, rate yourself honestly on this scale of 1 to 4 for each competency.

1. do not demonstrate at all
2. demonstrate occasionally (needs improvement)
3. demonstrate regularly (but can improve)
4. demonstrate always (highly developed)

• Reflecting on these domains, what did you find to be your greatest areas of strength and weakness relative to EI?

• Are others who know you or work with you likely to assess your competencies in a similar way?

• Once you complete the self-evaluation, repeat the assessment for someone for whom you currently work or have worked previously. Would you consider this person a resonant leader or a dissonant leader based on your evaluation? Has this person been a positive or negative influence on you and your performance in the organization?

Questions to Consider

1. Reflect on a situation in which you feel that you were anxious or were stressed by the need to manage the emotions of others. What did you do in this situation and how did it relate to elements of EI presented in this chapter?

2. Suppose that you are the senior director of a youth sport program and have just received notice that you will be named in a lawsuit for your indirect role in the injury of a participant in your sport program. What is your initial reaction? How does this relate to the EI elements of self-awareness and self-management?

3. Review one of the online sports news sites (e.g., espn.com, foxsports.com) and find a recent story that you think relates to EI and leadership (positive or negative). Given the information covered in this chapter, explain why the situation was handled either well or poorly. What recommendations for improvements would you make or what lessons would you take from this situation?

4. Why might it be important not simply to select any EI survey instrument and give it to all the members of an organization or team to determine their levels of EI?

5. Which of the two models of EI presented in this chapter do you think could be most useful to your current role or future role as leader of a sport organization? Why?

Recommended Readings

Antonakis, J. (2004). On why "emotional intelligence" will not predict leadership effectiveness beyond IQ or the "big five": An extension and rejoinder. *Organizational Analysis*, 12(2), 171-182.

Cherniss, C., Extein, M., Goleman, D., and Weissberg, R. P. (2006). Emotional intelligence: What does the research really indicate? *Educational Psychologist*, 41(4), 239-245.

Ciarrochi, J., and Mayer, J. D. (2007). *Applying emotional intelligence: A practitioner's guide*. New York: Psychology Press.

Goleman, D. (2006). *Emotional intelligence: The 10th anniversary edition*. New York: Bantam Dell.

Goleman, D., Boyatzis, R., and McKee, A. (2004). *Primal leadership: Learning to lead with emotional intelligence*. Boston: Harvard Business Review Press.

Waterhouse, L. (2006). Inadequate evidence for multiple intelligences, Mozart effect, and emotional intelligence theories. *Educational Psychologist*, 41(4), 247-255.

Building a Culture of Success

Learning Objectives

After reading and reflecting on the concepts, examples, and recommendations in this chapter, you will be able to

1. define and describe organizational culture;
2. discuss the relationship of organizational culture to organizational performance;
3. discuss cultural strength and explain its advantages and disadvantages;
4. identify and describe the levels of organizational culture and how culture is communicated in organizations;
5. discuss the sport-related research on organizational culture; and
6. explain ways in which a sport organization leader can go about analyzing, developing, or changing culture.

Self-Assessment

1. How do leaders effectively develop and communicate desired values and expected "ways of doing things" for an organization?
2. How can you go about diagnosing the strengths and weaknesses of an organization's culture?
3. What findings from sport organization culture research could be helpful in your role as a current or future sport manager or administrator?
4. What do you feel are critical components of an organizational culture development plan for building and maintaining a healthy and effective culture?

If you have ever participated on an athletic team or worked within a group whose members have widely shared values, act consistently with those values, and are able to work closely together to address challenges and overcome problems, you likely have experienced what is often referred to as a strong positive organizational culture. In sport, as well as other industries, these "tight-knit" organizations are often capable of demonstrating long-term effectiveness in areas such as group member motivation, communication, and desired performance outcomes. In a recent book based on years of research and practical application regarding organizational culture, Cameron and Quinn (2011) acknowledged that organizational culture can have a powerful influence on the performance and long-term effectiveness of organizations.

The academic study of organizational culture in corporate business and in education over the last 30 years recognizes organizational culture as a key factor of success in many high-profile organizations. Additionally, it has become generally accepted among researchers and practitioners that a link exists between leadership, organizational culture, and organizational performance (Schein, 1992, 2004; Robbins, 1998; Smerek and Denison, 2007). Moreover, findings from studies over the last several years support that leadership style (e.g., transactional, transformational, and charismatic) is strongly linked to organizational culture and that these approaches to leadership can be an important part of successful culture change efforts (Sarros, Gray, and Densten, 2002; Sarros, Cooper, and Santora, 2008).

In relation to organizational change, leaders often find that attending to elements of the organizational culture can be a key strategy for success. For example, Yukl (2002) states that "Large-scale change in an organization usually requires some change in the organizational culture as well as direct influence over individual subordinates. By changing the culture of an organization, top management can indirectly influence the motivation and behavior of organization members" (p. 278).

As asserted by MacIntosh and Doherty (2005), "Organizational culture is relevant to sport organizations, which are often searching and struggling to enhance the satisfaction, commitment, and performance levels of their employees, and to maintain a competitive advantage in the marketplace" (p. 2). In the world of sport, the numerous ways to measure effectiveness may involve winning, ticket and merchandise sales, sponsorships, and media contracts. At another level, effectiveness may also be measured by such things as participant satisfaction, safety, and community outreach and service. Developing a culture of success that consistently fosters achievement in these areas can be challenging for sport leaders. Given the implied importance of organizational culture to leadership and potential outcomes in sport organizations, this chapter

> *Culture does not change because we desire to change it. Culture changes when the organization is transformed; the culture reflects the realities of people working together every day.*
>
> *Frances Hesselbein*

- provides readers with a foundational understanding of organizational culture,
- identifies and summarizes a selected sample of the research to date in the study of sport organization culture, and
- offers ideas and strategies for applying culture development and management in the day-to-day practice of leading a sport organization.

Leadership and Organizational Culture: The Foundation

Slack and Parent (2006), in *Understanding Sport Organizations*, wrote that understanding more about organizational culture would lead to a better understanding of the structure and processes of sport organizations. According to Slack, "By studying a sport organization's culture, we are forced to pay attention to the somewhat intangible, but no less important, aspects of organizational life, such as the values and beliefs, the accepted modes of operation, and the shared assumptions that guide behavior within an organization" (p. 287). It is these values, beliefs, and shared assumptions that form the core of what many organizational scholars believe is the foundation of organizational performance and long-term effectiveness.

Research specific to sport organizational culture and its relationship to leadership and various outcomes in sport organizations is relatively new, but continues to provide insights into organizational leadership in sport. Examples of studies and findings that may be helpful to leaders in all types of sport organizations are provided later in this chapter. The next several subsections offer foundational information needed for a better understanding of organizational culture, how it is defined and studied, how it relates to leadership and organizational performance, and how it relates to organizational change.

Defining Organizational Culture

Organizational culture has been defined over the last few decades as a system of shared values, meanings, and assumptions that guide organizational members' attitudes and behaviors (Robbins, 1996; Schein, 1992, 2004; O'Reilly and Chatman, 1996). It has also been more informally described through such characterizations as "the way things get done around here" (Deal and Kennedy, 1982) and "the glue that holds organizations together" (Goffee and Jones, 1996). A formal definition for organizational culture recently offered by Schein (2004) is "a pattern of shared basic assumptions that was learned by a group as it solved its problems of external adaptation and internal integration, that has worked well enough to be considered valid and, therefore, to be taught to new members as the correct way to perceive, think, and feel in relation to those problems" (p. 17).

All sport organizations, to some extent, contain elements of these definitions. Some sport organization cultures are well defined and demonstrate evidence of widely shared values, while others are less clearly established. At any given time, many sport organization cultures are in the beginning stages of development with new leadership, and others are maintaining effective cultures and continuing to build on a rich history of success. In some instances, sport organizations are trying to overcome a negative and dysfunctional culture and need to undergo significant culture change.

Difference Between Culture and Climate

Organizational climate and culture is often graphically represented by an iceberg with its visible component above the surface of the water and a foundational component that is invisible, but often quite substantial, under the surface. Organizational culture, with theoretical roots in social anthropology, is typically recognized as existing "under the surface" at a deep level of core values and assumptions in an organization. Edgar Schein, often considered the "father of organizational culture," argues that culture is a deeply rooted phenomenon that cannot be easily revealed through external observation and is not easily measured through questionnaires and quantitative assessment (Schein, 1992, 2004).

Organizational climate, in contrast, has its theoretical foundation in social psychology and is composed of the more easily observable characteristics of an organization and its practices, procedures, and rewards (Schneider, Gunnarson, and Niles-Jolly, 1994). Some researchers believe that quantitative approaches to studying climate and culture are useful and that visible artifacts and organizational members' descriptions and perceptions of their work environment at a given time may be representative of the organization's culture (Cameron and Quinn, 1999, 2011; Hofstede, 1980; Quinn and Spreitzer, 1991).

Examples of more easily observable and measurable elements of the climate in a sport organization include such things as athlete or employee perceptions of leadership; evidence of team camaraderie and communication; and observable signs and symbols in offices, locker rooms, and meeting rooms that display the organization's espoused values.

Strong Versus Weak Cultures

Organizations with "strong cultures" are those in which the espoused values are widely shared and, more importantly, align closely with the actions and behaviors of both leaders and organizational members. According to Chatman and Eunyoung Cha (2003), strong cultures enhance organizational performance in two ways:

1. They energize employees through appealing to their higher ideals and values and rally them around meaningful and unified goals.
2. They shape and coordinate employees' behavior by focusing their attention on organizational priorities.

However, while strong cultures are often considered ideal, strong cultures are not always positive. For example, hazing issues in sport settings are often associated with a strong tradition of initiation or acceptance into a culture. In many cases, hazing rituals have resulted in injury or death to a young athlete and point to the need for both strong policies and a change of the culture toward more positive team-building activities. Another example in which a strong athletic culture was called into question was the recent Penn State child molestation case. As Bob Williams, National Collegiate Athletic Association (NCAA) vice president for communication, said about the situation, "One of the most challenging tasks confronting the university is an open, honest and thorough examination of the culture that underlies the failure of Penn State's most powerful leaders to respond appropriately to Sandusky's crimes."

Additionally, "strong cultures are by definition stable and hard to change" (Schein, 2004, p. 393). Thus, according to Schein, as the world becomes more turbulent, requiring more flexibility and learning, it is possible that strong cultures may be more of a liability than an asset.

With the rapid changes occurring in the development and implementation of technology in sport, a strong-culture manufacturing company that is developing and selling sport products (e.g., equipment, shoes, apparel) must also strive to have a flexible, adaptive, and responsive culture in order to capitalize on advances in technology and meet customer expectations.

On the other hand, some organizations have weak cultures that may not have had sufficient time to develop or in which there is internal disagreement with the organizational mission and little evidence of widely shared values. Weak cultures may also be positive or negative. In a weak positive culture, an organization can have an appropriate foundation of positive values and be moving toward positive outcomes. It is weak because the actions and behaviors of all organizational members, while moving in an appropriate direction overall, are not always congruent and the core values are not yet fully shared. In these organizations, leaders may be key in helping to nurture the culture and may need to educate, motivate, and support organizational members toward achieving successful outcomes. Weak cultures, however, may also be negative: The core values are loosely defined and shared, and the organization may also be dysfunctional, with some individuals or groups working against each other and some supporting leadership but not others. In many cases, weak negative cultures prevent an organization from reaching its goals and fully realizing its potential.

Healthy Organizational Culture

The term "healthy organizational culture," while common, is not generally used in a formal academic context. However, because trade-based articles and some business consulting firms refer directly or indirectly to the idea of a healthy culture, it is important to note that "healthy" cultures are often associated with overall organizational effectiveness. For example, Joel and Michelle Levey, founders of Seattle-based InnerWork Technologies, offering insights from more than 350 sources, suggest that "healthier" organizational cultures are associated with reduced workforce turnover; improved employee health, productivity, and performance; and ultimately improvements in business results.

Levels of Culture

In the context of deciphering and analyzing organizational culture, Schein (2004) identified three distinct levels at which culture manifests itself. These levels include elements ranging from those that are overt and tangible to those that are deeply embedded and reflect underlying assumptions of organizational members. The three levels are depicted in the iceberg graphic (figure 4.1) and then described.

1. **Artifacts:** Composed of elements that observers can see, hear, and feel. These include such things as the physical environment, technology, signs, symbols, rituals, ceremonies, products, attire, and communication. At this level, Schein points out that culture is easy to observe but difficult to decipher.

2. **Espoused beliefs and values:** These are the philosophies, goals, and strategies whose importance the organization states or advocates through its leadership. The issue at this level of analysis is that the stated beliefs and values may or may not be congruent with what actually occurs in the organization.

3. **Underlying assumptions:** These are the deeply rooted, unconscious perceptions, thoughts, and feelings that are the ultimate source of values and actions in the organization. The basic assumptions, according to Schein, become "so taken for granted that one finds little variation within a social unit" (p. 31). These assumptions, Schein says, become widely shared and strongly held by group members because of the repeated success of their implementation in the organization.

Schein argues that one can study a group's culture at the level of artifacts and espoused values, but to effectively analyze the true essence of the culture one must ultimately

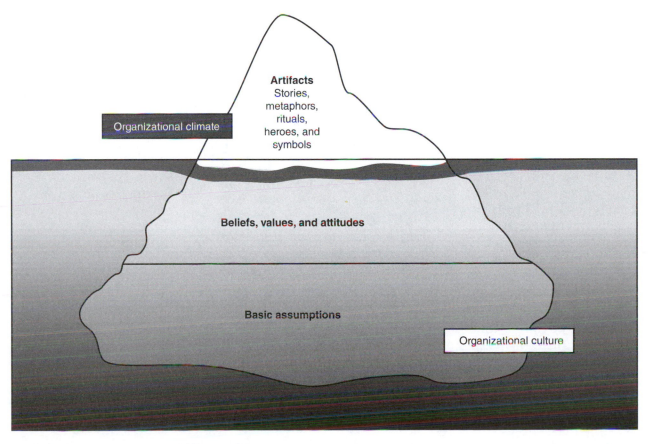

Figure 4.1 Organizational culture iceberg.

Based on Schein, 2004. *Organizational culture and leadership.*

Your Thoughts

Consider an organization you are very familiar with (e.g., your place of employment, team). Taking Schein's (2004) levels of culture into account, what are some of the visible artifacts of the culture in that organization? Are they clear and evident in the physical facilities? What do they communicate? Are there any rituals or ceremonies that offer insights into what is valued in the organization? Are the espoused beliefs and values reflected in what actually occurs, and are these values reinforced and rewarded? What do you believe are the underlying assumptions of this organization? Do you think others within the organization would say the same?

decipher underlying assumptions as well as the learning process that led to those assumptions.

Organizational Culture and Performance

One of the primary reasons that leaders of sport organizations need to better understand organizational culture—what it is and how it is created, managed, or changed—is the accountability that sport leaders assume for the overall "performance" of their organizations. While there are many different ways to measure performance across the numerous types and levels of sport organizations, the ability to produce positive outcomes relatively consistently is a critical factor in success for sport organization leaders. In a recent study of organizational culture in professional sport teams, Frontiera (2010) stated, "Inherent in culture change rationalizations is the basic desire to improve performance" (p. 74).

The relationship between organizational culture and performance is also acknowledged by Cameron and Quinn (2011) in the third edition of their book, *Diagnosing and Changing Organizational Culture*. According to these authors,

> *Culture is created in the first instance by the actions of leaders; culture also is embedded and strengthened by leaders. When culture becomes dysfunctional, leadership is needed to help the group unlearn some of its cultural assumptions and learn new assumptions.*
>
> *Schein (2004, p. 414)*

organizational culture has a powerful effect on organizational performance and long-term organizational effectiveness. In addition to its organizational effects, Cameron and Quinn suggest that organizational culture influences individuals in areas such as employee morale, commitment, productivity, physical health, and emotional well-being.

Organizational Culture and Leadership

Schein (2004), in the third edition of his widely referenced book *Organizational Culture and Leadership*, pointed out that leadership is a variable repeatedly touted as critical to defining the success or failure of organizations. He suggested that this makes it all the more important to look at how leaders create organizational culture, as well as how organizational culture defines and creates leaders. According to Schein, organizational culture and leadership are two sides of the same coin. "Leaders first create cultures when they create groups and organizations. Once cultures exist they determine the criteria for leadership and thus determine who will or will not be a leader" (p. 22). Schein later said in an interview with Doctor Duncan (2012) that an organizational culture is generally stronger than new leaders are and will serve to limit or even ignore leaders who do not fit with the culture. As an example, Schein mentioned Carly Fiorina, former CEO of Hewlett Packard: She was able to institute some new goals and values in the company, but her flamboyant style did not fit with the existing HP culture of relationships among people, teamwork, and humility. Schein suggested that this lack of congruence between Fiorina and the HP culture was the ultimate cause of her loss of credibility and effectiveness in the CEO position.

From a global socio-cultural perspective, it is also important to recognize the influence of ethnic, religious, and political culture on leaders and leadership style. The research of House, Wright, and Aditya (1997), as well as Project Globe (the Global Leadership and Organizational Behavior Effectiveness Research Project) (House, Javidan, and Dorfman, 2001), demonstrate that the expectations of leaders, what they can do, and the status bestowed upon them by constituents vary considerably as a result of the cultural forces associated with the countries or regions where they lead. In this context, leadership styles may need to vary or change based on the cultural influence and expectations relative to leader roles and behaviors.

The concept of cultural influence as a two-way street has not been explored to a great extent in business- or sport management–related studies. However, from a practical perspective, sport organization leaders should recognize that numerous aspects of organizational culture, as well as the national culture and ethnicity of followers, can have a strong impact on the leadership style and behaviors that are most appropriate to the situation. Failure to decipher, evaluate, and appropriately manage these elements can have a profound effect on the acceptance of the leader both within an organization and within a community.

Ultimately, according to Schein (2004), creating and managing organizational culture is the essence of leadership. Additionally, because leaders of organizations are typically held accountable for overall performance, there is adequate evidence of a link between organizational culture and organizational performance (Ogbanna and Harris, 2000). Numerous examples of this "leadership–culture–performance" relationship exist in sport—look at the impact of leaders such as Phil Knight with Nike; David Stern with the National Basketball Association (NBA); Lesa France Kennedy, CEO of International Speedway Corporation; and Pat Summitt with the University of Tennessee women's basketball.

How Culture Is Communicated and Learned

Employees and other members of organizations typically learn the culture through what they observe, participate in, and see as valued according to the words and actions of key lead-

ers and longtime members of the organization. The following areas of culture communication have been identified by Schein (1992, 2004) and more recently defined by Robbins and Judge (2008). According to Robbins and Judge, these are the four primary modes of culture communication:

- **Stories:** These anchor the present to the past and provide explanations and legitimacy for current practices.
- **Rituals:** These offer repetitive sequences of activities that express and reinforce the key values of the organization.
- **Material symbols:** These include such things as acceptable attire, office size, opulence of office furnishings, and executive perks that convey to employees who is important in the organization.
- **Language:** This comprises jargon and special ways of expressing oneself to indicate membership in the organization.

Sport organizations are among the best in the world at using elements of these four modes of culture communication. Some of the best-known examples are shown in table 4.1.

Culture and Subculture

Much of the organizational culture literature examines culture from an "integrated" or single-culture perspective (MacIntosh and Doherty, 2005). However, in many organizations, including those in the sport industry, people work within departments or work groups and at varying levels of the hierarchical structure (e.g., administrative, staff, player levels). Individuals in organizations may also develop unique subgroups with "close ties" based on various demographics, roles, experiences, or personal interest factors (Doherty and Chelladurai, 1999). These "subcultures" are often influenced by the larger organizational culture, but may have strong impacts on the behavior of individuals within the subgroup. For example, in intercollegiate athletic departments, numerous team subcultures (e.g., various men's and women's sports, revenue- and nonrevenue-producing sports) often operate independently with their own leadership, expectations, and value systems (Scott, 1997; Southall, 2001).

Table 4.1 Examples of Culture Communication in Sport

Mode of communication	Example
Stories	The story of Jackie Robinson, who became the first African American Major League Baseball player in 1947, ending more than 80 years of segregation in baseball in the United States. His story became a movie, *42*, in 2013 and offers inspiration for anyone overcoming cultural or racial biases and hardships.
Rituals	The haka "Ka Mate" dance, which has been performed by the New Zealand All Blacks national rugby team before each rugby match since 1905. The dance is a traditional expression of the Maori culture and is "performed with precision and intensity" by team members to symbolize both the culture and their approach to the game (allblacks.com, 2011).
Material symbols	The sign in the locker room at the University of Notre Dame with the slogan "Play Like a Champion Today." All players touch the sign on their way to the field. This symbolizes the players' and university's commitment to excellence (Sakakeeny, 2010).
Language	Numerous slogans and sayings used by intercollegiate athletic teams and fans in the United States that indicate membership and support for a school or team (e.g., University of Alabama, "Roll Tide"; Michigan State, "Sparty On"; Texas A&M University, "Gig-Em"; University of Oklahoma, "Boomer Sooner").

Research still needs to be done in this area, particularly in sport management, to provide a better understanding of the influence of subcultures on individuals and organizations. One study (MacIntosh and Doherty, 2005) in sport that addressed subculture pointed out,

> The further impact of subcultures at the organization level is an interesting consideration because organizational effectiveness is purportedly associated with a strong overall culture where common values are widely shared. Subcultures, by definition, imply a differentiated organizational culture. As such, subcultures may be considered to be detrimental to the long-term success of an organization. (p. 5)

However, MacIntosh and Doherty also suggested that strong subcultures may reduce uncertainty for group members, increase retention, and possibly contribute to performance and overall effectiveness of the group. Thus subcultures may be influential, positively or negatively, on the larger organizational culture. The challenge for organizational leaders is to keep these subcultures united and focused on core values of the larger organization (Deal and Kennedy, 1999; MacIntosh and Doherty, 2005). More information pertaining to the organizational culture research of MacIntosh and Doherty in sport- or fitness-related organizations is presented later in the chapter.

Organizational Culture and Change in Sport

Often, one of the most challenging of a sport organization leader's tasks is to actually bring about long-term and effective change. This is also frequently the reason an individual is hired into a position—to move a team, company, or other sport organization in the direction of desired performance outcomes. One perspective on why bringing about change in sport is difficult is that of Wayne Goldsmith, a professional sport performance consultant who has worked with leading sport organizations such as the Australian Sports Commission, the New South Wales Institute of Sport, British Swimming, and the United States Olympic Committee. According to Goldsmith (2012), "change is critical" to survival in competitive sport, but "sport is incredibly conservative" and may be more resistant to change than other areas of society. Goldsmith identifies several reasons for the difficulty of introducing change in sport, all of which relate to beliefs, values, and assumptions made in sport organizations. "On the Sidelines" presents examples of statements that Goldsmith identifies as reflective of these beliefs, values, and assumptions.

Research in Sport Organizational Culture

This section reviews and summarizes some of the key published research related to leader-

On the Sidelines

Why Change Is Hard to Introduce in Sport

Australian sport performance expert, Wayne Goldsmith (2012) suggests that "athletes, coaches and teams who are first at introducing new ideas and innovations are usually the winners, the gold medalists, the premiers – the success stories" (p. 1). Despite this, Goldsmith points to several reasons that people in sport are often unwilling to embrace a change process that can move them to new levels of achievement and performance. These are a few of the key examples on Goldsmith's list:

"It's different here": *The meaning is that this team, club, or sport is somehow different from others and does not need to change, evolve, or improve.*

"You don't understand the culture of this sport": *Although all sports and teams have unique cultures, it is also true that core principles of success apply to all teams.*

"We don't have the money to change": *Goldsmith suggests that this is rarely the real issue and that more often it is personalities or politics (or both) that are the real impediments to effective change.*

"I can't get people to buy into the need to change": *Goldsmith points out that resistance to change is a "fact of life." However, great leaders have the skill to convince people why change is necessary and help support them in moving in a new direction.*

"It's too difficult to change": *Goldsmith argues that everything changes and that if you can't change, you will be out of pace with the rest of the universe.*

These statements represent beliefs, values, or assumptions of organizational culture that may be hard for leaders of new or existing sport organizations to change. Are there instances in which you have felt these things yourself or heard others making these statements about a sport organization you are familiar with?

---

ship and organizational culture in sport. The discussion is divided into subsections reflective of various domains in the sport industry. The intent of the section is to provide insights into how organizational culture is examined and analyzed specifically in sport organizations, as well as to demonstrate the extent to which this topic has been and continues to be of interest among sport researchers. Much has been learned as a result of the research summarized; however, there are many unanswered questions, and more research is needed to lead to a better understanding of how sport leaders across the many sectors and levels of the industry interact with and influence culture.

Recreation and Fitness Industry

Recreation- and fitness-related organizations were the source for much of the original academic research in North America on organizational culture in a sport context. Wallace and Weese (1995), examining links between trans-formational leadership and organizational culture, found that Canadian YMCA organizations led by high transformational leaders carried out key culture-building functions to a greater extent than organizations with low transformational leaders. Weese (1995), in a similar investigation of campus recreation administration in the United States, determined that high transformational leaders direct more culture-building activities and build stronger organizational cultures than other leader types. In a follow-up study exploring relationships between transformational leadership, organizational culture, and organizational effectiveness in campus recreation programs, Weese (1996) found that no significant relationship existed between transformational leadership and organizational effectiveness. However, he did find that the perceived strength of the culture in these organizations was significantly related to organizational effectiveness. These findings led to questions for future study around the role that leadership and culture play relative to effectiveness in sport organizations.

Organizational culture research in the area of fitness management continued into the new millennium with studies of the Canadian fitness industry by Macintosh and Doherty (2005, 2008, 2010) and Macintosh, Doherty, and Walker (2010). These studies, using both qualitative and quantitative methods, yielded interesting findings relative to organizational culture in sport- or fitness-related organizations; some of these were as follows. (1) A significant culture gap existed between leaders' intentions and employee perceptions, and subcultures existed by organizational level (e.g., head office vs. club) (MacIntosh and Doherty, 2005). (2) Culture had a more direct influence on employees and a less direct influence, if any, on organizational performance (MacIntosh and Doherty, 2005). (3) The Canadian fitness industry has common dimensions of organizational culture that include such elements as organizational presence and member success and connectedness, and these dimensions appear to be predictive of organizational success (MacIntosh and Doherty, 2008). (4) Shared values appear to exist across both profit and nonprofit organizations in the industry, although a focus or value on sales productivity was related to an increase in intentions of staff to leave their positions.

International Sport Settings

One of the first studies in sport examining organizational culture was conducted by Pawlak (1984) on the Polish Weight-Lifting Association, the Polish Judo Association, and the Polish Kayaking Association. The author examined association publications, the press, and interviews with association officials. Key findings indicated that the associations valued success, development of the discipline, and the increasing popularity of the given sport. It was also shown that management value was attributed to centralization of decisions, decision-making processes, and clear and simple organizational structure.

Colyer (2000), in a study of selected state sport organizations in Western Australia, used the four-dimensional competing values approach for analyzing organizational cul-

ture (Cameron and Quinn, 1999; Quinn and Rohrbaugh, 1981; Quinn and Spreitzer, 1991). In the competing values framework, organizational values are distributed across four dimensions that to an extent are in competition with one another. The four dimensions are (1) *clan culture*, focusing on human relations and group cohesion; (2) *adhocracy culture*, recognizing innovation, flexibility, and change; (3) *market culture*, focusing on productivity, performance, and achievement; and (4) *hierarchy culture*, emphasizing internal efficiency, coordination, and control.

Colyer's study employed both qualitative (structured interviews) and quantitative (questionnaire) methods for the purpose of comparing the organizational culture profiles of the chosen sport organizations in Western Australia. The study also sought to determine differences in perception of the culture on the part of volunteers and paid staff working in the organizations. Findings of the research indicated that the three sport organizations included in the study had different profiles, including one with a very strong "people-oriented" or clan culture, another with moderate cultural strength across each cultural quadrant, and the third with a very balanced profile across each quadrant but with moderate to low evidence of cultural strength (shared values in each dimension). Colyer also found that tension existed between traditional voluntary management and emerging professional management. The study was the first in sport to use the competing values model, and the findings suggested that the model might be useful for defining culture profiles as a first step in diagnosing organizational culture in sport organizations. The competing values model has also been used in studies of professional baseball in Korea and in Triple A baseball in the United States and as discussed in the next subsection.

Professional Sport

Studies on leadership and sport organization culture in professional sport have only recently begun to appear in the academic literature. Choi, Martin, and Park (2008), also using the competing values approach to organizational culture (Cameron and Quinn, 1999), studied patterns of perceived culture and links between job satisfaction and culture among all seven baseball organizations in the Korean Professional Baseball League. Findings indicated that a market-oriented and results-driven culture was perceived to be the emphasis across the organizations, but that a clan-oriented and human relations culture had a significant influence on overall employee job satisfaction.

Choi and Scott (2009), in another study using Cameron and Quinn's (1999) competing values framework for analyzing organizational culture, examined employee perceptions of the organizational culture in 12 American Triple A baseball organizations. The purpose of the study was to describe the culture of these organizations; measure the strength of the four cultural dimensions; and determine if factors including geographic location, organizational size, or winning percentage were related to elements of the competing values cultural framework. Notable findings included the following: (a) The "market culture" was predominant across the Triple A baseball organizations; (b) the "clan culture" was also perceived to be a focus area; and (c) large organizations with high winning percentages obtained higher scores on cultural strength than mid-size or small organizations.

In a more recent qualitative study of leadership, organizational culture, and organizational change in professional sport, Frontiera (2010) set out to "explore how accomplished leaders in professional sport have been able to alter the culture of their respective organizations to improve on-field or on-court performance" (p. 71). In this study, Frontiera conducted in-depth interviews with six owners or general managers of organizations from the NBA, Major League Baseball (MLB), and the National Football League (NFL). These individuals were selected on the basis of their having successfully guided an organizational culture change as evidenced by a turnaround in overall team performance. The insights of the leaders in this study offer an applied foundation for culture development that can be very useful to sport organization leaders in all segments of the sport industry. A more in-depth review of Frontiera's work and its implications is provided in a special case study at the end of this chapter.

Intercollegiate Athletics

Studies of organizational culture in intercollegiate athletic organizations appeared in the mid to late 1990s. Scott (1997) provided one of the first conceptual articles in sport that specifically applied concepts of organizational culture to intercollegiate athletics. The article presented insights and recommendations regarding how intercollegiate athletic directors and head coaches could apply concepts and theories of organizational culture from business and higher education research to better decipher and manage the culture of athletic departments and teams.

In an empirical study, Scott (1999) used the multiframe leadership model of Bolman and Deal (1991) to explore predominant leadership behaviors of athletic directors in high-performing athletic departments (Sears Director's Cup finalists). The study also sought evidence of the extent of shared perceptions of leadership and organizational climate among head coaches within these departments. Findings supported the notion that "strongly shared agreement" among head coaches on various elements of leadership and organizational climate may be indicative of deeper underlying assumptions reflective of cultures that contribute to positive organizational performance within athletic departments.

Beyer and Hannah (2000), from both a sociological and a cultural perspective, examined how the deeply rooted cultural significance of athletics in higher education may present formidable barriers to reform in intercollegiate athletics. The researchers discussed three characteristics of college athletic cultures: (1) strong emotion of players and fans, (2) symbolic meaning of athletics in an institution, and (3) meanings based on the cherished history of institutions (e.g., mascots, traditions). As the authors pointed out, these elements of culture in intercollegiate athletics might be viewed by outsiders as insignificant, but the elements are "so interwoven with the practical and economic factors affecting universities that it cannot be ignored" (p. 127).

In other organizational culture–related studies, Southall, Wells, and Nagel (2005) used a multiple perspective of organizational culture to study college coaches' perceptions of organizational culture. They found that there were significant differences in organizational culture perceptions in intercollegiate athletics between male and female coaches and revenue and nonrevenue coaches.

More recently, Schroeder (2010), using a case study in NCAA Division III, proposed a new model for assessing culture in intercollegiate athletics. Schroeder argues that most of the frameworks used to analyze organizational culture in sport organizations come from corporate models (e.g., Schein, 2004). He also asserts that the inconsistency in values in intercollegiate athletics as a part of a larger higher education organizational culture presents challenges for the leaders of these organizations. Schroeder's model identifies four elements—institutional culture, internal environment, external environment, and leadership/power—that interact with one another to create a unique cultural environment in intercollegiate athletics. Readers of this textbook are encouraged to review Schroeder's article to obtain deeper insights into his proposed model.

Also recently, Charlton (2011), using a case study approach, examined the relationship between organizational culture and academic success in historically black college and university (HBCU) athletics. Charlton specifically explored the degree to which policy, language, and ritual "impacted the socialization of student athletes to an organizational culture that promotes academic success" (p. 121). Results and implications from the study indicated that a focus on three elements can shape a culture in athletics geared toward academic success: (1) purposefully designed policy; (2) transmission of values related to compassion and citizenship development; and (3) carefully planned ritual, such as regular recognition and honoring of academically successful athletes.

Other Related Areas of Research

Another area of sport research related to leadership and organizational culture focuses on cultural diversity and the management of diversity in sport organizations (e.g., Cunningham, 2008, 2009; Doherty and Chelladurai, 1999; Doherty et al., 2010). Because chapter 8 in this textbook is devoted to the topic of

diversity leadership, more information about these studies and this particular element of organizational culture is presented there.

Other organizational culture research in sport centers on culture within athletic teams and how it is influenced by coaches as leaders. The type and strength of team culture are thought by many to play a significant, if not primary, role in overall team performance in sport. For readers with a specific interest in research related to sport team culture, several studies (Lee, 1989; Weese, MacLean, and Corlett, 1993; Kao and Ceng, 2005; Schroeder, 2010) offer insights and recommendations regarding the development and management of sport team culture.

Building a Culture of Success in Sport Organizations

This section of the chapter provides an applied perspective on how one might approach culture development and management in sport organizations. It includes examples and key recommendations from some of the most widely recognized and cited organizational culture research in business and industry of the last several years. The section concludes with an in-depth case review of recent sport-specific research by Frontiera (2010), whose interviews with professional sport leaders provide timely insights into the effective creation and management of culture in sport organizations.

Organizational Culture and Leadership

Edgar Schein, mentioned numerous times throughout this chapter, has been at the forefront of organizational culture research for several decades. He offers a classic perspective on organizational culture and states that "culture and leadership are two sides of the same coin" (Schein, 2004, p. 22). Over years of research and consulting with organizations, Schein has identified several key mechanisms for influencing culture in organizations. Tables 4.2 and 4.3 list and describe Schein's "primary" and "secondary" mechanisms and may provide helpful ideas for leaders in sport organizations who want to build more effective organizational cultures.

Table 4.2 Schein's Primary Mechanisms for Influencing Culture

Mechanism	Description
Attention	Leaders communicate their priorities, values, and concerns through what followers see them pay attention to.
Reaction to crises	Leaders' responses to crisis situations send a strong message about values and assumptions. Leaders who faithfully support espoused values when under pressure provide evidence and communicate clearly that the values are really important.
Role modeling	Leaders communicate values and expectations by their *own* actions. Leaders who institute policies and procedures but do not act in accordance with those policies communicate an inconsistent message about what is really valued.
Allocation of rewards	Leaders also communicate what is valued in an organization through what is formally or informally rewarded. Differential allocation of rewards affirms the status of some organizational members compared to others. Failure to recognize accomplishments of individuals or groups communicates a message that they are unimportant.
Criteria for selection and dismissal	Leaders influence culture through the criteria used for recruitment, selection, promotion, and dismissal of organizational members.

Based on information in Schein 1992, 2004.

Table 4.3 Schein's Secondary Mechanisms for Influencing Culture

Mechanism	Description
Design of systems and procedures	The ways in which managerial leaders develop and implement such things as budgets, planning sessions, and performance reviews can reduce ambiguity and clarify role responsibilities. The more formal this process is, the more it is reflective of strong values around control and order.
Design of organization structure	Centralized structure is reflective of a culture in which only a leader or those in top management positions determine the best strategies and solutions for the organization. Decentralized structures are indicative of a culture that reflects values more oriented toward individual initiative and shared responsibility.
Design of facilities	In some situations, leaders can reflect basic values of the organization through the design of its facilities. For example, office layouts with open designs can indicate that the organization supports open communication and collaborative work.
Stories, legends, and myths	Stories about people and events contribute to how an organization transmits values and core assumptions. In order to be useful, stories must convey clear messages about what the organization values, and the stories must be based on real events.
Formal statements	Oral and written statements presented to the public about an organization can be very helpful in communicating values and assumptions, provided that they are supported by consistent actions and behavior of organizational leaders.

Based on information in Schein 1992, 2004.

Leadership Values That Enable Success

Kim Cameron, a noted expert in organizational culture and change management, provides 10 leadership values that he believes contribute to "spectacular, extraordinary and astonishing" organizational results (Cameron, 2006). While Cameron's list relates to the dramatic results achieved in a specific case (the cleanup of a nuclear power plant in the Rocky Mountains outside of Denver, Colorado), it also "explains the values that leaders in other organizations can apply in enabling their own spectacular success" (p. 132). Based on Cameron's recommendations, these values are listed here and may provide current or future sport leaders with areas of focus that can have a positive impact on their organizations.

Ten leadership values that enable success.

1. It is important to foster, enable, and encourage leaders throughout the organization and in other stakeholder relationships

to behave like leaders. *Do not rely on a single leader.*

2. Use incentives (specifically salary or compensation) to create fundamental transformational change only if it can change lifestyles (e.g., substantial pay increases).

3. A profound purpose for the organization's activities must be identified that affects human beings for the better over the long term.

4. Symbols (e.g., flags, logos, captions, signs) should be chosen that focus on what the organization desires to become.

5. The organizational control system must be well developed, and it must reinforce the achievement of extraordinary performance.

6. High-quality relationships must be built that permit perfect execution on commitments to external stakeholders (requires collaboration and mutual support to build trustworthiness).

7. Culture change requires a change in individuals—leaders and organizational members must believe differently, behave differently, and pursue abundance-based purposes and vision.

8. Learning from mistakes should have less priority than learning from successes (future strategies should be based on identifying the enablers and factors that have contributed to previous success).

9. Strategy should be established based on what the organization "can be" as opposed to what it has been or is now.

10. Virtuous behaviors and values (e.g., integrity, generosity, humility) should be enabled and reinforced throughout the organization.

Based on information by Cameron, K. in Hess and Cameron, Eds. 2006.

Diagnosing and Changing Organizational Culture

Cameron and Quinn (2011) offer a nine-step process that they recommend leaders follow when designing and implementing an organizational culture change effort. This plan is based on the widely used and referenced Organizational Culture Assessment Instrument (OCAI); Cameron and Quinn recommend that all individuals in an organization complete this assessment as the nine-step culture change process begins. The OCAI consists of 24 questions that measure participants' perceptions and is available in Cameron and Quinn's 2011 book. Table 4.4 summarizes the steps, key requirements and activities, and sample questions to consider when one is undertaking a culture change effort in an organization. Readers should refer to Cameron and Quinn (2011) for an in-depth explanation of culture change, the steps involved, and a more extensive list of questions.

Organizational Culture Transformation in Professional Sport

Frontiera (2010) has published one of the more recent studies with direct application for sport leaders attempting to embed a new culture into their organizations. His purpose was to examine the organizational culture change process in several organizations in the NFL, MLB, and NBA. His approach to the study and a review of results are presented in the special case study that follows. Review the details of the study and consider how you might apply them to an organization with which you are familiar.

Summary

Research over many years has broadly supported the notion that organizational culture can have a powerful influence on long-term organizational performance. Thus, understanding and managing organizational culture is one component of effective sport organization leadership. This chapter discusses how organizational culture reflects the shared values that guide decisions, actions, and learning in an organization. Strong-culture organizations are those with deeply rooted values in which group members recognize and act consistently with those values. Weak-culture organizations typically demonstrate less cohesiveness among group members and demonstrate less evidence of agreement or commitment to the organizational mission. Organizational culture is analyzed at three

Table 4.4 Summary of Steps for Initiating Culture Change

Steps for initiating culture change	Key requirements or activities	Sample questions to consider during the process
1. Reach consensus regarding current organizational culture.	Have all individuals who will be implementing or will be a part of the culture change effort complete the Organizational Culture Assessment Instrument (OCAI). Discuss the results within the organization.	• What fundamental assumptions drive the organization? • What events reflect the culture of the organization?
2. Reach consensus on preferred future culture.	Repeat step 1 and have organizational members focus on the "preferred or desired" culture.	• What will be needed for the organization to be successful in the future? • What will our customers or competitors require in the future?
3. Determine what the changes will and will not mean.	Plot the culture profiles from the results of the current and preferred responses on the OCAI and highlight discrepancies.	• What attributes and activities need to be emphasized in order to move toward a preferred cultural quadrant? • What is unique about each quadrant that should be preserved?
4. Identify illustrative stories.	Identify events or incidents within the organization that illustrate the key values desired in the future culture.	• What are some inspiring examples of the organization at its best? • What employees working in nonvisible positions exemplify the best aspirations of the organization?
5. Identify a strategic action agenda.	Have the group members reach consensus on new things that should happen and events or actions that should stop, and identify what we should do more of as the culture change process begins.	• Where should the process begin? • What processes or systems should be redesigned? • What environmental factors must be considered?
6. Identify immediate small wins.	Find things that can be changed easily, change them, and publicize the changes in order to create momentum for the culture change.	• What are some of the easy things to target for change? • What aspects of the organization can be visibly altered (e.g., the physical environment, celebrations, and recognitions)?
7. Identify the leadership implications.	Consider that leaders must have capabilities to lead both the change process and the organization of the future. Leaders must demonstrate total commitment to the culture change.	• What competencies will leaders need to lead the culture change effort? • What leadership training opportunities are needed?
8. Identify metrics, measures, and milestones.	Identify the measures, indicators, and milestones that will mark the progress of the culture change.	• What are indicators of progress? • What is success, and how often should progress be assessed?
9. Identify a communication strategy	Determine ways in which the message will be communicated and spread, including new symbols, icons, and visible representations of the new desired culture.	• How can members become involved in the communication? • What simple messages can be formulated to communicate the desired culture?

Based on information in Cameron and Quinn 2011.

levels: (1) artifacts, (2) espoused values and beliefs, and (3) underlying assumptions as proposed by Schein (2004). Also, leaders attempting to lead change efforts in their organizations should be highly cognizant of the elements of culture, which must be addressed effectively to achieve the desired results.

As also explored in this chapter, research in sport organizational culture has been conducted over the last two decades across several organizational types, including recreational sport, fitness organizations, intercollegiate athletics, and professional sport. Much of the research has been exploratory and has

Sport Research Case Study

Leadership and Culture Change in Professional Sport

Frontiera (2010) set out to "explore how accomplished leaders in professional sport have been able to alter the culture of their respective organizations to improve on-field or on-court performance" (p. 71). In the study, Frontiera conducted in-depth interviews with six owners or general managers of organizations involved in turning around low-performing NBA, MLB, and NFL organizations. He reported on five themes that emerged from the interviews:

- **Symptoms of a dysfunctional culture:** Five of the six participants in the study were aware of both physical and psychological dysfunctional elements of the organizational environment. This included elements of poor facilities as well as the absence of values such as trust, honesty, and integrity. In these organizations, Frontiera wrote, "a losing habit had become the norm, bad decisions were common and there was little confidence in the organization" (p. 77).

- **My way:** The participants discussed their roles in establishing a "new way to do things" in the organizations. According to Frontiera, five subthemes emerged in this category:

  - **Vision:** New tangible goals were provided through which members of the organization could come together.

  - **My values:** New values were brought to the organization, which became the foundation for decision making. These espoused values included "honesty, integrity, loyalty, trust, commitment, dignity, professionalism, philanthropy and team" (p. 78).

  - **Change personnel:** New people were introduced into the organization (e.g., head coach, front office personnel, players); this was considered necessary to begin the culture change.

  - **Grow people:** The importance of investing in and developing individuals within the organization was a common theme.

  - **Explicit communication:** A critical factor was for the leaders to "honestly and clearly

communicate their vision, plan and expectations to both players and staff" (p. 79).

- **Walk the talk:** All participants indicated the importance of the need for their actions as a leader on a day-to-day basis to be consistent with espoused values. This was true relative to their involvement in daily events as well as their reactions to critical events and involvement in critical organizational decisions.

- **Embedding new culture:** Participants identified two areas that were important to the embedding of a new culture in their organizations: (1) new success and (2) turning point. The *new success* component referred to a slow, steady improvement that reinforced the new culture and gained commitment from organizational members. The *turning point* referred to an event in which members of the organization came to a sudden realization that they had significantly improved and that the success they experienced was not fleeting.

- **Our way:** All participants in the Frontiera study also expressed that a culture shift had occurred in their organization as evidenced by how the organization selected new members, how organizational members made decisions, how things were run internally, and the organization's new collective values. All participants talked about the importance of valuing and respecting people including players, leaders, and fans.

According to Frontiera, several practical implications or "lessons" emerged from this study in relation to the culture change "process" for sport organization leaders. Key areas included (1) the importance of establishing a clear vision and adhering to the plan, even when pressured to change; (2) clearly communicating values verbally in the organization and consistently supporting those values through actions and critical decisions; (3) celebrating successes as they happen and communicating them throughout the organization; and (4) thinking independently and ensuring that the organizational culture can evolve to meet changing demands.

---

examined relationships between organizational culture, leadership style, performance, and various measures of organizational effectiveness and organizational change. Findings generally support the relationships between

leadership, organizational culture, and performance; however, more research is needed in this area to enable better understanding of how these relationships occur and whether they vary by organizational type and context.

Sport organization leaders attempting to develop a culture of success have several academic resources available to assist in this process. Schein (2004) offers both primary and secondary mechanisms for influencing culture that include the design and structure of the organization, the physical facilities, what leaders pay attention to, how they act and react relative to core organizational values, and what they reward in the organization. Cameron (2006) provides 10 leadership values proposed to have a powerful impact on organizational culture and organizational performance. Cameron and Quinn (2011) offer a nine-step process explaining the steps for initiating culture change, identifying key requirements and activities of those leading this process, and providing key questions to consider during the process. With respect to sport specifically, Frontiera (2010) identifies for practicing sport leaders five elements of culture transformation that emerged as important among selected professional sport team owners and general managers involved in successful culture change efforts.

Final Self-Assessment

After having read and reflected on the content in this chapter, consider your responses to the self-assessment questions presented at the beginning of the chapter. Have your perspectives changed, or do you have any new insights or additional questions regarding your understanding of the leadership–organizational culture relationship?

1. How do leaders effectively develop and communicate desired values and expected "ways of doing things" for an organization?
2. How can you go about diagnosing the strengths and weaknesses of an organization's culture?
3. What findings from sport organization culture research could be helpful in your role as a current or future sport manager or administrator?
4. What do you feel are critical components of an organizational culture development plan for building and maintaining a healthy and effective culture?

Game Plan Activity

Assume that you have just become the chief administrator or leader of a sport organization of your choice. Using one or more of the sets of recommendations for building a culture of success provided in the last section of this chapter, develop a draft plan that you would implement over the next several months, either to build on a strong culture or to attempt a culture change transformation in the organization. Use the following as guiding questions for your plan.

1. What would you pay attention to first?
2. What key values would you build on or need to introduce into the organization?
3. Who would you bring into the culture development or change process?
4. How would you attempt to "embed" desired elements of culture?
5. How would you know you were making progress?

Questions to Consider

1. What are some of the formal or informal organizational culture development activities you have experienced as a team member or employee of a sport organization? To what extent were they consistent with espoused values?
2. Hazing of new team members in a sport organization, often taken to extremes, has dangerous consequences (and is now prohibited by law in 44 U.S. states). Even so, it has historically been a part of the enculturation of individuals into many teams and

organizations. If you were administering a high school or college athletic department or coaching a team, what are other more constructive ways you can think of to effectively build team culture and cohesiveness?

3. Is it possible for subcultures within a parent organization to have more influence or power than the parent organization? Why or why not? If you think it is possible, what examples can you provide?

4. You are the new director of a large urban sport and fitness club. What are some examples of symbols, rites, and rituals you might incorporate to communicate core values in your organization?

5. A lack of focus or group cohesiveness in an organization may be a sign of a weak culture. Based on concepts and ideas presented in the chapter, how would you attempt to strengthen a weak culture and improve unity of purpose?

Recommended Readings

Argyris, C. (2012). *Organizational traps: Leadership, culture, organizational design.* Cary, NC: Oxford University Press.

Cameron, K., and Quinn, R. (2011). *Diagnosing and changing organizational culture: Based on the competing values framework.* San Francisco: Jossey-Bass.

Schein, E. (2004). *Organizational culture and leadership.* San Francisco: Jossey-Bass.

Vision and Strategic Leadership

After reading and reflecting on the concepts, examples, and recommendations in this chapter, you will be able to

1. give examples of visionary leadership in sport,
2. discuss ways in which a leader can develop and sustain a compelling vision,
3. facilitate an organizational meeting designed to develop a vision statement,
4. describe deliberate versus emergent strategy as it relates to strategic leadership,
5. discuss how the complexity of modern organizations influences strategic leadership, and
6. compare and contrast elements of traditional strategic planning with contemporary strategic thinking.

1. What are emerging and collective visions and how are they important for leaders of sport organizations?
2. What all is involved in the "practice" of visionary leadership?
3. What are the basic elements of traditional strategic planning and how might you effectively lead these efforts in an organization?
4. What is "strategic thinking" and how can it be applied to modern sport organization leadership?

One of the first questions often posed to individuals in new leadership roles is, "What is your vision for the organization and how do you plan to get us there?" Interestingly, while leaders are expected to be visionary as well as to have on-the-ground strategic planning skills, neither of these are innate abilities that come instinctively to anyone assuming a leadership position.

This chapter explores both vision and strategic leadership as expectations and requirements of sport organization leadership. The chapter begins with a focus on visionary leadership by providing a few historical examples of the transformation of sport-oriented visions into reality, as well as introducing examples of emerging visions arising from the collective thinking of individuals and organizations that are addressing sport-related challenges for the future. Attention then turns to the actual practice and process of developing vision for individuals in a leadership role. Questions that one can ask when attempting to develop a compelling vision, the importance of communicating and creating a "shared vision," and steps for how an organization can go about composing a vision statement are addressed. To complete this section, examples of recent research on organizational vision and its influence on employee satisfaction, adaptivity, and proactivity are included.

The next section of the chapter explores strategic leadership with emphasis on both traditional strategic planning and the more recent emerging strategy and strategic thinking in modern organizations. Elements of the strategic planning process, as well as recommendations for the role that leaders play in making the strategic planning process work more effectively, are discussed. The section then turns to a comparison of deliberate and emerging strategies and examines the challenges posed by the development of strategy in the context of complexity in modern organizations. The chapter ends with a discussion of the theoretical concepts associated with "strategic thinking" as well as leadership actions and behaviors associated with strategic leadership in this framework.

> *Vision—an imagined or discerned future state that clearly captures the organization's direction and defines its destination.*
>
> *Cartwright and Baldwin 2007, p. 15.*

Leadership and Vision in Sport Organizations

There are countless examples of visionary leadership in sport. There are also numerous indicators today of how important visionary leadership will continue to be in the future for addressing the many issues and challenges faced by sport leaders across the industry. This section provides only a few of many examples of what one can accomplish by beginning with a vision of the future. It is important when reading through these examples to consider that the critical element of visionary leadership is not limited to the creation of a new vision; it also includes the dedication and commitment necessary to advance that vision toward reality.

From Vision to Reality

One example of an individual's vision that evolved into a global sport movement is that of the late Eunice Kennedy Shriver and Special Olympics International. Shriver, in the early 1960s, based her vision on the belief that people with intellectual disabilities could accomplish more than was thought possible and that sport and physical activity was an avenue through which they could realize their potential ("Eunice Kennedy Shriver," 2012). Through her commitment and will to move a vision forward, Shriver began providing organized activities for children with disabilities at a summer day camp in her backyard. Since that time, her vision evolved into what is now known as Special Olympics International, a global organization that serves over 3.7 million people in 170 countries (specialolympics. org, 2012).

Another example of extraordinary visionary leadership is that of former tennis star, women's sport leader, and social advocate Billie Jean King. Among her numerous honors, King has been awarded the Presidential Medal of Freedom and named Global Mentor for Gender Equality by the United Nations Educational, Scientific and Cultural Organization (UNESCO); she was acknowledged in 1990 by *Life* magazine as one of the 100 most important Americans of the 20th century (Mylan WTT, 2012). King has provided vision, guidance, and support to organizations including the Women's Tennis Foundation, World Team Tennis, and the Women's Sports Foundation; most recently, in 2007, she cofounded GreenSlam, an initiative to make sports environmentally friendly. King's leadership demonstrates how linking vision with commitment has produced extraordinary outcomes leading to significant advancements in gender equity as well as social, cultural, and environmental responsibility in sport.

Emerging Visions in Sport

Many of the challenges facing the sport industry today call for visions that emerge out of *collective* thinking and create a *collective* impetus for change within or across organizations. In an article addressing visioning as an essential element for the overall future of the sport industry, Jean-Loup Chappelet (2009) points to several problems that he believes must be collectively addressed in order for sport to continue to play a positive role in 21st-century society. According to Chappelet, the core problems, particularly in competitive sport today, include (a) increased use of doping substances; (b) increased violence on the part of fans, players, and coaches; (c) corruption among athletes and officials; and (d) "gigantism." By gigantism, Chappelet means the "sheer scale of many sport events and facilities, which makes them difficult to maintain and sustain" (p. 484).

On the Sidelines

Roone Arledge: Visionary

Roone Arledge (1931-2002) has long been recognized in the sport industry as a true visionary in sport marketing and broadcasting. Among his many accolades, Arledge was selected by *Life* magazine as one of the 100 most important Americans of the 20th century and was placed in the top 10 by the Sports Broadcasting Group (SBG). SBG recognized Arledge as responsible for crafting "the modern link between sports and entertainment, transforming ABC Sports from a financial disaster to the world's go-to destination for athletics entertainment" (p. 1). Arledge was known for using "unheard-of technical innovations to make the Olympics some of the most important programming on television and creating a staple of modern American sports, Monday Night Football" (p. 1). The innovations in sport television broadcasting introduced by Arledge included slow motion, freeze frame, instant replay, and split screen, which added drama to sporting events. He was also known for adding "up-close and personal" features on athletes to help transform "obscure international athletes into instant celebrities."

Given your television viewing experience with sport events today, imagine that experience without the visionary innovations (e.g., slow motion, instant replay) attributed to Roone Arledge.

- How do you think his vision has affected your experience today?
- What can you envision for the future that, in your opinion, would further enhance the experience for television or online viewers of sport events?

Excerpts from "Roone Arledge: Management," retrieved February 12, 2012 from www.sportsvideo.org/halloffame/management/roone-arledge.

As a first step in developing a foundational vision for how those in the sport professions might conceptualize these problems and begin to propose solutions, Chappelet refers to a key question posed by Earle Ziegler (2007): "What kind of sport should the profession promote in order to shape the world in the 21st century?" According to Chappelet, a possible way to think about this question and its relationship to a future vision of sport is to consider the benefits of what he refers to as "good sport" (p. 484). These benefits can be classified into four categories:

1. Sport brings good health and quality of life for those who practice it.
2. It is a means of physical and moral education.
3. Sport provides role models and helps in the social integration of young people and other minority groups.

4. As a crucial global industry, sport contributes to economic and social development in the areas where it is organized.

Chappelet goes on to suggest that sport managers ask themselves four key questions when considering the future vision of sport. These questions, simply stated, are (1) "Do we promote health?", (2)"Do we encourage education or violence?", (3)"Do we provide good role models or encourage corruption?", and (4) "Do we promote balanced development of sport in cities?"

In summary, according to Chappelet, effectively addressing these four questions can lead to emerging visions and changes capable of producing sport that he describes as "Sustainable, Addiction-Free, Fair and Ethical—SAFE" (p. 485). In his view, this can occur through use of a holistic approach that operates at both the local and global levels.

In this example of visioning in sport, Chappelet lays a foundation for how leaders of sport organizations could collectively begin to visualize an ideal future. He also cites examples of work associated with this vision that is already in progress at various organizations, including the International Olympic Committee, the Union of European Football Associations (UEFA), and the European Olympic Committee. Each of these organizations, according to Chappelet, is contributing directly to initiatives designed to address some of the current challenges and issues related to doping, violence, and ethics in sport.

Another example of how leaders can collectively identify problems and begin to envision a different future relates to college sport reform in the United States. The challenges and issues associated with college sport, particularly in National Collegiate Athletic Association (NCAA) Division I, are mentioned almost daily in the news and have become a key focus of many individuals and organizations. These include university presidents, the NCAA, the American Association of University Professors (AAUP), the Knight Commission, the Drake Group, and the Coalition on Intercollegiate Athletics (COIA) (Benford, 2007). As pointed out by Benford, COIA, which is composed of 52 Division IA university faculty senates, is dedicated to promoting comprehensive reform in intercollegiate sports. Issues identified by COIA to be addressed include academic integrity, welfare of athletes, governance, finance, and commercialization.

According to *College Sports Business News* (December, 2011), the positive virtues of college athletics (including institutional pride; strengthening connections to alumni; and creating educational, competitive, and physical development and socialization opportunities for athletes) are often overshadowed by the demand for "sports-generated dollars." Among reform efforts, new *visions* for college athletics supported by Division I presidents include significant revisions to NCAA rules, improving academic standards and tying academic performance to participation in championships, and revamping the penalty structure for rule violations (Ramos, 2011). It is likely that the ultimate outcome of any college sport reform efforts will be directly influenced by the extent to which all of the individuals and organizations involved are able to align their collective visions and work together to create the impetus for lasting change.

Visioning as Effective Leadership Practice

The examples presented in the previous section provide evidence of how visions of individuals and groups in the sport industry can create change and begin to improve sport in society. In the next few sections, the focus shifts to identifying what is entailed in the actual *practice* of visionary leadership and how you, as a current or future sport organization leader, can perhaps become a better visionary leader.

Visionary leadership, while clearly evident in many organizations and noticeably absent in others, does not necessarily come naturally or easily to those in leadership roles. Jay Conger, professor of organizational behavior and author of numerous books and academic articles on leadership, reported in a 2001 interview the results of a visionary leadership research project that he and his colleague John Alexander had executed. This project was designed specifically to learn more about visionary leaders and how visionary leadership occurs ("Visionary Leadership," 2001). One of the key objectives of the project was to determine if one could "distinguish truly visionary people and organizations from those that merely had vision statements" (p. 19). Conger and Alexander conducted interviews with leaders and other employees of 11 visionary companies. They supplemented the interviews with historical research on noted visionary leaders, including Walt Disney, Ray Kroc of McDonald's Corporation, and Steve Case of AOL-Time Warner. Among the conclusions from the research, the investigators dispelled the myth that visionary leaders are a type of gifted individual and found instead that they often follow very different paths to becoming visionary. In the poststudy interview, Conger pointed to several other key findings that can provide insights into elements of effective practice for visionary leadership. These findings, along with recommendations, are summarized in table 5.1 and can be useful for gaining a better understanding of how visionary leadership may develop.

Visionary Process

In his 1992 book, *Visionary Leadership*, Burt Nanus (1992) stated, "If there is one thing that can profoundly increase a leader's chance of success, it is developing and sustaining a compelling organizational vision" (p. xxii). However, Nanus also indicated that developing a compelling vision is not an easy task because "rampant complexity, change, and choice conspire to blur images of the future and make the selection of the right vision more complicated, even as it becomes more critical" (p. 21).

Managerial leaders of sport organizations, by virtue of their positions and frenetic pace of work, are often preoccupied with tasks and responsibilities associated with day-to-day demands. These demands can delay or even prevent individuals in these roles from spending the time needed to engage in visionary thinking. Moreover, even if a sport organization leader devotes time to specifically pursuing visionary practice, it is often not readily apparent how the leader can effectively engage in the *process* of visioning in any systematic way.

Nanus (1992) identified applicable categories of visionary leadership practice and posed numerous key questions that provide a foundation for any leader engaging in the process of visioning. He identified these categories as (a) developing a vision, (b) determining its scope, (c) making the vision future oriented, (d) choosing the right vision, and (e) turning the vision into reality. Table 5.2 provides examples of questions posed by Nanus that may be useful for leaders of sport organizations engaging in systematic visioning as a leadership exercise.

Nanus (1992) proposed several additional characteristics of powerful and transforming visions for an organization. Visions

- are appropriate for the organization and for the times,

Table 5.1 How Leaders Develop Vision

Elements of visionary leadership	Description
Vision from ideas	Some leaders develop vision based on an idea that they believe the world is heading toward and then use that idea to create and build an enterprise aligned with the vision.
Vision from opportunity	Some visionary leaders are *opportunists*, who see specific gaps in the marketplace and seek to capitalize on them through experimentation.
Vision from adaptation	Visions often result from crises, accidents, experiments, and customer feedback that force leaders to readapt and stay flexible.
Support and collaboration	Visionaries all have other people who help them shape and implement a vision. This support may come from formal business partners and from employees, customers, and other key stakeholders.
How to become better at being a visionary leader	Leaders become better at *being visionary* by constantly listening to customers and listening for problems that must be solved. They find partners for brainstorming and spend time with leading-edge thinkers in the industry. They sense the ways in which the world is changing and learn to draw connections between their businesses and the changes that are occurring.

Based on information from J. Conger, 2001, "Visionary leadership: A talk with Jay Conger," *Leadership in Action* 21(2): 19-22.

Table 5.2 Key Questions in Developing a Compelling Vision

DEVELOPING A VISION (THE VISION AUDIT)	
Key Questions	What is the mission or purpose of your organization?
	What value does the organization provide (e.g., local, regional, national, global)?
	What are the values and organizational culture to which the vision must be aligned?
	What are the organization's current strengths and weaknesses?
	If continuing on its present path, where is the organization headed over the next decade?
DETERMINING THE SCOPE AND TARGET FOR THE VISION	
Key Questions	Who are the most critical internal and external stakeholders?
	What are the primary interests and expectations of these stakeholders?
	What are the boundaries and constraints to your new vision?
	What must the new vision accomplish, and how will you know when it is successful?
IDENTIFYING FUTURE DEVELOPMENTS RELATED TO THE VISION	
Key Questions	What future changes can be expected relative to the needs and wants of those served by your organization?
	What future changes can be expected in the social environment of your organization?
	What future changes in the relevant political environment can be expected?
	What future changes in the technological environment may affect your organization?
CHOOSING THE RIGHT VISION	
Key Questions	To what extent is the vision oriented toward the future?
	To what extent is it appropriate for the organization and its history, culture, and values?
	To what extent does it set standards of excellence?
	To what extent will organizational members likely be inspired by and committed to the vision?
TURNING THE VISION INTO REALITY	
Key Questions	Will the vision be pursued alone or in strategic alliances?
	What goals and objectives are needed as the foundation for achieving the vision?
	What resources (e.g., cash, human capital, facilities, equipment) will be needed?
	What changes may be needed in organizational structure to make the new vision a reality?
	What new policies or procedures may need to be developed?
	What individuals or groups will be assigned specific tasks?
	What new support services may need to be available?
	What new or revised incentive systems may be necessary?
	Who will lead the work groups or teams?
	What will be the goals and expectations of each unit involved in the process?

Based on information in Nanus 1992.

- set standards of excellence and reflect high ideals,
- clarify purpose and direction,
- inspire enthusiasm and encourage commitment,
- are well articulated and easily understood,
- reflect the uniqueness of the organization, and
- are ambitious—that is, they expand organization's horizons.

In addition to the points made by Nanus regarding the development of transforming visions as a component of effective leadership, the literature shows consensus that visions must be widely communicated across an organization and that individuals affected by the vision must be empowered to assist in its development or refinement. In relation to the importance of involving others in visioning, Kouzes and Posner (2007) stated,

Visions seen only by leaders are insufficient to create an organized movement or a significant change in a company. A person with no constituents is not a leader, and people will not follow until they accept a vision as their own. Leaders cannot command commitment, only inspire it. People must believe that leaders understand their needs and have their interests at heart (p. 17).

Communicating and Creating a "Shared Vision"

As already indicated, leaders who can develop personal visions but cannot effectively communicate and involve others in embracing those visions are destined to fail as change agents for organizations. Cartwright and Baldwin (2007), in an article addressing leadership and vision, suggest that "Having a vision but not communicating it isn't much of an improvement over not having a vision at all. A vision has to be shared in order to do the things it is meant to do: inspire, clarify and focus the work of your organization" (p. 24).

In sport organizations, the responsibility for communicating and creating a shared vision is generally assumed by a senior executive or upper management team. In the case of Special Olympics, the organization that grew out of Eunice Shriver's original vision now has a senior management team and seven regional offices around the world with directors who share a common vision for the continued growth and development of the programs in their countries (specialolympics.org, 2012).

While the final *responsibility* for creating a shared vision typically rests with upper management, the *process* by which this occurs often depends on the context of an organization and the stakeholders who should be included. For example, Dave O'Brien, former Division I athletic director and current educator and consultant with a focus on college sport, suggests that inspiring a shared vision for a college athletic department should follow a process that includes (a) understanding the history of the department, (b) listening closely to the perspectives of internal and external stakeholders (e.g., athletes, coaches, boosters, fans), (c) identifying strengths of the department that provide a sustainable competitive advantage, (d) building support for areas of program differentiation, and (e) using a disciplined market-ing and public relations campaign to sell the emerging vision (O'Brien, 2011).

There are also many other practical recommendations for how to communicate and create a shared vision that may be useful for individuals across all domains and levels of sport organization leadership. One such recommendation is presented in figure 5.1, which shows a flow chart with ideas for how an organizational leader might specifically lead a collaborative process of creating a *shared vision statement* in an organization. This process can be employed and adapted as needed in a variety of sport organization settings.

Once a vision statement has been created through a process such as that described in figure 5.1, leaders must find effective ways to communicate that vision within and outside of their organizations. Putting theory into practice, Cartwright and Baldwin (2007) offer several suggestions and strategies for communicating a vision once it is developed. Their key recommendations include (a) giving the vision a "personal touch" by engaging others in one-to-one conversations; (b) identifying key stakeholders and supporters who can help motivate others to be engaged with the vision; (c) being a "visible ambassador" of the organization's vision; (d) creating slogans, mottos, songs, and other means of communicating the vision; (e) rewarding behaviors, actions, and involvement consistent with the vision; and (f) connecting the vision to real, tangible outcomes.

Recent Research on Organizational Vision

A recent study from a corporate vision perspective that may provide questions to explore in sport organization research is that of Slack, Orife, and Anderson (2010), who looked at the relationship between employee perceptions of organizational commitment to organizational vision and employee satisfaction. The researchers administered surveys to approximately 900 employees of a robotics technology organization. They hypothesized that overall employee satisfaction would be more favorable based on (a) the degree of employee understanding of the vision statement, (b) the employee perceived importance of the vision statement to the success of the company, (c) the degree of perceived

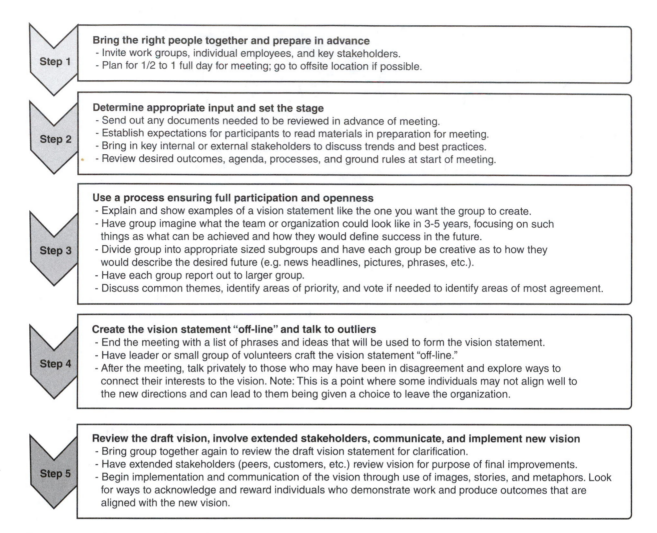

Step 1
Bring the right people together and prepare in advance
- Invite work groups, individual employees, and key stakeholders.
- Plan for 1/2 to 1 full day for meeting; go to offsite location if possible.

Step 2
Determine appropriate input and set the stage
- Send out any documents needed to be reviewed in advance of meeting.
- Establish expectations for participants to read materials in preparation for meeting.
- Bring in key internal or external stakeholders to discuss trends and best practices.
- Review desired outcomes, agenda, processes, and ground rules at start of meeting.

Step 3
Use a process ensuring full participation and openness
- Explain and show examples of a vision statement like the one you want the group to create.
- Have group imagine what the team or organization could look like in 3-5 years, focusing on such things as what can be achieved and how they would define success in the future.
- Divide group into appropriate sized subgroups and have each group be creative as to how they would describe the desired future (e.g. news headlines, pictures, phrases, etc.).
- Have each group report out to larger group.
- Discuss common themes, identify areas of priority, and vote if needed to identify areas of most agreement.

Step 4
Create the vision statement "off-line" and talk to outliers
- End the meeting with a list of phrases and ideas that will be used to form the vision statement.
- Have leader or small group of volunteers craft the vision statement "off-line."
- After the meeting, talk privately to those who may have been in disagreement and explore ways to connect their interests to the vision. Note: This is a point where some individuals may not align well to the new directions and can lead to them being given a choice to leave the organization.

Step 5
Review the draft vision, involve extended stakeholders, communicate, and implement new vision
- Bring group together again to review the draft vision statement for clarification.
- Have extended stakeholders (peers, customers, etc.) review vision for purpose of final improvements.
- Begin implementation and communication of the vision through use of images, stories, and metaphors. Look for ways to acknowledge and reward individuals who demonstrate work and produce outcomes that are aligned with the new vision.

Figure 5.1 Creating a shared vision statement.

Based on information in McCarthy 2009.

The IFP Vision

"In 2011, the International Powerlifting Federation will continue to be the world leader in Powerlifting, having taken that sport to an unprecedented level of recognition and respect in the sporting world. We will be delivering high level competitive and promotional opportunities to the widest range of athletes, administrators, government and the public. The International Powerlifting Federation will be an organisation of advanced integrity, administrative capability and financial stability."

From *International Powerlifting Federation strategic plan* 2008-2011. Available: www.powerlifting-ipf.com/fileadmin/data/IPF_Strategic_Plan.pdf

coworker commitment to the vision, and (d) the degree of employee perceived department management commitment to the vision. Results of the study indicated support for each of the hypotheses and included statistically significant evidence of a favorable relationship between vision, organizational commitment, and employee satisfaction. Managerial impli- cations noted by the authors included the idea that a clear vision understood and practiced at all levels is likely to positively affect employee satisfaction. Additionally, the researchers suggested that a company's performance management process should reward managers who effectively demonstrate commitment to the organizational vision.

In another study on visionary leadership, Griffin, Parker, and Mason (2010) investigated how the change-oriented behaviors of employee adaptivity and proactivity are influenced by leader vision. As pointed out by the researchers, few other studies had addressed how organizations can increase these two factors in employees, especially during times of transformational change. The authors employed a survey designed to measure employee adaptivity, proactivity, and proficiency over two time periods, one at the beginning of the study and the other a year later. Results clearly suggested that leaders who present a strong, clear, and compelling vision of the future motivate more proactivity and adaptivity among employees with a propensity for these behaviors. From a sport perspective, the results reported by Griffin, Parker, and Mason appear to align with what one would expect in a sport organization context, especially from athletes or employees who are eager to be part of a transformational change in their team or organization. However, similar studies would need to be conducted in sport to explore and possibly confirm these findings.

Visionary Leadership: Summary

The purpose of this section of the chapter was to highlight the importance of visioning as a critical element of effective leadership for sport organizations. Perhaps too often, leaders of sport organizations are faced with extraordinarily high expectations for performance and immediate outcomes. While this is the reality in most competitive sport organizations, leaders who have greater understanding of both the theory and practice of visioning may be more effective in producing and sustaining outcomes. The great scientist and inventor Thomas Edison once said, "Vision without execution is hallucination." This statement implies what can happen when individuals or groups conceptualize new and innovative ideas and propose new ventures without connecting them with the actions necessary to turn vision into reality. Making this connection is part of the challenge of strategic leadership, which is addressed in the remainder of the chapter.

Strategic Leadership

This section begins with a case study on the strategic work of the Department for Culture, Media and Sport in London, England, in partnership with Sport England. The case study provides an introduction to strategic leadership in sport that addresses both traditional strategic planning and elements of modern strategic thinking for complex sport organizations.

As you read and study the elements of strategic leadership presented in the remainder of the chapter, reflect back on the strategic directions in this case and consider how these elements apply not only to Sport England, but also to your own observations or experiences with sport organizations you are now connected with or aspire to be a part of in the future. Note that a critical factor in effective strategic leadership is to ensure that resources are in place to support the efforts as evident in the case of DCMS and Sport England.

Traditional Strategic Planning

Sport organizations must periodically evaluate where they are relative to their goals and desired outcomes and determine what strategies are needed to meet future goals and expectations. Historically, this has been accomplished through a systematic and deliberate strategic planning process typically led by individuals at the top levels of an organization. The traditional strategic planning process involves five steps that are followed in a linear sequence and help an organization identify a pathway to change and improvement:

1. Clarifying vision and mission
2. Analyzing external and internal environments (SWOT analysis)
3. Formulation of strategy
4. Strategy implementation
5. Evaluation and reassessment

By working through these five steps, organizations can define or redefine the purpose and goals of the organization, evaluate internal strengths and weaknesses along with external opportunities and threats, and begin to

Department for Culture, Media and Sport (DCMS) in Partnership With Sport England Strategy 2012-2017

Creating a Sporting Habit for Life

The DCMS in London, England, in partnership with Sport England, a nondepartmental public body (NDPB), recently released a new five-year youth and community sport strategy designed to increase participation and transform sport so that it becomes a "lifelong habit for more people and a regular choice for the majority" in the country by 2017. The strategy is associated with increased emphasis on and visibility of sport resulting from the 2012 London Olympic and Paralympic Games. According to Jeremy Hunt, secretary of state for Culture, Olympics, Media and Sport, the United Kingdom has promised to "inspire a new generation to take up sport" and wants to "harness the power of the Olympics and Paralympics to create a deep and lasting legacy of sports participation in every community." A particular focus of the commitment and strategy is to raise participation among 14- to 25-year-olds.

According to a recent news posting on Sport England's website, more than £1 billion of National Lottery funding had been designated for 2012 through 2017 to help create a "meaningful and lasting community sport legacy by growing sports participation at the grassroots level." To accomplish these goals, numerous entities including national governing bodies (NGBs), county sport partnerships, and organizations at the community level would be engaged to assist in the effort.

Key elements central to the new youth sport strategy identified by the Department for Culture, Media and Sport in partnership with Sport England include the following:

- **Building a lasting legacy of competitive sport in schools.** This will be accomplished through the "School Games" as a framework for inspiring young people across the country to participate in competitive school sport. Additionally, maintaining physical education in schools will be a compulsory component of the National Curriculum.

- **Improving links between schools and community sports clubs.** This includes the establishment of at least 6,000 partnerships between schools and local sports clubs so that it will be easier for school participants to continue playing sport after they leave the education setting.

- **Working with the sports governing bodies: focusing on youth.** NGBs will be asked to spend approximately 60 percent of their funding on various activities that will promote sport as a habit of life for young people.

- **Investing in facilities.** £160 million will be spent on new and upgraded sport facilities that will include funding to allow schools to open up many sport facilities to the public.

- **Communities and the voluntary sector.** Over £250 million will be invested to work with local authorities and voluntary groups to make the broadest possible offering of sport participation available to young people in their communities.

In relation to the new strategy for creating a sporting habit for life, Sport England Chief Executive Jennie Price stated, "Changing the sporting behaviour of a generation is a major challenge which has not been achieved by any other Olympic host nation. With a new focus on young people and an even tougher, government-backed, regime of payment by results, Sport England and its partners are determined to deliver."

Based on information in Sport England, 2012, *Creating a sporting habit for life.* Retrieved April 12, 2012, from www.gov.uk/government/uploads/system/uploads/attachment_data/file/78318/creating_a_sporting_habit_for_life.pdf and in Department for Culture, Media and Sport, Creating a sporting habit for life: A new youth sport strategy, January, 2012.

formulate a strategy that will help it meet its objectives and gain a competitive advantage.

Evidence of this approach to traditional strategic planning can be seen across many sectors of the sport industry. For example, leaders of a community-based youth sport program may follow this formal step-by-step strategic planning process to formulate and implement a long-term strategy designed to maximize participation, provide high-quality programs, and maintain financial sustainability. A sporting goods manufacturing company may also use a traditional strategic plan to identify its current strengths, evaluate its competitors, and examine current cost structures as well as the economic environment so that it can effectively stay abreast of consumer demand and a rapidly changing market.

Much of the academic literature on strategy has also focused on use of the strategic planning process to devise and implement a plan that addresses strategic development at two primary levels: corporate level and business level. These levels of strategy, along with the various types of strategy within each level, are explained in detail relative to sport in other sport management texts (Slack and Parent, 2006; Lussier and Kimball, 2009). To summarize, corporate-level strategies in sport are required when an organization competes in more than one industry and must make strategic decisions about selected products and markets (Slack and Parent, 2006). Examples provided by Slack and Parent include Rogers Communication ownership of the Toronto Blue Jays and the involvement of Brunswick Corporation in multiple industries (e.g., bowling, fitness, power boats). Slack and Parent explain and give sport-related examples of several types of corporate strategies: *growth* (diversification, horizontal integration, vertical integration), *stability* (harvesting), *defensive* (turnaround, divestiture, liquidation), and a *combination* of all of these strategies.

Slack and Parent also review three key business-level strategies, attributed in the business literature to the work of Porter (1980), that can be used by a sport organization to gain a competitive edge in the marketplace. These are (1) *cost leadership strategy*, whereby an organization prices its products lower than its competitors through various means including economies of scale and use of cheaper labor; (2) *differentiation strategy*, whereby the organization gains a competitive advantage by presenting the product or service as unique in relation to others in the market; and (3) *focus strategy*, whereby the organization concentrates on serving the needs of a very specific market defined by such things as geographic area or other demographics of a particular market segment. Readers of this text are encouraged to consult the work of Slack and Parent and Lussier and Kimball for more detailed descriptions of these business-level strategies as well as sport-specific examples.

Goals, Strategic Priorities, and Key Performance Indicators

After a thorough SWOT analysis (evaluation of the internal strengths and weaknesses and external opportunities and threats), leaders using a traditional strategic planning process determine the general type of strategy appropriate to the sport organization. It then becomes necessary for leaders to effectively facilitate, through an inclusive process with internal and external stakeholders, the development of goals, strategic priorities, and key performance indicators for the future.

In the strategic planning process, goals and long-term objectives are established for a three- to five-year time frame; it is often recommended that these satisfy the criteria known as SMART (specific, measurable, achievable, realistic, and time-bound). Strategic priorities are then established that help the organization achieve its SMART objectives. The Australian Sports Commission in its good practice guide for sporting organizations, *Planning in Sport* (2004, p. 14), suggests that strategic priorities address the following questions:

- Do the strategies address the internal strengths and weaknesses and external opportunities and threats?
- Are the strategies actionable?
- Are they building on the successes of the previous plan?
- Do they enable the organization to achieve its long-term objectives and performance indicators?
- Does the sport have the capacity (resources, skills) to achieve them?
- Will key stakeholders support them (buy-in)?
- Will they provide a competitive advantage for the sport?

Based on the strategic priorities, the Australian Sports Commission guide recommends that key performance indicators (KPIs) then be established to enable an organization to identify criteria against which the strategic priorities can be measured. KPIs should provide feedback on performance and achievement of objectives. Examples of KPIs identified in the guide include the following:

- Increased levels of funding and services between the sport and key stakeholders
- 5 percent increase in registered members
- 90 percent member satisfaction with upgraded web-based communication systems

Effectively Leading Strategic Planning

Leaders of sport organizations, in addition to needing to give careful consideration to the type of strategy and key questions for identifying strategic priorities, can benefit from ideas and recommendations concerning a leader's role in making the process of strategic plan-

ning more effective. Bryson and Crosby (1995) offered several recommendations regarding the role of leadership in strategic planning for both profit and nonprofit organizations. Several of these recommendations are identified in table 5.3.

Strategic Planning Research in Sport

Academic studies of strategic planning specific to sport organizations, both conceptual and empirical, began to appear in the literature in the early 1990s. Work over the last two decades has been representative of international interest in the topic and has addressed strategic management and planning for various sport-related projects and organizations. These include (a) the 2008 Beijing Olympics (Tong, 2009), (b) public and nonprofit sport organi-

Table 5.3 Leader's Role in Making Strategic Planning Work

Sponsor the process	Articulate the importance of the planning effort. Commit necessary resources. Emphasize that action and change will be the result. Exercise authority if needed to keep the process on track.
Champion the process	Keep planning high on people's agendas. Attend to the process without promoting solutions. Organize time, space, materials for the process to proceed. Keep pushing the process along.
Facilitate the process	Explain how the process works at the beginning and at various points along the way. Tailor the process to the organization and groups involved. Press groups toward taking action and assigning responsibility for specific actions. Congratulate people along the way.
Foster collective leadership	Rely on teams where possible. Focus on network and coalition development. Establish mechanisms for sharing power, responsibility, and accountability.
Create a meaningful process	Help followers frame and reframe issues and strategies. Offer compelling visions of the future. Champion new and improved ideas for addressing strategic issues. Detail actions and expected consequences.
Implement decisions in arenas	Mediate and shape conflicts within and among stakeholders. Understand the dynamics of political influence and how to target resources appropriately. Build winning, sustainable conditions.
Enforce norms, settle disputes, manage conflicts	Always be ethical. Foster organizational integrity and educate others about ethics, constitutions, laws, and norms. Adapt constitutions, laws, and norms to changing times. Resolve conflicts among constitutions, laws, and norms.

zations in Canada (Kriemadis and Theakou, 2007; Thibault and Slack, 1993; Thibault, Slack and Hinings, 1994), (c) economic development of sport tourism in South Africa (Swart, 2005), (d) university athletic departments in the United Kingdom (Kriemadis, 2009), (e) the English Football Association (Grundy, 1999), and (f) interscholastic athletics in the United States (Crow, Higgs, and Branson, 2008). In addition, strategic planning has been identified as important to the training of sport organization employees (Davakos, 2006). Three of these studies are discussed next as examples of areas for exploration in sport research on strategic leadership and planning.

Tong (2009) published an overview and summary of four strategic planning documents for the 2008 Summer Olympic Games in Beijing, providing a broad perspective of the strategic leadership and planning involved in an event of this magnitude. Of key interest to those studying strategic planning is the fact that the plan included a strategic overview that was issued by the Beijing municipal government for public review and comment. The public review resulted in more than 300 letters and 2,000 phone calls and e-mails from domestic and international constituents, which reflects the importance of including external constituents in the strategic planning process. Tong's article includes overviews of three areas within the operational plan (Ecology Plan, Transportation Plan, and Sports Action Plan), exemplifying the breadth of the Olympics strategic planning process.

Kriemadis and Theakou (2007), using the British Columbia Rugby Union (BCRU) as a case study for public and nonprofit sport, examined the extent to which five models of strategic planning were employed and integrated in this organization. These included (a) basic strategic planning, (b) issue- or goal-based planning, (c) alignment model, (d) scenario planning, and (e) organic or self-organizing planning. The study showed that BCRU developed its own model, using elements of mostly the basic strategic planning model and the issue- or goal-based model, and modified them as needed relative to the organization's processes and activities.

Thibault, Slack, and Hinings (1993, 1994) examined and verified a framework for analyzing strategy in Canadian nonprofit national sport organizations. Within their proposed framework were two dimensions of strategy that a nonprofit organization should consider based on (1) program attractiveness and (2) competitive position. The variables considered as "imperatives" for program attractiveness included a program's fundability, the size of the client base, volunteer appeal, and support group appeal. Imperatives in the dimension of competitive position included equipment costs and affiliation fees. The study identified four types of strategy that a nonprofit sport organization might pursue based on whether it is high or low in program attractiveness and strong or weak in competitive position. Thibault, Slack, and Hinings (1993) labeled and defined these four strategic types as shown in table 5.4.

Table 5.4 Nonprofit Sport Organization Strategic Types.

Type	Characteristics	Strengths and weaknesses
Refiner	Strategic focus is on fine tuning already existing and mature programs, but finding ways to reduce or eliminate costs that may act as entry barriers for members.	High in program attractiveness Weak in competitive position
Enhancer	Strategic focus is to enhance already strong programs and develop new ones. New programs have the advantage of using already existing networks of members and coaches.	High in program attractiveness Strong in competitive position
Explorer	Strategic focus is on developing programs that attract people to their sports and reduce the costs of entry.	Low in program attractiveness Weak in competitive position
Innovator	Strategic focus is on developing innovative programs, getting more people involved in their sports, and developing more coaches.	Low in program attractiveness Strong in competitive position

Based on information in Thibault, Slack and Hinings 1993, 1994.

Modern Approaches to Strategic Leadership

While strategic planning in the traditional sense is still commonly practiced, there has been increasing interest in the last several years in how leaders "think strategically" and what they can do to facilitate strategic leadership in modern organizations. Recent ideas, research, and practice around strategic thinking suggest that it is a way of conceptualizing strategy in an organization that may or may not result in the traditional strategic planning process discussed earlier. Although traditional process-based strategic planning is widely used and even required by policy in some organizations, many researchers and organizational consultants have emphatically argued that the traditional deliberate and rational approach to strategic planning has limited value and often fails completely. These experts claim that strategic planning in its traditional form can easily reduce flexibility, discourage change, inhibit innovation, impede organizational learning, and create a planning environment that becomes more focused on environmental analysis and implementation than on actual strategy formation (Holland, 2008; Mintzberg, 1994; Moore and Lenir, 2011). Also, it has been argued, from a research perspective, that the establishment of a clear construct of strategic planning has been challenged by inconsistencies in its underlying theoretical framework and by problems with determining the reliability or validity of its measurement (Boyd and Reuning-Elliot, 1998; Karami, 2007).

Proponents of strategic thinking suggest that the traditional approach to strategic planning is not as responsive and dynamic as is needed for modern organizations. It is argued that leaders today must think strategically on a *continual* basis and must *regularly* monitor internal and external factors influencing the organization's work and mission. Strategic thinking, as opposed to more traditional strategic planning, cannot easily be done in sequential steps and the plan effectively implemented without change over a three- to five-year period. The argument is that today's leaders must be prepared to think creatively and must be attuned to a rapidly changing business and technological environment. In addition, it is increasingly expected that individuals in leadership roles will effectively facilitate strategic thinking by directly engaging organizational members and key constituents at various levels, both internal and external to the organization.

Knowledge, understanding, and the ability to think strategically are thought by many to be a key element of effective leadership and are often considered a requirement of those in leadership roles. However, many sport organization leaders, depending on academic preparation and work experience, have little background or formal training in this area. The remainder of this chapter focuses on how strategies emerge in organizations and how the complexities of modern organizations influence leadership and strategy, as well as the concepts associated with strategic thinking across an organization. Thoughtful and adaptable strategic thinking and strategic leadership are likely essential for sport organizations to survive, prosper, and effectively reach their goals now and into the future.

How Do Strategies Come Into Existence?

When considering leadership and strategy development, it is important to understand the basic concepts of "deliberate" and "emergent" strategy. These concepts originally appeared in the academic literature as central themes of research on organizational strategy by Bryson (1988; Bryson and Crosby, 1995), Mintzberg (1973, 1994), and Mintzberg and Waters (1982, 1985), and have more recently been addressed in the work of Moore and Lenir (2011) and Maritz, Pretorius, and Plant (2011).

According to Mintzberg and Waters (1985), *deliberate* strategies are those that are "realized as intended" as opposed to *emergent* strategies, which are "patterns or consistencies realized despite, or in the absence of, intentions" (p. 257). Deliberate strategies are most associated with the traditional form of strategic planning described previously, while emergent strategies are thought to be more flexible and appropriate for many of today's strategic change efforts. When thinking of these forms of strategy development in today's sport industry environment, one can see how it could be difficult for a deliberate and long-term strategic plan to effectively realize its original intentions without having to adapt or respond to changes and to internal or external forces during the implementation of the plan. An example is the previously discussed case of the Department for Culture, Media and Sport in England and its strategies for creating sporting habits for life among citizens in the United Kingdom. One can see how a plan involving multiple constituents at many levels of government and community over a period of several years would likely depend on elements of both deliberate and emergent strategy to ultimately achieve its intended goals. The following list provides an overview of the characteristics of deliberate and emergent strategies.

Deliberate strategy

- Often begins with vision of success
- Goal driven
- Uses systematic process to move toward desired future
- May reduce flexibility and response to change

Emergent strategy

- Often exploratory and must develop quickly out of opportunities or challenges
- Responsive to unexpected circumstances or situations
- Is exploratory and dynamic
- Should involve all levels of managers and employees

The interest in and perceived importance of emerging leadership has been acknowledged in recent academic research (Maritz, Pretorius, and Plant, 2011) connecting strategy development to responsible leadership. In addition, recent research conducted by Song and colleagues (2011) on deliberate and emergent strategy showed that although deliberate strategic planning contributed to overall better firm performance, it also significantly impeded the number of new product development projects in the firms studied. As suggested by the researchers, this study provided evidence that traditional strategic planning actually reduced improvisation and "thinking outside the box," which impeded innovation and resulted in the development of fewer new products. While this study was not conducted in a sport context, it has important implications for sport organiza-

> **Your Thoughts**
>
> Reflecting on your direct experience with, or observation of, a sport organization in your area of interest, what approaches to strategy development do you see as most appropriate? Are both deliberate and emergent strategies necessary? Would one be preferred over the other? Why or why not?

tions such as sport equipment and manufacturing companies trying to innovate and produce new and enhanced products for the market.

Complexity and Strategy in Modern Organizations

Modern organizations have been increasingly described in the academic literature as demonstrating characteristics of "complex adaptive systems" (Uhl-Bien, Marion, and McKelvey, 2007; Senge, 2006; Painter-Morland, 2008, 2009), meaning that they are open, dynamic, and nonlinear, with component parts that interact in multiple ways and that must continually respond to new developments (Painter-Morland, 2009). Because of the complexity of these organizational systems, it is also increasingly suggested that new approaches and perspectives on leadership are necessary to address their strategic needs.

Bovaird (2008) notes that "recent applications of the theory of complex adaptive systems have opened up major theoretical questions about the role of strategic management and governance" (p. 320). Relative to strategy, Bovaird argues that when organizations are treated as complex adaptive systems, "emergent strategic management approaches are more likely to be successful than traditional strategic planning" (p. 326). He also points out there are fundamental challenges to the concepts of "planning" in any open system where there is significant decentralization of decision making. Moreover, Bovaird notes distinct differences between the concepts and processes of traditional strategic planning and what he refers to as "strategic shaping" and "meta-planning." Meta-planning, according to Bovaird, does not involve the development of a single set of preferred strategic actions with specific targets. Rather, it "entails tracking how emerging situations offer the possibility of changing the 'opportunity-map' facing the organization, and developing the capability of the organization to influence the overall system" (p. 338). Also, according to Painter-Morland (2009), leadership within a complex adaptive system is very different from the traditional perspective of directing the behaviors of others and requires disrupting existing patterns, encouraging novelty, and enabling new perspectives through using conflict and embracing uncertainty.

Nike Corporation is an example of an extreme complex adaptive system in sport. The success that Nike has achieved, as well as the challenges it has faced regarding criticism for child labor and working conditions in Third World countries, relates to the complex interaction of numerous economic and sociocultural factors all emerging concurrently in a global business environment. This intertwining of complex factors contributing to Nike's corporate strategy has been described in the research of Carty (1999) as consistent with the conceptual framework of a global commodity chain (GCC). According to Gereffi, Korzeniewicz, and Korzeniewicz (1994), "a GCC consists of sets of interorganizational networks clustered around one commodity or product, linking households, enterprises, and states to one another within the world-economy" (p. 2). Gereffi (1994) also notes that commodity chains include specific processes or segments involving (a) the acquisition of raw materials or semifinished product, (b) provisioning of labor, (c) transportation, (d) distribution, and (e) consumption. Analyzing a commodity chain, according to these authors, reveals how all of these segments are also shaped by social relations in a global economy.

This information about Nike and the GCC framework makes the point that complexity in sport organizations, especially in multinational corporations, undoubtedly contributes to the necessity of a highly dynamic and adaptable approach to strategic leadership for dealing with emergent issues and opportunities.

At present there is little research on complex adaptive systems or complexity theory in sport organizations. However, one exploratory study (Smith, 2004) examined the extent to which complexity theory could explain "unintentional change" and "emergent behavior" in Australian national sport organizations (NSOs). Three organizational members (at different levels of the organization) from eight NSOs were interviewed to get their perspectives on change practices in their organization. Among the results and implications of the study, Smith reported not only that change is pervasive in organizational life, but also that sport organizations can be subject to both the strategic whims of leaders and the pressures of the institutional environment in which they operate. In some cases, members reported that new practices and processes were introduced into the NSO apparently as random, unexplained changes without the prior knowledge or consent of managers. As suggested by Smith, this appears to indicate that that emergent change can manifest itself independently of strategic change efforts that are deliberate or planned.

Sport organizations are navigating the same rapidly changing political, economic, social, and technological environment as the rest of society. Consequently, elements of complexity theory and an emergent approach to strategy development appear to be highly applicable to both practicing leaders and academicians studying sport organizations.

Strategic Thinking

The term strategic thinking and the associated concepts have received considerable attention in the academic literature (Goldman, 2008; Fairholm, 2009; Fairholm and Card, 2009; Liedtka, 1998; Fontaine, 2008). Goldman, drawing on the work of Hanford (1995) and Liedtka, recognized strategic thinking as

1. **conceptual**—reflects ideas, models, and hypotheses;
2. **systems oriented**—takes into account the interaction of the organization's parts and relationships with the external environment;
3. **directional**—focuses on an "aimed-for" future state different from the present one; and
4. **opportunistic**—takes advantage of an organization's past achievements and present competitive and environmental conditions.

According to Fairholm, in order for strategic thinking to be different or distinct from strategic planning, it must go beyond just a focus on goals and outcomes and embrace concepts like purpose, meaning, and values, which in Fairholm's view support strategic thinking in terms of the activities of values, trust cultural, or whole-soul leadership. Fairholm says that traditional strategic planning has proven useful but limited, and that the notion of strategic thinking has emerged to help overcome those limitations. He points out that strategic planning relies heavily on concepts such as mission, objectives, key results areas, long- and short-term goals, metrics, performance measurements, action plans, and tactics. These are essential to good management of the organization, but they are also concepts that reflect many false assumptions, such as the ability to control and predict and the flawlessness of analysis and procedure. Fairholm and Card identify five elements necessary to thinking strategically, which are summarized in table 5.5.

Also in relation to strategic leadership and strategic thinking, Paul Schoemaker, research director for the Mack Center for Technological Innovation at Wharton Business School, recently stated, "It's hard to be a strategic leader if you don't know what strategic leaders

Table 5.5 Five Elements of Strategic Thinking

Element of strategic thinking	Strategic leadership actions
View yourself as an organizational philosopher more than a technical expert.	• Learn about the contexts in which your organization operates. • Focus on untangling the complexities of organizational life and see patterns of action in the culture of the organization that can influence members toward the wisest use of resources and the wisest relationships among people. • Ask questions such as these: What is the purpose of the organization? Why does this organization exist? Where did it come from? What might make it go away? What makes life in the organization meaningful?
Distinguish strategic planning from strategic thinking.	• Recognize strategic thinking as a "why–what–how" approach as opposed to just a "how" approach. • Strategic thinking demands that you synthesize rather than analyze and allows for flexibility, innovation, and creativity more than procedure and routine.
Adopt a values, vision, and vector orientation rather than a goals, objectives, and metric mentality.	• Recognize that strategic thinking views leadership as a precursor to strategic planning in which you focus on the following: • *Values*—to reflect meaning, purpose, and commitment of organizational members • *Visions*—to operationalize the values and make sense of what the values mean now and in the future • *Vectors*—to operationalize the magnitude and direction of vision-driven actions • *Voice*—to emphasize interaction between leader and led and to emphasize that the relationship is essentially voluntary based on the level of alignment with the values, vision, and vectors at play
Concentrate on the flow of information and the quality of relationships rather than the control of information.	• Recognize that the organization is unique and bound in its scope and purpose yet at the same time constantly interacting with outside forces. • Rather than trying to restrict and control information, recognize the importance of free and easy access to information. • Communication is two-way, and leaders must both share information with and receive information from others.
Learn to accept and work with ambiguity rather than trying to control and quantify all organizational endeavors.	• Have the maturity and wisdom not to try to control what may be inherently uncontrollable. Become more comfortable with ambiguity. • Understand the need for innovation, but recognize that innovation may create future areas of competition and ultimately can shape the need for more future innovation. • Gain an understanding of how people in the organization cope with change, and think strategically about how to lead individual and group transitions so as to deal with uncertainties in a productive rather than disruptive context.

Based on information in Fairholm and Card 2009.

are supposed to do" (Schoemaker, 2012, p. 1). Schoemaker identified what he refers to as "6 Habits of True Strategic Thinkers" that allow leaders to more effectively deal with today's environments of uncertainty (see "On the Sidelines").

Summary

Chapter 5 begins with a focus on visioning and includes historical examples from sport in which leaders have demonstrated commitment to a vision and have worked consistently over several years to bring that vision to reality. As shown by recent examples from sport, leaders are capitalizing on emerging opportunities to pose questions and develop strategic visions for what the true benefits of sport should be in the 21st century and the need for collective visioning to address issues of reform within intercollegiate athletics into the future.

The chapter next provides insights into and recommendations for how leaders go about developing vision, with examples from business practice and academic research. Key questions are identified from the literature (Nanus, 1992) that can help anyone in a sport organization leadership role begin the process of developing a compelling vision; this process includes determining the true mission and purpose of the organization; identifying the scope and target for the vision; anticipating future changes in the context, business, or political environment; choosing the right vision; and turning vision into reality. This discussion is followed by ideas for how a leader can put into practice the process of creating a shared vision statement in an organization.

The focus then shifts to strategic leadership and compares and contrasts the process of traditional strategic planning (deliberate strategy) with strategic thinking (emergent

---

On the Sidelines

What Do Strategic Leaders Do?

Paul Schoemaker recently identified what he refers to as "6 Habits of True Strategic Thinkers." He says that many leaders deal primarily with urgent issues that are directly in front of them, but in doing so, can miss strategic opportunities or signals that the organization may actually be on a road that is "leading off a cliff." Schoemaker points out that today's environment of uncertainty requires "adaptive strategic leaders" who can do six things well.

1. Anticipate: "Look for game-changing information at the periphery of your industry; Search beyond the current boundaries of the business; Build wide external networks to help you scan the horizon better."

2. Think critically: "Reframe problems to get to the bottom of things, in terms of root causes; Challenge current beliefs and mindsets, including your own; Uncover hypocrisy, manipulation, and bias in organizational decisions."

3. Interpret: "Seek patterns in multiple sources of data; Encourage others to do the same; Question prevailing assumptions and test multiple hypotheses simultaneously."

4. Decide: "Carefully frame the decision to get to the crux of the matter; Balance speed, rigor, quality and agility; Leave perfection to higher powers; Take a stand even with incomplete information and amid diverse views."

5. Align: "Understand what drives other people's agendas including what remains hidden; Bring tough issues to the surface, even when it's uncomfortable; Assess risk tolerance and follow through to build the necessary support."

6. Learn: "Encourage and exemplify honest, rigorous debriefs to extract lessons; Shift course quickly if you realize you are off track; Celebrate both success and (well-intentioned) failures that provide insight."

Carefully read and reflect on each of the six habits listed. If you are in a current sport leadership role, think about how you might introduce and facilitate core discussions about these habits with other leaders, middle managers, and staff in your organization. If you are currently a student planning to be in a sport leadership role, consider how you might use this list of habits as a tool to enhance your strategic thinking capabilities.

All quotes are reprinted from page 1 in Schoemaker 2012.

strategy). While both are often necessary in organizations, this section of the chapter makes the point that modern approaches to strategic leadership must recognize and be attuned to a rapidly changing societal, business, and technological environment. Traditional strategic planning with a focus of three to five years must now be highly adaptable and allow for improvisation and creativity. It is acknowledged, based on the work of researchers including Goldman (2008), Fairholm (2009), and Liedtka (1998), that in modern organizations, strategic thinking is a key responsibility of leaders; this includes being conceptual, systems oriented, and opportunistic based on competitive and environmental conditions.

Final Self-Assessment

After having read and reflected on the content in this chapter, consider your responses to the self-assessment questions presented at the beginning of the chapter. What insights do you now have or in what ways do you feel better prepared to be a visionary and strategic leader?

1. What are emerging and collective visions and how are they important for leaders of sport organizations?
2. What all is involved in the "practice" of visionary leadership?
3. What are the basic elements of traditional strategic planning and how might you effectively lead these efforts in an organization?
4. What is "strategic thinking" and how can it be applied to modern sport organization leadership?

Game Plan Activity

Using concepts presented in this chapter, develop the foundation or initial framework for a vision and strategic leadership approach addressing one of the following scenarios:

- Start-up of a new sport-related venture in a city of your choice (e.g., new team, facility, event)
- Emerging strategic plan for an existing sport program or athletic department (e.g., school district, college or university, youth sport)
- Creation of a business or development plan for a sport-related product
- Development of an initial planning document or electronic portfolio that includes sections such as the following:
  - Introduction
  - Core Values
  - SWOT Analysis
  - Vision
  - Mission
  - Goals
  - Strategic Priorities
  - Performance Indicators
  - Actions
  - Evaluation

Questions to Consider

1. What is an example of a personal, team, or overall sport organization vision that you have seen become a reality? How did this vision come into existence? How was it

communicated? What strategies or actions were put into place to help actualize the vision? How could the process have been improved in your opinion?

2. Consider your experience as a current or former member of a team or sport organization. Are there any ways in which you can see elements of a "complex adaptive system" at work in this organization? Explain why or why not.

3. You are the newly hired director for a large urban youth sport organization that has seen steadily declining participation and financial support. You are preparing to meet with the board to discuss the problems and begin to envision a new future for the organization. How might you use elements of strategic thinking to guide this conversation?

4. Using Shoemaker's list of "What Do Strategic Leaders Do" presented at the end of this chapter, evaluate yourself on a scale of 1 to 5 in each dimension where 1 is "not at all like me" and 5 is "always like me." Are there areas in which you believe you are stronger than in other areas? What can you do to demonstrate behaviors more aligned with strategic leadership?

Recommended Readings

Australian Sports Commission. (2004). Planning in sport. www.ausport.gov.au/__data/assets/pdf_file/0020/115535/2._Effective_Planning_in_Sport.pdf.

Bryson, J. M. (2011). *Strategic planning for public and nonprofit organizations* (4th ed.). San Francisco: Jossey-Bass.

Nanus, B. (1995). *Visionary leadership.* San Francisco: Jossey-Bass.

Read, D. (2012, June/July). All in the plan. http://athleticmanagement.com.

Wootten, S., and Horne, T. (2002). *Strategic thinking* (3rd ed.). London: Kogan Page.

6

Complexity and Problem Solving

Learning Objectives

After reading and reflecting on the concepts and examples in this chapter, you will be able to

1. understand how and why the environment for leadership is changing and becoming more complex for sport organizations,
2. explain the competencies and skills needed for effective problem solving,
3. identify and discuss examples of complex problems facing sport leaders,
4. explain the Cynefin framework relative to contextual placement of organizational problems from simple to chaotic,
5. discuss how the four frames of the multiframe leadership model can assist with problem solving in sport organizations, and
6. use the Vroom-Jago-Yetton decision tree for determining the style and level of involvement of groups in decision making.

Self-Assessment

1. In what ways do you feel that sport organizations are becoming increasingly complex?
2. What do believe to be your current strengths and weaknesses relative to your own competencies and skills as a problem solver?
3. What do you see as two or three of the complex problems facing sport organizations in your particular area of interest?
4. What tools or processes do you currently use (or have you observed being used) for addressing problems in a sport organization you are familiar with?

The sport industry across the globe is a very large, complex enterprise with high financial stakes. As pointed out by DeSensi and Rosenberg (2003),

> This is especially evident when one examines the amount of money paid for advertising during televised sport contests; the fees for rights to televise the Olympic Games; the gate receipts for attendance at professional sporting events; professional athletes' salaries, the costs of professional team franchises; government and organizational subsidies for sport; the investments needed to fund sport infrastructure including new stadiums and arenas; the financial scope of the sports equipment and apparel industries; the budgets of school, college, university and community sport programs. All of these examples attest to the fact that sport is an integral component of, and is driven by, the capitalist system in modern countries and contributes significantly to the economies of many nations. (p. 5)

In addition to the economic aspects and financial complexity, many sport organizations have large and complex organizational structures consisting of multiple departments and multiple levels of horizontal and vertical differentiation. Additionally, complexity in some sport organizations results from differentiation in geographical location such as that occurring in multiple athletic departments across a large urban school district or in a multinational sport corporation with sites in various countries around the globe. Moreover, organizations in the 21st century are becoming increasingly diverse and are transforming into more technologically enhanced, knowledge-age operations that create new challenges in leadership and problem solving. These examples provide a macro perspective of sport organizations and the sport industry in order to set the stage for discussion of why leaders in this field need to be adept at framing, diagnosing, and solving problems that will inevitably be part of this vast, complex, and changing industry.

This chapter introduces the idea of complexity and problem solving for leadership. It begins with a discussion of the changing environment for leadership and problem solving in modern organizations. For example, although traditional hierarchical and positional leadership are still in practice and in some cases necessary in sport organizations, the complexities of many problems, along with changing expectations of knowledge-age athletes and employees, have created new challenges for leaders.

The next part of the chapter identifies fundamental leader competencies and skills needed for effectively addressing complex problems. The information in this section relates to and expands on the foundational *skills approach* to leadership presented in chapter 1.

The chapter then provides examples of some of the macro-organizational and complex problems facing sport organizations. Subsections present information about problems related to economics and finance, legal issues, public relations, political factors, technology, and sociocultural issues in sport. The final section in the chapter explores three specific innovative approaches from business, education, and other settings that offer insights and tools to assist leaders in more effectively addressing the complex problems they encounter in modern sport organizations.

Changing Environment for Leadership

Much discussion currently appears in the literature about how and why leadership is changing in the 21st century. As we entered the second decade of the new millennium, a common theme among authors was the evolution in leadership from a more hierarchical, structural, and positional model to one that is more flexible, adaptive, creative, and transformational. Retired Colonel George Reed, in an article on leadership and systems thinking (Reed, 2006), stated that "leaders operate in the realm of bewildering uncertainty and staggering complexity" (p. 10). Reed suggested that today's organizations require us to *think differently about problems* and that we must get beyond the use of lower-level models to deal with the problems faced by higher-level systems.

Senge (1990), in his book *The Fifth Discipline*, recognized systems thinking as a core element of organizational learning and improvement. Senge points out that in the traditional view of leadership, leaders are special individuals who "set the direction, make the key decisions, and energize the troops" (p. 340). This, according to Senge, is based on an assumption that people are powerless, lack personal vision, and are unable to master forces of change. However, in Senge's belief, a new view of leadership is that leaders are "designers, stewards and teachers" who are responsible for "*building organizations* where people continually expand their capabilities to understand complexity, clarify vision, and improved shared mental models—that is, they are responsible for learning" (p. 340).

One of the reasons the overall environment for leadership is undergoing rapid change was proposed by McCrimmon (2008), who noted that we now operate in a knowledge-driven age in which the world is dynamic and rapidly changing, problems are increasingly complex, and innovation is critical. This change, partly resulting from advances in technology and access to information, has also influenced the nature of work and what is referred to as the "knowledge worker" in organizations. McFarlane (2008) suggests that managing knowledge workers today requires leaders to redefine their roles in order to develop systems of "participative knowledge sharing" in ways that can help solve organizational problems as well as manage crises and change. Moreover, McFarlane argues that knowledge workers in organizations today often possess specialized and valuable knowledge that they may be less inclined to share unless they perceive the compensation and reward system to be aligned with their contributions.

In relation to these examples of changing environments for leadership, work by Marion and Uhl-Bien (2001) initially set the stage for research and discussions around complexity leadership theory, which proposes that modern organizational leadership occurs in a complex adaptive system. In this perspective, leadership is thought of in terms of an "emergent event" and an interactive dynamic whereby individuals in organizations can participate as both leaders and followers depending on the situation (Lichtenstein et al., 2006).

To relate all this to its importance for sport leaders and problem solving, it is increasingly evident that sport organizations, particularly higher-level intercollegiate or professional sport teams and large multinational sport corporations, face issues that require new approaches to strategic problem solving and decision making. In this process, the complexity of the problems often demands specialized knowledge and multiple levels of leadership expertise. That knowledge and expertise frequently exists across varying departments and within individuals or groups outside of the traditional hierarchy. Sport leaders of organizations today should embrace this idea and create an environment in which the problem-solving contributions of employees (and even sport team or club participants) are welcomed, carefully considered, and valued in decision making.

Competencies and Skills for Creative Problem Solving

Solving problems is a typical expectation of organizational leaders. However, problems in sport range broadly, from simple, routine problems to those without easily discernible and concrete answers that involve significant complexity and sometimes overt conflict. Day-to-day managerial problems about such things as game scheduling or a decision about a promotional event may be easily addressed by a managerial leader with little to no interaction with others required. However, more complex and systemic problems, such as those discussed in the next section, tend to be less easily defined; effectively addressing these may require a consortium of individuals both within and outside of the organization. Mumford and colleagues (2000) pointed out that leadership is a form of social problem solving that addresses complex, often ill-defined, novel, and ambiguous problems. This frequently occurs in collaboration with others above and below the position of the leader in the organization.

So, what competencies and skills are foundational for leaders with regard to addressing complex problems? Mumford and coauthors (2000) proposed three elements that interact with one another and in their view involve "multiple forms of cognition" (p. 17). These three elements are listed and described in the sidebar "Competencies and Skills Needed for Problem Solving."

Competencies and Skills Needed for Problem Solving

Creative problem solving
- Defining problems and issues
- Gathering information on the problem
- Developing new or unique approaches or alternatives to the problem

Social judgment skills
- Working collaboratively with others in problem solving
- Social perceptiveness to the needs of various constituents

- Behavioral flexibility to adjust behaviors as needed to address the demands of the situation

Knowledge
- Mental structures or schemas needed to diagnose or assess complex issues
- Knowledge of situational factors regarding tasks, the organization, and the people
- Experiential knowledge helpful for defining problems, evaluating restrictions, and implementing plans.

Based on information in Mumford, Zaccaro, Harding, Jacobs and Fleishman 2000.

An important point as stated by Mumford and coauthors (2000) is that "leadership skills and subsequent performance are not viewed as the province of a few gifted individuals. Instead, leadership is held to be a potential in many individuals—a potential that emerges through experience and the capability to learn and benefit from experience" (p. 21).

Sources of Complex Problems in Sport Organizations

This section identifies many of the complex organizational and industry-wide issues in sport. These issues can pose complex problems for sport organization leaders and typically are not solved by individual leaders working in isolation or only from the top management positions in sport organizations. In addition, the size of a sport organization (defined here by such things as number of employees, number of participants or customers, physical facilities, and sales volume), as well as the organization's local, state, national, or international scope, has bearing on the complexity of leadership issues that must be addressed. It is also worth noting again (as discussed in chapter 1 in the context of followership) that key strategic constituents in sport (e.g., players, fans, boosters) have the capacity to exert powerful influence on sport organization leaders. Thus, internal

and external influence and pressures exerted upon leaders by their followers and stakeholders can also be a critical contingent factor to address when dealing with various issues in sport organizations. The following subsections overview some of the areas that currently present complex problems for sport leaders.

Economic Problems

Over the last few years, the United States and most of the world experienced a global financial crisis with declining stock markets, collapse of many financial institutions, and governments of even the wealthiest nations having to provide rescue packages for their financial systems (Shah, 2010). Concurrently, issues and challenges for professional sport organizations relative to the economy appeared ubiquitously in the news and on the Internet. For example, David Stern, commissioner of the National Basketball Association (NBA), reported that the NBA would lose $400 million in 2010; indications were that much of this was attributable to the economic downturn (Mahoney, 2010). Bad economic times starting in 2008 also affected the National Hockey League (NHL), Major League Baseball (MLB), minor league baseball, and NASCAR, with declining attendance and the tightening of corporate sponsorship budgets creating financial challenges. Additionally, CBS Money Watch online reported concerns in the National Football League (NFL), where over 15 percent of the league staff was reduced through buyouts, layoffs, and other reductions (NFL Tackles Tough Economy, 2009).

College athletics in the United States is also experiencing its share of challenges as a result of the economic conditions. The Knight Commission on Intercollegiate Athletics (2009), in a report offering an overview of the business and economic landscape of intercollegiate athletics, identified several issues that created leadership challenges at both the athletic department and institutional level. These were some of the key issues identified in the 2009 report (p. 25-26):

- "increased athletic costs at a time when other costs in the economy are rising faster than inflation and states are reducing appropriations for higher education"

- "intercollegiate athletic programs, particularly those in Football Bowl Subdivision institutions, have become heavily dependent on revenue from media and corporations that hopefully don't become so negatively affected by the economy that they cannot deliver on their sponsorships and/or contract obligations"

- "institutional subsidies to athletics are rising faster than educational subsidies for the student body, which means that colleges will have to expend a greater percentage on athletics than ever before"

Additionally, according to the Knight Commission report there were 25 top-tier football schools that produced average revenues of $3.9 million in 2008 while the other 94 operated with deficits averaging $9.9 million. According to the report, it was plausible that some universities might have to choose between funding academic departments internally and subsidizing athletics from other sources including state funding or student fees. In this environment, some student-athletes from nonrevenue sports could see their teams cut or funding reduced to help meet the needs of revenue sports. This economic environment in college sports certainly creates a problem-solving and strategic planning issue for university presidents, boards of regents, and athletic directors as they vision their programs into the short-term and long-term future.

Secondary schools and community and private recreational sport and fitness programs have also experienced financial challenges and have had to slash budgets in order to preserve core mission activities. In many cases, for school districts, this has meant having to cut back on sport programs and perhaps come up with increased revenue from such sources as student participation fees, private donations, increased booster club fund raising, and even corporate sponsorships. Numerous school districts across the United States, despite substantial community and parent opposition, have had to dramatically reduce budgets and in some cases totally eliminate various middle and high school sport programs.

What all of this means relative to leadership and problem solving for sport organizations is that leaders at all levels must carefully monitor the external economic environment, think prudently, and develop well-designed cost containment and strategic growth strategies that focus on the long-term viability of their programs and services. This is an area in which sport organization leaders, without what they feel is adequate training or solid enough experience, may need to consult with economists, financial specialists, or others who can provide guidance and assistance with strategic planning.

Legal Issues

The legal environment for sport organizations, especially in the United States, can also pose complex problems and is an area of priority responsibility for sport organization leaders. Sport-related legal problems and lawsuits are reported almost daily in the local and national news; and lawsuits can be very expensive to a sport organization, often in terms of negative publicity as well as risk to the financial resources of individuals and the organization. Depending on the setting and level of leadership, sport organization leaders must be highly cognizant of critical legal responsibilities, including constitutional law, tort law, contract law, employment law, the Americans with Disabilities Act, gender equity, intellectual property, and antitrust law. Currently, sport management academic programs provide required coursework that gives students both introductory and in-depth insights into these areas of legal responsibility. Additionally, numerous recent books in the field specifically address these topics as well as risk management for sport and recreation organizations.

An issue that often requires complex legal and financial problem solving by leaders of interscholastic and intercollegiate athletic programs in the United States is Title IX of the U.S. Education Amendments to the Civil Rights Act of 1972, which was designed to prevent discrimination based on gender in any education program or activity that receives federal financial assistance. While Title IX has been directly associated with the growth of women's sport programs over the last four decades, it also has also been controversial in cases around the country in which decisions were made to cut some men's sport programs in order to "achieve equity" in various school athletic departments. The following is an example of a statement about the legal and financial issues associated with Title IX, issued in 2009 by the National Women's Law Center:

"In difficult economic times, educational institutions at all levels face tight budgets. As a result, some schools may make grueling decisions to cut athletic opportunities or benefits ranging from delaying the purchase of new uniforms to reducing the number of scheduled games to totally eliminating certain teams. When making these hard choices, it is important for schools to remember that if they cut any athletic opportunities or benefits, they must do so in a way that does not discriminate on the basis of sex in violation of Title IX of the Education Amendments of 1972—that is, any cuts must not exacerbate existing gender inequities or create new ones." (p. 1)

Thus, leaders of school sport programs potentially facing financial cutbacks must address the complex problem of managing budget cuts to their institutions and departments while also maintaining compliance with federal law.

Public Relations Issues

Leaders in sport organizations must be constantly vigilant about every component of their organization relative to effective public relations. One negative incident or crisis may take years of public relations (PR) work to overcome; thus both prevention and creative problem solving are critical elements of effective and responsible PR leadership. Issues faced by sport organization leaders that can lead to complex PR problems are in the news almost daily. These are some prime, relatively recent examples:

• Michael Vick, American football player with the Philadelphia Eagles and formerly with the Atlanta Falcons, was convicted and served time in prison for his involvement in an illegal dogfighting ring.

• Nike was involved in the 1990s in human rights and labor issues in foreign factories; these included claims of coerced labor, poor working conditions, and lower than minimum wage payments to workers.

• Georgian luger Nodar Kumaritashvili was killed as the result of losing control on a straightaway during a practice run on the luge course at the 2010 Vancouver Olympics. The crash resulted in safety changes including more walls and padding, but concerns were raised over officials' reported refusal to admit that the course was dangerous (Male, 2010).

Political Issues

Sport organizations function within a local, state, national, and often international political environment. Depending on the organization and the component or setting of the sport industry in which it operates, it can be positively or negatively influenced by (or even have positive or negative influence on) its political environment. In addition, sport organizations, like all organizations, are composed of people and subgroups that typically have various enduring differences leading to internal political maneuvering. Politics can have a very negative connotation, implying perceived dishonesty, manipulation, and abuse of power; however, it can also be viewed constructively with regard to setting agendas, networking, building coalitions, and effectively influencing public policy (Slack and Parent, 2006; Bolman and Deal, 2008). Thus, organizational politics and the corresponding problems represent internal and external dimensions of organizations that must be addressed carefully and intelligently by astute leaders.

In sport, examples of problem solving related to politics and power negotiations are evident in many situations; these range from the jockeying of athletic programs for limited funding, to the symbolization of political ideologies in the Olympics, to the leveraging of power by professional sport franchises threatening to relocate.

Sociocultural Issues

This area represents one of both tremendous opportunity and significant challenge to sport organization leaders today. Certainly, race and ethnicity in sport as it relates to equal employment opportunity is an area that must continue to receive the attention of sport leaders. As indicated by Parks, Quarterman, and Thibault (2007), "Opportunities for people of color and women continue to lag behind opportunities for white males, both in the core sport industry (e.g. professional sport senior executives, athletic directors, general managers) and in the support industries (e.g. broadcast media, sport agents, concessions)" (p. 14). While progress has been made over the last several years, especially in the hiring practices of major professional sport leagues, with the NBA leading the way (Lapchick, 2010), there is still need for improvement. Addressing this issue from an ethical, legal, and sociocultural perspective is important to solving problems in this dimension of sport organization leadership.

Leaders of many sport organizations also face other pervasive and complex sociological problems such as increased commercialization, declining sportsmanship, deviant behavior of athletes, drug use, hazing, and other sources of social conflict. These issues, among many others, are addressed in the coursework preparation of students in sport management academic programs and in numerous textbooks in sport sociology. "Approaches to Problem Solving" later in this chapter offers ideas and

recommendations on how leaders can apply three specific strategies as at least a starting point in dealing with complex sociological issues.

Technological Issues

Sport leaders also face new problems and decisions related to pervasive and rapidly changing technologies, including technological infrastructure, information management, mobile communications, and social networking (Twitter, Facebook, LinkedIn, and so on). Computer and mobile technology along with social media have created an entirely new world of communications across the sport industry. For example, twittercounter.com (2011) reports that Shaquille O'Neal (SHAQ) has over 4.1 million followers on Twitter. It is also reported that Cristiano Ronaldo, soccer (football) player for Real Madrid, has a combined total of over 36 million fans and followers on Facebook and Twitter (fanpagelist.com, 2011). Online communication among players, fans, and media creates exciting new opportunities for sport organizations, but also can create new problems and the need for careful monitoring, education on the use of social media, and in many cases new policies. In the NFL, for example, league policy prohibits players, coaches, and football operations personnel from using social media from 90 minutes before kickoff until after the game, following media interviews (nfl.com, 2010).

Given the degree of social connection and influence that athletes can generate through technology, leaders of sport programs at all levels must recognize and make strategic decisions around the many productive uses of social media while also addressing issues that arise from careless, unprofessional, and unethical use of this technology.

In addition to communications-related technology, leaders of sport organizations must deal with other technological advancements and the potential problems they can create. Table 6.1 presents just a few examples of other technology-related issues that have necessitated problem solving by sport leaders in the past and may continue to do so in the future.

Table 6.1 Examples of Technological Issues for Sport Leaders

Issues	Examples
Sports and digital rights	English Premier League and other sports rights holders issued a class action lawsuit against YouTube and Google for copyright infringement (Bilal, 2007).
Technology and refereeing	Issues around the increasing use of digital cameras, software, and even computer chips embedded in soccer balls are leading to questions about whether this technology will or should eventually replace referees (Repanich, 2010).
Genetic testing and sport performance	DNA scans have been developed by genetic testing companies specifically to help tailor sport participants' training to their innate skills, as well to spot children or adults who may be susceptible, because of their genes, to life-threatening health problems and other injuries (Stein, 2011).

On the Sidelines

A good example of how technology has created a legal issue in sport over athlete exploitation is a lawsuit filed by former University of Nebraska quarterback Sam Keller against Electronic Arts (EA), a leading interactive entertainment software company (Keller v. Electronic Arts, 9th Cir., 2010). In this suit, Keller contended that Electronic Arts and the NCAA owed him (and thousands of other former players) millions of dollars for using their nameless images in EA's NCAA Football video game (Former Husker Keller's Suit, 2011). According to the CBSSports.com article, the lawsuit had escalated into a First Amendment challenge that could end up in the Supreme Court and could threaten organizations such as Hollywood studios and media companies.

Do you think this issue represents a problem of exploitation of college athletes? If so, what role and responsibilities do you think that leaders of the NCAA have in addressing the problem?

Approaches to Problem Solving

Drucker's statement offers some important insights into the challenges of truly solving problems such that they will no longer need attention and can be considered 100 percent solved. Several domains and dimensions of complex problems in sport are extremely difficult to solve in such a way that they will never have to be dealt with again. However, staying ahead of these problems and working with an attitude of continuous improvement can and sometimes will eliminate some of the issues or at least reduce them to a more manageable level in a reasonable time frame.

It is beyond the scope of this section to cover the plethora of historical and contemporary theoretical, mathematical, and computerized models of problem-solving and decision-making approaches available in the literature. For example, systems theory and complexity science offer insights into problem solving that can be very helpful for dealing with modern sport organizational issues. The "Recommended Readings" section at the end of the chapter lists resources in these areas. Also, readers interested in learning more about new approaches to decision science, computer-aided decision making, decision support, and artificial intelligence in sports are encouraged to pursue academic literature searches specifically in these areas.

While I have chosen to focus primarily on three approaches to leadership problem solving and decision making that can be useful in addressing the complexities encountered by leaders of sport organizations, it is important to acknowledge the work on problem solving and decision making done by 1978 Nobel Prize and 1986 National Medical of Science awardee Herbert Simon. Simon (1986) described the work of solving problems and

> *Most problems can't be solved, you can only stay ahead of them.*
>
> *Peter Drucker*

making decisions as "choosing issues that require attention, setting goals, finding or designing suitable courses of action, and evaluating and choosing among alternative actions" (p. 19). Within this description, Simon stated that the activities of fixing agendas, setting goals, and designing courses of action were the domain of problem solving, while decision making involved the two activities of evaluating options and choosing among possible actions. He argued, however, that numerous factors and complexities, including emotions, cognitive capacities, and time constraints, prevent managers and leaders from evaluating every possible decision alternative and thus, in reality, create the need to limit alternatives often to those that reflect personal preferences. Simon referred to this as "bounded rationality." The following sections reflect my preferences for problem-solving approaches that are well researched across various organizational contexts, offering what I believe are useful approaches to creative problem solving and decision making in sport environments.

The Cynefin Framework

The Cynefin framework (Kurtz and Snowden, 2003; Snowden and Boone, 2007) is described as a "sense-making device" that can help leaders better understand the context and complexity of organizational problems so that they can approach these issues and make decisions using different and appropriate actions as needed. Snowden and Boone point out that "leaders who understand that the world is often irrational and unpredictable will find the Cynefin Framework particularly useful" (p. 70). The framework consists of four domains as shown in figure 6.1.

For each domain or context in the framework are a description and recommendations for leader actions as proposed by Snowden and Boone (2007). In addition, examples of sport-related problems that fit into each context are provided. See table 6.2. While this framework has not been specifically researched in sport, the domains and recommendations are very applicable to many sport organization issues.

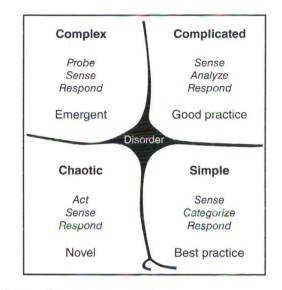

Figure 6.1 The Cynefin framework.
Based on Kurtz and Snowden 2003.

Multiframe Leadership and Problem Solving

Often leaders tend to approach organizational problems and decisions by turning to the style and approach that they are comfortable with and that have worked in previous situations. While this may work out fine in many instances, other circumstances and contexts call for a more flexible approach. When leaders become unidimensional, they may ultimately fail to see key components of problems and potentially overlook more effective solutions.

An interesting and useful approach to organizational leadership that addresses this issue is the multidimensional "framing" concept provided over the last two decades by Bolman and Deal (1991, 2008). This perspective has been researched and applied in a variety of organizational settings ranging from corporate and education settings to the military. It has additionally been applied in research related to leadership, problem solving, and organizational climate in intercollegiate athletic departments (Scott, 1999). From Bolman and Deal's (2008) perspective, dealing with organizational issues requires that leaders develop mental models or "a set of ideas and assumptions" (p. 11) that help them begin to understand and navigate various problems. These mental models, referred

Table 6.2 Domains of Complexity in Problem Solving and Decision Making

Context of problem	Sport-related examples
SIMPLE	
Problems characterized by clear cause-and-effect relationships. Issues are subject to little change, and the most appropriate or correct answer to the problem is often self-evident. Problem-solving approaches are typically based on best practices and may require a straightforward command and control leadership style. Leaders are advised to use a "sense, categorize, and respond" approach.	• Online sporting goods retail company resolving a straightforward processing and shipping issue • Ticket office resolving issue with an unsatisfied customer • Coach or athletic director dealing with athlete violating team or department policy
COMPLICATED	
Problems may have more than one right answer. Direct cause and effect, while existing, may not be clear to everyone. Outside experts or consultants may be needed to address the problem. Solutions may need to be based on good practices instead of best practices. Leaders are advised to use a "sense, analyze, and respond" approach.	• Declining participation in a youth sport program • NCAA conference realignment • Effective communication with international athlete • Making budget cuts while achieving Title IX compliance in athletic departments
COMPLEX	
Problems are multifaceted and often unpredictable. Cause and effect is difficult to establish. Potential solutions may create unintended consequences that affect other parts of the system. Leaders must try to refrain from quickly trying to impose a simple command and control approach and rely more on thoughtful and experimental strategies. Often the path forward emerges from careful and collaborative thought. Leaders are advised to use a "probe, sense, and respond" approach.	• Resolving issues related to commercialization in sport • Dealing with "digital media rights" issues of sport leagues and broadcast companies over online content and live streaming of games and events • Universities resolving budgetary issues around academic priorities and increasing costs of athletics
CHAOTIC	
Problems characterized by severe turbulence or crisis. Cause and effect may not be immediately known or may be impossible to determine. Problems typically require immediate and decisive action. Leaders must attempt to initially establish reasonable order and to sense where stability exists. Leaders are advised to "act, sense, and respond."	• Fan riot or terrorist activity at stadium or arena • Injuries or fatalities of sport team members in a travel accident • Natural disaster during sport event

Based on information in Snowden and Boone 2007.

to by Bolman and Deal as "frames," often require that leaders frame and reframe situations in order to see solutions more clearly. It is important to note that Bolman and Deal see frames as analogous to tools with their distinctive strengths and limitations. "The right tool makes the job easier, but the wrong one gets in the way" (p. 13). Also, one must frame situations accurately before choosing the appropriate tool, and it may be that one or two tools can be used in some situations but that multiple tools are needed for more complex tasks.

The multiframe perspective of Bolman and Deal (2008) consists of four unique lenses or perspectives, described next. These authors suggest that leaders often have a predisposition to one or two of the frames, but that developing the flexibility and capacity to use multiple frames in addressing issues may result in more effective outcomes.

An example of a problem that affects many interscholastic and intercollegiate sport organizations—one that might be addressed through the multiframe leadership approach—is hazing. According to an Alfred

Bolman and Deal's Frames of Reference

1. The **structural frame** emphasizes goal attainment, is task oriented, and is typically characterized by rules, policies, and traditional division of labor. Coordination and control is viewed as essential to effectiveness. Leaders in this frame stress accountability and efficiency and are outcome oriented. Leaders may also try to design and implement structured processes that help with solutions to problems in this frame.

2. The **human resource frame** views organizations as existing to serve human needs. This frame is attuned to effective relationship building, with facilitation and empowerment considered important to success. Leaders in the human resource frame demonstrate support and concern for organizational members and "work on behalf of the organization and its people, seeking to serve the interests of both" (p. 331).

3. The **political frame** recognizes that conflict is inevitable and that a feature common to many organizations is competition (both internal and external) over scarce resources. Leaders in this frame work at being skilled negotiators and build a power base that they use very carefully. They also attempt to manage conflict in productive ways and negotiate skillfully to help competing or conflicting groups reach compromises.

4. The **symbolic frame** emphasizes values and shared meaning in organizations. Attending to elements of the organizational culture is important in this frame. Thus, symbols, rites, and rituals are seen as important to the communication of values in the organization. Also, according to Bolman and Deal, "The symbolic leader believes that the most important part of a leader's job is inspiration—giving people something they can believe in" (p. 336).

Based on Bolman and Deal 2008.

University study in 1999, 80 percent of college athletes had experienced hazing. In addition, the National Study of Student Hazing (Allan and Madden, 2008) reported that 25 percent of athletic coaches were aware that hazing of team members occurred, and 47 percent of students entering college had experienced hazing when they were in high school. Even more concerning is that hazing in sport teams has escalated in seriousness over the last several years to include numerous cases of physical and sexual assault.

Approaching the issue of hazing through the multiframe perspective of Bolman and Deal provides some insights into what might be helpful for leaders addressing this situation. For example, a leader approaching hazing from the structural frame would likely see it primarily as a problem in need of a "no tolerance" policy. Strict rules and proper oversight of locker rooms and facilities by coaches and administrators would be essential. Swift punishment or removal from a team of any athlete involved in hazing another athlete would likely be a primary outcome of structural leadership in this situation.

While the structural frame is certainly appropriate to the situation, a leader could additionally frame the hazing problem through the human resource lens. From this perspective the leader would certainly want to demonstrate concern and support for the victims of hazing, but might also look to the perpetrators to determine whether they need counseling or whether there is any reason to believe that they could learn lessons from the situation and ultimately be reconnected to the team.

While the political frame might not initially seem directly applicable to this situation, it might be that the hazing incident was brought on primarily by conflict among team members or a power differential established by upperclassmen or upperclasswomen. It is also possible that a coach or sport administrator in this situation could use her own power base to productively move athletes toward compromises or negotiated agreements that eliminate hazing or reduce it to socially acceptable activities as deemed appropriate by team members, coaches, and administrators.

The symbolic frame offers another unique perspective for dealing with the problem of hazing. Hazing is often considered a ceremony or rite of passage whereby team members are fully accepted into the group. Thus coaches and administrators may consider educating athletes on the dangers of hazing and provide new activities and ceremonies based on core values that are considered essential to team development and team culture. In this way, hazing in its destructive and abusive form is no longer considered an acceptable way of doing things among the members of the team.

These examples suggest that many problems in the sport industry may be embedded in one or more of the four frames identified by Bolman and Deal. The challenge for sport leaders using this approach is to effectively frame and reframe problems until they are able to think from different perspectives and "be more versatile in their leadership approach" (Scott, 2008, p. 16).

Vroom, Yetton, and Jago (Normative Decision Model)

The decision model originally developed by Vroom and Yetton (1973) and later refined by Vroom and Jago (1988) has been used for several years in many organizational contexts as a model for improved leadership decision-making process among leaders. This model can be especially useful to sport organization leaders in situations that begin to require more organizational involvement in problem solving and decision making. The decision tree used in this model is presented in figure 6.2. To use

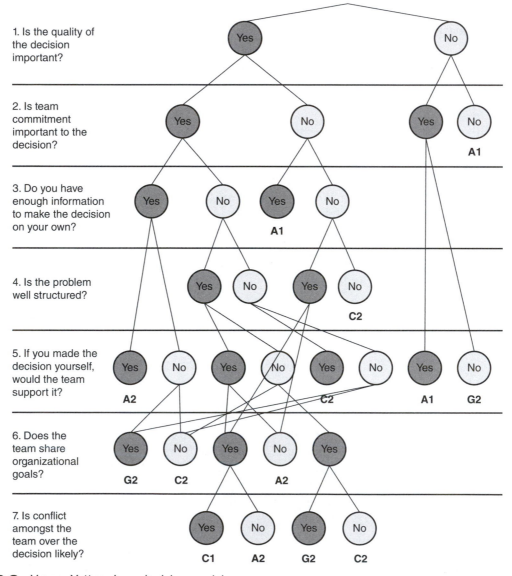

Figure 6.2 Vroom-Yetton-Jago decision model.

the decision tree, you begin with question 1 and answer Yes or No until you get to the decision-making process labeled A1, A2, C1, C2, or G2; these processes are explained next.

In this model, leaders may use three styles of leadership (autocratic, consultative, and collaborative) and five processes of decision-making to address organizational problems. The five processes are as follows:

A1 Autocratic I: Leader solves problem alone using information readily available.

A2 Autocratic II: Leader obtains information from group or team members and makes decision alone.

C1 Consultative I: Leader shares problem with group members individually, asks for information and evaluation, and makes decision alone.

C2 Consultative II: Leader shares problem collectively with group members but makes decision alone.

G2 Group II: Leader discusses situation with group. Leader directs discussion, but does not impose will, and final decision is made by the group.

In a sport context, the decision tree can be helpful, for example, when a community or commercial sport and fitness manager is evalu- ating the operation's budget and is attempting to make decisions regarding potential budget cuts to programs or services. Another real-world example, representative of the normative model in a sport context, was described by Sullivan (2011) in his news article about field manager Mike Quade's role in decision making with the Chicago Cubs. Read "On the Sidelines" for excerpts from Sullivan's article.

Summary

This chapter deals with the issue of complexity and its influence on leadership problem solving in sport organizations. Complexity within sport organizations is typically associated with dimensions of organizational structure, but is also influenced by the changing nature of organizations from hierarchically structured and managed entities to "knowledge-age" organizations that are rapidly changing, are technologically enhanced, and embrace a more inclusive and collaborative approach to problem solving.

Three key competencies and skills important for leaders relative to dealing with complex problems in organizations are (1) creative problem solving, (2) social judgment skills, and (3) knowledge. These skills are not limited to those in leadership roles and are considered important to identify or develop across individuals at all levels of an organization.

On the Sidelines

Excerpts from March 8, 2011, Chicago Tribune *article, "Final Cubs roster will be group decision," by Paul Sullivan,* Tribune *reporter:*

"In his 17 years as a minor league manager, Mike Quade simply handled the players who were assigned to him. In his first full season managing the Cubs, Quade now will be part of the decision-making process."

"Quade isn't sure how big a voice he will have in meetings later this month with general manager Jim Hendry and assistant GM Randy Bush. 'I can only speculate (until then),' Quade said. 'Jim has been very upfront about all these decisions being mine, But I'm always mindful in any decision of using the people I have available to me.'"

"So how much clout does Quade have? 'Some- times decisions will be made on what he thinks is best for the club, and other times, just in the normal process, you come down to tough decisions that obviously Randy and I would have final say in,' Hendry said. 'It's best when you do it mutually.'"

"Hendry said if Quade is adamant about keeping a player who has options remaining, he will tend to go with the manager's choice."

"Quade conceded he needs guidance, but he has waited a long time to have some say in his team. 'I fully expect to have the loudest voice, at least of the (field staff),' he said. 'But if (owner) Tom Ricketts or Jim Hendry or Randy Bush shot me down, that's because they're ahead of me. They're my bosses. It will be a group effort and we'll put our heads together.'"

Based on information in Sullivan 2011.

Several broad areas of complex issues in sport organizations are identified in the chapter. Economic problems associated with recent declining financial conditions across the globe are discussed as a primary area presenting complex problems for leaders across all types and levels of sport organizations. Sport-related legal as well as financial and sociological problems (with specific emphasis on Title IX) are identified as complex issues that continue to face leaders of interscholastic and intercollegiate sport organizations in the United States. Complexities associated with public relations issues, sociocultural problems, and the impact of technology and social networking in sport organizations also create challenges for sport organization leaders. Additionally, the growth of sports into an increasingly global enterprise is discussed relative to complexities created by growing internationalism among both participants and coaches and sport-related businesses increasingly operating in a cross-cultural, multinational environment.

Three specific problem-solving approaches useful for complex problem solving are rec-ommended for consideration by leaders of sport organizations. The Cynefin framework (Kurtz and Snowden, 2003) is a "sense-making device" that can help leaders identify and better understand both the content and complexity of organizational problems. Recommendations for how leaders can use the framework for both analysis and action are presented.

The multiframe perspective of Bolman and Deal (1991, 2008) is discussed as an approach through which organizational problems can be categorized into one of four frames: (1) structural, (2) human resource, (3) political, and (4) symbolic. Leaders can use these frames to diagnose and develop strategies for how to more effectively deal with internal and external issues.

Finally, the Vroom-Yetton-Jago (1988) normative model for decision making is presented as a decision tree that leaders can use to help determine the extent of autocratic, consultative, or group decision making that should be employed when making organizational decisions.

Final Self-Assessment

After having read and reflected on the content in this chapter, consider your responses to these self-assessment questions, slightly modified from the beginning of the chapter. Have your perspectives changed, or do you have any new insights or additional questions regarding your understanding of complexities and problem solving in sport organizations?

1. In what ways do you recognize that sport organizations are becoming increasingly complex?

2. What areas would you like to improve relative to your own competencies and skills as a problem solver?

3. What have you learned from the tools or processes presented in this chapter that you think could benefit your approach to organizational problem solving?

Game Plan Activity

You can do this activity on your own as a professional development exercise, or your instructor may want to make the activity a course assignment that can be presented or submitted as a problem-solving plan either by individuals or by small groups.

Choose one of the complex problem areas identified in this chapter or from your own experience that you would like to use as the focus for developing a problem-solving strategy. Use the Cynefin framework to diagnose the level of complexity of the problem or select Bolman and Deal's four-frame model to frame the problem and determine various approaches for how you would address the issue. Finally, employ the Vroom-Yetton-Jago decision tree for determining how you would go about making decisions in the organization.

Questions to Consider

1. What are some of the primary contributors to complexity in sport organizations?

2. Because of increasing complexity and rapid societal and technological change, many argue that it is now more difficult than in the past for only one person in a leadership role to solve problems in an organization. Do you think this is true for most sport organizations? Why or why not?

3. The problem-solving competency of *social judgment* is one of the skills considered important to effective leadership. What are the specific component skills associated with this particular competency?

4. Scan the Internet and identify at least two or three sport-related issues that you think pose complex problems. What types of solutions does it appear are being proposed and how, if at all, do they relate to the approaches presented in this chapter?

5. Do some additional research in the areas of decision making and problem solving, and identify at least one approach not covered in this chapter that you find interesting or potentially useful for addressing micro (internal organizational) or macro (external or industry-wide) issues in sport organizations.

Recommended Readings

Bolman, L., and Deal, T. (2008). *Reframing organizations: Artistry, choice, and leadership.* San Francisco: Jossey-Bass.

Chelladurai, P. (2009). *Managing organizations for sport and physical activity: A systems perspective.* Scottsdale, AZ: Holcomb Hathaway.

Marquardt, M., and Yeo, R. (2012). *Breakthrough problem solving with action learning: Concepts and cases.* Palo Alto, CA: Stanford Business Books.

Senge, P. (1990). *The fifth discipline.* New York: Doubleday Business.

Change, Turnaround, and Crisis Leadership

Learning Objectives

After reading and reflecting on the concepts and examples in this chapter, you will be able to

1. discuss organizational change relative to sport organizations and apply Kotter's change model to a sport organization;

2. define and give examples of turnaround situations in sport;

3. discuss and apply findings and recommendations from research on turnaround leadership;

4. discuss how turnaround situations may influence leadership style;

5. explain and give examples of obstacles that must often be overcome in turnaround situations;

6. identify types and levels of crises that can occur in sport organizations;

7. explain how decision making differs in crisis environments;

8. identify and provide examples of various crisis leadership competencies; and

9. understand and apply elements of effective crisis preparation, crisis response, and crisis recovery as a leader.

Self-Assessment

1. What do you currently think are key strategies for effectively leading change or a sport organization turnaround?

2. What do you believe are the most appropriate leadership styles for leading a turnaround? Does this depend on the situation? Why or why not?

3. How prepared do you currently feel if you were to be placed in a role of crisis leadership? What do you see as your strengths and weaknesses relative to knowledge, skills, and behaviors in a crisis situation?

4. What processes and recommendations are you familiar with for leading people and organizations through a crisis?

Being an effective and respected leader of a sport organization or team, at any level, is a challenging task. This task becomes even more demanding when one is required to lead individuals and organizations through change, turnaround, and crisis situations. Every year the sport industry witnesses significant turnover of top executives, coaches, or employees resulting from failures to perform or produce results at levels satisfactory to constituents. These situations often call for well-designed and systemic change initiatives and sometimes necessitate the implementation of dramatic turnaround leadership strategies. In addition, potential or actual crisis situations in sport that involve loss of lives or massive scandals require significant leadership efforts to demonstrate leader responsibility in crisis prevention, response, and recovery.

This chapter begins by reviewing some of the most pertinent organizational change research that has occurred relative to sport management over the last two decades. Pressures within the operating environment for sport organizations today indicate the need for sport leaders to be knowledgeable about and committed to effectively leading change. To address this need, the chapter presents information regarding the foundational and broadly accepted approach to change leadership offered by Dr. John Kotter, internationally known expert on leadership and change. An example of a change effort relative to the Professional Golfers Association (PGA) in the United Kingdom is included to demonstrate elements of effectively preparing for and leading sport organization change.

The chapter then defines and describes turnaround situations and processes in sport. Examples demonstrate the influence and impact that top executives can have as leaders of a turnaround. Research and practical applications for leading turnaround are covered; these include identification of a two-stage model for turnaround based on stabilization and repositioning of an organization during turnaround. Research investigating the impact of environmental changes and personnel on turnaround in public not-for-profit organizations is included to provide ideas for both practicing sport leaders and academic researchers interested in the effects of these factors on turnaround. To conclude this part of the chapter, reviews of research addressing elements of psychological turnaround and how to navigate cognitive, resource, motivational, and political hurdles are presented.

The second part of the chapter concerns crisis leadership and the roles and responsibilities that leaders assume relative to crisis situations. Concepts and definitions of crisis along with examples of the various levels and types of crisis are presented. The chapter then provides information on the decision-making environment and proposed competencies of effective crisis leaders. Finally, the last few sections of the chapter present concepts and recommendations associated with a crisis leadership progression that includes crisis prevention, crisis response, and action during a crisis situation, as well as effective leadership in a postcrisis recovery.

Change Leadership

Sport organizations, like all other organizations, are operating in a rapidly changing and complex world. However, interest in better understanding organizational change in sport is not new. Identification of various theoretical approaches and practices associated with understanding and leading change appeared in sport management research literature over two decades ago (Slack and Hinings, 1992). Using theories including resource dependency theory, institutional theory, organizational culture, and the role of transformational leadership in change, Slack and Hinings evaluated the change process affecting structure, strategy, and processes in Canadian national sport organizations. A few years later, Stevens and Slack (1998) used a case study of a Canadian amateur ice hockey association to further examine the notion of a deterministic approach and voluntary strategic choice in organizational transformation or change. Findings of this study indicated that institutional pressures and strategic choice were interconnected and instrumental in the change process.

After several years of little further research in sport-related organizational change, Zakus and Skinner (2008) examined organizational environment disturbances and external pressures (e.g., growing commercialism, ethical scandals, television rights, sponsorships) relative to their impact on organizational change within the culture, structure, and processes of the International Olympic Committee (IOC). Acknowledging various limitations of their theoretical approach, Zakus and Skinner concluded that varying levels of change had occurred in the evolution of the IOC and that while there was evidence of a new value system in some components of the organization, evidence also suggested the presence of historically embedded values and beliefs that continued to be deeply rooted in the organization.

Currently, there continue to be enormous pressures on all organizations in sport to be able to respond and change to environmental, social, political, economic, and technological changes. The responsibilities and accountability of leaders and leadership teams for effectively leading change continue to require commitment and knowledge to address these pressures.

One of the most highly recognized approaches to effectively leading organizational change has been provided by Dr. John Kotter, who is recognized internationally as the expert in change leadership. Kotter, who began publishing on the topic in 1995, identified an eight-stage process, along with the specific actions in each stage, as well as pitfalls to try to avoid when leading change. Kotter points out in the most recent edition of his book, *Leading Change* (2012), that while his concepts and approach to leading change have not altered, the speed at which change is occurring continues to make his concepts and recommendations even more relevant. Kotter also notes that one of the biggest problems and obstacles to initiating change is created by complacency and an inadequate sense of urgency on the part of leaders. Kotter's eight-stage process is summarized in the sidebar, which is followed by an "On the Sidelines" sport organization example that demonstrates how some of the change leadership concepts can be used.

Eight Stage Process for Leading Change

1. Establish a sense of urgency.
   - Evaluate market and competitive environment for opportunities and potential crises.
   - Overcome complacency and convince majority of managers that change must occur.

2. Create a guiding coalition.
   - Build a guiding team with a high level of trust, commitment, and shared goals and objectives.
   - Team must have enough power to lead the change effort.

3. Develop vision and strategy.
   - Create a clear vision to effectively direct changes.
   - Develop and implement appropriate strategies aligned with the vision.

4. Communicate the change vision.
   - Make use of every communication vehicle available to communicate the new vision and strategies.
   - Model the new behaviors and send consistent messages.

5. Empower employees or others for action.
   - Remove obstacles or alter structures and systems that might undermine the vision.
   - Encourage followers to take risks and develop new ideas and actions.

6. Generate short-term wins.
   - Define and monitor visible performance improvements.
   - Recognize and reward individuals for their contributions to the improvements.

7. Consolidate gains and produce more change.
   - Use the increased credibility from early wins to continue changing systems, structures, and policies.
   - Hire and develop personnel who are capable of implementing the changes.

8. Anchor new approaches in the culture.
   - Explain the connections between the change-related behaviors and success.
   - Create further leadership development and succession consistent with the change.

Based on information in Kotter 2007, 2012.

On the Sidelines

The following blog post appeared on the sports coachuk.org website and provides an example of *elements of effectively leading change in a sport organization.*

PGA Case Study: Managing and Communicating Change

We asked the PGA how the UK Coaching Framework had caused change within the sport of golf, how this change is being managed and communicated, and what the implications will be for their sport. Having recently completed an MBA with a dissertation focusing on Change Management, Jane Booth was unsurprisingly at the helm of this for Golf.

Fundamentally, the UK Coaching Framework provided us with a sense of direction and an impetus to look at things differently; it gave individuals within the sport of golf a reason to work together. We were definitely drawn to the idea of creating a cohesive coaching system but although we took guidance from the UK Coaching Framework and used it as a reference, it was important to us to translate this into our own language and work out what coaching means to us.

For us, the management of this change has firstly been about developing a common story and a collective vision that everyone understands, and which can be adapted to different people's worlds. Key partners were brought together to shape this vision and it is now important to get commitment and buy-in from all levels – from board level down to the clubs. We have always had quite a fragmented structure and we needed something common to bring bodies and individuals together. Plus, golf is quite a traditional sport, and also a multi-million pound industry, and we needed to make sure that we considered practical issues within the vision – for example, how can our coaching vision help address the issue of falling membership in the current economic climate?

We are at a place where consistent communication with all partners is crucial and this will continue to be a focus over the next 12-18 months. By working together, we will gradually get the coaching message out in the form of a common story that everyone understands.

In terms of implications for our sport, we would hope to see the emergence of a change in coaching culture and a different way of thinking and looking at things, and of course the whole sport working together across Great Britain and Ireland. Specifically, this would involve the delivery of a world-class coaching system that supports the growth and development of golf by helping to attract more golfers into the sport and helping them to achieve their potential (whatever that may be). Our ultimate aim is our simple vision: 'right coach, right place, right time'.

Jane's Guide for Managing Change

1. Develop a shared vision and create (and collectively agree) a 'story' that tells and sells the vision in simple terms.

2. Engage the right people in telling the story – identify leaders at all levels that will inspire others to follow.

3. Communicate the story consistently at all levels and help people understand what it means for them . . . keep on telling the same story until people truly understand.

4. 'Walk the talk' – visibly show people what the new system looks and feels like . . . if it is better than the current one, they won't want to go back!

5. Take time to develop the right solutions – major change takes time and tomorrow's answer may not be the right one in the long run; but don't forget to keep delivering the high quality day-to-day business to maintain the momentum for change.

Reprinted, by permission, from SportsCoachUK, 2012, *PGA case study: Managing and communicating change.* Available: www.sportscoachuk.org/blog/pga-case-study-managing-and-communicating-change

Turnaround Leadership

From a corporate-level strategy perspective in sport, turnaround is considered a defensive strategy by which an organization tries to reverse the situation when the demand for its product or service starts to decrease and it develops strategies to counter increasing costs and falling revenues (Slack and Parent, 2006). Turnaround in sport can also refer to dramatic or rapid improvement in team performance, fan interest, and ticket sales. Turnaround also may occur in community-based recreational or sport programs when significant declines in interest and participation are followed by a period of sustained recovery and growth. This section defines turnaround, provides sport-related examples of turnaround, and presents related information from research and practice across other academic domains to help prepare leaders for effectively addressing turnaround situations.

Defining Turnaround

The term "turnaround" in its broadest sense refers to the reversal of performance in an organization from negative to positive. In a corporate context, turnaround is often associated with a period of decline in profits and market share followed by a subsequent rejuvenation and return to a profitable environment and increased shareholder value. Turnaround has also been defined as the need to bring about rapid, dramatic, and lasting change, often with limited resources (Kim and Mauborgne, 2003).

The turnaround process has historically been associated with two stages: retrenchment and recovery (Robbins and Pearce, 1992). According to Robbins and Pearce, *retrenchment* places strong emphasis on cost and asset reduction in a company as a way to mitigate conditions that led to a financial downturn. *Recovery*, Robbins and Pearce say, refers to the process whereby an organization then shifts its focus toward a growth and development objective and emphasizes an increase in market share.

In many cases, turnarounds in sport organizations are led by an individual or a new leadership team (e.g., new CEO, team owner, GM, athletic director, head coach and staff) hired for the purpose of leading a turnaround effort. In these situations, expectations are typically high for the new leaders to demonstrate tangible results and marked improvements within a relatively short amount of time—often within one or two years.

Sport Turnarounds

Many examples exist of successful turnaround situations in sport over the last decade. While turnarounds occur across all levels of sports, the following paragraphs describe some of the ones that have attracted national media attention.

One of the well-recognized sport franchise turnarounds in recent history is that of the National Hockey League (NHL) Chicago Blackhawks. In what Vardi (2009) on forbes.com called "the greatest sports-business turnaround ever," the Blackhawks experienced dramatic changes in the franchise in 2007 after Rocky Wirtz took over from his father, Bill Wirtz. Rocky Wirtz has been credited with making sweeping changes to previous policies and practices that, over the course of three years, resulted in the growth of season ticket purchases from 3,400 to 14,000 and the growth of regular-season attendance from 522,000 to 912,000, the top attendance in the NHL (Vardi, 2009). In addition, the Blackhawks won the Stanley Cup, in 2010, for the first time since 1961. One of the key elements of the franchise turnaround has been attributed to Wirtz's bringing in a new team president, John McDonough, to improve the team's marketing and promotions (Clark, 2008). As noted by Clark, the hiring of McDonough resulted in the creation of the Blackhawks fan convention and a decision to broadcast all Blackhawk games on television for the first time in history.

Another well-publicized turnaround of the last decade was that of Major League Baseball's Minnesota Twins from 2000 to 2010. In 2000, the Twins were considered one of baseball's weakest franchises, with a small payroll (only 1/10 that of the New York Yankees), poor team performance, and attendance reaching just over 10,000 per game (Schoenfeld, 2010). Additionally, the Twins were sharing the Metrodome, home of their local National Football League (NFL) counterpart, the Vikings, which was not a good financial arrangement or highly attractive to fans. With the franchise at its nadir, then-owner Carl Pohlad had reportedly agreed to a $150 million buyout to dissolve the team. However, shortly thereafter, Carl's son Jim Pohlad took over the team and started a turnaround process that resulted in the planning and construction of Target Field, five postseason playoff appearances for the team, and a payroll that increased to 11th in the league (Schoenfeld, 2010). Schoenfeld recognizes

Pohlad as the leader of the Twins' dramatic turnaround and describes his approach as "thinking like a small business" (p. 1). See the "On the Sidelines" story titled "Turnaround Artist" for details on Pohlad's approach to the turnaround.

In intercollegiate athletics in the United States, one of the most notable turnarounds in all of sport occurred with the Kansas State University football program under the leadership of Head Coach Bill Snyder. In 1988, just before Snyder became the head coach of the Wildcats, the team had experienced two straight winless seasons, and at one point in 1987 they had lost three consecutive games by a combined 151 points (Mays, 2011). In addition, as noted by Mays, the Wildcats had been last in the nation in scoring offense and scoring defense over the previous 40 seasons, and were considered by objective measures the worst program in the history of college football. After the hiring of Bill Snyder in 1989 and on his return from retirement in 2005, the program experienced a dramatic turnaround, with postseason bowl appearances in 12 of 14 seasons (1993-2006), including 11 straight bowl games under Snyder between 1993 and 2003 (kstatesports.com, 2013). While many factors can contribute to

On the Sidelines

Turnaround Artist

Jim Pohlad, owner of the Minnesota Twins, is credited with a dramatic turnaround of the Twins Major League Baseball (MLB) franchise between 2000 and 2010. Pohlad was featured in *Entrepreneur* magazine as "The Turnaround Artist" (Schoenfeld, 2010) who was able to guide the Twins to new success by running the team more like a small business. Schoenfeld's article identifies five strategies associated with the Twins' turnaround during the 2000-2010 period that can offer lessons for other small businesses and organizations.

1. **Identify your strengths:** The Twins, as a small-market franchise in MLB, were not able to compete with large-market teams for top players. By identifying and developing young talented players and promoting from within their own farm system, they were able to build a team that went from a 42.5 percent winning percentage to winning the American League Central Division in 2002.

2. **Offer a unique experience:** Until Target Field was completed for the 2010 season, the Twins shared the Metrodome with the NFL's Vikings as well as the University of Minnesota Gophers. With this arrangement, the Twins could not generate income from premium seating or suites and had only partial control of concessions. Since the completion of the new open-air facility, luxury suites are available and fans are treated to unique food and shopping experiences. In addition, the ballpark offers conference space for lease so that the franchise can generate revenue at times when the team is on the road and during the off-season.

3. **Connect with your customers:** The team made players as personally accessible as possible to fans by expanding their traditional "winter roadshow" so that it included more stops over a longer time period in a five-state region. Keeping the roster stable enabled fans to better connect to their favorite players, and the Twins also committed to keeping tickets affordable when they moved from the Metrodome to Target Field.

4. **Remain loyal to your employees:** Operating in a way noticeably different from other franchises in baseball, the Twins have numerous employees who have been with the club for 20 years. Evidence of loyalty to the franchise is also evident in top management, and the Twins maintain strong relations with their previous players as well.

5. **Know when it's time to act like a big business:** When faced with the possibility of losing Joe Mauer, American League MVP and local icon, Jim Pohlad offered Mauer a franchise-high eight-year $184 million deal. While this seemed inconsistent with the small business approach, it indicated the importance of demonstrating financial commitment to a star player and an intent to keep fans engaged with the team.

turnaround performance, in the case of Kansas State football, the leadership of Bill Snyder was certainly a critical element. In the foreword to *Leadership: Lessons from Bill Snyder* (Shoop and Scott, 2000), Jon Wefald, president of Kansas State University from 1986 to 2009, wrote,

"I know of no one that better understands the key ingredients of leadership than Coach Bill Snyder. He has been stressing the qualities and meaning of leadership for over a generation. Bill Snyder not only teaches the principles of leadership every day of the week, he lives by them. For years and years, Coach Bill Snyder has been articulating to his players and fellow coaches the principles and concepts of hard work and dedication, the setting and meeting of goals, the vital importance of loyalty and integrity, the value of dependability and credibility, and the championing of a caring attitude for fellow student athletes and friends." (p. viii)

Readers are encouraged to refer to the book by Shoop and Scott (2000) mentioned above for details and examples of 20 leadership lessons as they were put into practice by Coach Snyder with the Kansas State Wildcat football program.

Frontiera and Leidl (2012), in *Team Turnarounds: A Playbook for Transforming Underperforming Teams*, use information gained from team managers in the National Collegiate Athletic Association (NCAA), NFL, and MLB, along with top executives from companies that successfully led turnaround efforts, to illustrate specific steps teams need to take in order to turn performance around. These are the six elements or stages of turnaround identified by Frontiera and Leidl:

1. Leading past losing
2. Commitment to growth
3. Behavioral change
4. Embracing adversity
5. Achievement of success
6. Nurturing a culture of excellence

The commonalities among turnaround teams pointed out by Frontier and Leidl include

a committed leader who can help teams be resilient throughout the turnaround process and the ability to overcome deep-rooted beliefs that may lower their internal expectations (e.g., seeing themselves as a small-market team).

Research on Turnaround Management and Leadership

Turnaround situations occur fairly often in sport at all levels. In most cases, local, regional, and national sport news offers various explanations and internal or external observations regarding how the turnaround was achieved. Stories of turnaround and how they came about also appear in commentaries and reflections in business- and sport-related magazines as well as online articles. However, academic studies specific to turnaround situations in sport are scant. At the time of this writing, a review of the research databases and indexes revealed no empirical research specifically addressing "turnaround management" or "turnaround leadership" in sport. This represents an area of opportunity for those interested in conducting research on the causes, recovery strategies, and dynamics of turnaround in sport organizations.

Although research on turnaround in the sport-related academic literature is limited, there is considerable research regarding turnaround management and leadership in the business literature. Some of the studies and recommendations are reviewed here to provide examples of the types of research and various research questions that could be addressed by sport researchers interested in turnaround management or leadership. The studies reviewed also provide ideas that may be helpful to sport managers who find themselves in positions in which they must lead turnaround efforts.

Two-Stage Model for Turnaround

Arogyaswamy, Barker, and Yasai-Ardekani (1995) proposed that firms attempting to turn around from declining performance exhibit two classes of response that occur in stages. First, the organization exhibits decline-stemming strategies intended to halt and reverse dysfunctional consequences of a decline. At stage I, these strategies involve creating efficiencies and stabilizing the internal environment of the organization. This component of the strategy often involves cost containment or reduction and is sometimes referred to as retrenchment. Also at stage I, strategies to garner external stakeholder support along with stabilizing the firm's internal climate and decision processes must be implemented. Once the organization's decline has been halted and the stage I issues have been addressed, Arogyaswamy and colleagues say the organization can move into stage II, in which implementation of recovery strategies begins. These strategies, often referred to in other academic works as "repositioning," broadly include new strategic management actions and changes to policies that will attempt to eliminate or effectively manage what caused the decline and are designed to bring performance back to acceptable levels.

While this study was outside the realm of sport, there are many indications that the two-stage model proposed by Arogyaswamy and coauthors is followed by sport organizations. For example, one often sees stage I of the model put into effect when a sport organization in decline stops production and promotion of one or more of its products or fires and replaces top executives, coaches, and other organizational leaders because they are identified as a primary cause of the decline. Stage II of the model, as applied to sport, often results in new policies and procedures (e.g., allowing television broadcasts of all games, as in the case of the Chicago Blackhawks mentioned earlier) or the hiring of new leaders to take the organization in new directions (e.g., Bill O'Brien, head football coach of Penn State; Kristina Keneally, new CEO of Basketball Australia).

Environmental Change, Human Resources, and Turnaround

Boyne and Meier (2009), in a study of turnaround in failing school districts, pointed out that previous research in turnaround had focused primarily on retrenchment and repositioning, but had paid less attention to the influence or impact of changes that occur in the task environment and in human resources on an organization's recovery effort. This study is included in this chapter because it is one of the first applications of a turnaround model to public organizations as opposed to private sector companies. Thus, for sport researchers, this study could serve as a foundation for research on turnaround and organizational performance in public and nonprofit sport organizations.

Boyne and Meier note that the model used in their study has its foundation in three of the main literatures of organizational performance and turnaround. The first element draws on research suggesting that external factors and circumstances beyond the control of managers lead to organizational failure and affect subsequent turnaround efforts (Dess and Beard, 1984; Castrogiovanni, 2002). According to Boyne and Meier, this issue may be very relevant in public organizations (such as schools) because they don't usually have the ability to easily exit their environment. The second component of Boyne and Meier's model is aligned with previous research (Zajac and Kraatz, 1993; Wiersma and Bantel, 1992) suggesting that internal adjustments brought on by new senior managers and better human resources are likely to be adaptive rather than disruptive and are likely to be successful in situations in which performance is unsatisfactory. The third component of the model is based on the classical strategic management theory of Miles and Snow (1978) suggesting that failing organizations are able to rescue themselves through both retrenchment and repositioning.

Using the components of this model, Boyne and Meier set out to test their hypotheses in three categories as indicated in the sidebar "Boyne and Meier's Proposed Categories of Factors Influencing Turnaround."

Collecting and analyzing data on turnaround strategy from 140 low-performing schools, Boyne and Meier reported that their model explained 78 percent of the variation in the extent of turnaround in the school districts studied in the period from 1995 to 2002. The results showed that school turnaround appeared to be associated with positive changes in the task environment. Changes in human resources also had a significant and

Boyne and Meier's Proposed Categories of Factors Influencing Turnaround

Environmental change and turnaround

- Increases in the munificence (e.g. availability or abundance of resources) in the task environment are positively associated with turnaround.
- Increases in complexity (number of market domains served) of the task environment is negatively associated with turnaround.

Human resources and turnaround

- Appointment of a new top level manager from within the organization is positively associated with turnaround.

- Turnaround is associated more positively with insider succession than outsider succession.
- An increase in the ratio of core staff to total employees is positively associated with turnaround.
- An increase in the quality of core staff is positively associated turnaround

Retrenchment, repositioning, and turnaround

- Retrenchment is positively associated with organizational turnaround.
- Repositioning is positively associated with organizational turnaround.

Based on information in Boyne and Meier 2009.

positive effect on the improvement of performance in schools, with turnaround more likely to be achieved by insiders than by outsiders. Finally, the results indicated that the extent of school turnaround additionally appeared to be influenced by retrenchment and repositioning. Importantly, however, it was noted that retrenchment, specifically the strategies associated with cutting costs and raising efficiencies, actually exacerbated a school district's decline.

This research provided some important conclusions that could have implications for future empirical studies of turnaround in sport organizations. For example, Boyne and Meier indicate that the impact of environmental changes on turnaround appears likely to apply in other organizational settings and that the constraints imposed by task environments (e.g., availability of resources and complexity of the environment) are stronger for public organizations that cannot easily shift focus to new markets. When one considers the situation of a community or recreational sport organization or a public school athletic department trying to overcome financial difficulties or a decline in participation and support, focusing on a new market may not be a viable alternative. Also, Boyne and Meier suggested from their findings that the knowledge of insiders about an organization may be more valuable than a radical turnaround strategy introduced by an outsider in a turnaround situation. For

example, people who have been working within an organization may have specific knowledge needed by outsiders (e.g. external consultants or newly hired leaders from the outside) that can be of crucial importance in producing an effective turnaround effort.. This is also an area that provides opportunity for sport organization research, given the extensive turnover each year among head coaches of professional teams and Division I intercollegiate athletics.

Leadership Style and Turnaround

Muczyk and Steele (1998) addressed the issue of what type of leadership style is most appropriate for corporate turnaround situations. They point out that while democratic and participative leadership is widely supported and has been a cultural norm in the United States since World War II, there is also recognition that situations such as retrenchment and turnaround may require a more directive and autocratic leadership, especially in the initial stages. Muczyk and Steele note that the reversal of a business experiencing backward movement requires doing things in "different, unfamiliar, and often unpleasant ways" (p. 41). In turnaround situations, it is common for managers to be replaced and employees to be terminated. Additionally, the urgency of a turnaround does not easily lend itself to participative management, which can be very time-consuming. According to Muczyk and Steele, although many companies do well under leadership and management styles reliant on participation and worker autonomy, it must not be assumed that this is effective for organizations in declining and desperate situations. Finally, the authors acknowledge that while a more autocratic, top-down approach to leadership is appropriate for turnaround situations, leaders should also recognize the need to treat organizational members with courtesy, dignity, and respect in the process. They also suggest that when the difficult stages of the turnaround have been navigated, autocratic leaders may then need to be replaced with more democratic and participative leaders.

Your Thoughts

Based on your own experiences or observations in sport organizations, do you agree with Muczyk and Steele's perspective on the need for more autocratic and directive leadership when an organization is in need of turnaround? What examples have you seen of this approach working or not working in your program or interest area?

Psychological Turnaround

Kanter (2003), in the article "Leadership and the Psychology of Turnarounds," discusses issues and resolutions associated with bringing distressed and declining companies back to a healthy, profitable existence. Kanter bases her observations and recommendations on experience inside approximately two dozen turnaround situations and uses as examples three high-profile corporate turnarounds in the late 1990s and 2000s. She points out that while all cases involved smart financial and strategic decision making during the turnaround, another vital effort on the part of executives in each case was to restore people's confidence in themselves and each other. Kanter characterizes this effort as leading a psychological turnaround. While acknowledging that not every situation is the same and that turnaround situations often require cutting expenses, which can make initiatives challenging, Kanter

offers several real-world examples and recommendations for reversing attitudes in declining organizations.

According to Kanter, several dynamics are associated with the decline of organizations. Notably, these dynamics occur in similar patterns across organizations from many different industries. Kanter refers to these patterns as *organizational pathologies*—secrecy, blame, isolation, avoidance, passivity, and feelings of helplessness. Once these pathologies arise and are reinforced, a company enters a "death spiral"; reversal requires focused and deliberate efforts by the top executive to address each pathology.

Kanter asserts that in leading a turnaround, managers and leaders can introduce interventions that can begin to shift momentum back in favor of the company. The basic formula to achieve a successful turnaround is that the leader (the CEO in Kanter's article) must reverse the momentum and provide new ways to empower people, which involves replacing old attitudes and feelings with new ones as the organization moves into the future. See figure 7.1 for indications of the pathologies (arrows

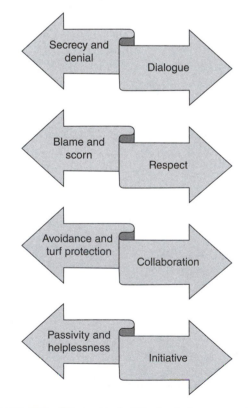

Figure 7.1 Reversal of attitudes in turnaround situations.

to the left) and the new attitudes and actions that must replace them (arrows to the right).

Describing each of these interventions or reversal strategies, Kanter says that turnaround leaders must initially open channels of communication at the highest level of the organization. In one company she used as an example, this involved exposing performance data of senior managers and creating opportunities for questioning and group dialogue as opposed to individual reports. This created a new, more open and transparent environment where secrecy and denial were no longer possible.

In the next stage of attitude reversal, Kanter suggests that turnaround leaders must move the organization away from a culture of blame and move toward a culture of respect, recognizing that colleagues who respect one another are more likely to collaborate and shape a better future together. This may involve the leader's showing trust in current organizational managers and employees by giving them opportunities to demonstrate talent and to contribute to new strategic thinking efforts.

As the third component of attitude reversal, Kanter describes the problem-solving process across departments and indicates that turnaround leaders must recognize and facilitate collaboration and collective commitment to new courses of action. In one example, a new corporate leader, shortly after his arrival, started a campaign to obtain more collaboration in the organization. As part of the initiative, executive meetings became more devoted to interdivisional themes, and organizational members found areas in which combining forces allowed them to address new opportunities. Kanter also suggests that in turnaround situations, leaders can often use flexible temporary work groups to open relationships rather than continually reorganizing, which can be very disruptive.

Finally, after establishing structures in which people are allowed to collaborate, Kanter suggests that turnaround leaders empower employees to initiate actions designed to improve the financial or strategic position of the company. In one example, the leaders of a company empowered organizational members in new ways. Several strategy teams composed of organizational members were developed, provided with information and resources, given a deadline, and then left on their own to produce ideas for new company strategies, resulting in improved feelings of empowerment and sense of pride and control.

Tipping Point Leadership

Kim and Mauborgne, authors of the marketing and strategic leadership book *Blue Ocean Strategy*, also provide insights and recommendations related to leading turnaround situations, discussing what they refer to as "tipping point leadership" (2003, 2006). Using a case study of leadership in the New York Police Department as the foundation, Kim and Mauborgne assert that successful turnaround leaders in organizations have to overcome inertia and navigate through four obstacles in order to reach the "tipping point" of successful turnaround. According to these authors, "in any organization, once the beliefs and energies of a critical mass of people are engaged, conversion to a new idea will spread like an epidemic, bringing about fundamental change very quickly" (p. 62). Managers and leaders attempting turnaround efforts can benefit from recognizing the four hurdles or obstacles presented in the "Four Hurdles to Navigate in a Turnaround" sidebar. These hurdles are common in all organizations, and sport leaders may be able to recognize and use the model and recommendations provided by Kim and Mauborgne as an important tool for navigating a turnaround.

Crisis Leadership

At no time in the life of a sport leader is the expectation for visibility, influence, and accountability higher than in a time of organizational crisis. Crisis situations can bring out the worst as well as the best in individuals and groups in an organization. In many cases, especially in large and highly recognized sport organizations (e.g., Nike, IOC, U.S. Olympic Committee, professional teams worldwide, NCAA Division I athletic departments and universities), leaders may have multiple individuals or even crisis teams that they can pull together for initial response and to develop crisis recovery plans into the future. In smaller organizations such as local community recreation organizations,

Four Hurdles to Navigate in a Turnaround

1. Cognitive Hurdle. The first and often hardest battle—getting people to agree on causes of problems and the need for change. This step involves more than just looking at the numbers and insisting that the company or organization achieves better ones. (In sports, this would be like a team owner, at the end of a poor season, meeting with coaches and players and just demanding that the team improve the next year). Key managers and leaders in the organization must be placed face-to-face with the operational problems as a first step in the process.

2. Resource Hurdle. Recognizing the reality of scarce or limited resources. This step often leads to either a decision to reduce ambitions for the change or develop a focused campaign for more resources, which takes time and can divert attention from problems. The resource hurdle is often unavoidable, however, as suggested by Kim and Mauborgne, and leaders should concentrate the available resources on the places that are (1) most in need of change and (2) have the largest payoff potential. Careful analysis of facts may also identify where changes in key policies or procedures can reduce the need for resources (e.g. distribution of work or technological advancements).

3. Motivational Hurdle. Getting employees to recognize what needs to be done and motivating them to want to do it. An effective approach can be to identify individuals who are key influencers inside or outside the organization and to get them motivated first. These individuals then serve to spread motivation among the groups they influence. Another approach can be to develop a clear culture of performance where individuals are held accountable for results. Also, people can be more motivated if they believe the results are attainable and realistic. (In other words, in a sport context, it may not be a good idea to set a league title, national championship, or world championship as an immediate goal if you are in the first year of a turnaround situation).

4. Political Hurdle. Organizational politics are a reality and overcoming them can be extremely challenging. As an organization reaches the "tipping point" and change appears likely, powerful individuals and groups may become more vocal and willing to fight for their position. This has the potential to damage or derail turnaround efforts. In some situations, leaders may have to identify those most opposed to the effort, seek to understand their positions, and then find ways, if necessary, to minimize their impact. This may be accomplished through building coalitions of supporters that ultimately have more influence in the organization. In some cases, it may result in the need to make personnel changes in an organization.

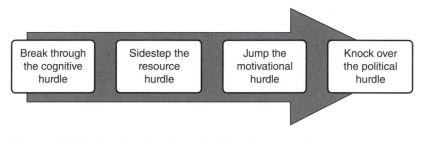

Figure 7.2 Four hurdles to navigate in a turnaround.

Based on information in Kim and Mauborgne 2003, 2006.

youth sport clubs, and high school athletics, this responsibility may fall primarily on one person or on a small group of key individuals in leadership roles.

Of course, the best and most effective approach to crisis management and leadership is careful, proactive, and purposeful avoidance or prevention where possible. Scanning the environment and planning in advance for possibilities and situations that can create a crisis, as well as carefully considering decisions and actions that can further contribute to a crisis (e.g., the Penn State sexual abuse situation), are essential leadership responsibilities. However, because we live in a world of uncertainty, where disasters are not always easily predictable and where there is no fail-safe assurance of physical and financial safety, crisis situations will continue to occur. In addition, despite the strongest efforts of leadership policy creation and enforcement, history suggests that crisis situations in sport resulting from extreme lack of professionalism and ethical decision making, sometimes even at the highest levels of an organization, may continue into the future. Consequently, effective crisis leadership will continue to be a primary challenge and, in many cases, a defining moment for sport organization leaders. The next few sections address crisis leadership and provide ideas and recommendations for current and future sport leaders.

Concept of Organizational Crisis

Often cited for their contributions to theory and practice of crisis management and crisis communications, Seeger, Sellnow, and Ulmer (2003) offer the following insight about crisis in modern organizations:

> "Increasingly, crises are common parts of the social, psychological, political, economic, and organizational landscape of modern life. They affect more people than ever before, are more widely reported in the media, and have a wider impact on increasingly interconnected, dynamic, and complex social-technical systems. . . . Understanding the complex dynamics of crises is imperative for both researchers and practitioners as they seek to reduce the frequency of crises and the level of harm they cause." (p. 3)

Seeger and colleagues offer descriptions of crisis that apply across all organizations. For example, they depict a crisis as "an unusual event of overwhelmingly negative significance that carries a high level or risk, harm, and opportunity for further loss" (p. 4). They point out that a crisis may represent a profound personal loss for individuals internal and external to an organization, and that it usually begins suddenly with a dramatic and surprising event and "ends with some resolution and return to near normalcy" (p. 4). Crisis survivors, they say, are typically central to postcrisis efforts associated with cause, blame, and liability, and organizations that are seen as causing a crisis "may lose legitimacy, credibility, reputation, and ultimately income" (p. 5).

In another characterization of organizational crisis, Pearson and Clair (1998) suggest that it is an event with low probability of occurring, but with very high impact that can threaten an organization's viability. The authors also suggest that the cause of a crisis, its potential outcomes, and the best approach to its resolution may not be immediately clear. Even so, decisions often have to be made swiftly based on the best available information. It is important to recognize, however, that despite the seriousness of crisis situations and the organizational and personal stress they elicit, these situations often provide important opportunities for growth, development, and education of others regarding crisis leadership (Pearson and Clair, 1998; Seeger, Sellnow, and Ulmer, 2003).

Another important concept with regard to crisis is the emotional element and behaviors that people may exhibit during and after crisis situations. As suggested by Klann (2003), crisis is emotional chaos, and these emotions can trigger both positive and negative behaviors in people. Some individuals may act with compassion, courage, and self-sacrifice, while others may display fear, anger, selfishness, cowardice, and greed. What is critical, according to Klann, is that leaders understand and be prepared to lead in a chaotic, ambiguous, and highly charged emotional environment.

Types of Crises

Crises can occur in many forms and degrees of intensity. Klann (2003) categorizes crises based on the seriousness of the threat and the severity of the impact that it will have on people and organizations, as follows:

Level 1 crisis: Organization is publicly embarrassed by such things as allegations of wrongdoing, lawsuits, or various forms of unethical, politically incorrect, or socially irresponsible behavior.

Level 2 crisis: Situation that results in personal injury, property loss, and possible loss of life and has the potential to seriously damage a company's reputation.

Level 3 crisis: Situation that results in loss of life, significant property damage, or a perceived threat to the survival of the company.

The majority of crisis situations in sport fall into level 1 of Klann's typology. These situations pose threats to the credibility and reputation of the organization and often include such things as college recruiting scandals and criminal activity of athletes or employees. However, crisis situations in sport can reach Klann's level 2 or level 3; these stem from accidents and disasters that result in multiple fatalities and severe injuries.

Numerous types of crises are identified in the crisis management and crisis communications literature, ranging from natural disasters and severe accidents through to malevolence, organizational scandals, and employee-centered crises (Lerbinger, 1997; Wooten and James, 2008). Using cluster analysis research, Coombs (2000) identifies four families of crisis: (1) natural disasters, (2) tampering/terrorism, (3) accidents, and (4) transgressions.

Natural disasters

- Eleven members of Congolese soccer team were killed by lightning in 1998.
- A hailstorm at a soccer match in Nepal caused fans to rush for cover, resulting in 70 fans trampled to death.
- The Japan earthquake and tsunami of 2011 killed over 10,000 people and injured hundreds of others. As a result of the disaster, there were multiple cancellations or rescheduling of both local and international sport events throughout the country.

Accidents

- Airplane crashes
  - 1961, U.S. figure skating team (72 killed)
  - 1970, Marshall University football team (75 killed)
  - 2001, Oklahoma State University basketball team (10 killed)
  - 2011, Yaraslov Lokomitiv, Russian hockey team (44 killed)
- Fire
  - 1985, fire at Valley Parade Stadium, Bradford, England (56 deaths and over 200 injuries)
- Bleacher collapse
  - 2010, collapse of a section of bleachers at a car race in Brazil (111 injuries)

Tampering or terrorism

- In 1972, 11 athletes and coaches of the Israeli national Olympic team were taken hostage and killed at the Olympic Games in Munich.
- In 1997, the Grand National horse race in the United Kingdom received bomb threats, resulting in evacuation of 60,000 spectators and participants. Approximately 20,000 people were stranded when cars and buses were locked inside the facility (Levy, 2012, p. 8).
- In 2008, a bomb was detonated at the start of a marathon in Sri Lanka, killing 12 people and injuring almost 100 (Levy, 2012, p. 9)

Transgressions

- Penn State University child molestation case
- Multiple issues and investigations related to inappropriate activity by boosters of college athletic programs in the United States
- Public criticism of Nike in the 1990s regarding accusations of producing goods in "sweatshops" in Asian countries
- Attack on Nancy Kerrigan at the 1994 U.S. figure skating championships
- Scandal associated with pre-2002 Salt Lake City Winter Olympics with accusations of bribery associated with members of the SLOC

Based in part on information from Coombs 2000.

Crisis Management Versus Crisis Leadership

As discussed in chapter 1, individuals in modern sport organizations who occupy management and leadership roles assume responsibilities and perform tasks associated with both management and leadership. In many ways, crisis management and crisis leadership involve activities that are integrated with one another in practice. However, just as there are conceptual differences in definitions and descriptions of leadership and management, so too are there differences with regard to crisis management and crisis leadership. According to Pearson and Clair (1998), "organizational crisis management is a systematic attempt by organizational members with external stakeholders to avert crises or to effectively manage those that do occur" (p. 61). Ridley (2011) suggests that crisis management is process driven, reactive, inward focused, and bureaucratic, whereas crisis leadership is strategic, visionary, proactive, and outward focused. Klann (2003) suggests that crisis management deals primarily with operational issues while crisis leadership is associated with how leaders handle human responses, needs, emotions, and behaviors caused by a crisis.

The following sections discuss various activities and responsibilities associated with effectively preparing for and dealing with crisis situations. The intent is to focus primarily on ideas and recommendations that will be of practical use to those in various roles in sport organization leadership as opposed to conceptually distinguishing crisis management from crisis leadership.

The Crisis Decision Environment

Crisis situations often require complex decisions to be made swiftly in an ambiguous environment, as mentioned previously. Muffet-Willett and Kruse (2009) hold that crisis leadership moves along a continuum. In normal organizational situations, decision making is routine, consequences are understood, and organizational processes follow established protocols. However, as a crisis situation escalates, it can create a severe threat to the viability of an organization. The decision environment is more highly scrutinized and complex, which results in increased levels of stress, lack of established protocols, and nonroutine decision making. Consequently, according to Muffet-Willet and Kruse, a key foundation of crisis leadership is the ability of a leader to effectively adapt in a rapidly changing and complex environment.

Crisis Leadership Competencies

Wooten and James note that little research has been done to systematically identify the leadership competencies necessary in crisis situations. They argue that the gap in the literature regarding crisis leadership competencies exists in part because crisis research is housed primarily within the communications domain. Consequently, developments in the field of crisis management center mainly on development of communication strategies. The authors also argue that viewing crisis management only through a communication lens may neglect other important leadership responsibilities.

Wooten and James (2008) conducted an in-depth ethnographic content analysis from printed news articles related to 20 high-profile business crisis situations. From this research, they argue that crisis leadership occurs across several phases and involves a number of leadership competencies. These are listed and described in table 7.1, along with hypothetical or actual examples of application to sport organizations.

Crisis Prevention and Training

It is important to recognize that certain types of crisis situations are unpredictable and may not be completely preventable, specifically those created by natural disasters and other unexpected events. However, crises often ensue from events that are indeed predictable, and these are the ones that can cause excessive problems for an organization and the leaders who ultimately are seen as accountable for the results of the crisis. As pointed out by Watkins and Bazerman (2003), many organizations are caught unaware by events that they refer to as "predictable surprises." These surprise events can take many forms and result in short-term losses or distraction as well as catastrophe, such as that occurring on September 11, 2001, in New York City.

Watkins and Bazerman posit that while many crisis events happen that are truly not predictable, leaders should be held accountable for damage from events that indeed were foreseeable and preventable. With regard to legal, professional, and ethical responsibility, leaders should give close attention to thinking about crisis situations that should have been predicted. The authors propose three primary ways in which leaders can fail with regard to predictable crises. In order to proactively address their responsibility for crisis leadership, organizational leaders need to follow a procedure that Watkins and Bazerman refer to as the "RPM process: recognition, prioritization,

Table 7.1 Crisis Leadership Competencies and Sport Examples

Crisis leadership competency	Description	Sport example
Sense making	Looking for pre-crisis warning signals and taking action to help prevent crisis	Indianapolis Power & Light Company spends $180,000 to install locking manhole covers in Super Bowl village and other high-traffic areas before Super Bowl XLVI. This is the result of several underground explosions since 2005 that turned manhole covers into flying projectiles.
Perspective taking	Putting oneself in the place of those affected by a crisis; focusing on the needs and ensuring the well-being of those affected	Philadelphia Eagles owner, GM, and team unite to provide support for Head Coach Andy Reid upon the death of his oldest son.
Issue selling	Directing attention and strategy of the organization toward crisis planning and preparedness	Sheik Salman bin Isa Al-Khalifa of Bahrain reassures Formula One racing teams and fans that antigovernment unrest and violence have been addressed and that all measures will be taken to preserve the safety of participants and fans at the 2012 Bahrain Grand Prix.
Organizational agility	Developing a thorough knowledge of all aspects of a business and working across organizational functions and departments in crisis preparation, prevention, and response	Sebastian Coe, head of the London Olympic Committee, works with committee and the British military to bring additional security to the London Olympic Games after private security company fails on promises to deliver 10,000 security guards.
Creativity	Thinking creatively about an organization's vulnerability to crisis and brainstorming about ways to be prepared and deal with crisis situations	GE Security develops the Itemiser, which is a direct transfer trace detector using a finger sample wheel that can detect trace particles of explosives and narcotics at the point of entry into a sport venue.
Decision making under pressure	Ability to work with and around negative emotions and make sound decisions in crisis situations	University of Arkansas athletic director makes hard decision to fire winning head football coach after scandal involving coach.
Communicating effectively	Identifying and connecting with key organizational personnel; attempting to restore calm and provide reassurance to those affected by the crisis	Puma CEO Jochen Zeitz reassures employees that the temporary closure of its production shops in Japan will not affect business after the 2011 Japan earthquake and tsunami.
Risk taking	Not becoming too risk averse in crisis situations; thinking creatively and in novel ways regarding approaches to overcome a crisis	The executive director of Pop Warner youth football leads effort to change practice rules so as to prohibit full-speed head-on blocking and tackling and reduce exposure of youth players to head impact and concussion.
Promoting organizational resilience	Using a crisis to help promote moving an organization positively and effectively beyond where it was prior to the crisis, not just a return to normal	Hoover Wright, former coach of the Prairie View A&M University track team, is able to lead the team back to defend the Southwestern Athletic Conference indoor track championship after several members of the team were killed and several others injured in a van crash earlier in the season.
Acting with integrity	Building trust by engaging in ethical decision making and behavior; crucial in situations when the organization may be perceived to be at fault	Recent firings of several high-profile college coaches associated with scandals or misdeeds at their institutions.
Learning and reflection	Engaging in purposeful activities to reflect on decisions, actions, and experiences during a crisis and developing ideas for new training and ways to improve for the future	This competency will be critical to the postcrisis actions at Penn State University, where rebuilding trust and credibility is essential to overcoming negative public perceptions.

Based on information in Wooten and James 2008.

mobilization" (p. 74). The following are questions related to RPM:

1. **Did the leader recognize the threat?** This is usually determined by whether or not the leader can demonstrate that resources were devoted to scanning the environment for emerging threats and whether or not it appears that the leader did a reasonable job of data analysis and interpretation.

2. **Did the leader prioritize appropriately?** Leaders can encounter problems in this area when they recognize a crisis threat but do not deem it serious enough to require immediate attention and thus do not give it priority relative to its potential costs to the organization. To avoid this, leaders should perform careful cost–benefit analyses and ensure that the threats representing the highest costs to the organization receive priority consideration.

3. **Did the leader mobilize effectively?** This question has to do with what occurs once a serious crisis threat has been identified. Leaders should be able to demonstrate that precautionary measures commensurate with the risks were appropriately instituted.

Regarding training and preparation for potential crisis situations, Muffet-Willett and Kruse (2009) point to the importance of leaders' selecting appropriate training opportunities for organizational employees and ensuring that training includes those employees who are most likely to be affected by a crisis. Training exercises can include simulations or scenarios with opportunities to practice interpersonal communication and cognitive and decision-making skills during a crisis. Muffet-Willet and Kruse also offer a number of ideas for preparing leaders to be effective in crisis situations. These ideas and descriptions of each are presented in table 7.2.

> **Your Thoughts**
>
> Consider various crisis situations in sport that you would categorize as "predictable surprises" as described by Watkins and Bazerman. What examples can you think of that demonstrate where a sport organization leader either failed or could have responded more effectively with regard to the three areas of "recognition," "prioritization," and "mobilization?"

Table 7.2 Key Ideas for Training Effective Crisis Leaders

Key ideas for improving crisis leadership	Description
Effective crisis leaders are not made in a workshop.	Attending a workshop does not in and of itself automatically create an effective crisis leader. This involves not only a willingness and enthusiasm of the individual being trained, but also collaboration of supervisors and support for training to be implemented in the organization.
Effective crisis leaders are used to being pushed.	Training needs to be realistic. It is better to put trainees "on the spot" in hypothetical training conditions than to see them fail in real crisis situations. Crisis leaders need to become familiar with what it is like to operate under demanding conditions.
Effective crisis leaders must be immersed in a wide variety of issues within the company from an early stage.	Leaders can be better prepared to effectively address crisis situations if they have had the opportunity to be challenged by difficult situations in early stages of their careers. Providing these opportunities will better prepare individuals to lead through actual crises that occur in the future.
Effective crisis leaders listen.	Individuals leading others through crisis must be careful listeners and information processors under stress. They must ensure that they listen to all those involved in the organization in crisis situations.
Effective crisis leaders learn from others.	Leaders watch and study how other organizations navigate crisis situations. Various types of crises appear almost daily on a national and global scale and can provide excellent learning opportunities through observation of the actions of others going through a crisis.
Effective crisis leaders make decisions.	Leaders need to step forward and make decisions in times of uncertainty. "Crisis leaders have the ability to make a decision on limited information and carry it out to the best of their ability" (p. 257).

Based on information in Muffet-Willett and Kruse 2009.

Dealing with Crisis in Progress

As discussed in chapter 2, a key component of effective leadership is the demonstration of legal, professional, and ethical responsibility. When a crisis situation is in progress, all these components of responsibility become simultaneously paramount, and leaders must often make very fast decisions in highly complex or threatening situations involving people's lives and their organization's future. It is beyond the scope of this book to discuss all of the legal considerations related to tort law, duty owed, and issues of nonfeasance, misfeasance, and malfeasance covered in legal texts and sport management courses; suffice it to note here that sport organization leaders must be cognizant of these considerations and their implications during crisis situations.

It is very important for top leaders of an organization to be out front and visible during a crisis. Recognized for his outstanding leadership during and after the September 11 terrorist attack in New York City, Rudolph Giuliani points to four key elements of effective crisis leadership: being visible, composed, vocal, and resilient (Giuliani, 2002). From his experiences and actions at a time of extraordinary crisis, Giuliani points out that leaders must be able to control their emotions, maintain their poise, be reassuring, and provide a sense of hope of overcoming a crisis.

From a communications and public relations perspective, Schoenberg (2005) offers a model of crisis leadership according to which leaders must have access to ongoing information, have training in dealing with the media, and have the experience and ability to take command during chaos. Schoenberg regards authenticity and influence as the pillars of effective crisis leadership. To be authentic during a crisis situation, leaders must communicate the realities and possibilities of the situation with uncompromising honesty. Effective crisis leaders must also attempt to positively influence, to the extent possible, the messages and outcomes of the situation.

Klann (2003), in his book on crisis leadership, provides specific recommendations for leaders when a crisis is imminent or in progress. Leaders first need to gather reliable information regarding the crisis; determine the emotions and behaviors that are occurring (including their own emotions); and focus on meeting the social, security, and acceptance needs of the people involved. Balancing the demands of external stakeholders and the media with the emotional needs of the organizational members is essential. Klann also points out that communication during a crisis is critical and that senior leaders must keep employees continually and accurately informed of developments. Leaders must also meet regularly with media representatives to update them on what is occurring and how it is being dealt with. Leaders may not have all the information they are asked to share with the media at any given time, and saying so is totally acceptable. Klann also suggests that leaders need to live by the values that have been defined and communicated in the organization so as to set the appropriate example and take leadership responsibility in the situation.

Recovering From Crisis

After the critical phase of a crisis situation has subsided and an organization is attempting to recover, leaders must think carefully through the processes and approaches for restoring order, confidence, and trust among all internal and external stakeholders. In relation to sport, the recovery and restoration process in progress at Penn State over the next several years will be a case study in postcrisis leadership and crisis recovery.

One approach to recovery that can be useful for sport leaders to consider is provided by O'Callagan (2010), who specifically addresses five areas of expertise that leaders should attend to when helping an organization recover or turn around from a crisis. These five areas, questions leaders should ask themselves, and related requirements of leadership are provided in table 7.3.

Response to Social Crisis

While this part of the chapter has been about planning for, responding to, and recovering from crisis within sport, another consideration for leaders of sport organizations is how they

Table 7.3 Leader Responsibilities and Requirements for Crisis Recovery

Leader expertise and responsibility	Questions for you and your team	Requirements
Making the right promises	"In our current situation, do we understand what all our key stakeholders are focusing on and the promises they are seeking from us and our company?" (p. 5)	Requires leaders who can master the challenge of effectively balancing competing interests among customers, investors, lenders, employees, and suppliers.
Gathering multiple new viewpoints	"As leaders, have we taken a complete 360 degree view of the business, its stakeholders and the market in the current environment?" (p. 5)	Requires leaders to obtain viewpoints on the crisis from across the organization (e.g., financial, human resources, legal) so as to increase the possibility of producing "more innovative and deliverable actions" (p. 9).
Core business skills	"Do we have the necessary expertise, experience and insights to make decisions about the issues that matter most in our post-crisis situation?" (p. 5)	Requires leaders to develop skills specifically in the areas of cash flow and time management, develop postcrisis strategy, and maintain sales and cost base restructuring.
Delivering results through relationships	"What are the right implementation models and leadership styles to employ to ensure that the promises we make are delivered?" (p. 5)	Requires leaders to extract the best possible delivery from the organization in difficult circumstances through focused direction and purpose and also through effective relationship building.
Rebuilding trust through authentic communication	"How will we build and maintain the level of trust with employees, customers, suppliers, lenders and investors that will be necessary to deliver the recovery plan?" (p. 5)	Requires leaders to communicate carefully and make sure that their actions are always aligned with their words; trust must be improved by providing clear benefits to others of the relationship and effectively addressing the perceived risks from those whose support the leader is seeking.

Based on information in O'Callagan 2010.

can effectively respond to crises occurring in their communities and the nation. Multiple examples exist of ways in which sport organizations have given back to communities in crisis. One example is the delegation of New York Yankee players and Manager Joe Torre that visited emergency workers, victims, and their relatives after the September 11, 2001, terrorist attack in New York City. When Hurricane Katrina struck New Orleans in 2005, several New Orleans Saints players volunteered to assist with the rebuilding of homes destroyed by the storm. This activity provided needed help and goodwill, but also assisted in building a mutual respect on the part of the team and its fans that likely contributed to the subsequent turnaround of the team and Super Bowl championship.

The communities and people who support sport organizations across the globe should expect to see social responsibility and obtain assistance from these organizations in times of crisis. Sport leaders have numerous opportunities to assist when disasters and other crisis situations strike their communities. This is yet another key area of leadership responsibility that leaders of sport organizations must give special attention to.

Summary

Turnaround and crisis leadership are and will continue to be areas that provide defining career moments for sport leaders. It is frequently in these situations that leaders are most visible and influential and are also expected to demonstrate highly effective leadership. In each of these areas, the research specific to sport is currently very limited, which represents an academic opportunity; however, the business and communications literature provides substantial information and recommendations that may be applicable to sport organizations and their leaders.

The first part of this chapter provides examples of turnaround from sport, as well as concepts and strategies for leading turnaround. Sport leaders should be cognizant of the stages of turnaround and how they can be influential in both stabilizing a declining organization and leading a carefully planned and strategic repositioning and growth. Understanding that leadership style may be influenced by the intensity of the turnaround situation, leaders should be prepared to take an authoritative role when needed as well as to be accountable for results during a turnaround. Leaders in turnaround situations must also know how to reverse attitudes of key stakeholders and navigate cognitive, resource, motivational, and political obstacles as discussed in the chapter and must understand the importance of doing so.

The second part of the chapter addresses crisis leadership, which is likely the greatest challenge faced by any sport organization leader. To be as effective as possible, leaders must think proactively and be prepared to try to prevent a crisis; they also need to be visible, caring, communicative, and able to make difficult decisions swiftly. While crisis situations vary in type and intensity, having a basic understanding of the leadership competencies, training, and preparation during a crisis, as well as responsibilities after a crisis, can be helpful in improving leadership outcomes.

Final Self-Assessment

Now that you have spent time reading, discussing, and studying elements of turnaround and crisis leadership, consider your responses to the self-assessment questions presented at the beginning of the chapter. Do you have new or additional thoughts about your role and responsibility as a leader in these situations?

1. What do you currently think are key strategies for effectively leading change or a sport organization turnaround?

2. What do you believe are the most appropriate leadership styles for leading a turnaround? Does this depend on the situation? Why or why not?

3. How prepared do you currently feel if you were to be placed in a role of crisis leadership? What do you see as your strengths and weaknesses relative to knowledge, skills, and behaviors in a crisis situation?

4. What processes and recommendations are you familiar with for leading people and organizations through a crisis?

Game Plan Activity

Individually or with a partner or small group, create a change, turnaround, or crisis plan for a sport organization based on the types and examples of each given in this book. Develop this plan and prepare it as a presentation that you would give to a board of directors or a strategic planning leadership team. Use concepts, theories, and models presented in this chapter as well as any other resources that you find as support for your final product.

Questions to Consider

1. Consider the challenges faced by sport organizations relative to the athlete head injury and concussion issue, especially in American football at all levels. What do you consider the leadership challenges and responsibilities associated with effectively addressing this situation? How might Kotter's approach to change leadership be useful in bringing about long-term change to improve athlete safety?

2. Review the four "hurdles" in the model by Kim and Mauborgne (2003, 2006). Considering the sport organization you are most familiar with, how would you overcome these hurdles if you were leading a turnaround in your organization?

3. Assume that you are the owner or CEO of a company that produces a sport drink for athletes. A year or two after your product has been in wide use across the nation, several team members of one or more teams become gravely ill after drinking your product. What should be your initial response? What will you do in the immediate and short-term future to address this situation? What communication strategies will you use during and after the crisis in order to be viewed as having responded in an appropriate and effective way?

4. In a recent unprecedented move, the NCAA gave unilateral authority to its president, Mark Emmert, to impose sanctions on the Penn State athletic department for its role in the child molestation scandal. Do you think this will set precedent for other decision-making processes in the NCAA in the future? Do you agree or disagree with this level of authority in crisis situations? Why or why not?

5. What are possible ideas for how a small sport organization (e.g., youth sport club, high school athletic department, community recreational facility) could respond to a disaster in a community?

Recommended Readings

Brown, R. (2004). Sport and healing America. *Society*, 42(1), 37.

James, E. H., and Wooten, L. P. (2010). *Leading under pressure*. New York: Routledge.

Klann, G. (2003). *Crisis leadership*. Greensboro, NC: Center for Creative Leadership.

O'Callaghan, S. (2010). *Turnaround leadership: Making decisions, rebuilding trust, and delivering results after a crisis*. London: Kogan Page.

Romney, M. (2007). *Turnaround: Crisis, leadership and the Olympic Games*. Washington, DC: Regnery.

Diversity Leadership

Learning Objectives

After reading and reflecting on the concepts, examples, and recommendations in this chapter, you will be able to

1. define and discuss the meaning of the term "diversity" relative to sport organizations;

2. discuss the difference between surface-level diversity and deep-level diversity;

3. explain two perspectives on diversity and inclusion: (1) representation and (2) embracing and leading diversity;

4. discuss and give examples of the current state of diversity representation across professional, intercollegiate, and interscholastic sport organizations;

5. offer recommendations for leading and embracing elements of diversity and inclusion such as valuing and creating a culture of diversity, developing a proactive strategy, managing commitment and change, and improving cultural competence;

6. identify and explain leadership issues associated with diversity and inclusion of women and special populations, including LGBT and individuals with disabilities; and

7. conduct a self-assessment and provide recommendations for leadership competencies that can be associated with leader performance relative to diversity and inclusion.

Self-Assessment

1. How do you currently define or describe diversity, and what is your experience working with or leading diverse individuals, teams, or larger organizations?

2. What is your current perspective on the roles and responsibilities of leaders relative to equity and inclusion? Is it compliance oriented? Is it proactive?

3. What are ways you believe leaders can improve representation and better embrace and lead diversity in a sport organization?

4. What are the some of the critical issues, as you know of them now, in relation to women and special populations in sport?

5. How might you assess your own, or others', leadership competencies relative to diversity and inclusion? How could this information be used in leadership evaluation and professional development?

Leaders of sport organizations take on a responsibility, either directly or indirectly, for diversity and inclusion in their organizations. What is becoming increasingly evident, as indicated by prominent sport management researchers in this area, is that diversity will continue to be one of the most important issues for sport managers to address (Cunningham and Fink, 2006; Cunningham, 2010, 2012). As pointed out by Cunningham and Fink, several factors are contributing to the importance of this aspect of management and leadership. These factors include (a) dramatic changes in the nature of the workforce in relation to both demographic characteristics and personal values, attitudes, and beliefs; (b) changes in the way work is conducted in organizations (e.g., proliferation of work groups that must work more interdependently with others, creating more interaction among diverse individuals); (c) legal requirements relative to equal opportunity that managers and leaders must follow; (d) social pressures leading to moral obligations related to acceptance of diverse individuals; and (e) recognition of the value of diversity and benefits it can provide in an organization.

> *Imagine being placed into a scenario where language, familiarity with local culture, traditions, beliefs, gender, background, personalities, business climate, business practices and opinions are all in the mix. From a leadership perspective, it could be a challenge, but an evolutionary experience in creating a dynamic and flourishing team.*
>
> *Jim Holland (2011, p. 1)*

This chapter addresses the issue of diversity in sport organizations, including representation of diverse groups and the leadership associated with embracing and proactively addressing diversity. Recent statistics on diversity representation across primarily professional and intercollegiate sport organizations indicate that achieving appropriate representation of diverse groups in sport is an important leadership issue and continues to require attention both at the participant level and in management and leadership.

The chapter then discusses the importance of leaders' embracing and actively leading diverse sport organizations and individuals. Several academic studies from sport literature, both conceptual and empirical, are reviewed to point out important areas. These include (a) the value of diversity, (b) diversity and organizational culture, (c) diversity management strategy and organizational outcomes, (d) organizational commitment and change, and (e) cultural competence and leadership. Recommendations in each area will give sport organization leaders insights into responsibilities and actions associated with each area.

The next sections present information on three specific populations often associated with diversity and inclusion issues in sport: (1) women, (2) the LGBT population (lesbian, gay, bisexual, transgender), and (3) individuals with disabilities. While there is evidence of increasing participation of women and girls in sport at all levels, research supports that women still face multiple constraints and barriers and continue to be underrepresented in management and leadership. Legal requirements and ethical responsibilities associated with the inclusion of individuals in the LGBT population are presented and recommendations provided for more effectively and proactively addressing inclusion for this population. Issues associated with diversity and inclusion for individuals with disabilities are discussed. An integrated conceptual framework from the recent academic literature in sport offers leaders and researchers ideas for examining progression toward or regression from inclusion of individuals with disabilities in sport. The issue of technology and how it can now provide disabled athletes with unprecedented new ways of competing is discussed, along with the ethical, philosophical, and management challenges associated with the potential "transhuman" or super-abled athlete of the future.

The chapter concludes by presenting a diversity and inclusion model that, although developed outside of sport, has many potential applications for sport leaders. The model identifies trends affecting diversity including globalization, demographic shifts, technology, the sociopolitical climate, and the legal environment. Also included are suggested diversity and inclusion competencies for sport leaders.

Readers should note that this chapter is devoted primarily to leadership in relation to diversity and inclusion outside the realm of "legal responsibility" associated with discrimination and equal opportunity. While some elements of legal responsibility are included here, readers can find more information on this topic in sport and recreation law textbooks specifically addressing diversity, equal opportunity, and constitutional and employment law (e.g., Clement and Grady, 2012; Thornton, 2010; Sharp, Moorman, and Claussen, 2010).

Defining Diversity

There are numerous formal and informal definitions in the literature, many of which appear to be broadening what the term is intended to describe and how it is perceived across organizations. Merriam-Webster (m-w.com, 2012) defines diversity as "the condition of having or being composed of differing elements," especially "the inclusion of different types of people (as people of different races or cultures) in a group or organization." From a business perspective, Whitelaw (2010) points out that "while diversity has traditionally referred to categories like race and gender, companies and diversity experts are increasingly considering a wide range of factors from age and sexual preference to disabilities and even weight" (p. 1). Another element of diversity that is increasingly recognized is the various generations of people now working together in organizations (e.g., baby boomers, Gen X, Gen Y, millennials). As Whitelaw (2010) quotes Michael Hyter, president of Novations Group, "you have Gen Xers and millennials, whose definition of loyalty and what keeps them engaged is significantly different than for baby boomers. That's a huge diversity issue that, if you looked at diversity in the traditional sense, you'd miss" (p. 1). Also, some definitions include "diversity of thought" as another appropriate element of diversity among individuals.

Given the broadening definitions of the term, and in the context of this book, sport leaders must understand and gain appreciation for the many definitions and perspectives of diversity

and must be prepared to effectively design, implement, and evaluate organizational and communication strategies to embrace diversity among athletes and employees. Doing so may be a key factor in recruiting and retaining talent, as well as creating an environment conducive to reaching organizational goals and outcomes desired by the collective whole.

Perspectives on Gender, Culture, and Nationality

In addition to the definitions of diversity just presented, insights on the diversity elements of gender, culture, and nationality can be important to a sport organization leader's increased understanding of diversity and its influence on leadership. For example, Ayman and Korabik (2010) note the importance of differentiating between the terms *gender* and *sex*; *sex* is a biological term referring to whether a person is a man or a woman, and *sociodemographic gender* refers to a combination of elements that include gender schemas and stereotypes; gender-role identity; and gender-role traits, attitudes, and values. From this perspective, Ayman and Korabik point to the importance of including the social roles and expectations of each gender in society as part of a deeper understanding of diversity. For example, they suggest that the term *gender* may be linked to an ascribed status characteristic whereby men are considered to have higher social status and more access to power and resources than women.

Ayman and Korabik also identify some important elements of culture that should be considered relative to leadership and diversity. The authors acknowledge that most still agree with Kluckhohn's (1951) definition of culture as an acquired and transmitted pattern of shared meaning, feeling, and behavior that constitutes a distinctive human group. However, Ayman and Korabik argue that culture can be operationalized in two different ways, based on existing leadership research: (1) in terms of characteristics visible on the surface such as country boundaries and physical characteristics (skin color, hair texture, eye shape), which allow people to be categorized into social groups by country or nationality, and (2) in terms of more invisible and deeper differences (e.g., values and personalities). Regarding the second perspective on cultural differences, Ayman and Korabik allude to the research of Hofstede (2001) that identifies cultural values related to personalities and communication: (a) individualism-collectivism, (b) power distance, (c) uncertainty avoidance, and (d) masculinity-femininity.

Also in relation to aspects of culture and diversity, Ayman and Korabik offer the definition of culture provided by Connerly and Pederson (2005): a complex multidimensional, multilevel, and dynamic phenomenon consisting of both visible and invisible characteristics that may influence leadership. These characteristics may include demographics (e.g., place of residence and physical gender), status characteristics (e.g., socioeconomic status and educational attainment), and ethnographic characteristics (e.g., nationality, ethnicity, and language). Another underlying assumption related to cultural differences and diversity identified by Ayman and Korabik is that people who look alike, have similar languages, or live within the same geographic boundaries will have similar cultural values. However, this is not always the case, as evidenced in the United States and in many other countries where people live within the same geographic boundaries and generally speak a common language (e.g., English), but vary significantly in their appearance and cultural values.

One more term that is commonly associated with the diversity of people is *nationality*. Pittinsky (2010) notes that nationality is a "unique alchemy (blend) of history, politics, ethnicity, religion, values and educational systems" (p. 194). A critical element related to leading organizations with members of multiple nationalities is the recognition that differences and miscommunication among them may be a unique and challenging source of conflict; if managed appropriately this can be used positively, but if not, it can have negative consequences that can be devastating to an organization.

Surface-Level Versus Deep-Level Diversity

Research in organizational behavior and social psychology over many years has looked at the issue of workplace diversity and its relation-

ships to group cohesion, group performance, discrimination, leadership opportunity, and leadership effectiveness. Also, researchers over the last several years have addressed questions related to differences between "surface-level diversity" and "deep-level diversity" (Eagly and Chin, 2010; Harrison, Price, and Bell, 1998; Harrison et al., 2002; Klein and Wang, 2010). These terms are important in this chapter as they potentially relate to new areas of research and ideas for effective leadership practice in sport organizations. The following definitions come from Harrison, Price, and Bell (1998):

• **Surface-level diversity (demographic):** Differences among group members in overt and observable biological characteristics that are typically reflected in physical features including age, gender, race, and ethnicity.

• **Deep-level diversity (psychological):** Differences among members' deeper attitudes, beliefs, and values. Information about these factors can be communicated (or gathered) only through extended individual interaction.

According to Harrison, Price, and Bell (1998), theory from organizational behavior suggests that group members tend to base their initial categorization of other group members on surface-level stereotypes and then later modify or replace those stereotypes with deeper-level knowledge of group members' deep-level characteristics. When this occurs, further knowledge of similarities among attitudinal beliefs and values can form the foundation for group members' continued attraction and affiliation. Hypothesizing that time spent working together has an effect on work group cohesion among diverse members, the researchers proposed that deep-level diversity has a steadily stronger consequence for groups than demographic or surface-level diversity as group members spend more time together. Their findings indicated that the length of time group members worked together weakened the effects of surface-level diversity and strengthened the effects of deep-level diversity. This confirmed previous research (Amir, Halina, and Sagie, 1976) showing that as people spend more time getting to know each other, stereotypes tend to be replaced by more accurate knowledge of the deep-level characteristics and can result in reduced prejudice, decreased conflict, and increased group cohesiveness. More recently, Price, Harrison, Gavin, and Florey (2002), examined time, teams, and task performance in group interaction. The findings from their study suggested that frequent collaboration among work groups reduces the impact of surface-level diversity in group functioning.

Price, et al. also showed that "social integration" of a team (defined as the degree to which group members are psychologically linked in pursuit of a common objective) was a strong predictor of overall performance and that social integration absorbed the effects of perceived or actual diversity. This has implications for athletic teams as well as work teams within sport organizations relative to the critical importance of having shared vision and values regardless of the extent of surface-level diversity in a group.

Klein and Wang (2010), in a conceptual argument regarding surface-level diversity and leadership, suggested that it is critical to disentangle the two leadership-related variables supposedly affected by surface-level diversity: leadership opportunities and leadership effectiveness. These authors argue that surface-level or demographic characteristics can lead to discriminatory disparities in leadership "opportunities" whereas deep-level characteristics generally do not. They also suggest that research designed to explore the role of deep-level characteristics in leadership could help researchers and practitioners identify

fundamental psychological variables that may predict a host of outcomes, including leader effectiveness.

Klein and Wang propose that more research on deep-level diversity would complement the disproportionate focus to this point on surface-level diversity in leadership, which they say is not always useful for predicting and improving leadership ability. According to these researchers, identifying deep-level characteristics that significantly contribute to effective leadership might provide a diversity leadership theory that is universally applicable regardless of the leader's gender, skin color, or sexual orientation. The authors also suggest that by "promoting surface-level diversity in leadership *opportunities* and deep-level similarities in leadership *training*, it is conceivable that organizations could counter adverse impact in leader selection while also improving organizational outcomes" (p. 933).

Diversity Representation and Embracing Diversity

Diversity in sport organizations and its relationship to leadership roles and responsibilities are discussed in this chapter from two perspectives: (1) diversity representation and (2) embracing diversity as an organizational attribute through purposeful leadership strategy. These perspectives are presented in table 8.1.

Table 8.1 Two Perspectives of Diversity

Diversity perspective	Leadership roles and responsibilities
Representation in sports (addresses surface-level diversity)	• Increasing representation of diverse individuals and groups participating in sport • Ensuring appropriate recruitment, hiring, and retention of diverse groups (legal requirements and HR management) in compliance with OEO, EEOC, and so on • Title IX and gender representation • Commitment to improving diversity representation and addressing issues of "limited access" of those in leadership and organizational management positions (e.g., league and club front office, athletic directors, head coaches)
Embracing and leading diversity in sport (addresses deep-level diversity)	• Increasing understanding of diversity and inclusion in sport organizations • Improving cultural competence • Effectively communicating and creating a climate of acceptance and inclusion in the team or organization • Modeling and setting agendas that support commitment to diversity across key areas including not only gender, race, culture, and special needs, but also diversity of thought, ideas, attitudes, and values

The first perspective, *diversity representation*, is typically thought of in terms of ensuring representation and inclusion of individuals from all the legally recognized categories of diversity, including race, color, gender, religion, national origin, age, disability, and sexual orientation. Leaders of all sport organizations must follow policies and procedures and meet legal requirements of the Office of Equal Opportunity (OEO) and the Equal Employment Opportunity Commission (EEOC) related to recruiting and hiring individuals. Sport leaders must also be cognizant of and work toward improving diversity representation among participants of sport teams, clubs, leagues, and so on.

The second perspective, *embracing and leading diversity*, goes beyond the legal and compliance expectations of diversity and requires a commitment by leaders to developing vision, focused strategies, and collective input. This results in activities or initiatives specifically designed to address the needs, motivation, and performance of diverse individuals and groups in an organization.

Diversity Representation in Sport

Leaders of sport organizations have a professional, ethical, and legal obligation to provide opportunities for diverse participation (e.g., diversity among athletes) and employment (diversity among management and general staff). While many of the leadership responsibilities in this area are driven by laws protecting participants and employees of sport programs from discrimination, the legal requirements associated with equal opportunity are discussed in numerous other textbooks addressing law in sport and recreation and are not covered here. This section includes historical as well as recent examples and statistics related to diversity representation in sport in the United States; much this information comes from work conducted by The Institute for Diversity and Ethics in Sport (TIDES), located at the University of Central Florida. This institute, under the direction of Dr. Richard Lapchick, annually publishes the Racial and Gender Report Card "to indicate areas of improvement, stagnation and regres-

sion in the racial and gender composition of professional and college sports personnel and to contribute to the improvement of integration in front office and college athletics department positions" (Lapchick, 2010, p. 2).

While diversity representation is now common in sport organizations, this has not always been the case in the United States with its historic segregation, especially with regard to African American participation in team sports and lack of gender representativeness across the various levels of professional and amateur sport. Table 8.2 provides examples of historical events and individuals related to diversity representation in a variety of sports.

Participant Diversity in U.S. Sport

This section provides information on diversity representation of participants in various sport organizations in the United States within the last few years as reported by the Institute for Diversity and Ethics in Sport. See table 8.3 for summary information on racial diversity among professional sport leagues. Table 8.4 provides summary information on racial diversity in Division I intercollegiate athletics. This information, while not inclusive of every sport at all levels of competition, provides sport leaders with examples and insights into the current status of diversity representation at the highest levels of sport in the United States. For example, for the 2012 major league professional baseball season, the Racial and Gender Report Card (Lapchick, 2012a) showed that 38 percent of participants were players of color, 27 percent being Hispanic. It was notable, however, that the percentage of African American players had decreased over the last 15 years, with only 8.8 percent on the rosters at the beginning of the 2012 season. See "On the Sidelines" in this section for more information on African American participation in baseball. Of interest in relation to international player diversity is that Major League Baseball (MLB) reported 28.4 percent of players from outside the United States, and the National Basketball Association (NBA) report (Lapchick, 2012b) indicated that 17 percent of NBA players were international.

Table 8.2 Historic Events and Individuals Representing Diversity in Sport

Time period	Events
1920-1939	1920 - Fritz Pollard is first African American to play in the American Professional Football Association (now the NFL).
	1924 - Edith Cummings, female golfer, appears on cover of *Time* magazine.
	1927 - Iowa Girls High School Athletic Union founded. The organization is still in existence today and is solely devoted to interscholastic athletics for girls.
	1936 - Jesse Owens, African American, wins four gold medals at the Berlin Olympics.
1940-1959	1941 - Joe Aguirre, first Hispanic American to be drafted in the NFL.
	1943 - All American Girls Softball League formed to maintain baseball because men are away serving during World War II.
	1947 - Jackie Robinson is first African American to play Major League Baseball.
	1954 - Babe Zaharias, famous female athlete in multiple sports, wins the U.S. Women's Open golf championship only months after colon cancer surgery.
1960-1979	1960 - Wilma Rudolph is first woman (also African American) to win three gold medals in a single Olympic Games.
	1966 - Texas Western men's basketball team is first basketball team with all African American starting lineup to win the NCAA basketball championship.
	1968 - First Special Olympics held in Chicago.
	1972 - Congress passes Title IX to prohibit discrimination based on sex in any education program or activity receiving federal financial assistance.
1980-1999	1982 - Gay Olympics, now called the Gay Games and held every four years, is started in San Francisco.
	1986 - Debi Thomas becomes first African American woman to win the singles U.S. figure skating championship.
	1996 - Sheryl Swoopes becomes first player to sign with the WNBA.
2000-present	2001 - Women's United Soccer Association begins initial season as the first female soccer league in the world with all players compensated as professionals.
	2002 - Yao Ming from Shanghai, China, becomes first international player selected as a first-round pick in the NBA draft.
	2003 - Grant Fuhr is first black player to be inducted into the National Hockey League Hall of Fame.
	2012 - U.S. Olympic team sends more women than men to the Olympics for the first time in history.

The National Hockey League (NHL), not included in the Racial and Gender Report Card or in table 8.3, continues to be the least racially diverse of the professional sport leagues in the United States. This has been attributed by sport journalists and hockey officials primarily to financial costs of equipment and lack of access to ice rinks for all socioeconomic classes. However, in a diversity initiative begun in 1995, the NHL started a program called "Hockey Is for Everyone" that provides support and programming to youth hockey organizations across North America. It is estimated that the program has given more than 40,000 economically disadvantaged boys and girls the opportunity to experience hockey (nhl.com, 2012).

In a research report released by the National Golf Foundation (ngf.org, 2010), it was estimated that minority golfers (amateur and professional) in the United States totaled 5.7 million of the overall total of 27.1 million golfers, or 21 percent. Of the minority groups represented, it was estimated that there were 1.4 million African American, 1.1 million Asian, and 3.2 million Hispanic golfers. According to a 2005 United States Tennis Association survey, 87 percent of players nationwide were white, 10 percent were black, and 3 percent were other minorities; this suggested opportunities for expanding diversity and inclusion in tennis.

On the Sidelines

Baseball and African American Diversity

Concerns have been raised in recent years among MLB, the National Collegiate Athletic Association (NCAA), and African American communities about declining participation of African Americans in baseball throughout the United States. While there was a slight increase in the percentage of African American players in MLB between 2011 and 2012, the total as of 2012 was only 8.5 percent (Lapchick, 2012). Similar declines have occurred in college baseball; the 2009 Racial and Gender Report Card: College Sports (Lapchick, 2010) showed that only about 6.0 percent of the Division I baseball players in 2007-08 were African American. The lack of African American players is also contributing to diversity issues among spectators; a Scarborough Marketing Research study (Nightengale, 2012) showed that only 9 percent of fans who attended a MLB game in 2011 were African American.

Speculation varies as to the reason for the declining participation of African Americans. One suggestion is that it has to do with inner-city African American youths' limited access to quality youth baseball programs; another possibility is that more African American boys are finding their heroes in other sports, primarily basketball and football. However, it appears that some progress is being made to address the lack of representation in baseball. In a recent FOXSports.com report, Rosenthall (2012) noted that MLB had made significant progress toward improving the number of African American players in the amateur draft. Seven African Americans were included among the 31 first-round picks, representing the highest percentage and total in 20 years. The report also acknowledged that MLB had made progress through opening urban youth academies and the Reviving Baseball in Inner Cities (RBI) program as tools to increase its African American talent pool and renew interest in baseball among African American youth.

Table 8.3 Racial Diversity in Professional Leagues in the United States

League	Diversity breakdown
NFL (2011)	• 67% African American • 31% White • 2% all other races
NBA (2012)	• 78% African American • 18% White • 3% Latino • 1% all other races
WNBA (2011)	• 69% African American • 21% White • 3% Latino • 7% all other races
MLB (2012)	• 61% White • 27.3% Latino • 8.8% African American • 2.9% all other races
MLS (2010)	• 54% White • 26% African American • 17% Latino • 3% all other races

Based on information in the Racial and Gender Report Cards Lapchick 2010, 2011, 2012.

Table 8.4 Racial Diversity in Division I NCAA Intercollegiate Athletics

Sport	Diversity breakdown
Football	• 47.2% White • 41.4% African American • 8.7% all other races
Men's Basketball	• 59.3% African American • 28.8% White • 11.3% all other races
Women's basketball	• 50.6% African American • 36.8% White • 12.6% all other races
Men's baseball	• 82.2% White • 6.3% Latino • 5.1% African American • 6.4% all other races
Women's softball	• 75.3% White • 8.2% African American • 7.9% Latino • 8.6% all other races

Based on information in the NCAA Division I race and ethnicity report for championship participation 2011.

In other NCAA Division I sports, the racial diversity composition in 2011 was predominantly white. Exceptions were men's and women's track and field, where minorities composed approximately 40 percent of participants, and men's and women's tennis, where approximately 50 percent of participants were from races classified as other than white.

Diversity Representation in Management

While data on racial and gender representation throughout all of the sport industry are not readily available, significant data on diversity in management and leadership positions in professional sport leagues and intercollegiate athletics in the United States have been collected over the last decade by TIDES at the University of Central Florida as well as by the NCAA. The research efforts and publications from TIDES and the NCAA provide important information to individuals currently in or preparing for leadership roles, not only within professional and intercollegiate sport but also in sport- and fitness-related commercial or community organizations. In particular, TIDES provides examples and a perspective on data collection and tracking relative to gender and racial diversity that can be used as a model in sport organizations outside of professional and intercollegiate sport. The information collected by TIDES can also inform strategy and decision making across all domains of the sport industry where leaders are working toward continuous improvement as to representation of diverse individuals and groups in front office managerial or other professional positions.

Some of the most recent outcomes of diversity research conducted by TIDES provide insights into the current state of diversity representation in professional sport. For example, in the 2012 Racial and Gender Report Card for the NBA, the NBA received an A+ for racial hiring practices, an A– for gender hiring practices, and an overall combined grade of A, which was the highest combined grade in the history of men's professional sport. According to the report, there were more head coaches of color (53 percent) than white head coaches, which was a first-time occurrence in the NBA's his-

tory. Lapchick stated, "The standard for racial and gender diversity is led by Commissioner David Stern. He has continually been at the forefront of the issue and has led the charge for the NBA's progress in racial and gender equality, which featured an historic set of accomplishments in 2012" (p. 1). The report additionally pointed out that diversity hiring had progressed in the NBA office, where 34 percent of current professional employees were people of color and 42 percent were women.

In MLB, the 2012 report card showed consistency in terms of a high grade for racial hiring practices but showed a drop in hiring practices for women. Lapchick indicated that MLB had done very well in increasing the number of people of color in the league office and recommended that this occur with senior staff and professional positions in the front office of all the teams in the league. Major League Soccer (MLS) and the National Football League (NFL) continued to score high in racial hiring practices but lower in the gender hiring category. Patterns in the data suggest that significant opportunities still exist for leadership to commit to improving the hiring and retention of women across all leagues.

According to the College Racial and Gender Report Card in 2010, college sport had made substantial improvements overall on both racial and gender hiring practices since 2008. However, the report also indicated significant areas of concern, including a drop in the percentage of African American head coaches in NCAA Division I men's basketball, which had historically had an outstanding record of equal opportunity. In 2010, the percentage of African American men's basketball head coaches was 21.0, down 1.9 percent from 2008 and down 4.2 percent from 2006. The 2010 report also showed that only 8.3 percent of Division I athletic directors were women and that all commissioners of Football Bowl Subdivision (FBS) conferences were white men (college sports received Fs in these categories). Lapchick (2012) reported that significant progress had occurred in college football; at the beginning of the 2011 season, the number of head coaches of color (19, of whom 17 were African American) was at an all-time high, and six new coaches of color were hired for the 2011 season.

Organizational Leadership and Diversity

This section identifies several topics and issues pertaining to diversity research in sport organizations. Discussion of each area begins with examples and brief summaries of related research and then presents recommendations for how leaders may facilitate or improve diversity leadership.

The majority of the research related to these topics in sport management has been done only in the last 20 to 25 years, and much of the empirical work has been conducted in intercollegiate athletics. Summaries of the research pertaining to each topic are limited to explaining the fundamental purposes of the studies and highlighting key findings or implications. Readers with specific interest in the details of this research are encouraged to refer to the articles cited for more information about research questions and methods and more specific results.

Value of Diversity

In a 1995 article, DeSensi addressed the philosophical basis for *why* diversity is important in sport and physical activity and discussed the professional and ethical responsibilities associated with managing multiculturalism and diversity. DeSensi referred to the changing demographics of both society and the labor force and discussed the importance of assisting all individuals in achieving their potential. She stated that "this approach is not and does not involve 'political correctness' or 'superficial tolerance', but involves increasing the consciousness and appreciation of differences associated with *heritage, characteristics* and *values* of different groups" (p. 35). The author also suggested that when people broaden their understanding about differences in others and examine per-

sonal feelings associated with their experience, this can ultimately help them understand themselves better, improve interpersonal relationships, and allow them to better appreciate diversity in their organization.

> **Leadership Recommendation 1**
> Develop an understanding and appreciation of the value associated with multiple types of diversity in a sport organization.

Diversity and Organizational Culture

Doherty and Chelladurai (1999) proposed that whether cultural diversity is constructive or destructive in an organization is a function of how that diversity is managed and the extent to which diversity is valued within the overall organizational culture. The authors point out that research in organizational culture supports the idea that organizational culture can be improved and that what organizational leaders pay attention to and reward become what people recognize as desired values that can begin to shape attitudes and behaviors. More specifically, relative to creating a sport organizational culture that values diversity, Doherty and Chelladurai introduced the idea that task interdependence (the extent to which tasks require group members to interact and collaborate with one another), as well as task complexity (extent to which tasks are difficult and multifaceted), could influence the positive or negative impact of cultural diversity. They proposed that when diverse individuals work together in an organizational culture that values diversity and perform complex tasks that permit the expression of diverse perceptions and ideas, the benefits of cultural diversity are more likely to be realized.

> *The 21st century leader will have to be comfortable in dealing with diversity. Such a person will not seek comfort in sameness, but will celebrate differences and see the concomitant tension as an avenue for pursuing a higher order of things.*
>
> Bagchi (2006, p. 9)

Diversity Management Strategy and Organizational Outcomes

Fink and Pastore (1999) introduced a framework for diversity management in sport based on an integration of research studies from business management published in the 1990s. Fink and Pastore's framework identified four categories or descriptors of an organization's approach to or strategy for diversity management:

1. **Noncompliant:** The organization is unaware of or does not follow policies and federal laws, considers diversity as a liability.

2. **Compliant:** It is aware of and makes great efforts to comply with laws and regulations regarding appropriate representation of diverse individuals and groups (e.g., Title IX).

3. **Reactive:** It views diversity as an asset but often focuses only on racial and gender diversity and tends to offer such things as workshops or mentoring programs on a one-time basis.

4. **Proactive:** It views diversity more broadly to include other differences beyond race and gender; leaders examine policies and processes regarding diversity before problems occur and also show commitment to diversity through the allocation of resources.

According to the authors, proactive management of diversity would be considered the goal for an organization, as it would be expected to produce more positive and lasting organizational outcomes.

Fink, Pastore, and Riemer (2001), building on this theoretical framework, surveyed NCAA Division I athletic directors (ADs) as well as head coaches of women's softball and men's baseball regarding their beliefs and perceptions about (a) the benefits of diversity management, (b) approaches to or strategies for diversity management, and (c) diversity management and organizational outcomes. Beliefs in the benefits of diversity management among ADs (particularly female ADs and those from larger departments) were positive and higher than expected, which possibly indicated that ADs were becoming more aware of and beginning to believe in the advantages of diversity. Relative to diversity management and organizational outcomes, the researchers reported that different strategies for diversity management resulted in different organizational outcomes. For example, compliance strategies were associated with "retaining talented workers," "avoiding lawsuits," and "having a diverse fan base" (p. 43) while proactive strategies were more predictive of all other outcomes including employee satisfaction, involvement in decision making, perceptions of a creative workplace, and overall workplace diversity.

Following up on the 2001 study, Fink, Pastore, and Reimer (2003) examined diversity management among athletic directors, senior women's athletic directors, and men's and women's head basketball coaches in NCAA Division III. Findings from the study again supported the idea that strategies for managing diversity, particularly compliance and proactive practices and strategies, were related to positive organizational outcomes. A recommendation from the study was that it is very important for top-level managers who value and believe strongly enough in diversity, to provide the resources (both personnel and monetary) that are necessary for change.

Organizational Commitment

Research specific to sport organizations with regard to diversity-related organizational commitment, as well as the change process related to diversity, has been conducted primarily by Cunningham and Sagas (2004) and Cunningham (2008). In the 2004 study, Cunningham and Sagas examined the effects of racial dissimilarity on the organizational commitment of NCAA Division I men's assistant basketball coaches. The study addressed the question, "Do coaches racially different from other coaches on the staff have less organizational commitment than do coaches racially similar to other coaches on the staff?" (p. 128). Findings indicated that within this population, being racially different from others in the work group does have an impact on coaches' commitment to their organizations, although racial dissimilarity did not affect black and white coaches' commitment in the same way.

Using a perspective of how an organization's commitment to diversity across multiple dimensions can influence athletic department outcomes, Cunningham (2008) administered a survey to 258 NCAA Division I athletic departments to examine the influence of variables including sex diversity, race diversity, and categories of organizational commitment on the outcomes of (a) attracting diverse fans, (b) having satisfied employees, and (c) offering a creative workplace. Results indicated that departments demonstrating collective commitment to diversity were more likely to achieve these desired outcomes. Cunningham pointed out from the research that focusing primarily on department demographics or commitment to diversity alone is not sufficient, and that athletic administrators should look for ways to increase demographic diversity while also fostering a commitment to diversity among department employees.

> ### Leadership Recommendation 4
> Understand and communicate that commitment, on the part of both organizational members and the organization itself, is a key element of diversity management.

Cultural Competence and Leadership

Cultural competence has multiple definitions and meanings across various contexts but is a term that is commonly used in health care and education. Cultural competence generally refers to such things as (a) having an awareness of one's own cultural identity and an appreciation for the cultures of others, and (b) providing assistance or services in a way that recognizes and responds appropriately to differences in beliefs, attitudes, languages, and behaviors of those being served.

Many of the academic articles addressing cultural competence in sport have been in the field of athletic training (Ford, 2003; Marra et al., 2010; Rodriguez and Romanello, 2008). However, several studies more broadly examine cultural competence or recommend the need for enhancing cultural competence among sport management professionals across all sport domains (Gill et al., 2006; Xian-feng, 2009).

In an article offering recommendations for how athletic trainers can work toward improving cultural competence, Ford (2003, p. 60) identified four key points pertaining specifically to athletic training, though they could be considered applicable in other sport environments:

1. The willingness of certified athletic trainers and therapists to increase awareness and to confront biases and stereotypes will lay the groundwork for a culturally sensitive environment.

2. A culturally sensitive environment is influenced by physical factors, as well as style of communication, values, behaviors, and attitudes.

3. Certified athletic trainers and therapists should recognize that an individual's

> ### Leadership Recommendation 5
> Develop and grow personal and organizational capacity to value cultural differences among all races, ethnicities, cultural and religious beliefs; acquire cultural knowledge and respond effectively to the needs of the diverse constituents served by the organization.

choices, behaviors, and responses are affected by culture.

4. Optimal outcomes in clinical settings are achieved when health care practitioners possess more knowledge and respond with sensitivity to cultural issues.

Women and Special Populations in Sport

In addition to general organizational leadership issues in sport that span race, ethnicity, and all other categories of diversity, this chapter includes three specific populations: (1) women, (2) LGBT (lesbian, gay, bisexual, transgender), and (3) individuals with disabilities. In each of these areas, issues of diversity and inclusion, legal challenges, and moral or ethical decisions must be thoughtfully and carefully addressed by leaders of sport organizations.

Women in Sport

Likely the strongest and most persevering leadership effort related to diversity and inclusion in sport in the United States has occurred relative to women's participation and employment in the field. At the time of this writing, the 40th anniversary of Title IX, the federal law prohibiting sex discrimination in any educational program or activity receiving federal financial assistance, had just been celebrated. However, Title IX and its enforcement, from a leadership perspective, still present both a challenge and an opportunity for sport leaders in programs subject to the legislation. One of the primary challenges typically identified by athletic administrators in educational institutions has to do with effectively and appropriately managing budgetary and resource issues while concurrently trying to achieve gender equity. This challenge also presents significant opportunities for leaders to develop new, creative, and proactive approaches that truly improve opportunities and provide equitable resources for women's sport programs at their institutions.

It is important to note that while significant and encouraging progress has occurred over the last 40 years relative to women's participation and employment in sport, many schools still do not abide by the law and acknowledge that the chances of their being investigated are small and that even fewer will be meaningfully punished (Thomas, 2011). Thomas points out that although the Office of Civil Rights has the power to enforce the law such that any school found in violation could lose its federal funds, punishment to this extent has never been used since the law was passed in 1972.

However, there have been recent legal cases with outcomes suggesting stronger enforcement of Title IX. For example, in 2012, the University of California at Davis agreed to a $1.35 million settlement in a discrimination case brought by three female wrestlers who were not given an opportunity to participate on a women's team and were subsequently cut from the men's team. While it was found that university officials did not discriminate against the wrestlers when they were cut from the men's team, it was determined that the university failed to sufficiently expand intercollegiate athletic opportunities for female students during the period between 1999 and 2005, when the plaintiffs were attending (AAUW, 2012).

Although the statistics are encouraging, there continue to be concerns regarding representation and inclusion of women in sport.

> *While we were proud to stand up with these plaintiffs for what's right and fair, we look forward to the day when it doesn't take a lawsuit to enforce Title IX.*
>
> Linda D. Hallman, AAUW Executive Director

Olympics

- 1900 Paris Olympics had 19 women competing in two sports (lawn tennis and golf).
- 2012 London Olympics has women's competition in all 26 sports.
- The number of women on the 2012 United States Olympic team (269) outnumbered the men (261) for the first time in history.

Intercollegiate sport

- In 2012, approximately 200,000 females participated in intercollegiate athletics in the United States, the highest number in history (Acosta and Carpenter, 2012).
- The average number of women's teams per institution grew from 2.5 in 1972 to 8.73 in 2012 (Acosta and Carpenter, 2012).
- The highest ever number of female professionals (13,792) are employed in college athletics (Acosta and Carpenter, 2012).
- 42.9% of women's teams are coached by females, with the highest ever total number of female coaches (3,974) coaching women's teams (Acosta and Carpenter, 2012).

High school sport

- The National Federation of State High Schools Association reports that female participation in high school athletics has reached an all-time high of 3.1 million (compared to 1972 when Title IX was enacted into law) (Gardner, 2012).
- While there are still 1.3 million fewer girls than boys in high school sports, the gap has closed considerably since 1972 (Gardner, 2012).

Despite indications that more females are participating in sport than ever before (Acosta and Carpenter, 2012; Grappendorf, 2011), issues of representation of female leaders persist across all levels of sport (Massengale and Lough, 2010; Pederson and Whisenant, 2005; Sartore and Cunningham, 2007; Whisenant, Pederson, and Miller, 2005). The following are examples that support these claims:

- Women hold only 20.3 percent of athletic director positions in intercollegiate athletics (Acosta and Carpenter, 2012).
- Only 1 of 10 head sport information directors is female (Acosta and Carpenter, 2012).
- Out of approximately 4.1 million youth sport coaches, 654,000 are women (16 percent) (De Lench, 2006).

These data provide examples of not only problem areas, but also areas of significant opportunity for sport organization leaders to address in the future. It is well known that males (typically white males) continue to hold the majority of professional leadership positions across all levels of sport. This brings up the question of the "glass ceiling" and whether or not sport will continue to be a patriarchal institution where the power structure will keep women marginalized (Dickerson Lynes, 2007). It is obvious from data presented previously that participation of females at the youth, interscholastic, and intercollegiate levels is rapidly and continually increasing, which appears likely to continue into the future. Thus, it is essential for 21st-century sport organization leaders to address appropriate and equitable numeric representation, as well as meaningful social and professional inclusion of women in coaching, administrative, and other professional managerial roles. By doing so in a proactive rather than reactive way, leaders may be able to reduce tension and truly improve opportunities for all women in sport.

On the Sidelines

There are other notable indications that work is developing worldwide to provide increasing opportunities and improve the representativeness of women in sport. For example, in 2008, the Australian Government Sports Commission made $400,000 available to help women gain more opportunities to become leaders in sport ("Grants will deliver," 2008). Also, UK Sport in partnership with the British Olympic Foundation in the United Kingdom has developed the Women and Leadership Development Programme to increase representation of women in leadership positions in sport, build competence and confidence of women in decision-making positions, increase support among organizations for the contribution women can make to sport leadership, and foster networking among female leaders, both in the United Kingdom and internationally (UK Sport, Women and Leadership Development Program, 2012 [www.uksport.gov.uk/pages/women-and-leadership-development-programme]).

Selected Academic Research

A large volume of academic studies from sport management, sociology, and business has been published in areas related to women in sport. The focus of these studies ranges from gender equity among participants, employees, and leaders of sport organizations to the media portrayal of women in sport. Table 8.5 is a summary of studies representing various perspectives. Readers are encouraged to review these studies in more detail and further consider how the findings can affect leadership and decision making in this area of sport organization diversity.

Table 8.5 Selected Studies of Representation and Inclusion for Women in Sport

Researchers	Purpose of study	Major findings or implications
Inglis, Danylchuk, and Pastore (1996)	Understand factors of retention in coaching and athletic management positions to help explain social conditions of the workplace and identify factors important for individuals (particularly women) to stay in their jobs	Retention factors identified and empirically supported were (1) work balance and conditions, (2) recognition and collegial support, and (3) inclusivity.
Pederson and Whisenant (2005)	Assess the status and success rates of interscholastic athletic directors, focusing primarily on gender	Confirmation that interscholastic athletic administration continues to be male dominated (90% of ADs were male), but that females in these positions were equally successful in relation to their male counterparts given the same opportunities.
Sartore and Cunningham (2007)	Apply a symbolic interactionist perspective to help explain underrepresentation of women in sport organization leadership positions; model proposes that gender-role meanings and stereotypes may limit capacity of females	Proposed research model suggests that persons (women in this case) may not seek higher-level opportunities in an organization if there is a discrepancy between their own self-perception of identity and that of others. For example, female assistant coaches may exhibit self-limiting behavior driven by an internal identity issue that results from environmental input counter to that identity (e.g., idea that it is somehow inappropriate for a woman to be a head coach).
Stevenson (2010)	Examine the implications of Title IX and the growth of high school female athletic participation relative to future educational attainment and workforce participation	Participation in high school sport has a significant effect on both educational attainment and workforce participation. Stevenson reported that a 10% rise in female sport participation generates a 1% increase in female college attendance and up to a 2% increase in labor force participation of females.
Fink, Borland, and Fields (2011)	Examine reaction of the media as well as the perpetrators and defenders to five sexist incidents that occurred in sport from 2004 to 2007: 1. Firing of a college women's volleyball coach after she made gender equity complaints 2. Inappropriate comments made by the president of Formula One racing with regard to a white female race car driver 3. Inappropriate comments made by a former male NBA player and radio announcer regarding a black female NBA referee 4. Inappropriate comments made by radio host directed toward a college women's basketball team 5. Media coverage of sexual harassment trial between a former black female executive for the New York Knicks and the coach and president of the team	• Most of the stories received little attention in the national media, although each involved blatant sexism. Incidents receiving the most media attention were those (4 and 5) that involved both racism and sexism. Strategies for apology from sources including the perpetrators, members of the media, top management, and family and friends were reported to occur in the categories of denial, bolstering, transcendence, and differentiation along with either silence or marginalized sexism. • Authors suggest that "the fact that particularly sexist comments go mainly unnoticed, or ignored, by the sport media further entrenches the 'acceptability' of sexism in sport" (p. 204).

LGBT (Lesbian, Gay, Bisexual, Transgender) Diversity

All individuals in roles of leadership in sport organizations, from CEOs to coaches and athletes, must recognize and be prepared to effectively lead and manage diversity relative to lesbian, gay, bisexual, and transgender (LGBT) participants and employees. While progress is being made across sports regarding the acceptance of individuals with sexual orientations that differ from heteronormativity, this is an area in which negativity, discrimination, and even hostile behaviors (homophobia) continue to exist. It has also been argued that sport is an environment that may foster the development of homophobic attitudes and behaviors, specifically in cultures where masculinity is valued as a path to manhood (Plummer, 2006).

LGBT, Discrimination, and the Law

It is very important for leaders of sport organizations to understand the laws and legal obligations associated with LGBT participation and employment. While I refer readers interested in specific details to the sport law textbooks, leaders should be aware of the laws that currently exist. See table 8.6 for the most recent (2012) information on federal, state, and local laws pertaining to employee discrimination relative to sexual orientation.

Regarding participant discrimination, leaders of school-based or other community sport programs should refer to their state statutes for more information. In many cases, states require administrators and coaches to ensure that the conduct of athletes (and coaches) does not create a hostile environment based on sexual orientation.

LGBT Research in Sport

A large volume of research addresses issues associated with LGBT, especially in sport psychology and sport sociology, and there are several recent conceptual articles and empirical research studies related to LGBT in the sport management literature. For example, Gill and colleagues (2006) conducted a study to obtain and evaluate data regarding attitude and sexual prejudice toward gays, lesbians, and other minority groups. The researchers surveyed a large sample of undergraduate students along with upper-level preprofessional exercise and sport science students and members of a campus organization with significant representation of sexual minorities. Findings indicated that attitudes overall were generally in the midrange of the scale, with females expressing more positive attitudes than males toward gay men. The upper-level students surveyed were more positive than the undergraduate students, but were still negative overall with respect to attitudes toward lesbians and gay men. These results suggested that sexual prejudice was persistent among the participants in this study. The authors pointed to the need to give attention to sexual minorities in diversity management and to continue to pursue research and develop educational

Table 8.6 Federal, State and Local Law Regarding Sexual Orientation Discrimination

Federal Law	State Law	Local Law
Currently in 2012, no federal law specifically outlaws workplace discrimination *in the private sector* based on sexual orientation.	Many states have laws that prohibit sexual orientation discrimination *in both public and private* workplaces.	While dependent on the location, many cities and counties prohibit sexual orientation discrimination in some workplaces.
Federal government workers *are* protected from discrimination based on sexual orientation.	These states are California, Colorado, Connecticut, Hawaii, Illinois, Iowa, Maine, Maryland, Massachusetts, Nevada, New Hampshire, New Jersey, New Mexico, New York, Oregon, Rhode Island, Vermont, Washington and Wisconsin. The District of Columbia is also included.	More information regarding city and county legal protection can be found at the Lamda Legal Defense and Education Fund Website www.lambdalegal.org.

Based on information in *NOLO law for all* (2012), www.nolo.com/legal-encyclopedia/sexual-orientation-discrimination-rights-29541.html.

programs that will enhance cultural competence among sport managers.

Barber and Krane (2007) discussed the importance of creating inclusive and positive climates in girls' and women's sport for all female athletes regardless of sexual orientation. These authors suggested that elimination of prejudice based on sexual orientation and gender identity is important and that all athletes should have the opportunity to gain the benefits of sport participation.

Sartore and Cunningham (2010), addressing the existence of a lesbian stigma in sport, proposed a conceptual model to evaluate potential causes and consequences of the heteronormativity in sport and to study how stigmatization of women can affect their personal, social, and work-related outcomes as well as reinforcing continued marginalization of women. The model, using social identity, self-categorization, and status characteristics theories, recognizes that people tend to classify themselves and align with other like individuals, constituting an "in-group," while individuals with other characteristics constitute what one perceives to be an "out-group." Referring to the work of Fink, Pastore, and Reimer (2001), Sartore and Cunningham in their model suggest that within sport, white, Protestant, heterosexual males (in-group members) continue to possess a higher contextual status, are able to maintain their ideals, and also are able to exert power over others (e.g., females, minorities, homosexuals) who would be considered out-group members. From that foundation, the authors set forth several propositions for future study: that women are susceptible to the lesbian stigma in sport; that as a result of the stigma, they may experience threats to social identity; and that as a result of both stigmatization and social identity threat, women in sport may adopt strategies for identity management.

In a study of NCAA Division II athletic departments, Cunningham (2010) examined antecedents that contribute to sexual orientation diversity at this level of college athletics. Data were collected from 653 top administrators in 199 athletic departments; the results indicated that 46 percent of participating departments had low sexual orientation diversity and 17 percent demonstrated no sexual orientation diversity. For the participating departments that were identified as having high sexual orientation diversity, size of the university, racial diversity of employees, and gender diversity of employees were all factors positively associated with sexual orientation diversity.

Leadership Actions and Recommendations

All sport organization leaders, including executives, athletic directors, coaches, and program directors of leisure and recreational sport, are in roles that require knowledge, recognition, understanding, and in many cases the ability to develop specific strategies and initiatives related to diversity of LGBT participants and employees. This section provides resource information and recommendations intended to be useful for increasing proactivity in this area.

A focused leadership effort related to LGBT diversity has been organized by the Women's Sports Foundation, which includes the It Takes a Team! Education Campaign for LGBT Issues in Sport. This campaign focuses on eliminating homophobia in sport and provides educational information and resources to administrators, coaches, parents, and athletes designed to help make sport a safe and welcoming place for all involved. The It Takes a Team program establishes "five basic rights" of athletes and coaches:

1. Safety from physical and verbal harassment or violence
2. Fair treatment in all aspects of programming
3. Equal access to all aspects of programming
4. Support for developing positive self-esteem and acceptance of others
5. Education about social diversity, prejudice, and discrimination

In addition, the Women's Sports Foundation website provides numerous links to reports and to statements on its position on various issues related to LGBT in sport. Topics include access for transgender athletes to school sport teams, fair employment practices based on sexual orientation or gender identity, and unethical recruitment strategy perpetuating myths and misconceptions. The information in these reports is highly recommended for those in leadership roles needing to consider the ways in which their organizations are affected by and can provide a safe environment for LGBT participants and employees.

Your Thoughts

Review the five "basic rights" of athletes and coaches advanced by the It Takes a Team program. Consider your current sport organization or one you are familiar with and reflect on the extent to which these five statements are true about the organization. What ideas do you have for improving each of these areas, if needed?

Other recommendations for proactive diversity management in this area include elements of policy as well as professional development. For example, Carol (2006) recommends that athletic leaders consider pursuing sexual orientation clauses in their institutional antidiscrimination policies as well as in the athletic department policy regarding professional ethics (Carol, 2006). Carol also suggests that it is a responsibility of leaders to educate all personnel, including coaches, athletes, and department staff members, about tolerance and equal treatment of LGBT athletes, and that this education can be incorporated into existing training and professional development offered within a department.

Individuals With Disabilities

Another key area of responsibility for sport organization leaders is diversity and inclusion for people with disabilities. According to a 2005 U.S. Census Bureau report (Brault, 2008), 54.4 million people in the United States (18.7 percent of the population) had some level of disability, while 35.0 million (12.0 percent) had a severe disability. The report identifies three primary domains of disability:

1. *Communication:* Disabilities related to vision, hearing, or speech disorders
2. *Mental:* Includes learning disabilities, mental retardation, any mental or emo-

tional disability interfering with daily activities, attention deficit hyperactivity disorder, autism, dementia, Alzheimer's disease
3. *Physical:* Includes difficulty walking, lifting, grasping objects, getting in and out bed; use of wheelchair, cane, or walker; arthritis; back injuries, head or spinal cord injuries; missing one or more limbs; deformity; paralysis; diabetes; heart disease; cancer; and numerous other medical conditions that interfere with everyday life

Obviously, almost all individuals at some point in their lives are going to experience disability, and many are going to desire to participate, seek employment, and possibly pursue leadership roles in competitive and recreational sport despite a disabling condition. Innumerable people with varying impairments and disabilities are able to compete safely and intensely and able to be employed in sport. Many athletes with disabilities or impairments have overcome physical, mental, or societal impediments and have competed at the highest levels of sport competition. Examples include Natalie du Toit, swimmer; Rocky Bleier, professional football player; Bethany Hamilton, surfer; Kyle Maynard, wrestler and mixed martial arts competitor; Anthony Robles, wrestler; and Jim Abbott, professional baseball.

However, despite the fact that many individuals with disabilities are getting to pursue their interests and participate in sport at all levels, many young people with disabilities still do not get the opportunity to do so or have highly negative experiences with schools or organizations when they try to participate in sport activities. As indicated by Lakowski (2009) in a reflection on the state of opportunities for athletes in school sports, although many schools and programs are taking affirmative action to include students with disabilities, the experiences of these students often paint a negative picture. Many disabled athletes (a) have few opportunities for participation; (b) are not provided with reasonable accommodation; and (c) if allowed to participate, may be ostracized or even excluded because of their disability. From a compliance perspective, Lakowski points out that the federal American with Disabilities Act of 1990 and specifically the federal Rehabilitation Act of 1973 provide legal protection and purported equal opportunity for students with disabilities. However, many questions and much lack of specificity still exist regarding what formally constitutes "equal opportunity" in school sport. For example, Lakowski asks whether "equal" means that disabled students can try out for teams but that no accommodations need be made for their disability. Also, does "equal" mean that disabled students should be provided opportunities for meaningful participation as defined by having access to all of the benefits of participation including facilities, equipment, uniforms, and trained coaches? Lakowski concludes by arguing that sports are a potent force in society that can have a strong impact on the health, confidence, and self-esteem of individuals. Consequently, Lakowski suggests, we must do everything possible to ensure that boys and girls with disabilities have the same meaningful sport participation opportunities as do those without disabilities.

The following subsections provide insights into a few recent perspectives on disability in sport. These are not intended to represent all of the available literature on the subject but are especially pertinent to proactive leadership and decision making in this area for the future.

Disability Sport Versus Disability in Sport

It is important to clarify some terminology as currently used in sport with regard to the difference between sport experiences specifically designed for individuals with disabilities and those that result from the inclusion and support of individuals with disabilities in mainstream sport activities and events. Fay and Wolff (2009) highlight these differences as follows:

• **Disability sport:** A construct used in the recent book *Disability Sport* (DePauw and Gavron, 2005) to refer to those sports and events that are created uniquely for people with certain disabilities and use technologies (e.g., Special Olympics, Paralympics, wheelchair sports, beep baseball). Beyond the national and international organizations that exist for disability sport, numerous state athletic

associations for interscholastic athletics in the United States are now providing adaptive events so that disabled boys and girls can participate in various state championship events (Lakowski, 2009).

• **Disability in sport:** Focuses on issues "pertaining to labeling, identity and classification systems used either to include or exclude based on self and/or organizational descriptors" (Fay and Wolff, 2009, p. 234). Fay and Wolff point out that "disability identity becomes a socially constructed paradigm promulgated through cultural and sport classification systems that can become an internalized, as well as externalized, paradigm similar to race and gender" (p. 234).

Note: Because this chapter primarily addresses issues of diversity and inclusion broadly within sport organizations, the information presented in this section pertains mostly to "disability *in* sport" as opposed to "disability sport." This is not intended in any way to downplay the extraordinary leadership and support associated with all of the organizations, activities, and events worldwide that exist specifically for social inclusion of individuals with disabilities so that they can participate or compete in sport. For more information on disability sport organizations and the leadership of these organizations, readers are encouraged to refer to the textbook *Disability Sport* by DePauw and Gavron.

Fay and Wolff: Sport Opportunity Spectrum

Fay and Wolff (2009), addressing new concepts and ways of approaching disability in sport in the 21st century, argue that many governing bodies and sport systems perpetuate a false premise that having separate, segregated opportunities for persons with disabilities is desirable and equitable. Thinking into the future and questioning what the sport opportunities will be for individuals with disabilities over the next 50 to 100 years, Fay and Wolff make several arguments and raise an intriguing question that should be carefully considered by leaders of sport organizations: "Will there be a shift from the 'norms of naturalism' to trans-humanism that will yield new paradigms and understanding of what is sport and who are athletes?"

While some individuals have disabilities so severe that they legally preclude mainstream sport participation, Fay and Wolff point out that many athletes with disabilities are able to compete successfully with others who do not have the same disabilities. This raises the question, as suggested by Fay and Wolff, "Where do these athletes fit and how do they define or identify themselves?" (p. 243). The authors propose five conceptual frameworks that may allow researchers to evaluate both progression toward equity-based inclusionary practices for athletes with disabilities and regression back to discriminatory and segregationist practices. These conceptual frameworks are summarized in table 8.7. Readers may wish to consider the

Table 8.7 Interlinking Conceptual Frameworks for Evaluating Progression Toward (or Regression From) Equity-Based and Inclusionary Practices in Sport

Conceptual framework	Description and examples
Critical change factors model	The model identifies factors used to determine differences in the progression toward inclusion of disabled individuals among working class, management, and the upper organizational executive or ownership level. Examples of factors include, but are not limited to: • Change in laws and court actions involving disabled individuals • Change in level of influence of high-profile role models on public opinion • Change in the critical mass of disabled athletes attaining high athletic achievement • Change in beliefs about medical and intellectual stereotypes of individuals with disabilities • Change in hiring practices and use of strategic processes to include and integrate more individuals with disabilities into managerial and leadership roles
Organizational continuum of sport governance	The framework examines inclusion at various levels of sport, the role of the individual (e.g., working class, management, ownership), and the progression of a specific identity group (e.g., able-bodied individuals vs. individuals with a disability) across the spectrum of sport from the play or recreational level on up to scholastic, intercollegiate, and national, international, or professional sport.
Criteria for inclusion in sport organizations	The framework provides a means of assessing and scoring an organization with regard to its practices of inclusion for individuals with disabilities. Organizations range from exclusive clubs (fewest points) to very diverse and accepting organizations (most points). Categories in which organizations could be assessed include governance, management, funding or sponsorship, education of organizational membership, events and programs, awards and recognition, philosophy, and advocacy.
Individual multiple identity sport classification index	This classification index recognizes that athletes, in addition to the typical personal identity factors of age, race, gender, nationality, and so on, use various sport-related identity factors that include the federation, league, or specific sport they belong to as well as their role, position, performance, and records held. According to Fay and Wolff, the index is intentionally constructed to "expose the futility of stereotyping and labeling persons with a disability, similar to the use of racial or gender labels" (p. 244). For example, some athletes with disabilities have an identity as a world-class competitor in a specific sport even if they also have a disability (e.g., Natalie du Toit).
Sport opportunity spectrum (SOS)	Five hypotheses proposed by Fay and Wolff for evaluation related to athletes with disabilities and the opportunity to compete: 1. The SOS for individuals with disabilities will be perceived by the majority of any given society's population as more limited than the SOS for able-bodied athletes in the same society. 2. The SOS within a society will be perceived to be significantly different by athletes with a disability as compared to those identified as able-bodied. 3. Sport governance systems use classification and performance standards intentionally as strategies to control participation. 4. Sport governance systems use classification and performance systems also to create different sport opportunity spectrums for able-bodied versus disabled athletes. 5. Athletes with disabilities often reinforce the acceptance of different sport opportunity spectrums for able-bodied athletes through an acculturation process referred to as *internalized ableism,* meaning that they internally stereotype and devalue themselves similar to the way other devalued people internalize racism and sexism.

various components of this model relative to how they could affect sport organization leaders' knowledge of and actions toward diversity and inclusion of individuals with disabilities.

Technology, Disability, and Leadership

Continued advancements in sport technology are creating new questions and challenges to old assumptions regarding not only participation of individuals with physical disabilities, but also possible competitive advantages of these individuals over "able-bodied" participants. New materials and designs that integrate knowledge and expertise from medicine, engineering, biomechanics, physics, chemistry, and other related fields are giving disabled athletes exciting opportunities to participate as never before. The development and utilization of sport technology is also creating interdisciplinary research opportunities in STEM fields (science, technology, engineering, math) as well as opening up new dialogue in areas such as physical education, coaching, sport sociology, sport psychology, and sport management.

From an ethical and philosophical perspective, questions of whether or not technology and the ability to enhance performance of individuals with disabilities introduce new inequities and issues of fair play have recently appeared in the academic literature (Van Hilvoorde and Landeweerd, 2010). According to the authors, "transhumanism is a movement that seeks to advance technology in such a way that it would alter the human condition to something to which the term human may no longer be applicable" (p. 2224).

While technology, no doubt, will continue to offer the possibility of enhancement to athletic performance for disabled individuals, leaders

On the Sidelines

The following quote from a high school sport participant in a recent academic article provides a strong example for coaches and sport administrators at all levels of sport to consider relative to professional responsibility and their roles as mentors and leaders.

I do not have a physical disability but I have a learning disability. While the effects of physical disabilities are much more severe, learning disabilities affect people greatly in the athletic arena. Some coaches will tell you to run a drill and because you cannot understand them very well, you get into trouble and it makes it look as though you're disobeying them. I have been publicly humiliated because of a disability I could not control. Sometimes you just want to give up because you cannot understand the drill and the coach keeps yelling at you and your teammates blame you for all the running they are doing. I have been called dumb, stupid, idiot, slow, and the list goes on. I just would like coaches out there to understand that there are athletes out there with learning disabilities and its not that we are not trying, it's just that we have a hard time understanding. But please do not give up on us or call us names, we will get it! Learning disabilities will never leave a person even if they come up with ways to hide them. Please open your eyes to those athletes with learning disabilities and give them a chance.

High school student, Virginia

From Women's Sports Foundation from 2007-2008, *Share your story,* as quoted in T. Lakowski, 2009, "Athletes with disabilities in school sports: A critical assessment of the state of sports opportunities for students with disabilities," *Boston University International Law Journal* Vol. 27: 283.

of sport organizations across all levels will need to be prepared for the challenges and ethical questions that will follow. Will a future vision of elite sport include a transhumanist view of human performance? Is it possible that there will eventually be another division or level of sport for "super-abled" athletes? These questions suggest issues that are interesting yet in some ways troubling for current and future sport leaders to address.

Leadership Competencies and Diversity

This chapter concludes by presenting a model that is outside the specific realm of sport but that I believe offers excellent and highly applicable information relative to leadership and diversity in sport. The information comes from *Council*

Perspectives, a report on competencies of diversity and inclusion professionals (Lahiri, 2008). This report, developed from the deliberations of many highly experienced executives worldwide, identifies five key trends driving changes and defining a need for new thinking regarding the competencies of diversity and inclusion professionals. I suggest that leaders of sport organizations across all domains may benefit from thinking about these trends and identifying those that currently affect or have the potential to affect the work of their specific sport organization. See the following list for trends affecting the role of diversity and inclusion professionals.

- **Globalization:** Employees and customers coming from around the world leading to cultural competency as a leadership imperative.
- **Demographic shifts:** Changes in labor pool (e.g., aging) requiring flexibility and redefining of employee needs and expectations.
- **Technology:** Simpler and faster global communication, more access to information, can increase employee expectations regarding flexibility and openness to culture.
- **Socio-political climate:** Strong religious, political and nationalist divides emerging in communities worldwide offering a significant challenge tor leaders attempting to create and manage a culture of inclusion.

- **Legal environment:** Increased regulation and media attention add new dimensions to compliance and concerns about damage to reputation, brand image and community relationships.

Based on information in Lahiri (2008), Creating a competency model for diversity and inclusion practitioners, *Council Perspectives*™, Insights from The Conference Board Council on Workforce Diversity.

Additionally, Lahiri (2008) offers a competency model for diversity and inclusion professionals that broadly addresses the various knowledge, skills, abilities, and behaviors appropriate to more effectively address diversity in organizations. In this model, Lahiri provides insights into the responsibilities and actions one could regard as competencies that metrics could be developed for to evaluate progress and identify areas in need of improvement. The model includes multiple competencies in the categories of (a) change management; (b) diversity, inclusion, and global perspective; (c) business acumen; (d) strategic external relations; (e) integrity; (f) visionary and strategic leadership; and (g) human resource disciplines. From the numerous competencies included in the model, I have selected 10 that I believe are highly relevant for leaders in sport organizations striving to improve diversity leadership. These 10 competencies are presented in the sidebar list.

Diversity and Inclusion Competencies for Sport Leaders

1. "Offers useful and timely interventions in cases where progress is impeded due to a diversity-related issue" (p. 11).
2. "Understands multiple cultural frameworks, values, and norms" (p. 13).
3. "Negotiates and facilitates through cultural differences, conflicts, tensions, or misunderstandings" (p. 13).
4. "Commits to continuous learning/improvement in diversity, inclusion, and cultural competence" (p. 13).
5. "Knows and applies best practices in diversity and inclusion practices, strategies, systems, policies, etc." (p. 13).
6. "Understands and is current on global and local trends/changes and how they inform and influence D&I" (p. 14).
7. "Determines and communicates how D&I contributes to core business strategy and results" (p. 14).
8. "Acts as a voice for perspectives, levels, and cultures that are not otherwise represented" (p. 16).
9. "Understands how to motivate and work with both minority and majority groups" (p. 16).
10. "Collaborates appropriately with others to envision and convey an inspiring, compelling, and relevant D&I future state" (p. 17).

Important Practices for Successful Diversity Leadership

The Lead Change Group, a global community, states that its mission is to instigate a character-based leadership revolution. A recent blog posting by Holland (2011) offers the following very practical and useful recommendations for effectively leading diversity efforts in an organization:

1. "Practice the art of listening with the intent to understand" (p. 1). Ask more questions, consider insights and responses, and work to overcome barriers in communication.

2. Recognize the styles and preferences of those you are working with. In diverse organizations, not all individuals will communicate in the same way. For example, individuals from some cultures find strength in one-on-one discussion, others find it in small groups, and some are highly enculturated to the idea that whoever is the leader deserves respect and honor.

3. Develop and cultivate trust. Help group members develop association, acceptance, and support. This helps individuals become more comfortable with the organization, team, expectations, roles, and interactions. Be sure to recognize and reward *all* people for outstanding performance, work ethic, and efforts.

4. Accept *all* people for their contributions, character, and capabilities. If this is at the forefront of a leader's goals, a person's heritage, background, culture, or other element of diversity should not make a difference. People who are willing to give their best to the organization deserve acceptance and support on a continuous basis.

There are other practical ideas offered by the Lead Change Group for improving leadership competency to more successfully lead diversity. See the "Important Practices for Successful Diversity Leadership" sidebar.

Summary

Recent statistics on diversity representation across primarily professional and intercollegiate sport organizations indicate that while improvements are occurring, achieving appropriate representation of diverse groups continues to require attention at the participant level as well as in management and leadership. As underrepresentation by gender and race continues to be an issue, leaders of organizations across all domains of sport must continue to address and assume primary responsibility for improving representation of all diverse individuals and groups.

Beyond the quantitative issue of representation, sport leaders must also actively embrace diversity and work to improve organizational life for all individuals. Recommendations include (a) developing understanding of and appreciation for the value of diversity in an organization, (b) evaluating current organizational culture for evidence that its actions regarding diversity are consistent with espoused values, (c) implementing proactive as opposed to reactive strategies for diversity management and leadership, (d) communicating and demonstrating commitment to change toward a culture that values diversity, and (e) developing personal cultural competence to better address the needs of diverse individuals and groups.

Current and future sport leaders must also be prepared to address diversity issues related to women in sport, LGBT participation and employment, and the inclusion of athletes and employees with disabilities. While participation and representation of women in sport are improving, the research reviewed in this chapter suggests that multiple constraints and barriers must still be overcome. Sport leaders must also recognize the responsibility to provide safe environments for participation and work for all individuals, including LGBT populations. Leaders in sport must be knowledgeable about and effectively address increasing interest in and demands for participation from individuals with disabilities. Helpful in this regard are new conceptual frameworks presented in the chapter that offer ideas for examining progression toward or regression from inclusion for individuals with disabilities in sport. Also, as technology continues to advance, disabled athletes are being provided with unprecedented ways of competing, which creates new ethical and philosophical challenges for leadership.

Final Self-Assessment

After having read and reflected on the content in this chapter, consider your responses to the self-assessment questions presented at the beginning of the chapter. What insights do you now have or in what ways do you feel better prepared to effectively lead an organization in the area of diversity and inclusion?

1. How do you currently define or describe diversity, and what is your experience working with or leading diverse individuals, teams, or larger organizations?
2. What is your current perspective on the roles and responsibilities of leaders relative to equity and inclusion? Is it compliance oriented? Is it proactive?
3. What are ways you believe leaders can improve representation and better embrace and lead diversity in a sport organization?
4. What are the some of the critical issues, as you know of them now, in relation to women and special populations in sport?
5. How might you assess your own, or others', leadership competencies relative to diversity and inclusion? How could this information be used in leadership evaluation and professional development?

Game Plan Activity

With one or more of your colleagues or fellow students, use the leadership competencies listed in the sidebar "Diversity and Inclusion Competencies for Sport Leaders" as a foundation to develop a quantitative (e.g., Likert scale) and qualitative (e.g., open-ended questions) instrument that could be used to evaluate sport organization leaders relative to diversity and inclusion. Choose a domain of sport (e.g., professional, intercollegiate, interscholastic, youth) as the context for the evaluation, and feel free to add questions or delete any competencies that you don't feel are appropriate for the domain. After you have completed the instrument, write a summary that explains how, where, and by whom you think the instrument could be used effectively to improve leadership for diversity in sports.

Questions to Consider

1. Beyond policy and legal implications, why do you believe diversity and inclusion is a key area of importance for effectively leading a sport organization?
2. Suppose that you have just assumed a key leadership role in a sport organization. How would you go about trying to better understand individuals and groups representing various races, cultures, nationalities, social classes, religions, sexual orientations, abilities, and various perspectives within the organization?
3. As a leader within a sport organization at any level, what are tangible activities or processes that you might use to ensure that diverse individuals and groups have a voice in the plans and strategies of the organization?
4. Choose a sport organization that you are familiar with and identify what evidence exists that diversity is valued in the organization. What, in your opinion, could be done to improve in this area?
5. In the sport organization chosen for question 4, how would you go about actively addressing diversity representation in the areas of both recruitment and retention?

Recommended Readings

Cunningham, G. (2010). *Diversity in sport organizations* (2nd ed.). Scottsdale, AZ: Holcomb Hathaway.

DePauw, K. P., and Gavron, S. J. (2005). *Disability sport* (2nd ed.). Champaign, IL: Human Kinetics.

Griffin, P., and Carroll, H. (2010). On the team: Equal opportunity for transgender student athletes. www.womenssportsfoundation.org.

9

Globalization and Leadership

Learning Objectives

After reading and reflecting on the concepts and examples in this chapter, you will be able to

1. define and describe globalization and related terms;
2. identify and give examples of various forms of globalization;
3. provide examples and evidence of the increasing globalization of sport;
4. discuss sport and its fundamental influence on both nationalization and globalization;
5. identify and give specific examples of problems and complexities that globalization presents for the sport industry;
6. recognize areas of social and ethical responsibility that must be addressed by leaders of global sport organizations;
7. define and describe the term "global leadership";
8. apply findings from research including Project GLOBE and the Global Mindset Project to sport leadership challenges and opportunities; and
9. identify and describe global leadership competencies, stages, and behaviors.

Self-Assessment

1. What is your current knowledge of global leadership issues in sport?
2. How prepared would you feel to assume a leadership role if you were assigned responsibility for a major international sport project?
3. What are elements of "global" leadership that you think may differ from "local" leadership?
4. What are key leadership behaviors that you think would be effective in any country across the globe?

This chapter is about the challenges, opportunities, and considerations that current and future sport organization leaders should recognize when tasked with leadership in a global context and in an increasingly interconnected, technological world. Much of the information in this chapter is based on what I consider a comprehensive and powerful statement from a group of the most predominant researchers in global leadership:

> "The essence of global leadership is the ability to influence people who are not like the leader and come from different cultural backgrounds. To succeed, global leaders need to have a global mindset, tolerate high levels of ambiguity, and show cultural adaptability and flexibility." (Javidan et al., 2006, p. 85)

The chapter is divided into three major sections, on (1) terminology and forms of globalization, (2) globalization in a sport context, and (3) globalization and leadership. In the first section, the meaning of the term globalization is introduced along with how it differs in meaning from "internationalization." Other related terms are also introduced and defined. The section additionally includes reference to and description of six different forms of globalization that apply to all organizations around the world.

The second section addresses globalization in a sport context. This is intended to provide readers with a foundational understanding of the history of globalization in sport and its increase today, as well as the influence that sport has on globalization and the reciprocal effect that globalization has on sport. A case analysis of the Manchester United football (soccer) club is included in this section as evidence of a successful global sport franchise. The section also discusses identification of the dynamics of contemporary globalization and the problems and complexities it creates. The final topic is the sociocultural and economic tensions created as a result of globalization in sport. Included is a review of the 2008 Dr. Earle Ziegler lecture to the North American Society for Sport Management, "Globalization of Sport: An Inconvenient Truth" (Thibault, 2009), which addresses key issues and asks questions critical

to responsibility-based leadership in a global context.

The focus for the third section of the chapter shifts to defining global leadership and presenting the results of key research in this area to provide a conceptual framework for understanding the essential elements of leading in a global context. International research and models reviewed and summarized in this section include Project GLOBE (House et al., 2004), the Global Mindset Project (Javidan and Walker, 2012), and the 10 key behaviors defining great global leaders as identified in the research of Gundling, Hogan, and Cvitkovich (2011). Additional information is presented relative to the developmental shifts that are seen as necessary for producing effective global leadership (Holt and Seki, 2012).

Terminology and Forms of Globalization

It is important to begin with a clarification of terminology regarding globalization, its forms, and other terms and jargon related to the concept. One of the original descriptions or interpretations of globalization was provided by Robertson (1992), who suggested that it represents the consolidation of the world into a whole space or "global community." Robertson further explained that globalization is "the compression of the world and the intensification of consciousness of the world as a whole" (p. 8). Several years later, Aninat (2002, p. 4) defined globalization as "the process through which an increasingly free flow of ideas, peoples, good and services and capital leads to the integration of economies and societies." Sport sociology professor Joseph Maguire, author of *Global Sport: Identities, Societies, Civilizations*, described globalization as occurring when "every aspect of social reality – people's living conditions, beliefs, knowledge and actions – is intertwined with unfolding globalization processes. The processes include the emergence of a global economy, a transnational cosmopolitan culture and range of international social movements" (Maguire, 1999, p. 3).

A term often confused with globalization is "internationalization," which actually represents something very different. According to Daly (1999), with internationalization, the basic unit of analysis remains at the national level, but the term refers to the increasing importance of international trade, international relations, and the formation of treaties, alliances, and so on with other nations. In contrast, the term "globalization," according to Daly, specifically involves the global economic integration of formerly independent national economies into one global economy with free trade and easy or uncontrolled migration. In this sense, according to Daly, globalization occurs when there is an "erasure of national boundaries for economic purposes" (p. 1).

Another term often used in business is "transnational," which simply refers to anything extending or going beyond national boundaries (Merriam-Webster, m-w.com, 2013). This term is often used in descriptions of corporations or organizations that cross national boundaries in their scope of work.

An additional term that has more recently appeared in the literature is "glocalization." This term refers to products or services that are designed to benefit a local market but at the same time are developed and distributed on a global level (businessdictionary.com, 2013). Glocalization is occurring regularly in the interconnected digital world of today but is also leading to increased challenges and opportunities. For example, Giulianotti and Robertson (2004) describe how, within the context of international football (soccer) tournaments, individual members of a local society are expected to identify with their team (localization). However, at these same tournaments, there are often thousands of supporter groups from different nations who interact and

display distinctive dress, song, music, and other patterns of behavior that turn the event into a "glocal" experience.

In addition to terminology associated with globalization, several distinct forms of globalization have been proposed. See table 9.1 for the forms of globalization that De Carvalho (2010) suggests have taken hold in the world today.

Regarding the impact of all of these forms of globalization, De Carvalho refers to Friedman (2006), who, in examining the impact of the "flattening" world, argued that the world has been changed permanently by globalized trade, outsourcing, supply chaining, and various political forces. Friedman argues that the pace of globalization is quickening and will continue to have a growing impact on business organization and practice.

Finally, information that leads into the following section comes from sport management academician Lucie Thibault, who has summarized literature on globalization and identified several factors that have played a key role in the movement toward this phenomenon. These factors include "pressure from transnational corporations, international capital, neoliberal economies and right-wing governments where markets have become deregulated and trade relations among countries have increased" (Thibault, 2009, p. 2).

Globalization in a Sport Context

The slogan of the 2008 Beijing Olympics, "One World, One Dream," is very representative of the globalization occurring in sport organizations. According to SportAccord (2010),

Table 9.1 Forms of Globalization

Form	Characteristics
Economic globalization	Deregulation of commodity, capital, and labor markets
Political globalization	Emergence of transnational elite
Cultural globalization	Homogenization of cultures worldwide
Ideological globalization	Merging of similar paradigms of thought
Technological globalization	Integration of technologies throughout societies
Social globalization	Development of social networks in all sectors of society

Based on information in De Carvalho 2010.

the umbrella organization for Olympic and non-Olympic sports, 89 international sport federations and 15 organizations that conduct similar sport-related activities are currently recognized around the globe. These are other facts of interest relative to globalization and sport:

- Volleyball is the most widely played organized sport in the world with 218 national federation organizations, followed by basketball (212), track and field (211), soccer (205), and tennis (203) (World of Sport, 2013).

- The 1936 Berlin Olympic Games were broadcast by short-wave radio to 40 other countries (Toohey and Veal, 2007). In contrast, broadcast coverage of the 2010 Vancouver Winter Olympic Games was available on more than 100 websites worldwide. The television broadcast was available in over 220 territories around the world, and this was the first-ever Olympic Games to be fully covered in high-definition television (Vancouver 2010 Olympic Winter Games, 2010).

- The opening ceremony of the London 2012 Olympics was watched by an estimated global television audience of 900 million people worldwide (Ormsby, 2012). Additionally, the London Olympics have been referred to as the "first social media Olympics"; mobile devices and social networking platforms allowed around-the-clock access to results and images, which magnified and created sustained interest in athletes (Siang, 2012).

- Global spending on sport is estimated to increase by 3.7 percent a year to $145 billion by 2015, according to a study by PricewaterhouseCoopers LLP (Elser, 2011).

- "The television contract through 2010 for the English Premier League (soccer) was reported to cost broadcasters £1.7 billion and an additional £625 million for overseas rights, which is the largest overseas deal in the history of sport" (Neubauer, 2008, p. 17).

- Nike is the most valuable sport brand in the world, recognized as worth $15.9 billion in 2012 (Ozanian, 2012). Nike has over 500 factories worldwide with offices in 45 countries and sells its products to more than

20,000 retailers in the United States, with international distribution to 110 countries (aboutus.org, 2013).

Given the increasing globalization in sport, in terms of both competitive sport and global products and services, individuals preparing for leadership roles need to have a foundational knowledge of the context of globalization in sport, its impacts on sport, and the influence of sport on globalization today and potentially into the future. The purpose of the next several sections is to provide information that can serve as an initial framework for preparation for global sport leadership.

The following case analysis provides a good starting point for demonstrating elements of successful global sport organization leadership. As you read through the case, look for examples of effective leadership previously presented in this book. Then move on to the remainder of the chapter to broaden your perspective of sport leadership in a global context.

History and Increase of Globalization in Sport

Sport sociologists and historians acknowledge that sport has been pervasive throughout the world for centuries. The first recorded Olympic Games were held at Olympia in Greece in 776 B.C.; in the fourth century A.D., the Games were banned by Roman Emperor Theodosius I. They were reborn after 1,500 years, in 1896 in Athens, where athletes from 13 nations competed before a crowd of approximately 60,000 spectators (history.com, 2013). Since that time, as suggested by Maguire (1999), "it is impossible to overlook the pervasive influence of modern sport on the lives of people from different parts of the globe" (p. 1). It has been suggested by Smart (2007) that the global spread of sport federations between 1870 and the 1920s ultimately shaped the global nature of sport, and that this occurred initially through the universal standardization of playing norms, rapid growth of broadcast coverage, and improved access to remote continents by better air travel. Smart (2007, p. 6), referring to the 20th century, also noted, "As the century progressed, the commercial world drew increasingly on sport's cultural

Case Analysis

Manchester United's Global Brand and Leadership

Manchester United is identified on its website as the "World's Most Popular Football Team." It is also recognized as the most valuable sport franchise in the world, with a net worth of approximately $3 billion (Blitz, 2013). The club has demonstrated a successful evolution from provincial to national to global brand status (Hill and Vincent, 2006), has won a record 13 English Premier League titles, and has a record 11 Football Association Challenge Cup (FA Cup) titles. In May 2005, the club was bought by a U.S. businessman, Malcolm Glazer; a major reason for the takeover was proposed to be the club's position as the most prominent global brand in sport with proven worldwide appeal (Hill and Vincent, 2006). Hill and Vincent, in their research case study of Manchester United, pointed to results that highlighted the interaction among global, industry, and resource factors contributing to its success. Some of the specific factors identified by Hill and Vincent were on-field success, commercial success, and astute off-the-field management. Relative to club management off the field, Hill and Vincent's study identified these factors behind the realization of success:

- "extensive leveraging of the club's name through branded products and service that raised its market profile both nationally and internationally" (p. 214)

- "proactive marketing that takes prime advantage of industry developments that have moved English football into the global arena through worldwide media" (p. 214)

In addition to off-the-field management, a great deal of the success of the Manchester United club has been directly attributed to the leadership of Sir Alex Ferguson, manager of the club from 1986 until his retirement in 2013. Notable regarding the announcement of his retirement was its impact on the stock market; shares in Manchester United fell 4.1 percent on the following day (Blitz, 2013). In a review of Ferguson's tenure as manager of the club, Blitz points to several elements of effective leadership that contributed to its success,

including his development and management of talent and his ability to extract competitive advantage, manage boardroom relations, and ultimately build a legacy over his time as club manager and leader. Blitz recounts how Sir Alex would bring in new untried players, sometimes dumping fan favorites and changing the team's style of play. Blitz also quotes Jim O'Neill, a fan of Manchester United and chairman of Goldman Sachs Asset Management, who said of Sir Alex, "He's not scared of taking a risk and changing his mind, whether it's player purchases, tactics, or employing very different sorts of managers. He is not really bothered about getting it wrong." O'Neill also described Sir Alex as a "protector of a brand and a concept." "When situations put themselves up, he would defend the club and use it to the side's advantage." Ferguson's loyalty to the new ownership assumed by the Glazer family was also identified by Blitz as a critical component of his leadership. His loyalty during the changeover resulted in his getting virtually a free hand to demand new players. According to Blitz, Ferguson acknowledged the strong backing he received and the time that he was given to build the club in his early years. However, in Blitz's view, the new manager will not likely be afforded the same luxury of time that Sir Alex had and will "need immediate results."

Hill and Vincent (2006) note that the study of Manchester United has direct relevance to sport management with regard to "how to raise and maintain club profiles in national and global contexts; how to leverage brand names commercially to complement on-field success with off-field activities; and how to harness technology to broaden appeal" (p. 214). These authors point out how the combination of on-the-field management relative to the product and astute marketing-oriented management off the field led to the overall success of the club in a global market. "The common denominator," they say, "has been total commitment to and single-minded pursuit of excellence" (p. 214).

Based on information in Hill and Vincent 2006; Blitz 2013.

---

capital to raise the global profile and appeal of corporate brands and to expand the global markets for their products." Along with this progressive development came the continued growth of transnational companies like Nike and Adidas and an increasing sponsorship

culture related to corporate association with global sport events.

Two of the most predominant global sport entities that have been identified as primarily responsible for the global influence of sport are the International Olympic Committee and the Fédération Internationale de Football Association (FIFA). As Cronin and Holt (2003, p. 29) wrote,

> The IOC and FIFA have been the most successful advocates of a global adherence to positive aspects of sport. During the twentieth century, as formal imperialism went into decline, these two bodies became the most active advocates of globalized sport and became the new agents of an informal process of sporting imperialism. From small beginnings with limited memberships, both organizations have grown to the extent that there are few nations in the world which are not affiliated to both. (p. 29)

It is also important to recognize that many sports have benefitted from the international media exposure that originated with their appearance in the Olympics. For example, Hill and Vincent (2006) point out that sports like tennis and golf, as well as the colonial sports of cricket, rugby, squash, and badminton, have been global for decades. Other sports named by Hill and Vincent that have benefitted from international exposure include equestrian, motorsport, table tennis (Ping-Pong), boxing, hockey, ice hockey, and lacrosse. In the United States, according to these authors, sports such as basketball, American football, and baseball have also become established in foreign markets as a result of the broadening of their appeal around the world through global media.

Many sport organizations worldwide are also experiencing growing internationalism internally. For example, in the United States, roughly 20 percent of National Basketball Association (NBA) players and 28 percent of Major League Baseball (MLB) players are foreign born. Another example of internationalism is Women's National Basketball Association (WNBA) player Becky Hammon, who was originally from South Dakota and became a naturalized Russian citizen in 2008 in order to compete in the Olympics in Beijing. Additionally, many college athletic programs in the United States are experiencing increased interest from international athletes and are recruiting higher numbers of these athletes into their programs.

Sport and Its Influence on Globalization

Relative to globalization in general, sport has had a significant influence around the world, especially with regard to elite-level sport such as the Olympics and world-class international football (soccer). Chung (2010) points out that both of these organizations have larger memberships (203 and 208, respectively) than that of the United Nations in 2008. Chung notes that the Olympics and World Cup not only attract millions of people around the world to view games and matches, but also offer a platform for interaction and exchange among small nations of the world.

Another point Chung makes in relation to global accomplishment and achievement is the medal count made public through all global media sources as part of the Olympic Games. This information is important not only to athletes and teams, but also to politicians and the media as a measure of international success.

Relating sport and globalization to socioeconomic development, De Carvalho (2010) argues that sport is a part of the sustainable development in countries that enlarges people's choices and increases opportunities available to all members of society. However, according to De Carvalho, it is important for these choices and opportunities to be based on inclusion, equity, and sustainability. From a political perspective, Bairner (2001), in *Sport, Nationalism, and Globalization: European and North American Perspectives*, recognizes the close link between sporting nationalism and political nationalism whereby group identification with sport can be strongly connected to identification as a nation. Bairner also suggests that it is important to understand sport-national identity formation in order to appreciate the full complexity of nationality.

In the environment described by the examples presented here, leaders of sport organizations, especially those who operate global enterprises or work with employees or athletes from various countries, must not only recognize the powerful influence that sport can have in a global context, but must also be cognizant of the numerous potential challenges and opportunities that present themselves in a cross-cultural, multinational environment. These leaders must effectively demonstrate cultural competence and solve problems related to communications and expectations that may arise from the interactions of employees, athletes, or other organizational members in a global context. The next section outlines some of the key challenges sport leaders face as a result of globalization in sport.

On the Sidelines

In May 2013, it was announced that the National Football League (NFL) in the United States was planning to work jointly with England's Premier Rugby Limited to back the development of an innovative rugby union competition in the United States (Dart, 2013). This joint endeavor involved an initial match between an invitational U.S. team and the London Irish. The match, scheduled to take place in August 2013, was considered the initial step toward the establishment of an East Coast league in the United States that would include six teams representing cities from Boston to Miami. The first match was to occur at Gillette Stadium near Boston, and NFL Network television would broadcast the event. A return match was to be scheduled one week later and would take place in London. Dart (2013) reported that based on success of the events, the plan was to build on momentum and seek potential investors willing to pay for a new franchise and finalize deals to play future matches in NFL stadiums. Part of the plan was for the NFL Network to offer live sports on television outside of the American football season.

Based on information in Dart (2013).

Influence of Globalization on Sport: Problems and Complexities

While sport has exerted a significant influence on globalization over the last century, numerous factors associated with contemporary globalization create challenges and issues for all organizations operating in a global context. Many of these concerns are associated with mass media and technology, as well as with issues related to labor, commerce, migration, and international politics, all of which are addressed in *Globalizing Sport: How Organizations, Corporations, Media and Politics Are Changing Sports* (Sage, 2011).

Another consideration related to globalization is the constant and rapid change that is ongoing in world markets, international trade, and technological advancements in communications, science, engineering, medicine, education, and so on. To explain the impact of the speed of change, Neubauer (2008) points out that while the term globalization is in common use, what is actually meant by globalization often differs. Many researchers view globalization as having a long history; within this, the social history of mankind is seen as a long journey toward greater integration of people and places. However, a more recent perspective, which Neubauer refers to as "contemporary globalization," holds that over the last 40 to 50 years, several new structures and processes have emerged that drive this rapidly developing contemporary phenomenon. Neubauer identifies six of these dynamics as shown in table 9.2.

In relating the six dynamics presented in table 9.2 to the globalization of sport, Neubauer makes several points that I think are important for future leaders of the global sport enterprise to be aware of and consider in the strategic leadership of their organizations. Following each point are questions that warrant careful consideration relative to leadership and decision making.

- The collapse of time and space enables global sport. "The instantaneous movement of images across time and space makes possible the sense of team and athlete identification on which sport marketing depends" (p. 12). *How can sport organization leaders capitalize on this element of contemporary globalization? What ethical or professional responsibility issues does it raise?*

- The global media fully support globalization of sport by providing large sums of money to support the leagues, teams, and athletes so that they gain recognition by billions of people throughout the world. *What problems does this solve for a growing sport enterprise, and what issues does it create relative to power and decision making?*

Table 9.2 Dynamics of Contemporary Globalization

Dynamics of contemporary globalization	Description
Collapse of time and space	Technological developments in transportation and communication that have allowed such things as travel to any place on the globe within 24 hours, instantaneous communications through satellite, 24/7 currency markets, and off-shoring of many customer services.
Migration and urbanization	Many cities across the globe are experiencing massive population growth to an extent that challenges both the governmental definition of a city and the source of its authority. This growth into urban conglomerates has created factors that combine in various ways to speed up processes of social and cultural change.
Wealth creation and distribution	Globalization has contributed to an enormous growth in overall wealth, but the distribution of wealth and income has become more uneven, with a growing gap between rich and poor worldwide. Also, in the globalization era, the interdependence of financial markets can lead to dire consequences across the globe as seen in the recession of the late 2000s and the dynamics of the American housing market relative to its impact on financial instruments traded throughout the world.
Transformation and global media	The last several years have resulted in changes to the global media involving "rapid and extensive distribution of capacity and content and relative consolidation and integration of media industries" (Neubauer, 2008, p. 6). Global media companies such as Time Warner, Walt Disney, The News Corporation, Vivendi, and Comcast have become powerful transnational firms. Some argue that the size of global media companies increases their capacity to dominate, set agendas, and determine "what is being said and seen by whom, and . . . the ability of the largest firms to assure their access to the highest levels of decision making throughout the world" (Neubauer, 2008, p. 7).
Primacy of trade and consumption	Global interconnectedness and interdependence are at the core of the dynamics, interactions, and structures that are referred to as globalization. Neubauer describes this as Sassen's "circuits," made up of a "myriad of exchanges, each with a content and a flow, each with a pattern of origination and distribution. Increasingly, what we trade is what we are, and seemingly we trade everything" (p. 8).
Transformation of values	Neubauer says that "globalization has capitalized (literally) on a value shift that reorients other historically relevant values on which society has traditionally been based, values that assign status and place within communities, guide behavior, and purport to give meaning to life. The economic imperatives of globalization either act to replace such values with those of the marketplace or to diminish the relative status that non-economic values—the meaning assigned to goods—have within a nation or community's social cosmology" (p. 11).

Based on information in Neubauer 2008.

- In areas where substantial urbanization has occurred, both the concentration of wealth and the density of the population provide acceptable economic return to sport teams and, in some cases, extraordinary financial success (e.g., New York Yankees). *What implications does this have, both positive and negative, for various sport clubs and leagues worldwide?*

- As access to and use of digital technology increase in an interconnected world, this leads to uncertainty as to how digital personalized media may affect or disrupt the current business model of global media and large-scale sport. *As a leader of a transnational media company or sport organization, how would you respond strategically to this issue?*

- In a published report from the Geneva International Academic Network titled "Fair Play for Housing Rights: Mega-Events, Olympic Games and Housing: Opportunities for the Olympic Movement" (COHRE, 2007), it is alleged that as part of preparation for the Olympic Games in Beijing, over 1.25 million people were displaced from their homes. The report was disputed by an Olympic Games spokesperson, who indicated that 6,037 households were demolished to make room for venues and that generous compensation for relocation was provided to these households (Neubauer, 2008). Neubauer points out that reports and rebuttals like this represent a tension between globalization progress and disaster narratives relative to sport. *What is your perspective on this "tension" and how, as a leader, would you propose addressing these issues?*

Also related to challenges of globalization in sport, evidence of inequities still appears to exist, according to De Carvalho (2010). For example, one category of globalized sport is practiced by elite athletes and coaches in a market designated for the elite and socioeconomically privileged. These sport organizations make up a set of rich clubs with sources of bond capital or specific investors who play the game employing strategies similar to those used in their own firms. De Carvalho point out that sports such as tennis, horse racing, golf, and automobile racing, as well as football, basketball, hockey, rugby, and cricket, can be included in this classification.

De Carvalho also points to the role of globalization at a grassroots level with regard to community development. In this context, sport can be used as a tool to meet personal, national, and international development goals and to address societal challenges. De Carvalho suggests that future research in this area can explore the potential as well as the limitations of sport as it increasingly becomes a part of humanitarian and development work (which is part of globalization), as well as a component of social responsibility for corporate and private sectors.

Tensions Related to Global Sport

Despite the virtues and opportunities associated with global sport, considerable challenges and political, financial, socioeconomic, and sociocultural tensions will continue to create dilemmas that need to be addressed by current and future sport leaders. Safety of participants and spectators in countries experiencing social unrest, violence, and instability in leadership will be of paramount importance to global sport leaders. Developing

infrastructure for massive global sporting events such as the Olympics will continue to provide extraordinary financial and logistical challenges for host cities. Also, staying ahead of the technology and digital media communications curve will require additional resources as well as extreme adaptability and flexibility of sport organization leaders and members of their teams.

Beyond all this are additional tensions that warrant careful consideration as we move into the future of sport globalization. Many of these tensions and their potential influence in sport management are well communicated by Thibault (2009) in her article addressing aspects of globalization in sport as "inconvenient truths." Thibault points out that "although there are many virtues associated with the global movement in sport, globalization has not been favorable for all" (p. 4). Thibault specifically refers to four issues that must be considered relative to the globalization of sport: (1) the division of labor on an international scale as a result of transnational corporations drawing on the workforce of developing countries to manufacture sportswear and sport equipment; (2) the flow of athletes in and out of countries in which country and origin of birth do not limit where athletes can play or compete; (3) increased involvement of global media conglomerates; and (4) the environmental impact of sport. These issues represent a convergence of thought between the management approach to globalization and the sociological perspective of social and ethical responsibility. Additionally, Thibault (2009, p. 13) poses several questions that should be carefully considered by anyone preparing for or assuming a leadership role in a global context.

1. "What are we willing to give up to promote sport and the sport industry to ensure a more globally egalitarian situation with respect to sport?"

2. "Should rich professional sport leagues in developed countries invest a portion of their profits in the countries where they acquired talent for their teams or leagues?"

3. "Should sport management students and scholars be sensitized to the impact that

sport has beyond economic and financial terms of developed countries' sport teams and leagues?"

4. "How do we ensure that these students understand the impact that sport has on developing countries, on sport systems from poorer countries, on workers producing our sportswear and sport equipment?"

5. "What choices and decisions can we make as consumers, as sport participants, as teachers, as researchers, and as sport leaders to redress the imbalances that have occurred in sport as a result of globalization?"

I would suggest that the issues and questions raised by Thibault relate back to the responsibility dimension of leadership discussed in chapter 2. Professional and ethical responsibility of leadership demands that questions such as these be considered carefully by global sport leaders in addition to the focus they must place on financial results and the development of strong international and political relationships.

Another example of how sport in a global context can help overcome local tensions is provided by Jun and Lee (2012) in an article examining how globalization of sport has influenced and transformed the ways in which national identity is defined, as well as how the identity of cross-national athletes can be disseminated and marketed by the media. Using a case study approach, Jun and Lee point out how Hines Ward, MVP of Super Bowl XL, became a national sport celebrity in South Korea. The authors suggest that although Hines is only part Korean, what made him a national celebrity was an underlying social shift in the ways in which national identity and citizenship are conceptualized and defined in South Korea. They point out that new sophistication in local media relations, along with the global management and marketing of cross-national athletes, made this possible. For example, "as cultural intermediaries, South Korean journalists produced and circulated symbolic and cultural meanings of Hines Ward and, hence, established his national identity in Korea, which seemed to be conducive to his marketing and promotional values

at a local level" (p. 109). This, according to the authors, resulted in the "mediazation" of Hines Ward that occurred primarily through television, the Internet, and the local media in Korea. Ultimately, this exposure created extensive commodification of Hines Ward through various endorsements, corporate sponsorships, and commercials. Consequently, he became identified as a "cross-national" athlete and ultimately a national sport hero of Korea. Also, according the Jun and Lee, Hines Ward contributed $1M to the establishment of a foundation for the education of "half-blood" children in South Korea. Ward subsequently was granted honorary citizenship in South Korea, which was recognized by the authors as "extremely rare and remarkable" given the historical and political context of South Korea. As stated by Jun and Lee, "Although Hines Ward is a half Korean, he is by all means a foreigner with U.S. citizenship in light of South Korea's long held definition of national identity, which strictly emphasizes pure Korean blood and complete Korean ethnicity" (p. 106). However, as the authors point out, the extensive media coverage of the success of Hines Ward in Korea "awoke public awareness and social discourse of abolishing the deep-rooted racial discrimination in South Korea..." (p. 107). This case shows how globalization of sport, particularly the popularization of athletes by international media, can contribute to changes in perspectives related to local tensions.

Globalization and Sport Management Professional Development

It is important to note in this chapter that numerous national and international organizations now exist that facilitate and support sport management practice for executives, as well as the academic study of sport management. For example, Evanta, a company serving the leadership development and information-sharing needs of high-level executives, includes the Sports Leadership Institute, which was founded in 2011 to explore ways in which sport can maximize its impact on business, the community, and the overall quality of life (Sports Leadership Institute, 2013). According to its website, this institute brings together team owners, retired professional athletes, college athletic directors, and professional sport executives from around the globe to foster collaboration and share information relative to industry trends and ways in which sport can maximize its impact on society. Each year, the Sports Leadership Institute holds a global sport management summit, bringing together leaders from many high-profile sport organizations.

From an academic perspective, numerous national and international organizations provide a forum for exploring theoretical concepts and practical ideas related to sport management. These organizations offer annual conferences and opportunities for sport management faculty and students to interact and share the latest in sport industry research. The following are some of these organizations:

Continental Sport Management Associations

ALGEDE—Latin American Association for Sport Management

AASM—Asia Association for Sport Management

ASMA—African Sport Management Association

EASM—European Association of Sport Management

MASMA—Malaysian Association for Sport Management

NASSM—North American Society for Sport Management

SMAANZ—Sport Management Association of Australia and New Zealand

TASSM—Taiwan Association of Sport Management

Globalization and Leadership

This part of the chapter concerns the theoretical, research-based, and practical connections between globalization and leadership. It is important to consider information presented previously in this chapter relative to how the various aspects and examples of leadership in a global sport context can apply. The following subsections define global leadership, provide insights into key research in this area, and present information regarding global leadership competencies.

Defining Global Leadership

According to Javidan and Walker (2012), no specific definition of global leadership existed before 2004. Since that time, however, at least two definitions have surfaced and are explored here. First, the definition provided by Beechler and Javidan (2007) and cited by Javidan and Walker (2012, p. 38) identifies global leadership as "the process of influencing individuals, groups, and organizations (inside and outside the boundaries of the global organization) representing diverse cultural/political/institutional systems to help achieve the global organization's goals" (p. 38).

From a slightly different perspective, the term global leadership is defined by Holt and Seki (2012) as applicable to "anyone who operates in a context of multicultural, paradoxical complexity to achieve results in our world—where everyone is entitled to use global leadership skills" (p. 199). According to Holt and Seki, "This situation is already a reality in some companies, where all employees are expected to practice global leadership as they interface with customers and coworkers around the world. Thus global leadership is not hierarchical per se, because anyone can be a global leader" (p. 199).

While top sport executives of transnational companies, professional sport franchises, and Olympic organizations are often considered the global leaders in sport, both of the definitions presented here are consistent with the idea that contemporary leadership is often team based and can emanate from within an organization. Leadership to address global issues and challenges in sport is not, or should not be, restricted to only the highest organizational echelon. Most certainly, individuals who have knowledge, proficiency, and the desire to make an impact both within their spheres of influence and beyond should be encouraged and supported to express this leadership.

Project GLOBE

One of the most widely published and highly recognized international research projects addressing leadership in a global context was Project GLOBE. This project was initiated in 1994 to examine relationships among culture, leadership, and organizational effectiveness around the world. After 10 years of data collection and analysis, the project culminated in the publication of the book *Culture, Leadership, and Organizations: The GLOBE Study of 62 Societies* (House et al., 2004). This project was mentioned in chapter 1 in connection with the researchers' culminating definition of leadership: "the ability of an individual to influence, motivate, and enable others to contribute toward the effectiveness and success of the organizations of which they are members" (p. 15).

In the project, approximately 170 researchers from around the globe studied how both national culture and organizational culture influence members' preferences for leadership; they also identified the leader attributes and behaviors that contribute to perceptions of leader effectiveness. The study involved collecting data from over 17,000 middle managers in 951 organizations based in 62 different societal cultures. An important part of the research was to identify cultural perspectives of leadership, ascertain the leadership dimensions considered to be facilitators or impediments to leadership effectiveness, and examine the extent to which certain leadership values and practices are universal.

Following up on the original study, Javidan and coauthors (2006) used both results from the GLOBE project and hypothetical examples of what an American executive could encounter when leading a project in four different countries (Brazil, France, Egypt, and China) to suggest "cross-cultural lessons" in leadership for global executives. The remainder of this section includes a summary review of the findings from Project GLOBE, as well as some of the key practical recommendations from Javidan and colleagues, to provide insights that can be useful to sport organization leaders involved in transnational efforts.

To begin, the GLOBE project empirically verified 10 cultural clusters that exist across the world (Javidan et al., 2006, p. 70):

1. Latin America
2. Anglo
3. Latin Europe (e.g., Italy)
4. Nordic Europe
5. Germanic Europe
6. Confucian Asia
7. Sub-Saharan Africa
8. Middle East
9. Southern Asia
10. Eastern Europe

The GLOBE study also identified nine cultural dimensions that can be used to distinguish the cultures of various countries or regions relative to both cultural practices and cultural values. These nine dimensions have managerial and leadership implications and are listed and described in table 9.3.

In addition to the cultural dimensions described in table 9.3, Project GLOBE empirically identified 21 primary leadership attributes and six global leadership dimensions that were considered to be either *contributors* to or *inhibitors* of outstanding leadership (Javidan et al., 2006). The six global dimensions and brief descriptions are presented in the "Six Dimensions/Profiles of Leader Behaviors" sidebar.

Given the variability in both the cultural dimensions identified in table 9.3 and the leadership profiles in the sidebar it is obvious that managerial leaders working with or in multiple countries or cultural contexts must be cognizant of these dimensions and how they can strongly influence interpersonal and business communications as well as overall leadership practices and strategies. Javidan and colleagues (2006) point out the need to understand that acceptable management practices in one country may be totally unacceptable in another country. However, they also note from the results of the GLOBE study that cultural differences are not so vast that there are no common management or leadership practices applicable across all cultures. Data collected in the GLOBE study revealed 22 leader behaviors that were considered desirable across all countries included in the project. There were also 8 behaviors considered universally undesirable and several others considered "culturally contingent." The contingent attributes must be

Table 9.3 Nine Cultural Dimensions Recognized by the GLOBE Project

Cultural dimension	Description and examples of differences in countries
Performance orientation	Degree to which performance improvement and excellence are encouraged and rewarded among group or organizational members. The United States and Singapore score high in this area while some other countries, including Russia and Greece, tend to score low based on their preferences for family and background.
Assertiveness	Degree to which individuals display assertiveness and aggressiveness in business relationships. Cultures that enjoy competition in business such as the United States and Austria tend to be more assertive, whereas countries like Sweden and New Zealand tend to emphasize loyalty and solidarity in relationships.
Future orientation	Extent to which future-oriented behaviors like planning, investing, and delaying gratification are demonstrated. Countries like Singapore and Switzerland tend to demonstrate more planning and future-oriented practices, whereas companies in Russia and Argentina tend to be more opportunistic in their values and actions.
Humane orientation	Degree to which such things as being fair, caring, generous, and kind to others are encouraged and rewarded. Egypt and Malaysia are examples of countries that ranked high in these practices whereas countries like France and Germany tended to rank lower.
Institutional collectivism	Degree to which the collective distribution of resources is encouraged and rewarded in organizations and society. Organizations in countries including Singapore and Sweden emphasize group performance and rewards, whereas others including Greece and Brazil tend to emphasize and reward individual achievement.
In-group collectivism	Degree to which pride, loyalty, and cohesiveness are expressed in organizations or families. People in some countries, including Egypt and Russia, express pride relative to their families and the organizations in which they are employed.
Gender egalitarianism	Degree to which gender inequality is minimized. In the GLOBE study, European countries tended to score high on gender egalitarianism whereas Egypt and South Korea were highly male dominated.
Power distance	Degree to which organizational members can expect power to be distributed equally. Countries that score high on this practice tend to be more stratified economically, socially, and politically, with individuals in positions of authority expecting and receiving obedience. The GLOBE Project found that companies in countries like Thailand, Brazil, and France tend to demonstrate more hierarchical decision making with limited participation and communication.
Uncertainty avoidance	Extent to which social norms, rules, and procedures are used to alleviate unpredictability of future events. Higher scores in this area indicate that people prefer orderliness, consistency, structure, and laws to cover situations. Organizations in countries like Singapore and Switzerland tend more toward elaborate processes, procedures, and detailed strategies. Organizations in countries like Russia and Greece are more opportunistic and risk taking and prefer broadly stated strategies.

Based on information in Javidan, Dorfman, Sully de Luque, and House 2006.

considered carefully depending on the region or country where business is occurring.

Table 9.4 includes examples from Javidan and colleagues (2006) of universally accepted facilitators of leadership effectiveness, as well as universal impediments and culturally contingent leader attributes. Corresponding leadership descriptors are included in parentheses.

Discussing these results from a practical perspective, Javidan and colleagues (2006) state that leaders working in a global context must be able to demonstrate the ability to be adaptable and flexible based on cultural norms and values in the countries in which they operate. In refer-

ring to cultural adaptability, the authors point to the importance for leaders to understand other cultures and to behave in ways that not only help with goal achievement but also build strong and positive relations with the local citizens. In addition, the authors note how important it is for leaders to recognize that every new country where they work may hold a different paradigm, which requires the ability to tolerate ambiguity and learn new ideas quickly. The game plan activity at the end of this chapter provides an opportunity to explore the elements of Project GLOBE in detail relative to the development of a hypothetical leadership plan in a sport context.

Six Dimensions/Profiles of Leader Behaviors

Charismatic/Values Based

- Ability to inspire, motivate, and expect high performance outcomes from others.
- Generally contributes to outstanding leadership

Team Oriented

- Emphasizes effective team building and common purpose or goals among team members
- Generally contributes to outstanding leadership

Participative

- Degree to which managers/leaders involve others in making and implementing decisions
- Generally reported to contribute to outstanding leadership with some differences in countries

Humane Oriented

- Leadership that reflects support, consideration, compassion, and generosity

- Considered neutral in some societies and moderately contributing to outstanding leadership in others

Autonomous

- Refers to degree of independent and individualistic leadership
- Considered to impede outstanding leadership in some cultures and to slightly facilitate outstanding leadership in others

Self-Protective

- Focuses on self-centered and face-saving behavior that ensures the safety and security of the individual
- Generally considered to impede outstanding leadership

Based on information in Javidan, Dorfman, Sulley de Luque, and House (2006).

Table 9.4 Cultural Views of Leadership Effectiveness

Facilitators and impediments to effectiveness	Associated leadership characteristics
Universal facilitators of leadership effectiveness	• Being trustworthy, just, and honest (integrity) • Having foresight and planning ahead (charismatic-visionary) • Being positive, dynamic, encouraging, motivating, and building confidence (charismatic-inspirational) • Being communicative and informed, a coordinator, and team integrator (team builder)
Universal impediments to leadership effectiveness	• Being a loner and asocial (self-protective) • Being noncooperative and irritable (malevolent) • Being dictatorial (autocratic)
Culturally contingent endorsement of leader attributes	• Being individualistic (autonomous) • Being status conscious (status conscious) • Being a risk taker (charismatic III: self-sacrificial)

Adapted from Javidan et al. 2006.

Global Mindset for Leadership

In 2012, Javidan and Walker published an article recognizing that traditional leadership development is not sufficient for the current globalization of business. The authors argue that global leaders of the 21st century must have more knowledge relative to navigating cultural management and the complexities of recruitment that are associated with globalization.

Additionally, Javidan and Walker suggest that an effective "global mindset" better allows leaders to influence people who are different from themselves: "Global leaders need to influence individuals, teams and organizations from different parts of the world to help achieve their organizations' objectives. And they need to do this without relying on traditional lines of authority" (p. 39).

While agreeing that leadership is about influencing others, Javidan and Walker point out that the key difference between "leadership" and "global leadership" is the capability to "influence others unlike yourself" (p. 38). To arrive at what they consider the three major constructs of a global mindset, the authors provide an overview of the Global Mindset Project (GMP) that started in late 2004 at the Thunderbird School of Global Management. In this project, a team of eight professors reviewed literature on global and cross-cultural leadership; conducted interviews with 26 professors considered experts in global business; and interviewed 217 global executives in the United States, Europe, and Asia. In addition, an invitation-only conference was convened to bring in over 40 academic experts from around the world to "test, stretch and refine" their thinking about global leadership. The process allowed the research team to identify the scope and components of the concept of

global mindset. The team then worked with a renowned instrument design group to empirically verify the construct of global mindset and to scientifically design an instrument that would measure an individual's global mindset profile. This involved conducting surveys and pilot tests with more than 200 MBA students and more than 700 managers working for two Fortune 500 corporations. The work resulted in a construct of global mindset that included three major dimensions: (a) intellectual capital, (b) psychological capital, and (c) social capital. The subelements of each of these areas are shown in figure 9.1, and descriptions and examples of each are provided in tables 9.5, 9.6, and 9.7.

In addition to all of the characteristics, abilities, and skills identified by Javidan and Walker, the research project revealed several other factors that are predictors of a high global mindset in individuals. These include (a) proficiency in more than one language; (b) number of countries in which one has lived, studied, and worked; (c) possession of an international graduate degree; (d) age (executives and officials in the low 40s to mid-50s had *lower* mean scores than older individuals on global

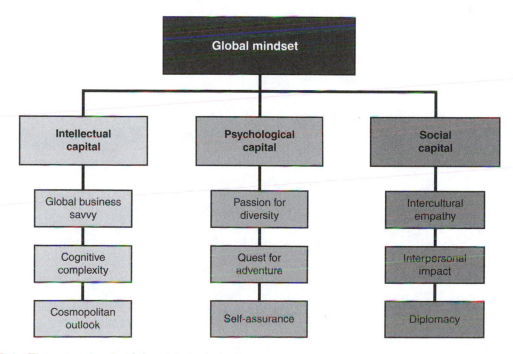

Figure 9.1 Three constructs of the global mindset.

Reprinted by permission, from M. Javidan and J.L. Walker, 2012, "A whole new global mindset for leadership," *People and Strategy* 35(2): 36-41.

Table 9.5   Construct of Intellectual Capital in Global Mindset

Construct	Building blocks	Examples
Intellectual capital Refers to leader's knowledge of global surroundings and ability to digest and leverage additional level of complexity involved in work in global environments	*Global business savvy* Knowledge of the way world business works	Knowledge of: Global industry, global marketing strategies, conducting business in other parts of the world, important world events
	Cognitive complexity Recognition that global is more complicated than domestic only	Ability to: Grasp complex concepts quickly, understand abstract ideas, take complex issues and be able to make them simple and understandable
	Cosmopolitan outlook Understanding that home country of manager is not the center of the universe	Knowledge of: Cultures in different parts of the world; geography, history, and important persons in other countries; economic and political issues in major regions of the world

Based on information in Javidan and Walker 2012.

Table 9.6   Construct of Psychological Capital in Global Mindset

Construct	Building blocks	Examples
Psychological capital Refers to the "affective" aspect of global mindset; this dimension helps managers leverage the construct of intellectual capital	*Passion for diversity* Not just tolerating or appreciating diversity, but thriving on it	Interest in exploring and getting to know people in other parts of the world, interest in variety and living in another country
	Quest for adventure The "Marco Polos" of the world	Interest in dealing with challenging situations, willingness to take on risks and test one's abilities, interest in dealing with unpredictable situations
	Self-assurance Source of psychological resilience and coping	Energetic, self-confident, comfortable, and witty in uncomfortable and tough situations

Based on information in Javidan and Walker 2012.

Table 9.7   Construct of Social Capital in Global Mindset

Construct	Building blocks	Examples
Social capital The behavioral aspect of global mindset; this dimension reflects an individual's ability to act in ways that build trusting relationships with people around the world	*Intercultural empathy* Displaying "global" emotional intelligence	Ability to work well with people from other parts of the world, understand nonverbal expressions of people from other cultures, emotionally connect to people from other cultures, engage people from around the world to work together
	Interpersonal impact Making a difference and seldom ignored across boundaries	Experience negotiating contracts in other cultures, develop strong networks with people from other cultures; reputation and credibility as a leader
	Diplomacy Seeks to understand before seeking to be understood	Ability and willingness to start conversations easily with a stranger, integrate diverse perspectives, listen carefully to what others have to say, collaborate with others

Based on information in Javidan and Walker 2012.

mindset, although most senior executives and government officials are in this age group).

The information in this section can be useful to current and future sport organizational leaders with the desire to work in a global leadership role. I suggest that carefully examining each of the constructs, building blocks, and examples in tables 9.5 through 9.7—and also considering your profile relative to the predictors of effective global mindset—would be an excellent starting point for preparing for or improving your current level of proficiency relative to global leadership.

Global Leadership Competencies and Behaviors

This final section of the chapter provides additional thoughts that can be related back to the results, relationships, and responsibility components of chapter 2. Expectations to produce tangible desired outcomes will become even higher in the future and will be a primary factor in success or failure for global sport leaders. This will be particularly true for leaders conducting business in transnational corporations, professional sport, and Olympic sport. However, high performance results will not occur or will not be sustainable if leaders neglect the critical importance of demonstrating inclusionary and effective interpersonal communications and professional relationships. Additionally, demonstrating consistent and principled leadership as well as professional and ethical responsibility to the industry, the environment, and humanity will be vital to overall global leadership effectiveness.

As discussed throughout this chapter, success in the complex and changing global sport business environment will require astute, flexible, and culturally competent leaders. These leaders not only must be cognizant of the multiple factors influencing performance and outcomes, but also must be agile in mobilizing people and resources quickly to take advantage of emerging opportunities in the world to come. This will require increased understanding of the global leadership challenges, a developmental shift, and development and improvement in key global leadership competencies. Additional research and writing

in each of these areas are summarized in the following pages.

First, to gain more insights into global leadership challenges and responsibilities from within the ranks of practicing leaders, Thorn (2012) interviewed 12 top executives from international financial and development institutions. These leaders identified the following primary challenges that they see facing global leaders:

- "Coping with the speed of interrelated international events and crises, including the speed of technology;"
- "Managing and leading in the growing complexity of a global society;"
- "Managing the instability and gap between world poverty and the rich;"
- "Becoming more adaptable and flexible in creating, accepting, and adapting to change;"
- "Maintaining a vision that incorporates people from different cultures;"
- "Recognizing the decline of nation states and boundaries" (Thorn, 2012, p. 160).

Additionally, the author and the leaders interviewed in the study made several points that reinforce elements of effective leadership mentioned previously in this chapter and throughout the book, with implications for developmental competencies for global leaders:

- Developmental competencies for global leaders included in this study include: "strategic vision, adaptability, fostering teamwork, creating open communications, and building relationships" (p. 161).
- "There was a strong view that leaders would need to strive to create a more generous (caring) society. [It was] felt that leaders of international organizations had a moral obligation, or a social responsibility, to the world at large" (p. 160).
- "International organizations are reported to be highly structured and bureaucratic environments in need of transformation" (p. 159).
- "Executives believe that developing leaders is the most important human resource issue for achieving global success" (p. 159).

Another important perspective on leadership competencies and the developmental shift taking place relative to leadership in a global context was recently offered by Holt and Seki (2012). These authors believe that a "huge shift is underway that will ultimately define all leaders as global leaders. This shift is blurring the distinction between leadership and global leadership due to the global complexity of the business and cultural context where leaders operate" (p. 198).

Holt and Seki point out from a practical reality perspective that global leaders have unique challenges and are especially busy people. They are often required to communicate across time zones, have to speak and read e-mail in other languages, and may have to spend anywhere from 8 to 20 hours traveling to corporate meetings. The authors suggest that global leaders today must operate in a context of multicultural, paradoxical complexity and argue that four distinct developmental shifts are required. These are listed and described in table 9.8.

In another study designed to examine how global leaders differ from domestic leaders and to identify what effective global leaders have in common, Gundling, Hogan, and Cvitkovich (2011) interviewed 70 international executives from 14 major organizations in different industries across North America, Europe, Asia, and the Middle East. An over-riding consensus among those interviewed was that, while global leaders carry out tasks similar to those of leaders in any location, they must also be able to shift their personal styles, strategies, and business processes to fit the various cultural environments in which they work. Based on the results of the study, Gundling and coauthors proposed that there are 10 global leadership behaviors that need to occur in five dimensions: (1) seeing differences, (2) closing the gap, (3) opening the system, (4) preserving balance, and (5) establishing solutions. The authors propose that each of the 10 behaviors (two in each of the five dimensions) should be used by global leaders to help move organizations toward constructive solutions while also maximizing the engagement of their global employees (see table 9.9). Readers are encouraged to explore the work of Gundling and colleagues in more depth for specific global leadership examples and potential applications of this information.

Summary

This chapter provides insights intended to set a foundational structure for individuals who are or may in the future be assuming global sport leadership roles. It is evident that the pace of globalization is increasing rapidly each year and will likely continue to do so into

Table 9.8 Developmental Shifts Necessary for Effective Global Leadership

Development shifts	Descriptions
Developing multicultural effectiveness (MCE)	While this is a primary area of responsibility for global leaders, it is not well understood in the research. Several challenges have been identified, including multiple tools and models used to assess MCE, inadequate validation research, and lack of performance measures in some intercultural research tools. Improvements will be necessary to assist in the developmental shift necessary for effective global leadership in this domain.
Becoming adept at managing paradoxes	Global leaders have the ability to manage contradiction between elements (e.g., being process oriented while also sensitive to the needs of people, firm while also flexible, disciplined while also entrepreneurial).
Cultivating the "being" dimension of human experience	Global leaders have exceptionally busy jobs that require them to be more mindful about their energetic presence based on who they are and not just what they do. They must be "'present in the moment' and pay attention to their being even while many strategic and operational priorities clamor for their attention" (p. 206).
Appreciating individual uniqueness in the context of cultural differences	Global leaders recognize the critical importance of eliminating stereotypes and learn to pay attention to the true uniqueness of other individuals. This includes the ability to focus on people, not just the job they do, and to try to understand the cultural groups they belong to.

Based on information in Holt and Seki 2012.

Table 9.9 Stages of Global Leadership and Leadership Behaviors

Stages of global leadership	Associated leadership behaviors
Seeing differences	*Cultural self-awareness:* Recognition that leadership practices are shaped by our environments and that there is more than one viable way to get things done. *Invite the unexpected:* Leaders process many stimuli on a daily basis and use mental models (images of reality based on experience) to help hone in on important facts and develop responses to the matters at hand. However, global leaders need to learn to suspend their mental models so as not to miss critical data that are not part of the normal routine.
Closing the gap	*Results through relationships:* Leaders must recognize that the doorway to getting things done in a global context is through effective relationship building. It is emphasized that building strong relationships typically comes before addressing work tasks. *Frame shifting:* Ability to shift perspectives and methods to fit the appropriate cultural context.
Opening the system	*Expand ownership:* Involves creating a sense of engagement in shared processes and accountability for setting and achieving target goals of both local and global significance. *Develop future leaders:* Identifying and cultivating high-potential leaders from anywhere in a global organization who can help provide leadership for future global growth.
Preserving balance	*Adapt and add value:* Ability to balance a change agenda with local practices and perspectives. This involves learning to use self-awareness, heightened sense of judgment, and restraint adapted to local circumstances. *Core values and flexibility:* Establishing an internal balance between the core values held by the leader and the flexibility to adapt to the personal and organizational values of foreign colleagues.
Establishing solutions	*Influence across boundaries:* Involves creating solutions without having direct authority, which involves diplomacy and political acumen. *Third-way solutions:* Draw on all of the behaviors previously mentioned to bring everything together into real business solutions.

Based on information in Gundling, Hogan, and Cvitkovich 2011.

Your Thoughts

Consider the stages of effective global leadership and the associated behaviors proposed by Gundling, Hogan, and Cvitkovich (2011). Do research on one or more of the following global sport leaders and determine where you think these individuals most demonstrate elements of these stages and behaviors:

- Jacques Rogge, president of IOC
- Heidi Ueberroth, president, International Business Operations for the NBA
- Mark Parker, president and CEO, Nike, Inc.
- Lesa France Kennedy, CEO, International Speedway Corporation
- Daniel E. Doyle Jr., founder and chair for the Institute for International Sport
- Stacey Allaster, chairman and CEO, World Tennis Association

future decades. Sport leaders must recognize that sport organizations both contribute to and are strongly influenced by globalization. It will be critical in the future for these leaders to have a strong framework of "global knowledge" and "global leadership" skills to guide them into this realm. The chapter includes examples of challenges facing global sport leaders relative to increasing complexity, rapid advances in technology and global communications, leading individuals and teams from different cultures, and recognizing and responding to social issues and tensions that can result from globalization in sport. It also includes specific models, examples, and evidence from international research of consistently identified elements of effective leadership in a global context. The information in this chapter is intended to serve as a guide and resource toolkit for those preparing to be effective global sport leaders of the future.

Final Self-Assessment

The self-assessment at the beginning of the chapter involved assessing your knowledge and experiences relative to your preparation for becoming a global sport leader. Unless you have had opportunities to be in a global leadership role, you may not have had direct experience at this point in time. This chapter provides information that hopefully has given you an opportunity to improve your overall knowledge of the challenges and opportunities in global sport leadership and also given you insights into knowledge and behaviors that you might improve in preparing to assume a leadership role.

Given your reading and study of this chapter, what has most affected your thoughts about global leadership? What problems and tensions related to globalization do you think will continue to affect sport, and how might they be dealt with more effectively in the future? What would be your list of priorities, if you were given an international assignment with a sport company or organization, based on your knowledge of the information provided in this chapter?

Game Plan Activity

Assume that you have just been hired as the new executive director of marketing and sales for an extreme sport equipment company located in your home country. You have been assigned a role to direct the expansion of the business into another country. The country you select for this activity should be one whose cultural values, norms, and business practices you currently have minimal knowledge of. You have been given authority to hire an assistant director and a marketing staff to execute the new business plan in this country. What you have been tasked to accomplish with this team is to evaluate the foreign market in the country, introduce the company products, establish a market presence, and work to set and achieve sales goals appropriate to the situation.

For this assignment, prepare a leadership project plan that includes the following elements:

1. A demographic and psychographic analysis of the country selected.

2. An analysis of the nine cultural dimensions recognized by Project GLOBE (see table 9.3). This should be the part of the plan that identifies what approaches to business will be most appropriate in the cultural context of the country.

3. A plan for the type(s) of individuals (relative to leadership attributes and skills) you will want to hire to your team. Indicate specific positions and whether you will plan to hire people from your home country, the country in which you will be doing business, or both. (Refer to the sidebar "Six Dimensions/Profiles of Leader Behaviors" for information on the six global leadership dimensions identified by the Project GLOBE study.)

4. A list and explanation of what you think will be the three to five most critical elements of leadership necessary to meet the goals of this project.

Questions to Consider

1. Choose a recent event or occurrence in sport from around the world that you think represents sociocultural, political, or economic tension created by globalization. What elements of effective global leadership do you think could be incorporated to lessen the tensions created by this situation?

2. In what ways do you feel that the growth of social media in the last several years has contributed positively or negatively to global sport?

3. What elements of the global mindset presented in this chapter do you think are essential for you to further develop if you decide to pursue a leadership role in a global sport organization?

4. Reflect on the "inconvenient truths" about global sport suggested by Thibault (2009) and presented in this chapter. What do you consider the most pressing and challenging issues that must be addressed in order to effectively demonstrate responsible global sport leadership in the future?

Recommended Readings

Giulianotti, R., and Robertson, R. (2007). *Globalization and sport*. Hoboken, NJ: Wiley-Blackwell.

Sage, G. (2011). *Globalizing sport: How organizations, corporations, media, and politics are changing sport*. Boulder, CO: Paradigm.

Westerbrook, H., and Smith, A. (2003). *Sport business in the global marketplace*. Basingstoke, UK: Palgrave Macmillan.

Developing Sport Leaders of the Future

Part III consists of chapters 10 and 11. Chapter 10 shifts to information intended to assist students in understanding more about the process of leadership learning and development. This chapter includes recent research and practical recommendations on individual self-directed leadership development, mentoring, experiential-based action learning, and new trends in leadership development through technology-based training media. The book concludes with chapter 11, which provides future considerations for leadership and an introduction to the concept of sport organizations as learning organizations. Several brief case studies representative of current and future challenges for sport leaders are included in chapter 11 to provide opportunity to apply many of the concepts presented throughout the book toward potential solutions to these issues.

Leadership Learning and Development

Learning Objectives

After reading and reflecting on the concepts and examples in this chapter, you will be able to

1. discuss why it is argued that leaders can be developed through various approaches;

2. identify and describe ways in which leadership learning occurs;

3. define and give examples of what is meant by leadership education, leadership training, and leadership development;

4. explain three purposes served by leadership development in organizations;

5. identify several types of leadership-related self-assessment instruments and describe the strengths and problems associated with 360-degree feedback processes;

6. define and describe mentoring as an approach to leadership development;

7. discuss and give examples of leadership development through experience and employer-based "action learning"; and

8. describe future trends in leadership development including technology-based training.

Self-Assessment

1. Reflect on experiences you have had, related to one or more of the previous chapters in this book, that you think have most contributed to your own leadership development.

2. What are elements of effective leadership learning?

3. What is your current knowledge of self-directed leadership development, 360-degree feedback, mentoring, action learning, and leadership succession planning?

4. If you are not currently in a top leadership role, how prepared do you feel to assume that role and what leadership development opportunities do you think would be helpful in preparation for that role?

The preceding chapters have provided insights about the many theories related to leadership style and behaviors and also addressed elements of leadership important to different organizational functions and situations in sport (e.g., strategy, problem solving, change, turnaround, crisis, diversity). What has not been addressed is the question, "How does one learn to become a better leader?" Certainly, having a foundational textbook knowledge of leadership is an important component, but what about the role of continuing professional development and advancement by means of in-the-trenches (on-the-job) experience, self-development, and professional advancement through other forms of training and development?

> *It may make more sense to say that in the present world, leadership is not learned but rather that it is learning.*
>
> Brown and Posner
> (2001, p. 3)

This chapter begins by providing the perspectives of leadership experts Howard Gardner and Jay Conger in relation to their beliefs that leadership is something that can be developed in individuals. The next section examines some basic ideas and research addressing questions associated with how we learn to lead. Following this is discussion of the concept of "leadership learning"; assumptions associated with learning; and the terms leadership education, leadership training, and leadership development.

The chapter then addresses concepts and ideas and presents various examples of leadership learning and development and its potential applications for sport organizations. Areas of emphasis in this section are (a) self-development, specifically related to available instruments that empirical research supports as helpful to self-awareness; (b) mentoring; and (c) learning through on-the-job experience, use of action learning projects, and leadership succession planning. The chapter concludes with some of the newest thoughts on leadership development by examining developmental readiness, authentic leadership, and the use of technology to provide web-based training, along with the use of "trigger events" that can result in short "micro training" sessions available immediately through mobile technology.

Perspectives on Leadership Development

This section introduces two perspectives from well-known leadership experts indicating their firm convictions that leadership can be developed and that it is not something to which only a few select individuals are capable. Throughout history, many people with varying personalities, backgrounds, education, ages, race, ethnicity, and social status have assumed or attained leadership roles. Howard Gardner (1995), in his book *Leading Minds*, identifies and discusses four factors that he suggests are at the foundation of leadership: (1) a sense of self or group identification based on beliefs, attitudes, and values; (2) the mind of a five-year-old who already recognizes elements of leading and following and who is full of wonder and is imaginative; (3) attainment of expertise in one or more disciplines or domains; and (4) expertise in the realm of people, which is simply described as the ability to understand other persons. All of these are areas that people can recognize and improve in themselves.

In Gardner's 1990 book, *On Leadership*, he dismissed the often made assumption that leaders are born, not made, and suggested that leaders can be developed and that leadership development can occur on a scale beyond anything we have attempted. Gardner's belief more than 20 years ago was that many people in society have untapped leadership capabilities or have not understood the need that society has for what they can offer. Gardner also suggests that leadership development is essentially a lifelong process that involves continued learning.

Jay Conger, recognized worldwide as an authority on leadership training and development, asserts that leaders are both born *and* made (Conger, 2004). Using research findings to support his claims, Conger suggests that on-the-job experience, work on special projects, and participation in assignments assist people in learning about building and leading teams. Conger says that leadership development has been found to have greater impact when it is customized around specific needs of those receiving training, and that programs considered rigorous and disciplined typically produce more leadership talent.

A point emphasized by Conger was that previous academic study of leadership had produced primarily normative models of leadership, which make the assumption that one of the many existing models (e.g., charismatic, emotional intelligence based, or transformational) is best across all situations. According to Conger, given the many different situations encountered by leaders, the ability to develop versatility and adaptability of style may be what is most needed but most difficult to develop. He suggests that this will continue to be one of the more challenging aspects of leadership development programs. Based on many of the important points identified by Gardner and Conger, the next sections focus on how we can improve knowledge, skills, and abilities of current and prospective leaders in our field.

How Do We Learn to Lead?

Research over the last couple of decades has attempted to answer this question by conducting case studies as well as interviewing or surveying hundreds of executives, midlevel managers, and other people in leadership roles. The key foundational studies in this area include those of Kouzes and Posner (1995), Zemke (1985), and McCall, Lombardo, and Morrison (1988). What this research collectively reports is that the key sources of learning to lead include a combination of experiential components (e.g., observation, trial and error, job assignments, communication with others, hardships endured) and formal and informal education and training programs.

Another area of study—one that goes beyond just identifying the sources of learning that help prepare better leaders—is aimed at advancing understanding about the actual relationship between learning tactics and improved leadership behaviors and actions. In an exploratory investigation addressing these factors, Brown and Posner (2001) studied 312 participants of an MBA program that included midlevel managers of a technology company, working professionals across a variety of technology organizations, and managers enrolled in the executive MBA program. Participants were asked to complete two inventories: the Learning Tactics Inventory (LTI) (Dalton et al., 1999) and the Leadership Practices Inventory (LPI) (Kouzes and Posner, 1997). The LTI examines participants' responses relative to the extent to which they report using each of four approaches as tactics to learn:

1. Action (trial and error)
2. Thinking (reading articles and books)
3. Feeling (e.g., self-reflection about worries)
4. Accessing others (talking about hopes and fears with someone who is trusted)

On the other side of the equation, the LPI scale used in the study focuses on the key constructs of the Kouzes and Posner leadership model and measures the extent to which participants indicate that they engage in each of the following five transformational leadership behaviors:

1. Challenging the process—seeking out opportunities to test skills and abilities
2. Inspiring a shared vision—describing a compelling image of the future
3. Enabling others to act—developing cooperative relationships
4. Modeling the way—setting a personal example of what is expected
5. Encouraging the heart—praising others for jobs well done

In Brown and Posner's study, results of the correlational analysis between these scales indicated that each of the learning tactics was significantly correlated with each of the learning practices. Detailed analysis of the data revealed that respondents frequently using any of the four learning tactics also reported engaging more frequently in the transformational leadership behaviors. While these results are not conclusive and are preliminary, allowing limited generalization based on the sample, the study calls for more research to further examine the relationships between learning approaches to leadership and leadership behaviors, processes, and outcomes.

Brown and Posner (2001) suggest from their results that approaches to leadership development need to attempt to reach leaders at a personal and emotional level that triggers self-reflection and can provide support for creating learning and leadership mindsets. Regarding other forms of learning leadership, Brown and Posner point out that more than two decades of research underscores that the majority of leadership skills are actually learned from naturally occurring experiences in the workplace. They also suggest that the ultimate act of leadership development is the creation of a culture of leadership and learning in an organization.

As of yet, studies specifically examining how leadership development or leadership learning occurs in sport organizations have not been attempted. Questions that arise regarding this area of potential study include "Are there unique contextual factors within sport organizations that influence how one would go about learning to lead in that environment?" and "What forms of leadership development are taking place in sport organizations, and are they producing the desired outcomes?"

Leadership Learning Applied

It is important to consider at this point in the evolution of leadership study that leadership is generally approached as a *process* that is capable of being learned. This goes back to trait theory as discussed in earlier chapters and the question of whether or not individuals possess inherent traits that naturally predispose them to be leaders. However, as stated by McCall (2010), "Even if some leaders are 'born,' there clearly aren't enough such gifted people to go around, and we need all the help we can get" (p. 705). It is also important to remember, as suggested by Allen and Roberts (2011), that "leadership learning is not simply a laundry list of programs, services and resources. Instead, it is an outcome of purposefully designed and integrated experiences that foster the development of human capacity for positive change" (p. 69). Allen and Roberts also offer thoughts and basic assumptions about leadership that relate to how leadership is improved through learning. See the following list for assumptions about leadership learning.

Leadership can be developed to some extent in all people.

- Leadership that will be most important in the twenty-first century is about adaptivity and solving adapted challenges.
- Leadership requires a focus by both leaders and followers on self-exploration and individual development.
- Leadership is contextual and involves relationships among leaders, followers, and context.
- Leadership is not position dependent. People step into and out of leadership roles when moving the organization's work forward.
- Leadership is a combination of personal attributes, practices, position, and purpose.

Based on Allen and Roberts 2011.

Allen and Roberts (2011) define some terms related to leadership learning that provide a good foundation for much of the information covered in the remainder of this chapter. Read these definitions and consider how each term, while similar to the others, represents a slightly different component of the leadership learning process:

- **Leadership education:** "A series of training interventions designed to enhance the knowledge, skills, and abilities of individuals interested in engaging in leadership" (p. 67). This domain typically refers to college courses, professional seminars, and so on.
- **Leadership training:** "Activities designed to develop an individual or group's ability to perform practical skills that facilitate effective leadership" (p. 66). Leadership training is typically focused on individuals who are already in leadership positions.
- **Leadership development:** "A continuous, systematic process designed to expand the capacities and awareness of individuals, groups and organizations in an effort to meet shared goals and objectives" (p. 67). Development may occur for both new and existing leaders.

In relation to these definitions, it is important to note a recommendation that Conger (2004) had made previously, pointing to the need for more research on whether managers and leaders have sufficient versatility of behavior to shift leadership styles in changing situations and contexts. This was based on the idea that leaders of modern complex organizations must have the versatility to adapt their behaviors as needed in their organizations. Certainly, if developing leaders through learning is something we believe is both possible and necessary to the future of our organizations, it will be important to consider how we address Conger's concerns across all levels of leader education, training, and development.

Planning and Implementing Leadership Development

In sport, while bringing in a new executive director, general manager, or head coach from the outside may at times be necessary, it is not always desirable or even feasible to replace everyone with a leadership role in an organization by bringing in a whole new team. Given the complexities and challenges of modern sport organizations, as well as the challenge of operating within financial constraints, it is important for organizations to invest in and develop leadership talent from within.

Thus, well-planned and well-executed leadership development within sport organizations is suggested as an essential follow-up to classroom learning on the topic. This development should include responsibilities on both the organization and on the individual desiring to be in a leadership role. Many of today's organizations have a flat or even a round organizational structure, and this will be the case in the future. It is likely that more and more individuals will assume leadership roles for various projects or situations but may not carry the formal title or position typically associated with leadership (e.g., executive director, president, GM, AD, head coach). Consequently, leadership development for sport organizations should not be thought of only as a succession planning exercise for a relatively few top-level positions; organizations need to consider preparing a variety of people for leadership roles they may assume.

As suggested by McCauley, Kanaga, and Lafferty (2010), developing organizational leaders involves enhancing their performance, improving their ability to lead congruently with chang-

ing realities, and expanding their capacity to move into higher organizational positions.

McCauley and colleagues recognize three different purposes that are served by leader development:

1. **Performance improvement:** May involve special training for first-time supervisors or the development of a performance management process to help new leaders develop plans for individual improvement

2. **Succession management:** Recognizes the need to identify and develop a strong "bench" or pipeline of high-potential leaders and provide them with opportunities to grow.

3. **Organizational change:** Many organizations, because of the need to constantly adapt in order to remain competitive, use strategies of new acquisition, tap into emerging markets, explore innovation, become global, or look at new ways to become more efficient. These changes often require new competencies and skills from leaders that may include targeted development programs and changes in the competency models and reward systems.

The next several subsections provide more specific information regarding leadership learning related to self-development, 360-degree feedback, mentoring, learning through experience, employer-based training, action learning, and leadership succession planning. A key component of overall leadership learning is that which occurs through a combination of self-development and the training that can be provided by an individual's organization. We also know from empirical research that quality experience is an important factor in leadership learning.

In some sport organizations, as well as organizations in other fields, formal leadership training provided by employers is completely absent and individuals must rely purely on self-development through online resources, reading from the hundreds of books and practical articles available in their area, deciphering academic research articles, attending university or continuing education classes, or what they pick up informally through on-the-job experiences. While these developmental activities can certainly be beneficial to some degree, it is important to note that many of the self-help books and guides, as well as formal training programs, have few or no valid empirical findings that link the developmental training and activities to actual leader or organizational performance outcomes. The next few sections present ideas and recommendations and discuss areas of leadership development and succession planning for which there is at least some level of research-based as well as practical evidence and support regarding their benefits.

Self-Development

A common approach to self-development in leadership is for people to gain a better understanding of themselves in areas related to personality, emotional intelligence, authentic leadership, and transformational leadership. This approach typically involves the use of self-rating instruments and focused reflection on occurrences or situations that one has experienced relative to leadership. Often, it is also necessary to obtain the perspective of those with whom the leader interacts so that

the followers' perspectives can be taken into consideration. It is not uncommon for a leader's self-perception to be different from those of followers, and both perspectives are often useful for growth and development of leaders. Table 10.1 lists and describes assessment instruments that are commonly used in research as well as for executive training and other developmental purposes. Several of these instruments are available only through purchase. These instruments all provide insights that may be helpful in improving and implementing components of self-understanding as part of leadership development.

360-Degree Feedback

What is known as 360-degree feedback has become an increasingly common way for managers and leaders to obtain feedback from their supervisors and peers and from employees who report to them. In this approach, also known as multirater feedback, a sample of these individuals are asked to complete an anonymous instrument or form on which they rate the manager or leader in several competency areas. The individual being rated also completes the

Table 10.1 Examples of Self-Rating Instruments Related to Leadership

Self-rating instrument	Description
Meyers-Briggs Type Indicator (MBTI) (meyersbriggs.org)	Commonly used personality assessment instrument that measures self-perceptions related broadly to the degree to which an individual demonstrates *extraversion* or *introversion*, along with the extent to which a person is *sensing, intuitive, thinking,* or *feeling*.
Keirsey Temperament Sorter (KTS-II) (keirsey.com)	Claimed to be the world's leading assessment for individuals, teams, and organizations (keirsey.com), the instrument addresses the extent to which individuals rate themselves in the categories of *artisans* (concrete and pragmatic), *guardians* (concrete and cooperative, *idealists* (abstract and cooperative), or *rational* (abstract and pragmatic).
Emotional Intelligence—EQ-I$^{2.0}$ (hpsys.com)	Instrument that identifies five domains and 15 subscales that interact to predict an individual's behaviors. The five domains are self-perception, self-expression, interpersonal skills, decision making, and stress management.
Authentic Leadership Questionnaire (ALQ) (mindgarden.com)	Leadership survey instrument that measures the components proposed to constitute authentic leadership. These components are self-awareness, transparency, ethical/moral, and balanced processing.
Multifactor Leadership Questionnaire (MLQ) (Bernard Bass and Bruce Avolio) (mindgarden.com)	Widely recognized instrument for measuring transformational leadership. Instrument measures leadership styles, including passive style, leadership based on contingent reward, and transformational leadership behaviors, and can be used for both self-rating and rating by others.
Leadership Orientations (Lee Bolman and Terrence Deal) (leebolman.com)	Brief self-rating instrument that examines leadership orientations in four frames: structural, human resource, political, and symbolic.

rating tool, and comparisons are then made between the self-rating and the rating offered by the others.

While 360-degree feedback is used widely across Fortune 500 companies and provides information that can be very helpful in making managers or leaders more aware of their strengths and weaknesses, several limitations and problems are also associated with this approach.

Nowack (2009) provides suggestions for how 360-degree feedback processes can leverage multirater feedback to improve behavioral change, but also points out that this type of feedback is a modest intervention that when poorly administered can potentially be emotionally harmful. Nowack (2010) identifies several common issues with 360-degree feedback processes along with recommendations for evidence-based practices that can help

ensure more effective feedback results (see the sidebar 360-Degree Feedback Processes: Issues and Recommendations). Sport leaders who consider using these types of tools as an element of leadership development should be aware of both the challenges and limitations of 360-degree feedback, as well as the positives, that is, how it can lead to behavioral change if used properly.

Mentoring and Leadership Development

A common approach to leadership development in many organizations is through mentoring. Conger and Riggio (2006) define "mentors" in the traditional way as individuals with advanced knowledge and experience who make active efforts to support the development and upward mobility of a junior individual's career.

360-Degree Feedback Processes: Issues and Recommendations

Issues with 360-Degree Feedback Approach

- Often not evaluated for reliability or to ensure usefulness to respondents.
- Measure competencies that are highly correlated with each other which makes it difficult to determine specific areas for development.
- Correlations both within and between rater groups (e.g. direct reports, supervisor, peers) are modest making it difficult to interpret properly.
- Individuals who underestimate their skills likely use 360 feedback results to focus more on what they are not doing well than on their strengths.
- Most 360 interventions can improve awareness of perceived strengths and weaknesses, but lack accountability for developmental planning toward behavior change.
- Feedback interventions are often not integrated with HR systems thus minimizing the impact of change on individuals, groups, and teams.

Evidence Based Practices to Ensure Effective 360-Degree Feedback Results

- Clarify the purpose of the feedback, who will receive it and who is accountable for planning developmental action based on results.
- Have an internal or external consultant provide facilitated feedback.
- Link the feedback to human resource development system (e.g. succession planning, performance review).
- Utilize only the 360-degree feedback tools with established scale reliability and solid factor structure.
- Focus developmental interventions on participant's strengths and any major weakness or "derailment" areas that can enhance the motivation to change.
- Hold participant's manager accountable for evaluating progress of the resulting development plan, which should be both measureable and behavioral.
- Design a separate evaluation that can help determine the usefulness of the process.

Based on information in Nowack 2010.

They point out that mentoring practices can be formal or informal, are often instituted by the organization, can use technology to connect mentors and protégés in different locations, can include mentoring networks, and can also include peer mentoring.

The following are aspects of mentoring identified by Conger and Riggio:

- Mentoring can help produce tangible outcomes for both employees and organizations.
- Mentoring has been found to have a positive impact on career and job satisfaction while concurrently decreasing turnover in protégés.
- It can include "reverse mentoring" relationships to help older or senior employees update skills.
- It can create new channels for communication regarding diversity and inclusiveness.

One example of an organization-wide mentoring program for leadership development in sport is the NACDA Mentoring Institute (National Association of Collegiate Directors of Athletics). According to information on the NACDA (2013) website (nacda.com), the focus of this institute is to assist and prepare individuals who are currently senior-level athletic administrators and are one step away from becoming athletic directors (ADs). NACDA website information indicates that participants in this program learn essentials about what is required to best position oneself for the AD role, along with how to manage a department after being hired as an AD.

The "NACDA Mentoring Institute Testimonials" sidebar provides examples from the NACDA website of testimonials from participants in this program.

Leadership Learning Through Experience

This section addresses on-the-job or on-site experience as a critical component of leadership learning and overall leadership develop-

---

NACDA Mentoring Institute Testimonials

The NACDA Mentoring Institute was a key component of my professional growth and in the continuing development of my leadership and administrative skills as I prepared for the opportunity to one day serve as a Director of Athletics. As I now grow into this role at Coastal Carolina University, I place an even greater value on the knowledge shared and learned at the Mentoring Institute and how it impacts me as a Director of Athletics.

—**Hunter Yurachek,** Coastal Carolina University

The NACDA Mentoring Institute covers the most relevant topics in college athletics in a thorough, honest, and open way. The vast amount of material covered in the agenda couldn't have been better at preparing me for the challenges we all face every day as college administrators. The added bonus of networking with leaders in our industry made for a tremendous experience. I was energized with new thoughts, ideas and relationships when the two days were complete. I wouldn't hesitate to highly recommend the Mentoring Institute to anyone in our industry.

—**Bob Grant,** Wright State University director of athletics

The NACDA Mentoring Institute is one of the most informative sessions I've attended. I was able to gain some 'real world' experience from successful administrative professionals at the top of this business. If you're looking for some practical knowledge that's applicable to every day situations, the NACDA Mentoring Institute is a great place to start.

—**Kevin L. Hatcher,** Cal State San Bernardino director of athletics

I found attending NACDA's Mentoring Institute to be informative, inspiring and fun. The programming was outstanding as the true leaders in intercollegiate athletics shared lessons learned and candid thoughts regarding the challenges and opportunities facing this profession. I came away from the two-day institute with a wealth of knowledge and an even higher level of enthusiasm to face the challenges ahead. In an era when both time and money are in limited supply, I am confident you will find NACDA's Mentoring Institute to be a good investment.

—**Beth DeBauche,** Ohio Valley Conference commissioner

ment. According to Conger (2004), research supports the idea that successful performance in work endeavors can be attributed to experience and coaching, rather than simply to inborn traits and early-life experiences.

Much of the foundational empirical research and academic writing supporting the role of experience as well as personal and professional transitions in leadership development is found in the work of McCall, Lombardo, and Morrison (1988), Howard and Bray (1988), and more recently Dotlich, Noel, and Walker (2004) and McCall (2010). However, although experience has been established as an important factor in assisting in leadership learning, McCall points out that all experiences are not created

> *Taking leadership development seriously means using experience wisely to help those with sufficient dedication and desire to learn the craft.*
>
> *McCall (2010)*

equal and that the developmental potential of experiences is not found in job titles, levels, or descriptions but more in the actual challenges that force new learning. In other words, according to McCall, it is not just "experience" that is needed for leadership development, but "experience that matters."

Given this foundation, McCall provides recommendations through five leverage points that he suggests may increase the probability of developing more effective leaders via experiential opportunities. These points, along with descriptions and key elements, are presented in table 10.2.

In relation to the leverage points in table 10.2, McCall also recognizes five demands that executives must meet in order to become more

Table 10.2 Five Leverage Points for Improving Leadership Development Through Experience

Leverage points	Key elements
Leverage point 1 *Identifying developmental experiences*	• Identify the situations and challenges that leaders or potential leaders in this organization will need to deal with effectively. • Determine what experiences would increase the ability of talented people in the organization to handle those kinds of situations. • Recognize where those experiences exist and in what ways they or other alternatives can be used to prepare leaders for that future.
Leverage point 2 *Identification of potential*	• Identify individuals in an organization who have potential. This may be based on results they have achieved, their ability to learn, or both. • Recognize that different people in an organization have different strengths and attributes and that there are different ways in which leaders can handle situations effectively. • Focus on increasing competency in handling demands and challenges of leadership roles instead of just on finding individuals who have a certain set of competencies.
Leverage point 3 *Right experience at the right time*	• Ensure that managers involved in hiring understand the leader development process. • Build a culture that specifically uses experience as part of leader development. • Increase accountability by measuring and sanctioning developmental activities.
Leverage point 4 *Increasing the odds that learning will occur*	• Make sure to enhance learning of desired lessons through ongoing experience. • Promote and reward those who learn and perform well and can help others grow. • Enlist several people in the development process (e.g., supervisor, business partner, peer).
Leverage point 5 *Career-long perspective and focus on transitions*	• Keep track of formal leadership learning experiences over time along with any evidence of increased mastery. • Recognize key transition points (e.g., from individual contributor to manager or from manager to executive leader). • Recognize that in some industries, leaders may have global assignments that require transitional preparation.

Based on information in McCall 2010.

effective as a leader. These demands include (a) *setting direction* (e.g., knowledge of business, strategic thinking, development of structure and control systems), (b) *alignment* (e.g., working with constituents and political situations, dealing with conflict, negotiation, developing people), (c) *setting and living values* (e.g., needing others, management values, sensitivity), (d) *executive temperament* (e.g., self-confidence, tough when necessary, coping with ambiguity and situations beyond one's control), and (e) *growth of self and others* (e.g., balance of work and life, personal limits, control of one's career). It is important to recognize regarding the development of leaders in these dimensions that people with high potential typically have qualities or experiences that demonstrate some level of knowledge and understanding across these domains.

The leverage points and five demands identified by McCall offer a good foundation for more formally developing effective on-the-job and transitional leadership learning experiences in sport management. For example, in his chapter on the career paths of Football Bowl Subdivision ADs, Wong (2009) identified four different tracks that ADs at this level used to transition into their current roles. These tracks included the athlete track, the coach track, the business leader track, and the entry-level administration track. According to Wong, in many cases, being a high school and college athlete leads individuals into the coach track and ultimately into an AD role. As Wong points out, the experience gained by working with athletes, coaches, and administrators, along with the transferability of leadership skills at each level, can be invaluable to becoming a college AD.

Wong recognizes that in some cases individuals transition into an athletic directorship from having been a business leader in another field or through an entry-level administrative track whereby the individual without playing or coaching experience begins working in an athletic department as an intern or staff member and then works up through the ranks. This path "requires a great deal of on-the-job training, which may be supplemented with graduate education" (p. 293).

In this example, the pathways to becoming a senior AD leader all require various transitions and formal or informal training. In the progression from athlete to coach to AD, it is interesting to note how the process unintentionally and indirectly follows many of the leverage points and demands for leadership development suggested by McCall (2010). On the other hand, it could be that McCall's recommendations provide a good template for athletic departments to consider when thinking about preparing future ADs who are following the business leader or entry-level administration track into the position. Various elements of McCall's five leverage points could also be adapted for use by corporate sport organizations, league offices, and other community-based sport and recreation organizations.

Employer-Based Action Learning

Depending on the size and complexity of a sport organization, employer-based leadership development programs may be informal and align more with the mentoring approach already discussed, or may be formalized as part of a corporate training program. One of the recommended approaches to leadership development is the action learning approach used across many corporate industries (Conger and Benjamin, 1999).

Action learning is defined by Conger and Benjamin as an educational approach whereby managers learn issues from working within their own companies and participate in various forms of experiential problem-solving activities. In these programs, learning by doing is emphasized, and much of the leadership development and problem-solving experience is conducted in teams. Another key element of these programs is placing the participants into problem-solving roles and assigning work issues and problems specific to the organization. Conger and Benjamin identify typical elements of an action learning project common to leadership development and training programs. Table 10.3 identifies these elements and provides an example of how each element could be included in a sport-related leadership development program.

Conger and Benjamin also believe organizations need to ensure they are developing leaders with the knowledge and skills that prepare them for the organization's leadership

Table 10.3 Action Learning for Leadership Development

Typical stages of action learning project	Sport-related example
1. Participant teams are "assigned" a real organizational problem to address and are provided with background information for review.	Junior marketing executives for an international sport marketing and public relations firm are tasked with developing a plan to address declining customer interest and sponsorship support for one of their top clients.
2. Learning teams begin research on the problem within their own company.	Executive teams are given access to and begin research on existing marketing and communication plans, sponsorship agreements, and so on to gather needed information.
3. Participants are given access to managers as well as customers.	The teams hold one or more meetings with senior executives assigned to the account to obtain more information. Client organization personnel are also contacted to notify them of the special project and to allow access to financial information, customer surveys, sponsor feedback, and so on.
4. Over the designated time period, team evaluates problem, meets, discusses plans and potential solutions, and develops draft solution plan.	After data gathering stage, junior executive teams meet to analyze and evaluate the situation, specifically identify problems, and develop initial draft solution plan.
5. Initial findings and draft plans are reviewed by an outside consultant (or internal midlevel manager) to identify gaps and potential issues.	Draft plans are provided to chosen outside consultant (e.g., retired marketing executive, PR consultant), who reviews the plan and makes final recommendations.
6. Project concludes with presentation to senior executives in the organization.	Junior executive team or teams present solution plan to senior executives within the firm.

Based on information in Conger and Benjamin 1999.

requirements in the decade ahead, as opposed to just those needed today. In the sport-related example in table 10.3, another step or component of the final project could be to ask the junior executive learning teams to develop a vision for what the needs of clients and possible solutions might be based on five- to 10-year predictive models or projections.

Leadership Succession Planning

Leadership succession in sport organizations tends to imply the change of leadership that results when an incumbent leader (e.g., CEO, AD, GM, head coach) is replaced by an external candidate brought in to change or turn the organization around. While this happens regularly in sport, another approach to succession planning is often used in both for-profit and nonprofit organizations. This type of succession planning involves the deliberate development of an internal talent pool that prepares individuals within the organization to assume future leadership roles. This section focuses on this approach to succession planning as it can apply to various types and levels of sport organizations.

Planning for internal leadership succession and preparing potential individuals for leadership roles is a process that takes time and care. Ultimately, the purpose is to effectively develop future leaders with both strategic vision and the ability to implement strategy (Cascio, 2011). According to Cascio, the best organizations are those that are "consciously strategic in their leadership planning" (p. 2). Cascio holds that the best organizations view people development as a leading indicator of organizational success over financial results. This is challenging for many corporate business organizations and can also be challenging for sport organizations that are under tremendous pressure to produce winning teams, products, or services. Failure to recognize and act on the critical need for leadership succession planning can lead to a future crisis if it becomes necessary to go outside the organization to find people who can adequately fill all leadership roles. In order to avoid this type of crisis, Cascio (2011) suggests five steps for designing a leadership succession plan:

1. Ensure that the current CEO or senior executive understands the importance of succession planning and makes it a priority.

2. Focus on future needs of the organization and not past accomplishments. New leaders in the future will need different strengths and talents.

3. Encourage prospective leaders to offer differences of opinion and disagree with management decisions.

4. Provide broad exposure to future leaders. Allow such things as job rotation and shadowing of senior managers so people can see how decisions are made.

5. Provide access to the board of directors or other governing body. Allow future leaders to make presentations to these groups so that they get a sense of what is important to the directors and so that the directors have an opportunity to view the talent in the pipeline.

Based on information in Cascio (2010).

Wolfred (2008) and the National Council of Nonprofits (2013) have offered additional approaches to internal leadership succession planning focused specifically on nonprofit organizations. According to Wolfred, succession planning is critical to ensuring organizational or agency viability, can help sustain leadership services through emergencies, and can help create an environment for shared leadership. Wolfred (2008, p. 6) presents three approaches to succession planning:

1. **Strategic leader development:** Involves defining strategic vision for organization, identifying the skills needed to carry out the vision, and recruiting talented individuals who either have or can develop those skills.

2. **Emergency succession planning:** Ensures that key leadership and administrative functions can continue without disruption when an unplanned or temporary absence of an administrator occurs.

3. **Departure-defined succession planning:** Recommended when a long-term leader has announced departure at least two years in advance. This approach includes identifying the goals moving forward and determining the tools a successor will need to achieve the goals.

Also recognizing the need for smooth and thoughtful leadership succession, the National Council of Nonprofits (2013) offers seven elements of planning that can be applied to most organizations:

1. Identify current challenges and those that lie ahead and the corresponding leadership qualities that are needed to navigate these challenges successfully.

2. Draft a timeline for leadership successions that are planned.

3. Create an emergency succession plan to address the timely delegation of duties and authority when there is an unexpected transition of leadership.

4. Identify leadership development opportunities for staff and board members to expand their leadership skills so that the organization will have a "deeper bench" of future leaders.

5. Cross-train current staff to minimize the disruption from unexpected staffing changes.

6. Make plans to adequately support newly placed employees, for example with coaching.

7. Identify how the organization will communicate with stakeholders before, during, and after a transition of leadership.

Reprinted, by permission, from National Council on Non Profits, 2013, *Elements of effective leadership succession plan.*

As mentioned previously, many sport organizations replace top executives, coaches, and other key leaders with candidates from the outside; however, sport organizations can, in many cases, achieve their future strategic goals by developing and implementing internal leadership succession plans as described in this section. See the case study "Build and Empower the Winning Team" from the Nikebiz.com (2013) website, which illustrates how Nike approaches elements of internal leadership succession in preparing its executives for the future.

Future Leadership Development

There are and likely will continue to be many formal and informal employee training pro-

Build and Empower the Winning Team

"NIKE, Inc. has unlimited opportunities to fuel profitable growth and to drive competitive advantage. Our leaders work every day to ensure NIKE, Inc. realizes its potential by inspiring every one of our more than 30,000 employees to realize their potential. Human Resources professionals at NIKE, Inc. operate as stewards of organization effectiveness, talent and change. The function works to ensure that NIKE, Inc. has talented, diverse and inclusive teams organized effectively against our biggest opportunities of driving innovation and business performance.

Deepening our Bench to Realize Potential

In building our teams, we focus on Nike's future business needs, deepening the "bench strength" of our talent through deliberate leader development.

Our talent strategy focuses on critical assignment planning, manager accountability for coaching and mentoring, and structured learning via individual- and team-based classroom and online learning.

Our commitment to growing the potential of our people and building leadership capability is carried out in organization and talent reviews directly linked to the business strategic priorities. In these reviews, leaders are held accountable for improving the performance, potential, diversity, position continuity and cost of their bench. This thoughtful and robust career management approach deepens the bench with globally diverse talent who gain the critical experiences and leadership skills they need to achieve business objectives and to realize their potential.

To ensure that we have the leadership required for NIKE, Inc. to continue to grow, our HR function is investing significantly in the areas of sustainable talent practices and infrastructure.

We continue to develop our premiere talent brand via the relentless Human Resources focus on talent and by working closely in partnership with Diversity and Inclusion on our culture." Nikebiz.com (2013).

---

grams that address elements of leadership development. Some of these programs, but not all, are evidence based, meaning that their effectiveness is supported by some level of empirical findings. Also, these programs may provide great training on the input side but do not always follow up over time to determine their true impact on individual and organizational performance.

Avolio (2010) asserts that in the quest to develop highly effective leaders, there is a distinct need to develop what he refers to as "practitioner-scientists" (p. 740). These individuals do not participate directly in the scientific research world, but they understand the discipline it takes to determine that a finding is evidence based. In this connection, Avolio suggests that as we move into the future, we must become more scientific about determining how to develop leaders and move away from approaches that are typically accidental or adventitious. This may provide directions for leadership development in the future in sport organizations. Both undergraduate and graduate preparation programs in sport management could engage students in ways that focus on evidence-based research for leadership development that is applicable in

our field. Another way to accomplish this is through more of a partnership with academia and industry relative to employee professional development.

Developmental Readiness and Authentic Leadership

Two areas identified by Avolio (2010) as currently undergoing research to guide future evidence-based leadership development are (a) developmental readiness and (b) use of authentic and genuine leadership development approaches. Regarding readiness, Avolio and Wernsing (2007) suggested that enhancing the readiness of participants to engage at a level that moves them toward more effective leadership is a key aspect of leadership development in organizations. Avolio (2010) points to the doctoral work of Hannah (2006), who developed a new theoretical framework for leadership development called agentic leadership efficacy (ALE). Hannah defines ALE relative to the appropriateness of the leader's role in the environment and the leader's self-confidence in his capabilities to organize the positive psychological capabilities, motivation, and courses of action needed to sustain performance. Using Hannah's research, along with other research conducted at the United States Military Academy, Avolio (2010) reported that developmental readiness could predict confidence to lead, as well as motivation and actual performance among cadets learning to perform in leadership roles.

In the area of authentic and genuine leadership development, Avolio refers to the recent work of several research teams (Luthans, Avolio, Avey, and Norman, 2007; Luthans, Avolio, and Youseff, 2007; Walumbwa et al., 2008) who examined the role of the psychological constructs of optimism, hope, resiliency, and efficacy and how they contribute to effective leader performance. This work resulted in the development of the PsyCap inventory (Luthans, Avolio, and Youseff, 2007), which was then merged with new validated constructs comprising authentic leadership, including self-awareness, balanced processing, moral perspectives, and transparency. Studies using these measures (Luthans, Avolio, and Youseff, 2007; Walumbwa et al., 2008) indicated that they predicted a wide array of performance outcomes and did so by augmenting other more established measures of leadership (Avolio, 2010).

Relative to sport, the work and findings of Avolio and colleagues suggest an area in need of exploration with respect to the psychological and authentic leadership constructs. For example, sport researchers could examine factors of authentic leadership relative to their importance in predicting leadership performance across various types and levels of the sport industry. Such studies could attempt to establish how these constructs relate to various leadership styles (e.g., transactional, transformational), as well as how leaders are perceived to perform and the organizational outcomes produced under their leadership.

Trigger Events

In the past, most leadership development programs took place over several hours or days and involved reading, reflecting, listening to lectures, and perhaps participating in role play activities or group discussions. A very intriguing element of future leadership development presented by Avolio (2010) involves the idea of trigger events that can occur at any moment

and that give individuals the motivation to reflect and learn from the event. This could be the beginning of what Avolio refers to as "genuine leadership development" and supports the notion of Luthans and colleagues (2006) that less could actually be more with regard to our traditional notion of developing leaders. Using another term, "micro-intervention," Avolio (2010) says that these "interventions" can be developed and delivered through online materials and even mobile technology (e.g., cell phones, tablet computers); these are "booster events" designed to last only for a few minutes to up to a day. These events, according to Avolio, are designed to have individuals reflect on and begin working on changing the various states of authentic leadership. In preliminary research, evidence is already accumulating that micro training interventions lasting less than a day can return over 200 percent of one's investment relative to its impact on performance (Avolio, 2010). Avolio states, "Teaching leaders and followers to process and reflect, as opposed to developing a particular style or behavior, will become more the norm than the exception" (p. 762).

Regarding the future, Avolio suggests that during the next few decades there is no reason why contextual and focused leadership development cannot be delivered through highly mobile technology that can enhance leader, follower, and organizational development. This direction corresponds favorably with what Avolio refers to as "return on development investment" (RODI), a calculation that determines the cost of a leadership development initiative relative to its potential benefits and outcomes.

> **Your Thoughts**
>
> Consider the idea of "trigger events" proposed by Avolio. What are some ideas you might have for developmental experiences in a sport context that could be maximized through short, well-timed learning events delivered through mobile technology?

Summary

This chapter addresses the overall concept of leadership learning and development and presents some common ways through which it occurs, including self-development, mentoring, on-the-job experience, action learning, and leadership succession planning. The evolving research and practice in this area provide ideas and directions that may improve our methods for developing sport leaders in the future. Many questions remain for research to address so as to help people more effectively develop their own leadership potential or improve an organization's capacity to do so through its internal training and promotion practices. As we address leadership development specifically in sport, we must look to current leaders in practice and academic researchers to work together to provide both experiential and empirical evidence regarding the approaches to leadership development that will be truly most effective in the industry.

Final Self-Assessment

Based on the self-assessment questions at the beginning of this chapter, what elements of leadership learning and development do you better understand? What do you feel about next steps in your own leadership development? What recommendations do you have or research ideas can you offer that would continue to improve leadership development for sport organizations?

Game Plan Activity

Select a sport organization of any type or level to which you have reasonable access. Do a small case study to determine the current status of leadership development in that organization. This might involve meeting with a senior leader in the organization if you can gain access to this individual. In this case study, try to identify the formal and informal means by which leadership development, succession planning, or both currently occur. If it appears that there is no plan or that there is a plan in need of improvement, determine how you would go about improving leadership learning and succession planning for the organization. Present your results to your instructor. If appropriate, you might discuss your ideas with the leader of the organization you selected as to their feasibility, strengths, and weaknesses.

Questions to Consider

1. What are the elements of leadership you consider most critical to learning to lead in the context of the sport organization with which you are most familiar?

2. What sources can you find, beyond those referred to in this text, that provide evidence-based research useful for leadership development?

3. Do research on the Internet to find two or three leadership development training companies or programs. What areas of leadership do they address? What do they have in common? What strengths and weaknesses do you find in their claims?

4. What demands are placed on the leaders in the sport organization with which you are most familiar? How do you see that they respond to and address those demands? What preparation do you think you would need to do that job well?

Recommended Readings

Avolio, B. J. (2010). Pursuing authentic leadership development. In N. Nohria and R. Khurana (Eds.), *Handbook of leadership theory and practice* (pp. 739-768). Boston: Harvard Business School Publishing.

Nowack, K. M. (2009). Leveraging multirater feedback to facilitate successful behavior change. *Consulting Psychology Journal: Practice and Research*, 61, 4, 280-297.

Van Velsor, E., McCauley, C., and Ruderman, M. (Eds.). *The Center for Creative Leadership handbook of leadership development*. San Francisco: Jossey Bass.

Future Considerations

After reading and reflecting on the concepts, examples, and case studies in this chapter, you will be able to

1. discuss leadership skills of the future as proposed by Johansen (2012) and apply them to various types and levels of sport organizations,

2. explain the difference between conventional and integrative thinkers and use the information to create new potential solutions to sport-related issues,

3. discuss the concept of sport organizations as learning organizations and give examples of these concepts applied to a sport organization, and

4. use information in this book to assist in resolving issues presented in case studies that illustrate future challenges for sport organization leaders.

This chapter, while it is the final one in the book, is only the beginning when one considers the challenges of leadership for sport organizations in the future. New problems and challenges will be brought on by a rapidly changing society, phenomenal advances in technology, and an uncertain global economic and environmental future. However, in view of these challenges and opportunities, much of what has been presented in this book will be of both research interest and practical value relative to continuous improvement of sport organization leadership.

> *"The empires of the future are empires of the mind."*
>
> *Winston Churchill*

This chapter is not organized in quite the same way as the other chapters, just as many organizations in our industry in the future will be structured differently from the way they are today. The first part of the chapter introduces new ideas and approaches to leadership, including proposed new skills, new ways of thinking, and ways to consider sport organizations as learning organizations in the future. The remainder of the chapter consists of case studies illustrating issues and dilemmas presented by developments today and into the future and the context for sport organizations over the next several years.

Leadership Skills of the Future

Many of the business, social, ecosystem, and economic issues to be addressed broadly in the world of the future are identified by Bob Johansen, author of *Leaders Make the Future* (2012). Johansen introduces a new acronym, VUCA, to indicate that our world is one that will be characterized by volatility, uncertainty, complexity, and ambiguity. In a "VUCA World," Johansen says, there will be both danger and opportunity, and traditional leadership will not be adequate to "take advantage of VUCA opportunities" and "sidestep the dangers" (p. 3). Johansen offers 10 new leadership skills that he proposes will be essential to the development and ongoing learning of future leaders (see "Ten Leadership Skills for the Future").

Another perspective on new ways of thinking for leadership comes from Martin (2007) in *The Opposable Mind: How Successful Leaders Win Through Integrative Thinking*. Using the results of interviews of more than 50 leaders with exemplary records, Martin determined that most of them shared an unusual trait or capacity. He described this as the predisposition and capacity to hold two opposing

Ten Leadership Skills for the Future

- **The maker instinct:** Exploiting your inner drive to build new things and connect to others

- **Dilemma flipping:** Recognizing problems and challenges as both threats and opportunities

- **Bio-empathy:** Developing a deeper understanding of and respect for the natural world

- **Quiet transparency:** Ability to listen carefully, explain one's thinking to others, and adopt more of a servant leadership framework

- **Smart-mob organizing:** Ability to bring together large groups using available media; learning to lead in an online world

- **Clarity:** Ability to see through complexities to envision a future that can be clarified to followers

- **Immersive learning:** Leaders must become direct and continual learners in unfamiliar environments

- **Constructive depolarizing:** Ability to calm tense situations and bring people together, especially those from divergent cultures

- **Rapid prototyping:** Learn-as-you-go approach and willingness to try things, learn from them and try again

- **Commons creating:** Ability to seed, nurture, and grow assets that benefit others and the common good

Based on information in Johansen (2012).

ideas in one's head at the same time and then, without choosing one alternative or the other, resolve the tension by generating a new idea that is superior to both alternatives. Martin proposes that, when responding to problems or challenges, leaders use a four-step approach. Within this approach, there are distinct differences between conventional thinking and integrative thinking. Table 11.1 demonstrates these differences in how leaders think.

Sport Organizations as Learning Organizations

Throughout this book, much has been said to help prepare leaders for the current and future challenges and situations facing sport organizations. Another concept and approach that has gained strength over the last decade is that of the "learning organization" and its importance to organizational leadership in the future. As complexity increases in all aspects of business and industry, organizations that create environments embracing continued learning and understanding of the forces and factors influencing business strategies and practices will likely be the organizations that best flourish in an increasingly interconnected and global economy. In these highly adaptable organizations, ongoing individual and group- or team-based learning, with people participating in formal learning opportunities and regularly exchanging ideas, is a critical element of an effective organization's culture.

As we move into an uncertain and complex future, I suggest that sport organizations must

Table 11.1 Differences in Approaches Between Conventional and Integrative Thinkers

Steps in responding to problems or challenges	Conventional thinkers	Integrative thinkers
Step 1: Determining salience	Focus on obviously relevant features	Seek less obvious but potentially relevant factors
Step 2: Analyzing causality	Consider one-way linear relationships between variables	Consider multidirectional and nonlinear relationships among variables
Step 3: Envisioning the decision architecture	Break problems into pieces and work on them separately or sequentially	See problems as a whole, examining how the parts fit together and how decisions affect one another
Step 4: Achieving resolution	Make either-or choices; settle for best available options	Creatively resolve tensions among opposing ideas; generate innovative outcomes

Based on information in Martin 2007.

also think of themselves as learning organizations. The seminal academic work in this field was presented by Peter Senge (1990, 2006) in his classic book, *The Fifth Discipline: The Art and Practice of the Learning Organization.* Senge defines a learning organization simply as one that is "continually expanding its capacity to create its future." Table 11.2 lists and describes the five core disciplines identified by Senge that contribute to an organization's capacity to improve and continue learning. The table also includes an example of each discipline as it relates to a sport organization.

Another leading authority in the field of organizational learning, Michael Marquardt, pointed out in his 1999 book, *Action Learning in Action: Transforming Problems and People for World-Class Organizational Learning,* several important characteristics of learning organizations:

- Learning is accomplished by the organization as a whole.
- Organizational members recognize the importance of ongoing learning to the organization's future success.
- Learning is a continuous, strategically used process, integrated and running parallel to work.
- There is a focus on creativity.
- "Systems" thinking is fundamental.

About a decade later, in *Building the Learning Organization: Achieving Strategic Advantage Through a Commitment to Learning,* Marquardt (2010) asserted that external change and forces at work today "demand either organizational adaptation or organizational extinction" (p. 1). Marquardt identifies eight forces occurring in organizations today that necessitate continual organization-wide learning:

1. Globalization and the global economy
2. Technology and the Internet
3. Radical transformation in the work world
4. Increased customer power
5. Emergence of knowledge and learning as major organizational assets
6. Changing roles and expectations of workers
7. Workplace diversity and mobility
8. Rapidly escalating change and chaos

In order to create the learning environment and experiences necessary to deal with these forces, Marquardt (2010) proposed that learning organizations must address three complementary dimensions or subsystems of learning:

1. **Level of learning:** Includes individual, group or team, and organizational learning
2. **Types of learning:** Includes adaptive, anticipatory, and action-based learning (an example of action-based learning for leadership development is presented in chapter 10)
3. **Skills:** Includes systems thinking, mental models, personal mastery, self-directed learning, and dialogue

I suggest that the forces listed earlier and the approaches to learning that can help address these forces are most certainly applicable to sport organizations in today's world and should be strongly considered by current and future sport leaders as part of the ongoing learning necessary to lead our organizations into a successful future. Readers are encouraged to further explore the work of both Senge (1990, 2006) and Marquardt (2010) for details on incorporating elements of learning into organizational learning strategies. Additionally, from a very applied perspective, Kline and Saunders (2010), in the second edition of their book *10 Steps to a Learning Organization,* outline a practical approach beginning with an *organizational assessment* and progressing through nine additional steps: *promoting the positive, safe thinking, risk taking, using people as resources, learning power, mapping a vision, modeling the vision, incorporating systems thinking,* and *getting the show on the road.* The work of Kline and Saunders provides another excellent resource for potential application in sport organization leadership.

The theories and practice of organizational learning present an emerging area for potential new research on sport organization leadership. At the time of publication, little to no formal academic research had been reported on the extent to which any of the learning organization

Table 11.2 The Five Disciplines of the Learning Organization

Senge's disciplines	Description of discipline and sport example
Personal mastery	Organizations are made up of individuals who learn; thus organizational learning does not occur without individuals who can clarify their personal vision, continually expand their ability to create results, and develop "creative tension" between where they want to go and current reality. Personal mastery goes beyond competence and skills, and "people with high levels of personal mastery are continually expanding their ability to create the results in life they truly seek" (Senge 2006, p. 131 ***Sport example:*** *South African cricket star Gary Kirsten describes personal mastery as including knowing and playing to your strengths and not dwelling on your weaknesses. Kirsten indicates that it requires conducting yourself like an athlete, demonstrating integrity, honesty, humility, and respect. He adds that this is a path that leads through all of life, bringing both improved performance on the field and a rewarding life off the field (Upton, 2012).*
Mental models	New insights and creative ideas often fail to make their way into practice because they conflict with deeply rooted internal images of what people consider to be the way the world works and how these images shape people's views and actions. Senge suggests that the ability to surface, test, and improve or change these internal pictures is a key element of building effective learning organizations. ***Sport example:*** *Based on a true story of racial integration in a Virginia high school in the 1970s, the movie* Remember the Titans *depicts how a high school football team, through the leadership of a black head coach and a white assistant coach, was able to ultimately overcome stereotypes, distrust, and prejudice to become a championship team. Many of the issues that had to be conquered related to deeply rooted images and beliefs that had to be surfaced, addressed, and improved in order for the team to achieve its ultimate goals.*
Shared vision	Focuses on what a group wants to collectively create. Allows people and organizations to be connected and bound together with common aspirations. Senge suggests that a shared vision can become a force in people's hearts that can be one of impressive power. ***Sport example:*** *In a recent decision to allow reserve players in Major League Soccer (MLS) to be integrated into United Soccer League Pro (USL Pro), an agreement was reached between Sporting Kansas City of the MLS and Orlando City of USL Pro. Peter Vermes, manager of Sporting Kansas City, indicated that the shared vision of the two organizations would provide "beneficial opportunities for players to develop within a competitive environment for a tremendous organization and fanbase"(Orlando City Soccer, 2013).*
Team learning	Associated with alignment and people learning to work together as a whole unit. Often individuals trying to work in teams are working in a disconnected and unaligned way. In this situation, Senge points out that people are working hard, but the energy is not harmonized and does not translate into a true team effort. When teams learn to have commonality of purpose and can learn and practice together, the outcome can be impressive. ***Sport example:*** *Senge (2006) relates a story from the ex-Boston Celtic great Bill Russell. Russell recounted how the Celtic team would occasionally play in a way he called "magical" to describe how, in some special games, the action would be moving very fast but things almost seemed to happen in slow motion. Russell described how he could sense how the next play would develop and where the next shot would be taken before it happened. This, according to Senge, is indicative of a team truly aligned and working as a whole unit.*
Systems thinking	Recognizes that business are like organisms with multiple parts that are interrelated and in many cases dependent on one another. Changes or problems in one part of the system can have effects in other parts of the system, and it can sometimes take years to understand these effects. Senge suggests that the four other disciplines of the model fuse together with systems thinking so that they all become part of how an organization can be transformed by individuals working and learning together to create a new reality for the future. ***Sport example:*** *Rose Mercier, Canadian sport leadership consultant, applied systems thinking as a way to better understand and address the lack of female coaches among Canada Games teams. By using a systems analysis approach, she was able to come up with a list of several factors, including the lack of female role models, the small number of female coaches with appropriate experience, the lack of recruitment of women into coaching, and the lack of incentives to continue coaching (Mercier, 2002).*

Based on information in Senge 1990, 2006.

concepts are being used and how they are being implemented.

Certainly effective leadership in sport organizations into the future will continue to be associated with positive results and success as defined by internal and external stakeholders including athletes, coaches, owners, boosters, fans, stockholders, media, and sponsors. However, an important suggestion by Hackman (2010), with reference to business organizations, is that conventional organizational outcomes such as productivity and profitability may too often be considered the ultimate criteria of leadership effectiveness. Hackman proposed another perspective: Leadership effectiveness enhances what he refers to as system viability (p. 109). Hackman suggested that viable social systems have three attributes:

1. Those who are affected by the work of the system are satisfied by the products of the system.

2. The system becomes more capable as a performing unit over time.

3. Individual members of the system derive at least as much personal learning and fulfillment as frustration and alienation from their work in the system.

Your Thoughts

The three components of system viability suggested by Hackman (2010) may provide an expanded and somewhat more pragmatic view of effective leadership.

Basing your thoughts on Hackman's perspective and your own experience, are there examples in which you see that future leadership effectiveness in sport can be related to the three attributes of system viability?

Case Studies

Now that some of the ideas and approaches to leading for the future have been presented, the remainder of this chapter is devoted to cases that provide examples of VUCA (volatile, uncertain, complex, and ambiguous)-related challenges for current and future sport organizations. Some of the issues relate back to earlier chapters in this book, as well as information presented previously in this chapter. I suggest that you read each case carefully and reflect on its elements before proceeding to develop potential solutions.

I recommend that readers along with instructors use these cases to develop further dialogue and work together in exploring how these situations will affect sport leaders, as well as how leaders may effectively respond to and lead others through these situations. Some elements of these cases are real and some are speculative but nonetheless important to consider in trying to envision the challenges and problems that sport leaders may face in the future. Also consider where these cases call for more research in our field to gain a better understanding of how to effectively develop leaders for the future in our industry. Finally, I encourage readers and instructors to come up with their own scenarios and examples for deliberation regarding future complex challenges for sport leaders.

Case 1: Sport Business Context of the Future

It is 2020 and you are a senior executive in a multinational sport equipment company. The company is in the process of moving completely into a cloud computing environment, and you are leading a diverse workforce composed of a few employees from the baby boomer generation (currently in their early 60s), but primarily a mix of employees from generation X (currently in their late 40s to early 50s), generation Y (currently in their 30s), and true digital natives (currently in their early 20s). The marketing and sales division of the business is evolving into the new cloud environment with all customer data stored in the cloud. Moreover, your company has recently employed social media analytics software to tap into the social media activities (e.g., Facebook, Twitter) of customers. Consequently, strategies need to be developed to deliver the right marketing messages to the right customers at the right time using mobile technology as a medium. Also, in this environment, much of your workforce can do their jobs "virtually" from anywhere and at any time. You find yourself part of a key leadership team trying to remain competitive and advance the company as a world leader in providing sport equipment for the modern athlete.

This is an example of what a sport organization work context will be like in the near future. Addressing the numerous issues effectively will require insightful, agile, and adaptive leadership. Given this leadership environment, develop answers, as well as additional questions, using the following as a starting point:

1. What will be some of the new roles and responsibilities of leaders in this company?

2. What elements of complexity leadership may be important to effectively leading in this environment?

3. How will strategic thinking perhaps be more important than traditional strategic planning in keeping the company competitive in the future?

4. How will leaders go about building relationships with employees in this environment, where many employees may not be physically present in an actual facility?

5. How will elements of diversity leadership influence practice relative to the generational differences of employees in this company?

Case 2: Is That Really Fair?

Issues with performance-enhancing drugs and related substances have been a problem faced by sport for many years. However, advancements in technology like three-dimensional printing, and advancements in biomedical engineering including such things as laser eye surgery, limb replacement, and gene therapy to repair muscular tissue and strengthen muscles, are creating new questions regarding the bioengineered athlete of the future. In fact, a term in the sport world that is gaining popularity is "technology doping," referring broadly to any technology that gives athletes an unfair competitive advantage.

The past decade has seen stories of athletes who gained a competitive advantage of some type as a result of advancements in technology including biomedical engineering. For example, in the 2008 Olympics, Speedo developed the LZR Racer series full-body swimsuit, which allowed swimmers buoyancy. That advancement led Fédération Internationale de Natation (FINA), the international governing body of aquatic sports, to impose new regulations on the materials used and the construction of swimsuits. In 2005, Tiger Woods won the Masters tournament partly as the result, some argued, of improved vision through laser optic surgery. In the 2012 Summer Olympics, Oscar Pistorius, the "Blade Runner," reached the 400 m semifinals running on carbon-fiber lower legs.

To fast forward to 2020 and beyond, even more technological advances will exist that may be viewed as giving athletes special competitive advantage. For example, three-dimensional printing is at the point, both technologically and with respect to cost, that a sport team could "print" shoes for players based on weather or field conditions (Chan, 2012). Imagine that at a time in the future, all professional baseball players had laser eye surgery in order to improve tracking of the ball from the pitcher and ultimate success at the plate. Given the rapid advances in technology, the increased globalization of sport, and the financial incentives and rewards for success, consider the questions listed next. Also think of additional questions and other possible technologies that will have ethical, legal, and policy implications in sport.

1. How will sport leaders in the coming years address these rapid advancements in technology? What are the ethical implications?

2. Will this be primarily through increased policy and monitoring to try to preserve fairness?

3. Will these advancements ultimately lead to other types of future leagues (e.g., Bionic Olympics)?

4. What are the potential impacts on younger athletes trying to advance into elite levels of sport?

5. Will future generations be so accustomed to technological advances that the current value system will have evolved into a new paradigm of fairness in competition?

Case 3: The Changing Environment for High School Sports

Currently in the United States, the number of students attending public charter high schools is dramatically increasing. The number of charter schools and the number of students enrolled in those schools are likely to continue to grow. For example, recently in the Dallas-Fort Worth area, former Dallas Cowboy Deion Sanders and his business partner completely funded both a new elementary and a new secondary charter school that collectively would hire 100 teachers and provide each student with a laptop computer (Smith, 2012).

Already, charter high school athletic associations have been created in many states, and each association is growing in the number of schools that join each year. One of the issues that has arisen from this dramatic change in the school and athletic environment is that charter schools can operate without the typical district boundaries imposed on traditional public schools. As a result, many charter schools around the country have attracted, or in the views of some critics "recruited," some of the top athletic talent in their area. More and more often, charter school teams from different sports are appearing in and winning state championships, especially in the lower divisions of enrollment. Given the growth and likely increase of charter schools into the future, consider the following questions as well as others that you can generate regarding this new environment for high school sport in the United States.

1. How does this changing landscape affect structure, policies, and planning for leaders in state high school associations?

2. What is your perspective on whether or not charter schools now have an unfair advantage in athletic competition?

3. What issues do athletic directors and coaches in traditional public schools face with the increasing potential for athletes to transfer out of their programs?

4. How are athletics funded at charter schools?

5. What does all of this mean relative to high school sport leadership in the future?

Case 4: eRecruiting Internationally

You are the AD at one of the NCAA Division II institutions in the Midwest. The advent of online recruiting sites allows your coaches to easily view profile information and video from athletes, not only from within the United States but also from across the globe. A few years ago, recruiting international athletes at your institution would not have been an issue because of the expenses associated with travel to find and meet athletes. However, online recruiting sites and mobile technology have opened the door to instant recruiting worldwide. Your women's basketball coach lets you know that she has electronically located several players from outside the United States who, if recruited successfully, could likely take the struggling program to a conference championship and to the national tournament in the near future—and you agree.

However, at the same time, the president of your university has just let you know that the institution is developing a campaign to increase enrollment focused on attracting more local and regional students. The president has suggested that you work with your coaches to try to recruit more local and regional athletes so as to increase interest in the university in area schools and media outlets. As the AD, you are aware that it is challenging to bring in international students, especially to an area of limited culturally diversity. You also know of the challenges associated with getting many international students into the university and eligible to play basketball. However, you fully recognize that the women's basketball program is struggling to be successful. Moreover, you feel that it is part of your leadership role to support your coaches as much as possible in building successful programs.

In this situation, you have both a challenge and a strategic opportunity that would not have existed before online recruiting sites made identifying international athletes such a simple process. Given both the problem and the context (e.g., level of competition, geographic location), consider the following questions related to this leadership issue.

1. What are the most critical elements of this leadership problem as you see it?

2. Do you think that recruiting international players represents more of a challenge or an opportunity in this situation? Why or why not?

3. What leadership styles or behaviors and approaches to problem solving do you think might be appropriate in this situation?

4. What components of Martin's (2007) approach to integrative thinking or Johansen's (2012) new leadership skills for the future do you think most apply?

5. Given your answers, how would you proceed to address this situation?

Case 5: FIFA and Qatar

In 2022, the FIFA (Fédération Internationale de Football Association) World Cup is set to take place in the Middle Eastern country of Qatar. In 2012, a great deal of controversy had already arisen regarding concerns around human labor rights related to work conditions for mostly Asian migrant workers who would be constructing nine stadiums and improving infrastructure in the country over the next 10 years (Terzieff, 2012). Terzieff indicates that millions of workers in Qatar, as well as in other parts of the Persian Gulf and North Africa, face abuses including substandard wages, no compensation for overtime work, and even physical assaults and retaliation for activities associated with worker unions. According to Terzieff, the International Trade Union Confederation (ITUC), a key labor rights stakeholder, has indicated that if conditions for workers in Qatar are not improved to meet international standards, it will initiate a boycott campaign for the 2022 FIFA event. Labor activists are putting pressure on FIFA to in turn press Qatari authorities to provide better conditions for laborers ("Fifa pressed over Qatar," 2011). However, Terzieff also points out that boycotts of sporting events have historically failed to produce effective results. For example, the boycott by the United States (and 50 other

countries) of the 1980 Moscow Olympic Games was not successful in getting the Soviet Union to remove its troops from Afghanistan and resulted in more diplomatic tension between the two countries.

It is evident that considerable political, business, ethical, and moral issues are all interacting regarding the current state of affairs with Qatar and the FIFA World Cup. At this point, the decisions and actions of leaders of FIFA as well as leaders of the ITUC and the Labor Minister of Qatar will likely determine the potential resolution of these tensions or whether the situation worsens over time. Based on the information given, address the following questions about leading in this complex, uncertain, and volatile situation.

1. What do you view as the most critical and pressing issue in this situation?

2. What are the pressures that the FIFA leaders are under in this situation, and what level of power or influence do they have?

3. What are elements of emotional intelligence that might be useful in dealing with this situation?

4. How would you deal with the conflict if it escalated into a boycott of the event?

5. Are there other influential organizations or leaders that could be consulted or asked to contribute to potential solutions?

Final Thoughts

Sport organizations are evolving as the world is evolving. With this come daunting challenges as well as emerging opportunities for the future in all areas of the sport industry. To become highly effective leaders, those pursuing leadership roles in sport must be equipped with competencies developed from the academic study of leadership theory and research, as well as through self-understanding, confidence building, quality leadership development, and hands-on experience. This book has focused primarily on the academic study of leadership and has attempted to provide a foundation for good leadership practice, as well as better understanding of leadership research, and hopefully ideas that may lead some readers to conduct future sport-related research in this area.

In conclusion, I offer that I am optimistic about the future of sport and sport leadership, despite negative events across all levels of sport that continue to plague the profession. Over the next several years, the sport industry will be influenced by many complex interacting factors and will require leaders, in my opinion, who are intellectual, strategic, adaptable, and values oriented and who have what Howard Gardner (1995, p. 30) refers to as "expertise in the realm of persons."

I strongly suggest that individuals pursuing leadership roles in this field need to give deep and thoughtful consideration to the elements of the three "Rs" presented in chapter 2 of this book—results, relationships, and responsibilities. A great deal of evidence in the world of sport each year suggests that at least one of these dimensions is often out of balance.

I also think that we must continue to collectively focus on improving leadership development in sport that begins with a focused commitment from academic programs to provide the best foundation possible for "leadership learning." Effectively preparing individuals through reflection, critical thinking, problem solving, collaboration, communication, social learning, and hands-on experience will be essential to develop the competencies that future sport leaders will need to address the complexities of the modern world and 21st-century sport organizations. As Johansen (2012) said, the future is volatile, uncertain, complex, and ambiguous. But your role as a sport leader in the coming years is to think, act, and lead others in ways that truly turn challenges into opportunities and generate trust and respect for the industry, at whatever level you pursue. I urge you to take the challenge, continually improve your leadership learning, and never sell yourself short on your ability to be a leader. Good luck!

References

AAUW. (2012). Parties announce settlement of UC Davis Title IX athletics discrimination suit brought by former students. Retrieved July 15, 2012 from www.aauw.org/article/settlement-of-uc-davis-title-ix-athletics-discrimination-suit.

aboutus.org. (2013). Nike. Retrieved May 22, 2013 from www.aboutus.org/Nike.com.

Acosta, R. V., and Carpenter, L. J. (2012). Women in intercollegiate sport: A longitudinal, national study. Thirty-five year update 1977-2012. Retrieved May 18, 2012 from http://acostacarpenter.org/AcostaCarpenter2012.pdf.

Allan, E. J., and Madden, M. (2008). *Hazing in view: College students at risk* (pp. 1-52). http://umaine.edu/hazingresearch/files/2012/10/hazing_in_view_web.pdf.

Allen, S. J., and Roberts, D. C. (2011). Leadership learning: Crucial conversations, next steps, and thoughts for consideration. *Journal of Leadership Studies*, 5(2), 64.doi: 10.1002/jls.20219

allblacks.com. (2012). Retrieved February 19, 2012, from www.allblacks.com/index.cfm?layout=haka.

Amir, Y., Halina, Y., and Sagie, D. (1976). Verbal and behavioral aspects of commitment among Arabs and Jews. *Journal of Cross-Cultural Psychology*, 7, 37-48.

Aninat, E. (2002). Surmounting the challenges of globalization. *Finance and Development*, 39(1), 4-7.

Antonakis, J. (2004). On why "emotional intelligence" will not predict leadership effectiveness beyond IQ or the "big five": An extension and rejoinder. *Organizational Analysis*, 12(2), 171-182.

Aoyagi, M. W., Cox, R. H., and McGuire, R. T. (2008). Organizational citizenship behavior in sport: Relationships with leadership, team cohesion, and athlete satisfaction. *Journal of Applied Sport Psychology*, 20, 25-41.

Arogyaswamy, K., Barker, V. L. III, and Yasai-Ardekani, M. (1995). Firm turnarounds: An integrative two-stage model. *Journal of Management Studies*, 32(4), 493-525.

Avolio, B. (1999). *Full leadership development: Building the vital forces in organizations.* Thousand Oaks, CA: Sage.

Avolio, B. J. (2010). Pursuing authentic leadership development. In N. Nohria and R. Khurana (Eds.), *Handbook of leadership theory and practice.* Boston: Harvard Business Press.

Avolio, B. J., and Gibbons, T. C. (1988). Developing transformational leaders: A life span approach. In J. A. Conger and R. N. Kanungo, *Charismatic leadership: The elusive factor in organizational effectiveness* (pp. 276-308). San Francisco: Jossey-Bass.

Avolio, B. J., and Wernsing T.S. (2007). Practicing authentic leadership. In S.J. Lopez (ed.), *Positive psychology: Exploring the best in people.* Westport, CT: Greenwood Publishing Company.

Avolio, B. J., Luthans, F., and Walumba, F. O. (2004). Authentic leadership: Theory building for veritable sustained performance. Working paper: Gallup Leadership Institute, University of Nebraska-Lincoln.

Ayman, R., and Korabik, K. (2010). Leadership: Why gender and culture matter. *American Psychologist*, 65(3), 157-170. doi: 10.1037/a0018806

Bagchi, S. (2006). Leadership challenges in the 21st century. *Mindtree*. Retrieved July 18, 2012 from www.mindtree.com/downloads/leadership_challenges_21st_century.pdf.

Bairner, A. (2001). *Sport, nationalism, and globalization: European and North American perspectives*. New York, SUNY Press.

Barber, H., and Krane, V. (2007). Creating inclusive and positive climates in girls' and women's sport: Position statement on homophobia, homonegativism, and heterosexism. *Women in Sport & Physical Activity Journal,* 16(1), 53-55.

Bar-On, R. (2000). Emotional and social intelligence: Insights from the Emotional Quotient Inventory (EQ-i). In R. Bar-On and J. D. A. Parker (Eds.), *Handbook of emotional intelligence.* San Francisco: Jossey-Bass.

Bar-On, R. (2006). The Bar-On model of emotional-social intelligence (ESI). *Psicothema,* 18(Suppl), 13-25.

Bass, B. M. (1985). Leadership: Good, better, best. *Organizational Dynamics,* 13(3), 26-40.

Bass, B. M. (1990). From transactional to transformational leadership: Learning to share the vision. *Organizational Dynamics,* 18(3), 19-31.

Bass, B. M., and Avolio, B. J. (1989). Potential biases in leadership measures: How prototypes, leniency, and general satisfaction relate to ratings and rankings of transformational and transactional leadership constructs. *Educational and Psychological Measurement,* 49(3), 509-527. doi: 10.1177/001316448904900302

Bass, B. M., and Avolio, B. J. (1990). The implications of transactional and transformational leadership for individual, team, and organizational development. *Research in Organizational Change and Development,* 4, 231-272.

Bass, B. M., and Avolio, B. J. (1993). Transformational leadership: Response to critiques. In M. M. Chemers and R. Ayman (Eds.), *Leadership theory and research: Perspectives and directions.* San Diego: Academic Press.

Bass, B. M., and Avolio, B. J. (1994). *Improving organizational effectiveness through transformational leadership.* Thousand Oaks, CA: Sage.

Beam, J. W., Serwatka, T. S., and Wilson, W. J. (2004). Preferred leadership of NCAA Division I and II intercollegiate student-athletes. *Journal of Sport Behavior,* 27(1), 3-17.

Beechler, S., and Javidan, M. (2007). Leading with a global mindset. In M. Javidan, R. M. Steers, and Michael A. Hitt (Eds.), *The global mindset: Advances in international management* (Vol. 19, pp. 131-169). Bingley, West Yorkshire, UK: Emerald Group.

Benford, R. D. (2007). The college sports reform movement: Reframing the "edutainment" industry. *Sociological Quarterly,* 48(1), 1-28. doi: 10.1111/j.1533-8525.2007.00068.x

Bennis, W. (1989). *On becoming a leader.* Reading, MA: Perseus Books.

Bennis, W. (2007). The challenges of leadership in the modern world. *American Psychologist,* 62(1), 2-5. doi: 10.1037/0003-066x.62.1.2

Bennis, W. (2009). *On becoming a leader.* New York: Basic Books.

Bennis, W. G. and Goldsmith, J. (1997). *Learning to lead: A workbook on becoming a leader.* Cambridge, MA: Perseus Books.

Bennis, W., and Goldsmith, J. (2003). *Learning to lead: A workbook on becoming a leader.* Cambridge, MA: Perseus Books.

Benton, D. A. (2003). *Executive charisma: Six steps to mastering the art of leadership.* New York: McGraw-Hill.

Beyer, J. M., and Hannah, D. R. (2000). The cultural significance of athletics in U.S. higher education. *Journal of Sport Management,* 14(2), 105-132.

Bilal, A. (2007). Premier league sues YouTube, no more free football videos? Retrieved August 1, 2011, from http://soccerlens.com/breaking-news-premier-league-sues-youtube-no-more-free-football-videos/1645/.

Blake, R. E., and Mouton, J. S. (1985). Presidential grid styles. *Training and Development Journal,* 39(3), 30.

Blitz, R. (2013). Manchester United's global brand reaches crossroads. www.ft.com/

intl/cms/s/0/6d8732ae-b7ed-11e2-9f1a-00144feabdc0.html#axzz2XB3W4UqA.

Bolman, L. G., and Deal, T. E. (1991). Leadership and management effectiveness: A multi-frame, multi-sector analysis. *Human Resource Management*, 30(4), 509-534.

Bolman, L. G., and Deal, T. E. (2008). *Reframing organization: Artistry, choice, and leadership*. San Francisco: Jossey-Bass.

Bourner, F., and Weese, W. J. (1995). Executive leadership and organizational effectiveness in the Canadian Hockey League. *European Journal for Sport Management*, 2(1), 88-100.

Bovaird, T. (2008). Emergent strategic management and planning mechanisms in complex adaptive systems. *Public Management Review*, 10(3), 319-340. doi: 10.1080/14719030802002741

Boxill, J. (2003). *Sports ethics: An anthology*. Malden, MA: Blackwell.

Boyatzis, R. (2011). Neuroscience and leadership: The promise of insights. *Ivey Business Journal*, 75(1), 1.

Boyatzis, R. (2012). Neuroscience and the link between inspirational leadership and resonant relationships. *Ivey Business Journal*, 76(1), 26-28.

Boyatzis, R. E., Goleman, D., and Rhee, K. S. (2000). Clustering competence in emotional intelligence: Insights from the Emotional Competence Inventory. In R. Bar-On and J. D. A. Parker (Eds.), *The handbook of emotional intelligence: Theory, development, assessment, and application at home, school, and in the workplace* (pp. 343-362). San Francisco: Jossey-Bass.

Boyd, B. K., and Reuning-Elliott, E. (1998). A measurement model of strategic planning. *Strategic Management Journal*, 19(2), 181.

Boyne, G. A., and Meier, K. J. (2009). Environmental change, human resources and organizational turnaround. *Journal of Management Studies*, 46(5), 835-863. doi: 10.1111/j.1467-6486.2008.00813.x

Brady, E. (2007). Three major sports must deal with credibility crisis. Retrieved April 23, 2011 from http://usatoday30.usatoday.com/sports/2007-07-24-sports-controversy_N.htm.

Branch Jr., D. (1990). Athletic director leader behavior as a predictor of intercollegiate athletic organizational effectiveness. *Journal of Sport Management*, 4(2), 161-173.

Brault, M. W. (2008). Americans with disabilities: 2005. Retrieved January 17, 2012 from www.census.gov/prod/2008pubs/p70-117.pdf.

Brown, G. (2011). Demographics data show more inclusive trends. www.ncaa.org/wps/wcm/connect/public/NCAA/Resources/Latest+News/2011/December/Demographics+data+show+more+inclusive+trends.

Bryson, J. M. (1988). A strategic planning process for public and nonprofit organizations. *Long Range Planning*, 21(1), 73-81.

Bryson, J. M., and Crosby, B. C. (1995). Leadership roles in making strategic planning work. In J. M. Bryson (Ed.), *Strategic planning for public and nonprofit organizations* (revised ed.). San Francisco, CA: Jossey-Bass.

Burns, J. M. (1979). *Leadership*. New York: Harper Collins.

Burton, L. J., and Peachey, J. W. (2009). Transactional or transformational? Leadership preferences of Division III athletic administrators. *Journal of Intercollegiate Sports*, 2(2), 245-259.

businessdictionary.com. (2013). Retrieved May 10, 2013.

Cameron, K. S. (2006). Leadership values that enable extraordinary success. In E. D. Hess and K. S. Cameron (Eds.), *Leading with values: Positivity, virtue and high performance*. New York: Cambridge University Press.

Cameron, K. S., and Quinn, R. E. (1999). *Diagnosing and changing organizational culture: Based on the competing values framework*. Reading, MA: Addison-Wesley.

Cameron, K. S., and Quinn, R. E. (2011). *Diagnosing and changing organizational culture: Based on the competing values framework* (3rd ed.). San Francisco: Jossey-Bass.

Campbell, D. T., and Fiske, D. W. (1959). Convergent and discriminant validation by the multitrait-multimethod matrix. *Psychological Bulletin*, 56, 81-105.

Carnegie, D. (1936). *How to win friends and influence people*. New York: Simon & Schuster.

Cartwright, T., and Baldwin, D. (2007). Seeing your way: Why leaders must communicate their visions. *Leadership in Action*, 27(3), 15-24.

Carty, V. (1999). Emerging post-industrial, postmodern trends and the implications for social change: A case-study of Nike corporation. Unpublished dissertation. University of New Mexico.

Caruso, D. R., Mayer, J. D., and Salovey, P. (2002). Emotional intelligence and emotional leadership. In R. E. Riggio, S. E. Murphy, and F. J. Pirozzolo (Eds.), *Multiple intelligences and leadership* (pp. 55-74). Mahwah, NJ: Erlbaum.

Cascio, W. F. (2011). Leadership succession How to avoid a crisis. *Ivey Business Journal*, 75(3), 6-8.

Castrogiovanni, G. J. (2002). Organization task environments: Have they changed fundamentally over time? *Journal of Management*, 28(2), 129-150.

Chan, J. (2012). A new breed of unfair advantage in sports - technology doping. Retrieved September 14, 2012, from www.engineering.com/3DPrinting/3DPrintingArticles/ArticleID/4519/A-New-Breed-Of-Unfair-Advantage-In-Sports-Technology-Doping.aspx.

Chappelet, J.-L. (2009). A global vision for sport (and sport management). *European Sport Management Quarterly*, 9(4), 483-485.

Charlton, R. (2011). The role of policy, rituals and language in shaping an academically focused culture in HBCU athletics. *Journal of Issues in Intercollegiate Athletics*, 4, 120-148.

Chatman, J. A., and Eunyoung Cha, S. (2003). Leading by leveraging culture. *California Management Review*, 45(4), 20-34.

Chatman, J. A., and Kennedy, J. A. (2010). Psychological perspectives on leadership. In N. Norhia and R. Khurana (Eds.), *Handbook of leadership theory and practice*. Boston: Harvard Business Press.

Chelladurai, P. (1984). Discrepancy between preferences and perceptions of leadership behavior and satisfaction of athletes in varying sports. *Journal of Sport Psychology*, 6(1), 27-41.

Chelladurai, P. (1990). Leadership in sport: A review. *International Journal of Sport Psychology*, 21(4), 328-354.

Chelladurai, P. (1993). Leadership. In R. N. Singer, M. Murphey, and L. K. Tennant (Eds.), *Handbook of research on sport psychology*. New York: Macmillan.

Chelladurai, P. (1999). *Leadership in human resource management in sport and recreation*. Champaign, IL: Human Kinetics.

Chelladurai, P., and Saleh, S. D. (1980). Dimensions of leader behavior in sports: Development of a leadership scale. *Journal of Sport Psychology*, 2(1), 34-45.

Cherniss, C., Extein, M., Goleman, D., and Weissberg, R. P. (2006). Emotional intelligence: What does the research really indicate? *Educational Psychologist*, 41(4), 239-245 doi: 10.1207/s15326985ep4104_4

Choi, Y. S., and Scott, D. K. (2009). Dynamics of organizational culture in professional baseball organizations: A cross-cultural comparison. *International Journal of Sport Management*, 10(2), 169-187.

Choi, Y. S., Martin, J. J., and Park, M. (2008). Organizational culture and job satisfaction in Korean professional baseball organizations. *International Journal of Applied Sports Sciences*, 20(2), 59-77.

Chung, P. K. (2010). Sport and globalisation: Elite sport development considerations. *ICSSPE Bulletin*, Issue 59.

Clark, G. (2008). Chicago Blackhawks: A turnaround worth remembering. Retrieved June 19, 2012 from http://bleacherreport.com/articles/97222-chicago-blackhawks-a-turnaround-worth-remembering.

Clement, A., and Grady, J. (2012). *Law in sport: Concepts and cases* (4th ed.). Morgantown, WV: Fitness Information Technology.

COHRE, (2007). Mega events. Retrieved May 10, 2013, from http://tenant.net/alerts/mega-events/Report_Fair_Play_FINAL.pdf.

College graduates get failing grade in professionalism. (2009). *O&P Business News*, 19(23), 15.

College Sports Business News (2011, December). National sports law institute founder has college sports concerns. Retrieved June 15, 2012 from http://collegesportsbusiness news.com/issue/december-2011/article/national-sports-law-institute-founder-has-college-sports-concerns.

Colyer, S. (2000). Organizational culture in selected Western Australian sport organizations. *Journal of Sport Management*, 14(4), 321-341.

Conger, J. A. (1991). Inspiring others: The language of leadership. *Academy of Management Executive*, 5(1), 31-45.

Conger, J. A. (2004). Developing leadership capability: What's inside the black box? *Academy of Management Executive*, 18(3), 136-139. doi: 10.5465/ame.2004.14776188

Conger, J. A., and Benjamin, B. (1999). *Building leaders: How successful companies develop the next generation*. San Francisco: Jossey-Bass.

Conger, J. A., and Kanungo, R. N. (1987). Toward a behavioral theory of charismatic leadership in organizational settings. *Academy of Management Review*, 12(4), 637-647. doi: 10.5465/AMR.1987.4306715

Conger, J. A., and Kanungo, R. N. (1988). The empowerment process: Integrating theory and practice. *Academy of Management Review*, 13(3), 471-482. doi: 10.5465/AMR.1988.4306983

Conger, J. A., and Riggio, R. E. (2006). *The practice of leadership: Developing the next generation of leaders*. San Francisco: Jossey-Bass.

Connerly, M. L., and Pedersen, P. B. (2005). *Leadership in a diverse and multicultural environment: Developing awareness, knowledge, and skills*. Thousand Oaks, CA: Sage.

Consortium for Research on Emotional Intelligence in Organizations (2012). Emotional intelligence measures. Retrieved May 24, 2012 from www.eiconsortium.org/measures/measures.html.

Conte, J. M. (2005). A review and critique of emotional intelligence measures. *Journal of Organizational Behavior*, 26(4), 433-440. doi: 10.1002/job.319

Coombs, W. T. (2000). Designing post-crisis messages: Lessons for crisis response strategies. *Review of Business*, 21(3/4), 37.

Copobianco, S., Davis, M., and Krause, L. (2004). Good conflict, bad conflict: How to have one without the other. *Mount Eliza Business Review*, 7(2), 31.

Covey, S. R. (1992). *Principle-centered leadership*. New York: Fireside.

Covey, S. R. (2004). *The 7 habits of highly effective people*. New York: Free Press.

Covey, S. R. (2006). *The speed of trust*. New York: Free Press.

Creating a sporting habit. (2012). Retrieved June 1, 2012 from www.gov.uk/government/uploads/system/uploads/attachment_data/file/78318/creating_a_sporting_habit_for_life.pdf.

Cronin, M., and Holt, R. (2003). The globalisation of sport. *History Today*, 53(7), 26-33.

Crow, B., Higgs, C., and Branson, A. (2008). Long-term strategic planning in inter-scholastic athletics: An athletic director's perspective. *Interscholastic Athletic Administration*, 34(4), 10-12.

Cunningham, G. (2008). Commitment to diversity and its influence on athletic department outcomes. *Journal of Intercollegiate Sport*, 1(2), 176-201.

Cunningham, G., and Fink, J. (2006). Diversity issues in sport and leisure. *Journal of Sport Management*, 20, 455-465.

Cunningham, G. B. (2009). Understanding the diversity-related change process: A field study. *Journal of Sport Management*, 23(4), 407-428.

Cunningham, G. B. (2010). Predictors of sexual orientation diversity in intercollegiate athletics departments. *Journal of Intercollegiate Sport*, 3(2), 256-269.

Cunningham, G. B. (2012). Sport, race, and ethnicity: Narratives of difference and diversity. *Managing Leisure,* 17(4), 363-364. doi: 10.1080/13606719.2012.670698

Cunningham, G. B., and Sagas, M. (2004). Group diversity, occupational commitment, and occupational turnover intentions among NCAA Division IA football coaching staffs. *Journal of Sport Management,* 18(3), 236-254.

Dale Carnegie Principles, The. (2010). Retrieved March 15, 2011, from www.dcarnegietrain ing.com/resources/relationship-principles.

Dalton, M., Swigert, S., Van Velsor, E., Bunker, K., and Wachholz, J. (1999). *The learning tactics inventory: Facilitator's guide.* San Francisco: Jossey-Bass.

Daly, H. E. (1999). Globalization versus internationalization. Retrieved May 22, 2013 from www.globalpolicy.org/component/content/article/162/27995.html.

Dansereau, F., Graen, G., and Haga, W. (1975). A vertical dyad linkage approach to leadership within formal organizations: A longitudinal investigation of the role-making process. *Organizational Behavior and Human Performance,* 13, 46-78.

Dart, T. (2013). NFL joins plan aiming to create professional rugby union league in US. Retrieved May 25, 2013 from www.guardian. co.uk/sport/2013/may/11/nfl-rugby-union-rugbylaw-barbarians-irish.

Davakos, H. (2006). An integral part of strategic planning for sport organisations: Training employees. *International Journal of Sport Management and Marketing,* 1(4), 7.

Deal, T. E., and Kennedy, A. A. (1982*). Corporate cultures: The rights and rituals of corporate life.* Harmondsworth, UK: Penguin Books.

Deal, T. E., and Kennedy, A. A. (1999). *The new corporate cultures.* New York: Basic Books.

De Carvalho, P. G. (2010). Evolution of sport, economics and globalisation. *ICSSPE Bulletin* (59), 10. Retrieved May 27, 2013 from SPORTDiscus database.

De Lench, B. (2006). *Home team advantage: The critical role of mothers in youth sports.* New York: Harper Paperbacks.

DePauw, K. P., and Gavron, S. J. (2005). *Disability sport* (2nd ed.). Champaign, IL: Human Kinetics.

DeSensi, J. T. (1995). Understanding multiculturalism and valuing diversity: A theoretical perspective. *Quest,* 47(1), 34-43.

DeSensi, J. T., and Rosenberg, D. (2003). *Ethics and morality in sport management* (2nd ed.). Morgantown, WV: Fitness Information Technology.

DeSensi, J. T., and Rosenberg, D. (2010). *Ethics and morality in sport management* (3rd ed.).Morgantown, WV: Fitness Information Technology.

Dess, G. G., and Beard, D. W. (1984). Dimensions of organizational task environments. *Administrative Science Quarterly,* 29(1), 52-73.

Dickerson Lynes, C. J. (2007). Women's athletics and the athletic patriarchy. Georgia Southern University. www.georgiasouthern. edu/etd/archive/spring2007/cynthia_j_lynes/ Lynes_Cynthia_J_200701_edd.pdf.

Doherty, A., Fink, J., Inglis, S., and Pastore, D. (2010). Understanding a culture of diversity through frameworks of power and change. *Sport Management Review,* 13(4), 368-381.

Doherty, A. J. (1997). The effect of leader characteristics on the perceived transformational/transactional leadership and impact of interuniversity athletic administrators. *Journal of Sport Management,* 11(3), 275-285.

Doherty, A. J., and Chelladurai, P. (1999). Managing cultural diversity in sport organizations: A theoretical perspective. *Journal of Sport Management,* 13(4), 280-297.

Doherty, A. J., and Danylchuk, K. E. (1996). Transformational and transactional leadership in interuniversity athletics management. *Journal of Sport Management,* 10(3), 292-309.

Dotlich, D., Noel, J., and Walker, N. (2004). *Leadership passages: The personal and professional transitions that make or break a leader.* San Francisco: Jossey-Bass.

Drucker, P. F. (2006). *Classic Drucker.* Boston: Harvard Business Press.

Duncan, D. (2012). Dr. Edgar Schein on culture, leadership, and performance. http://doctor duncan.com/2012/10/16/dr-edgar-schein-on-culture-leadership-and-performance.

Eagly, A. H., and Chin, J. L. (2010). Diversity and leadership in a changing world. *American Psychologist,* 65(3), 216-224. doi: 10.1037/a0018957

Elser, C. (2011). Global sports spending to rise 3.7% to $145 billion by 2013, study says. www.bloomberg.com/news/2011-12-09/global-sports-spending-to-rise-3-7-to-145-billion-by-2015-study-says.html.

Eunice Kennedy Shriver. (2012). Retrieved January 12, 2012, from www.specialolympics.org/eunice_kennedy_shriver_biography.aspx.

Evans, M. G. (1970). The effects of supervisory behavior on the path-goal relationship. *Organizational Behavior and Human Performance,* 5(3), 277-298.

Fairholm, M. R. (2009). Leadership and organizational strategy. *Innovation Journal,* 14(1), 1-16.

Fairholm, M. R., and Card, M. (2009). Perspectives of strategic thinking: From controlling chaos to embracing it. *Journal of Management & Organization,* 15(1), 17-30. doi: 10.5172/jmo.837.15.1.17

fanpagelist.com. (2011). Top athletes on facebook. Retrieved August 8, 2011, from http://fanpagelist.com/category/athletes.

Fay, T., and Wolff, E. (2009). Disability in sport in the twenty-first century: Creating a new sport opportunity spectrum. *Boston University International Law Journal,* 27(2), 231-248.

Fiedler, F. E. (1967). *A theory of leadership effectiveness.* New York: McGraw-Hill.

Fifa pressed over Qatar World Cup worker's conditions (2011). BBC News Middle East. Retrieved August 8, 2012 from http://www.bbc.co.uk/news/world-middle-east-15772284.

Fink, J. S., and Pastore, D. L. (1999). Diversity in sport? Utilizing the business literature to devise a comprehensive framework of diversity initiatives. *Quest,* 51(4), 310-327.

Fink, J. S., Borland, J. F., and Fields, S. K. (2011). Sexist acts in sports: Media reactions and forms of apologia. *International Journal of Sport Communication,* 4(2), 198-216.

Fink, J. S., Pastore, D. L., and Riemer, H. A. (2001). Do differences make a difference? Managing diversity in Division IA intercollegiate athletics. *Journal of Sport Management,* 15(1), 10.

Fink, J. S., Pastore, D. L., and Riemer, H. A. (2003). Managing employee diversity: Perceived practices and organisational outcomes in NCAA Division III athletic departments. *Sport Management Review,* 6(2), 147-168.

Fontaine, R. (2008). Teaching strategic thinking. *The Journal of Global Business Issues,* 2(1), 87-94.

Forbes.com (2010). Slide Show: The World's Most Valuable Sports Teams. Retrieved July 20, 2011 from www.forbes.com/2010/07/20/most-valuable-athletes-and-teams-business-sports-sportsmoney-fifty-fifty-teams_slide.html.

Ford, M. G. (2003). Working toward cultural competence in athletic training. *Athletic Therapy Today,* 8(3), 60-66.

Former Husker Keller's suit threatens NCAA, EA (2011). CBSSports.com. Retrieved July 10 2012 from www.cbssports.com/collegefootball/story/14685064/former-husker-kellers-suit-threatens-ncaa-ea.

Freeman, R. E., Wicks, A. C., and Parmar, B. (2004). Stakeholder theory and "The Corporate Objective Revisited." *Organization Science,* 15(3), 364-369.

Friedman, T.L. (2006). *The World is Flat—A brief history of the twenty-first century.* New York: Farrar, Straus and Giroux.

Frontiera, J. (2010). Leadership and organizational culture transformation in professional sport. *Journal of Leadership and Organizational Studies,* 17(1), 71-86. doi: 10.1177/1548051809345253

Frontiera, J., and Leidl, D. (2012). *Team turnarounds: A playbook for transforming underperforming teams.* San Francisco: Jossey-Bass.

Gardner, H. (1983). *Frames of mind: The theory of multiple intelligences.* New York: Basic Books.

Gardner, H. (1995). *Leading minds: Anatomy of leadership.* New York: Basic Books.

Gardner, J. W. (1990). *On leadership.* New York: Free Press.

George, W. W. (2003). *Authentic leadership: Rediscovering the secrets to creating lasting value.* San Francisco: Jossey-Bass.

Gereffi, G., (1994). The organisation of buyer-driven global commodity chains: How U.S. retailers shape overseas production networks. In G. Gereffi and M. Korzeniewicz (Eds.), *Commodity chains and global capitalism.* Westport, CT: Praeger.

Gereffi, G., Korzeniewicz, M., and Korzeniewicz, R. (1994). Introduction: Global commodity chains. In G. Gereffi and M. Korzeniewicz (Eds.), *Commodity chains and global capitalism.* Westport, CT: Praeger.

Gill, D. L., Morrow, R. G., Collins, K. E., Lucey, A. B., and Schultz, A. M. (2006). Attitudes and sexual prejudice in sport and physical activity. *Journal of Sport Management,* 20, 554-564.

Giuliani, R. (2002). *Leadership.* New York: Hyperion.

Giulianotti, R., and Robertson, R. (2004). The globalization of football: A study in the globalization of the "serious life." *British Journal of Sociology,* 55(4), 545-568.

Glosier, M. (2011). Learfield sports, NACDA renew Directors' Cup partnership through 2016. Retrieved July 10, 2011, from www.nacda.com/sports/directorscup/spec-rel/061711aac.html.

Goffee, R., and Jones, G. (1996). What holds the modern company together? *Harvard Business Review,* 74(6), 133-148.

Goldman, E. F. (2008). The power of work experiences: Characteristics critical to developing expertise in strategic thinking. *Human Resource Development Quarterly,* 19(3), 217-239.

Goldsmith, W. (2012). Ten reasons why change is so hard to introduce in sport. www.sportscoachingbrain.com/ten-reasons-why-change-is-so-hard-to-introduce-in-sport.

Goleman, D. (1998). What makes a leader? *Harvard Business Review,* 76(6), 93-102.

Goleman, D. (2000). Leadership that gets results. *Harvard Business Review,* March-April, 82-83.

Goleman, D. (2001). Emotional intelligence: Issues in paradigm building. In C. Cherniss and D. Goleman (Eds.), *The emotionally intelligent workplace.* San Francisco: Jossey-Bass.

Goleman, D. (2004). What makes a leader? *Harvard Business Review,* 82(1), 82-91.

Goleman, D., Boyatzis, R., and McKee, A. (2002). *Primal leadership: Realizing the power of emotional intelligence.* Boston: Harvard Business Review Press.

Goleman, D. P. (1995). *Emotional intelligence: Why it can matter more than IQ for character, health and lifelong achievement.* New York: Bantam Books.

Graen, G. B. (1976). Role making processes within complex organizations. In M. D. Dunnette (Ed.), *Handbook of industrial and organizational psychology.* Chicago: Rand-McNally.

Graen, G. B., and Uhl-Bien, M. (1991). The transformation of professionals into self-managing and partially self-designating contributions: Toward a theory of leader-making. *Journal of Management Systems,* 3(3), 33-48.

Graen, G. B., and Uhl-Bien, M. (1995). Relationship-based approach to leadership: Development of leader-member exchange (LMX) theory of leadership over 25 years: Applying a multi-level multi-domain perspective. *Leadership Quarterly,* 6(2), 219-247.

Grants will deliver more women leaders in sport (2008). Retrieved July 22, 2012 from www.ausport.gov.au/participating/news/grants_will_deliver_more_women_leaders_in_sport.

Grappendorf, H. (2011). Where we've been, where we are, where we're going: Girls and women in sport and physical activity. *Women in Sport & Physical Activity Journal,* 20(2), 93-94.

Greenleaf, R. K. (1977). *Servant leadership: A journey into the nature of legitimate power and greatness.* New York: Paulist Press.

Griffin, M. A., Parker, S. K., and Mason, C. M. (2010). Leader vision and the development of adaptive and proactive performance: A longitudinal study. *Journal of Applied Psychology*, 95(1), 174-182.

Grundy, T. (1999). Managing strategic breakthroughs—lessons from the football industry 1997–98. *Strategic Change*, 8(8), 435-444.

Gundling, E., Hogan, T., and Cvitkovich, K. (2011). *What is global leadership?: 10 key behaviors that define great global leaders.* Boston: Nicholas Brealey.

Hackman, J. R. (2010). What is this thing called leadership? In N. Nohria and R. Khurana (Eds.), *Handbook of leadership theory and practice.* Boston: Harvard Business Press.

Hackman, J. R., and Wageman, R. (2007). Asking the right questions about leadership: Discussion and conclusions. *American Psychologist*, 62(1), 43-47. doi: 10.1037/0003-066x.62.1.43

Hanford, P. (1995). Developing director and executive competencies in strategic thinking. In B. Garratt (Ed.), *Developing strategic thought: Reinventing the art of direction-giving.* London: McGraw-Hill.

Hannah, S. T. (2006). Agentic leadership efficacy: Test of a new construct and model for development and performance. Unpublished doctoral dissertation. University of Nebraska-Lincoln.

Harris, I. H. (2001). *Examining the relationship between emotional intelligence competencies in NCAA Division I athletic directors and the organizational climate within their departments.* Eugene, OR: Kinesiology Publications, University of Oregon.

Harrison, D. A., Price, K. H., and Bell, M. P. (1998). Beyond relational demography: Time and the effects of surface- and deep-level diversity on work group cohesion. *Academy of Management Journal*, 41(1), 96-107. doi: 10.2307/256901

Harrison, D. A., Price, K. H., Gavin, J. H., and Florey, A. T. (2002). Time, teams, and task performance: Changing effects of surface- and deep-level diversity on group functioning. *Academy of Management Journal*, 45(5), 1029-1045. doi: 10.2307/3069328.

Harter, N., and Evanecky, D. (2002). Fairness in leader-member exchange theory: Do we all belong on the inside? *Leadership Review, Summer 2002.* Retrieved July 8, 2011 from www.leadershipreview.org/2002summer/article1_summer_2002.asp.

Hemphill, J. K., and Coons, A. E. (1957). Development of the Leader Behavior Description Questionnaire. In R. M. Stogdill and A. E. Coons (Eds.), *Leader behavior: Its description and measurement.* Columbus, OH: Bureau of Business Research.

Hersey, P., and Blanchard, K. H. (Eds.). (1984). *Management of organizational behavior.* Englewood Cliffs, NJ: Prentice Hall.

Hersey, P., and Blanchard, K. H. (1988). *Management of organizational behavior* (5th ed.). Englewood Cliffs, NJ: Prentice Hall.

Hersey, P., and Blanchard, K. H. (2006). *Leader effectiveness and adaptability description (LEAD).* Binghamton, NY: Center for Leadership Studies.

Hersey, P., Blanchard, K. H., and Johnson, D. E. (2012). *Management of organizational behavior* (10th ed.). Englewood Cliffs, NJ: Prentice Hall.

Heydarinejad, S., and Adman, O. (2010). Relationship between coaching leadership styles and team cohesion in football teams of the Iranian university league. *Studies in Physical Culture and Tourism*, 17(4), 367-372.

Higgs, M. J., and Dulewicz, V. (2002). *Making sense of emotional intelligence.* Windsor: NFER-Nelson.

Hill, J. S., and Vincent, J. (2006). Globalisation and sports branding: The case of Manchester United. *International Journal of Sports Marketing & Sponsorship*, 7(3), 213-230.

history.com. (2013). First modern Olympic games. (2013). Retrieved May 18, 2013, from www.history.com/this-day-in-history/first-modern-olympic-games.

Hofstede, G. (1980). *Culture's consequences: International differences in work-related values.* Beverly Hills, CA: Sage.

Hofstede, G. H. (2001). *Culture's consequences: Comparing values, behaviors, institutions, and organizations across nations* (2nd ed.). London: Sage.

Holland, J. (2011). Leading Diversity. Retrieved August 14, 2012 from http://leadchange-group.com/leading-diversity.

Holland, J. F. (2008). The perils of strategic planning. *Associations Now,* 4(9), 72-78.

Hollander, E. P. (1992). Leadership, followership, self, and others. *Leadership Quarterly,* 3(1), 43-54.

Holt, K., and Seki, K. (2012). Global leadership: A developmental shift for everyone. *Industrial and Organizational Psychology: Perspectives on Science and Practice,* 5(2), 196-215. doi: 10.1111/j.1754-9434.2012.01431.x

House, R. J. (1971). A path goal theory of leader effectiveness. *Administrative Science Quarterly,* 16(3), 321-339.

House, R. J. (1977). A 1976 theory of charismatic leadership. In J. G. Hunt and L. L. Larson (Eds.), *Leadership: The cutting edge.* Carbondale, IL: Southern Illinois University Press.

House, R. J. (1996, Fall). Path-goal theory of leadership: Lessons, legacy, and a reformulated theory. *Leadership Quarterly,* 7(3) 323.

House, R. J., and Howell, J. M. (1992). Personality and charismatic leadership. *Leadership Quarterly,* 3(2), 81-108.

House, R. J., and Mitchell, T. R. (1974). Path-goal theory of leadership. *Contemporary Business,* 3(Fall), 81-98.

House, R. J., and Podsakoff, P. M. (1994). Leadership effectiveness: Past perspectives & future directions for research. In J. Greenberg (Ed.), *Organizational behavior: The state of the science.* Hillsdale, NJ: Erlbaum.

House, R., Javidan, M., and Dorfman, P. (2001). Project GLOBE: An introduction. *Applied Psychology: An International Review,* 50(4), 489-505.

House, R. J., Hanges, P. J., Javidan, M., Dorfman, P. W., and Gupta, V. (Eds.). (2004). *Culture, leadership, and organizations.* Thousand Oaks, CA: Sage.

House, R. J., Wright, N. S., and Aditya, R. N. (1997). Cross-cultural research on organizational leadership: A critical analysis and a proposed theory. In P. C. Earley and M. Erez (Eds.), *New perspectives on international industrial/organizational psychology* (pp. 535-625). San Francisco: New Lexington Press/Jossey-Bass.

Howard, A., and Bray, D. W. (1988). *Managerial lives in transition: Advancing age and changing times.* New York: Guilford Press.

Howell, J. M., and Avolio, B. J. (1992). The ethics of charismatic leadership: Submission or liberation? *Academy of Management Executive,* 6(2), 43-54.

Inglis, S., Danylchuk, K. E., and Pastore, D. (1996). Understanding retention factors in coaching and athletic management positions. *Journal of Sport Management,* 10(3), 237-249.

Jackson, M. (2001). Bringing a dying brand back to life. *Harvard Business Review,* 79(5), 53-61.

Javidan, M., and Walker, J. L. (2012). A whole new global mindset for leadership. *People & Strategy,* 35(2), 36-41.

Javidan, M., Dorfman, P. W., De Luque, M. S., and House, R. J. (2006). In the eye of the beholder: Cross cultural lessons in leadership from Project GLOBE. *Academy of Management Perspectives,* 20(1), 67-90. doi: 10.5465/AMP.2006.19873410

Johansen, B. (2012). *Leaders make the future: Ten new leadership skills for an uncertain world.* San Francisco: Berrett-Koehler.

Jones, D. (2011, May 8). Questions and answers with Florida AD Jeremy Foley. Retrieved from www.usatoday.com/sports/college/2011-05-08-florida-jeremy-foley-q-and-a_N.htm.

Judge, T.A. and Piccolo, R.F. (2004). Transformational and transactional leadership: A meta-analytic test of their relative validity. *Journal of Applied Psychology,* 89(5), 755-768.

Judge, T. A., Piccolo, R. F., and Ilies, R. (2004). The forgotten ones? The validity of consideration and initiating structure in leadership research. *Journal of Applied Psychology,* 89(1), 36-51.

Jun, J. W., and Lee, H. M. (2012). The globalization of sport and the mass-mediated identity of Hines Ward in South Korea. *Journal of Sport Management, 26*(2), 103-112.

Kanter, R. M. (2003). Leadership and the psychology of turnarounds. *Harvard Business Review, 81*(6), 58-67.

Kao, S.-F., and Ceng, B.-S. (2005). Assessing sport team culture: Qualitative and quantitative approaches. *International Journal of Sport Psychology, 36*(1), 22-38.

Karami, A. (2007). *Strategy formulation in entrepreneurial firms.* Surrey, UK: Ashgate.

Katz, R. L. (1955). Skills of an effective administrator. *Harvard Business Review, 33*(1), 33-42.

Kellerman, B. (2008). *Followership.* Boston: Harvard Business Press.

Keller sues EA Sports over images. (2009). http://sports.espn.go.com/ncf/news/story?id=4151071.

Kent, A., and Chelladurai, P. (2001). Perceived transformational leadership, organizational commitment, and citizenship behavior: A case study in intercollegiate athletics. *Journal of Sport Management, 15*(2), 135.

Kent, A., and Weese, W. J. (2000). Do effective organizations have better executive leaders and/or organizational cultures? A study of selected sport organizations in Canada. *European Journal for Sport Management, 7*(2), 4-21.

Kent, T. W. (2005). Leading and managing: It takes two to tango. *Management Decision, 43*(7/8), 1010-1017. doi: 10.1108/00251740510610008

Kim, W. C., and Mauborgne, R. (2003). Tipping point leadership. *Harvard Business Review, 81*(4), 60-69.

Kim, W. C., and Mauborgne, R. (2006). Tipping-point leadership. *Leadership Excellence, 23*(9), 5.

Kirkpatrick, S. A., and Locke, E. A. (1991). Leadership: Do traits matter? *Executive, 5*(2), 48-60.

Klann, G. (2003). *Crisis leadership.* Greensboro, NC: Center for Creative Leadership.

Klein, K. M., and Wang, M. (2010). Deep-level diversity and leadership. *American Psychologist, 65*(9), 932-934. doi: 10.1037/a0021355

Kline, P., and Saunders, B. (2010). *Ten steps to a learning organization.* Salt Lake City, UT: Great River Books.

Kluckhohn, C. K. (1951). Values and value orientations in the theory of action. In T. Parsons and E. A. Shils (Eds.), *Toward a general theory of action.* Cambridge, MA: Harvard University Press.

Knight Commission on Intercollegiate Athletics. (2009). College sports 101: A primer on money, athletics and higher education in the 21st century. Retrieved August 12, 2012 from www.knightcommission.org/index.php?option=com_content&view=article&id=344&Itemid=84.

Kotter, J. P. (1990). What leaders really do. *Harvard Business Review, 68,* 103-111.

Kotter, J. P. (1996). *Leading change.* Boston: Harvard Business Review Press.

Kotter, J. P. (2007). Leading change. *Harvard Business Review, 85*(1), 96-103.

Kotter, J. P. (2012). *Leading change.* Boston: Harvard Business Review Press.

Kouzes, J. and Posner, B. (2013). The five practices of exemplary leadership model. *The Leadership Challenge.* Retrieved July 24, 2013 from www.leadershipchallenge.com/About-section-Our-Approach.aspx.

Kouzes, J. M., and Posner, B. Z. (1995). *The leadership challenge: How to keep getting extraordinary things done in organizations.* San Francisco: Jossey-Bass.

Kouzes, J. M., and Posner, B. Z. (1997). *The leadership practices inventory: Facilitator's guide.* San Francisco: Jossey-Bass.

Kouzes, J. M., and Posner, B. Z. (2007). *The leadership challenge* (4th ed.). San Francisco: Jossey-Bass.

Kriemadis, T. (2009). Strategic planning in university athletic departments in the United Kingdom. *Sport Journal, 12*(2), 1.

Kriemadis, T., and Theakou, E. (2007). Strategic planning models in public and non-profit sport organizations. *Choregia, 3*(2), 27-37.

Kstatesports.com (2014). This is Kansas State football: Bowl tradition. Retrieved October 12, 2013 from www.kstatesports.com/feature/football-bowlgames.html.

Kurtz, C. F., and Snowden, D. J. (2003). The new dynamics of strategy: Sense making in a complex and complicated world. *IBM Systems Journal*, 42(3), 462-483.

Lahiri, I. (2008). Creating a competency model for diversity and inclusion practitioners. *Council Perspectives: Insights from The Conference Board Council on Workforce Diversity*. www.conference-board.org/pdf_free/councils/TCBCP005.pdf.

Lakowski, T. (2009). Athletes with disabilities in school sports: A critical assessment of the state of sports opportunities for students with disabilities. *Boston University International Law Journal*, 27(2), 283-315.

Lapchick, R. (2010). 2009 racial and gender report card: College sport. Retrieved July 3, 2012 from www.tidesport.org/RGRC/2009/2009_College_Sport_RGRC.pdf.

Lapchick, R. (2011). 2010 racial and gender report card: College sport. Retrieved July 3, 2012 from www.tidesport.org/rgrc/2010/2010_college_rgrc_final.pdf.

Lapchick, R. (2012a). 2012 Major League Baseball Racial and Gender Report Card. Retrieved July 3, 2012 from www.tidesport.org/RGRC/2012/2012_MLB_RGRC.pdf.

Lapchick, R. (2012b). 2012 National Basketball Association Racial and Gender Report Card. Retrieved July 3, 2012 from www.tidesport.org/RGRC/2012/2012_NBA_RGRC[1].pdf.

Lee, C. D. (1989). *The relationship between coaches' leadership style, strategy and organizational culture on success*. Eugene, OR: Microform Publications, College of Human Development and Performance, University of Oregon.

Lencioni, P. (2012). *The advantage: Why organizational health trumps everything in business*. San Francisco: Jossey-Bass.

Lerbinger, O. (1997). *The crisis manager: Facing risk and responsibility*. Mahwah, NJ: Erlbaum.

Levy, G. (2012). Top 10 worst sport terrorism attacks. www.time.com/time/specials/packages/article/0,28804,1882967_1882966_1882962,00.html.

Lewin, K., Lippitt, R., and White, R. K. (1939). Patterns of aggressive behavior in experimentally created social climates. *Journal of Social Psychology*, 10, 271-279.

Lichtenstein, B. B., Uhl-Bien, M., Marion, R., Seers, A., Orton, J. D., and Schreiber, C. (2006). Complexity leadership theory: An interactive perspective on leading in complex adaptive systems. *Emergence: Complexity and Organization*, 8(4), 2-12.

Liden, R. C., Wayne, S. J., and Stilwell, D. (1993). A longitudinal study on the early development of leader-member exchange. *Journal of Applied Psychology*, 78(4), 662-674.

Liedtka, J. M. (1998). Strategic thinking: Can it be taught? *Long Range Planning*, 31(1), 120-129.

London, C., and Boucher, R. (2000). Leadership and organizational effectiveness in Canadian University athletics. *International Journal of Sport Management*, 1(1), 70-87.

Lussier, R., and Kimball, D. (2009). *Applied sport management skills*. Champaign, IL: Human Kinetics.

Luthans, F., Avey, J. B., Avolio, B. J., Norman, S. M., and Combs, G. M. (2006). Psychological capital development: Toward a micro-intervention. *Journal of Organizational Behavior*, 27(3), 387-393.

Luthans, F., Avolio, B. J., Avey, J. B., and Norman, S. M. (2007). Positive psychological capital: Measurement and relationship with performance and satisfaction. *Personnel Psychology*, 60(3), 541-572. doi: 10.1111/j.1744-6570.2007.00083.x

Luthans, F. L., Avolio, B. J., and Youseff, C. (2007). *Psychological capital: Developing the human capital edge*. Oxford: Oxford University Press.

Maak, T., and Pless, N. M. (2006). Responsible leadership in a stakeholder society—a relational perspective. *Journal of Business Ethics*, 66(1), 99-115. doi: 10.1007/s10551-006-9047-z

MacIntosh, E., and Doherty, A. (2005). Leader intentions and employee perceptions of organizational culture in a private fitness corporation. *European Sport Management Quarterly*, 5(1), 1-22.

MacIntosh, E., and Doherty, A. (2008). Inside the Canadian fitness industry: Development of a conceptual framework of organizational culture. *International Journal of Sport Management*, 9(3), 303-327.

MacIntosh, E. W., and Doherty, A. (2010). The influence of organizational culture on job satisfaction and intention to leave. *Sport Management Review*, 13(2), 106-117.

MacIntosh, E. W., Doherty, A., and Walker, M. (2010). Cross-sectoral variation in organizational culture in the fitness industry. *European Sport Management Quarterly*, 10(4), 445-464.

Maguire, J. (1999). *Global sport: Identities, societies, civilizations*. Malden, MA: Blackwell.

Mahoney, B. (2010). David Stern: NBA losses could reach $400 million. www.huffington post.com/2010/02/13/david-stern-nba-losses-co_n_461614.html.

Male, B. (2010). The 10 worst winter olympics PR disasters of all time. Retrieved July 25, 2011, from www.businessinsider.com/the-10-worst-pr-scandals-of-the-winter-olympics-2010-2?op=1.

Marion, R., and Uhl-Bien, M. (2001). Leadership in complex organizations. *Leadership Quarterly*, 12(4), 389-418.

Maritz, R., Pretorius, M., and Plant, K. (2011). Exploring the interface between strategy-making and responsible leadership. *Journal of Business Ethics*, 98, 101-113. doi: 10.1007/s10551-011-1024-5

Marquardt, M. (1999). *Action learning in action: Transforming problems and people for world-class organizational learning*. Palo Alto, CA: Davies-Black Press.

Marquardt, M. (2011). *Building the learning organization: Achieving strategic advantage through a commitment to learning* (3rd ed.). Boston: Nicholas Brealey.

Marra, J., Covassin, T., Shingles, R. R., Canady, R. B., and Mackowiak, T. (2010). Assessment of certified athletic trainers' levels of cultural competence in the delivery of health care. *Journal of Athletic Training*, 45(4), 380-385.

Martin, R. L. (2007). *The opposable mind: How successful leaders win through integrative thinking*. Boston: Harvard Business School Press.

Massengale, D., and Lough, N. (2010). Women leaders in sport: Where's the gender equity? *Journal of Physical Education, Recreation and Dance*, 81(4), 6-8.

Mayer, J. D., and Caruso, D. (2002). The effective leader: Understanding and applying emotional intelligence. *Ivey Business Journal*, Nov/Dec, 1-5.

Mayer, J. D., and Salovey, P. (1997). What is emotional intelligence? In P. Salovey and D. J. Sluyter (Eds.), *Emotional development and emotional intelligence*. New York: Basic Books.

Mayer, J. D., Salovey, P., and Caruso, D. R. (2002). *Mayer—Salovey-Caruso Emotional Intelligence Test (MSCEIT) user's manual*. Toronto, ON: MHS.

Mays, R. (2011). The second act of Kansas State's Bill Snyder. www.grantland.com/blog/the-triangle/post/_/id/7152/the-second-act-of-kansas-states-bill-snyder.

McCall, M. (2010). The experience conundrum. In N. Nohria and R. Khurana (Eds.), *Handbook of leadership theory and practice*. Boston: Harvard Business Press.

McCall, M. W., Lombardo, M. M., and Morrison, A. M. (1988). *The lessons of experience: How successful executives develop on the job*. Lexington, MA: Lexington Books.

McCarthy, D. (2009). How to create a shared vision statement. Great Leadership [weblog post]. Retrieved June 22, 2012 from www.greatleadershipbydan.com/2009/07/how-to-create-shared-vision-statement.html.

McCauley, C. D., Kanaga, K., and Lafferty, K. (2010). Leader development systems. In E. V. Velsor, C. D. McCauley, and M. N. Ruderman (Eds.), *The Center for Creative Leadership handbook of leadership development* (3rd ed.). San Francisco: Jossey-Bass.

McCrimmon, M. (2008, March). 21st century leadership.. Retrieved July 30, 2010 from http://suite101.com/a/21st-century-leadership-a46534.

McFarlane, D. A. (2008). Effectively managing the 21st century knowledge worker. *Journal of Knowledge Management Practice*. Retrieved April 11, 2011 from www.tlainc.com/articl150.htm.

Mercier, R. (2002). Applying systems thinking to understanding Canadian sport. *Canadian Journal for Women in Coaching Online*, 2(3). Retrieved May 14, 2012 from http://23361.vws.magma.ca/WOMEN/e/journal/jan2002/print_developing.htm.

Merriam-Webster. (2012). Retrieved January 15, 2012, from www.m-w.com.

Merriam-Webster. (2013). Retrieved May 10, 2013, from www.m-w.com.

Miles, R. E., and Snow, C. C. (1978). *Organizational strategy, structure, and process*. New York: McGraw-Hill.

Mintzberg, H. (1973). *The nature of managerial work*. New York: Harper & Row.

Mintzberg, H. (1994). *The rise and fall of strategic planning*. New York: Free Press.

Mintzberg, H. (2009). *Managing*. San Francisco: Berrett-Koehler.

Mintzberg, H., and Waters, J. A. (1982). Tracking strategy in an entrepreneurial firm. *Academy of Management Journal*, 25(3), 465-499. doi: 10.2307/256075

Mintzberg, H., and Waters, J. A. (1985). Of strategies, deliberate and emergent. *Strategic Management Journal*, 6(3), 257-272.

Mitchell report: Baseball slow to react to players' steroid use. (2007). http://sports.espn.go.com/mlb/news/story?id=3153509.

Moore, K., and Lenir, P. (2011). Mintzberg's better way to do corporate strategy. www.forbes.com/sites/karlmoore/2011/06/21/emergent-strategy-demands-emergent-learning.

Morgan, W. (2007). *Ethics in sport* (2nd ed.). Champaign, IL: Human Kinetics.

Muczyk, J. P., and Steel, R. P. (1998). Leadership style and the turnaround executive. *Business Horizons*, 41(2), 39.

Muffet-Willett, S. L., and Kruse, S. D. (2009). Crisis leadership: Past research and future directions. *Journal of Business Continuity & Emergency Planning*, 3(3), 248-258.

Mumford, M. D., Zaccaro, S. J., Harding, F. D., Jacobs, T. O., and Fleishman, E. A. (2000). Leadership skills for a changing world: Solving complex social problems. *Leadership Quarterly*, 11(1), 11.

Murray, A. (2010). *The Wall Street Journal essential guide to management*. New York: Harper Paperbacks.

Mylan WTT. (2012). Billie Jean King, Mylan WTT presented by GEICO co-founder. Retrieved January 12, 2012, from www.wtt.com/page.aspx?article_id=1252.

NACDA. (2013). NACDA Mentoring Institute. Retrieved May 24, 2013, from www.nacda.com/nacda/nacda-mentoring-institute.html.

Nanus, B. (1992). *Visionary leadership*. San Francisco: Jossey-Bass.

National Council of Nonprofits. (2013). Leadership development and succession. www.councilofnonprofits.org/resources/leadership-development-and-succession.

Neubauer, D. (2008). Modern sport and Olympic Games: The problematic complexities raised by the dynamics of globalization. *Olympika: The International Journal of Olympic Studies*, 17, 1-40.

nfl.com. (2010). League announces policy on social media for before and after games. Retrieved August 7, 2011 from www.nfl.com/news/story/09000d5d8124976d/article/league-announces-policy-on-social-media-for-before-and-after-games.

NFL tackles tough economy with cuts (2009). CBS Money Watch. Retrieved May 20, 2012 from www.cbsnews.com/2100-500395_162-4828761.html.

ngf.org. (2010). Minority participation in the U.S. 2010. Retrieved March 10, 2012, from http://secure.ngf.org/ces3/default.asp?q=minority+golfers.

nhl.com. (2012). Diversity. Retrieved July 6, 2012 from www.nhl.com/nhlhq/community/diversity.html.

Nienaber, H. (2010). Conceptualisation of management and leadership. *Management Decision*, 48(5), 661-675. doi: 10.1108/00251741011043867

Nightengale, B. (2012). Number of African-American baseball players dips again. USA TODAY Sports. Retrieved July 8, 2012 from http://usatoday30.usatoday.com/sports/baseball/story/2012-04-15/baseball-jackie-robinson/54302108/1.

Nikebiz.com (2013). Build and empower the winning team. Retrieved February 10, 2013 from www.nikebiz.com/crreport/content/people-and-culture/6-2-0-human-resources.php?cat=human-resources.

Northouse, P. G. (2010). *Leadership: Theory and practice* (5th ed.). Thousand Oaks, CA: Sage.

Nowack, K. M. (2009). Leveraging multirater feedback to facilitate successful behavioral change. *Consulting Psychology Journal: Practice and Research*, 61(4), 280-297. doi: 10.1037/a0017381

Nowack, K. M. (2010). Warning: 360-degree feedback may be hazardous to your health. Retrieved August 27, 2012 from www.linkage inc.com/thinking/linkageleader/Documents/Kenneth_Nowack_Warning_360degree_Feedback_May_Be_Hazardous_to_Your_Health.pdf.

O'Brien, D. (2011). The leadership challenge for athletic directors: Inspire a shared vision. Retrieved June 3, 2012 from http://college sportsbusinessnews.com/issue/october-2012/article/the-leadership-challenge-for-athletic-directors-inspire-a-shared-vision.

O'Callaghan, S. (2010). *Turnaround leadership: Making decisions, rebuilding trust, and delivering results after a crisis*. Philadelphia: Kogan Page.

Ogbonna, E., and Harris, L. C. (2000). Leadership style, organizational culture and performance: Empirical evidence from UK companies. *International Journal of Human Resource Management*, 11(4), 766-788. doi: 10.1080/09585190050075114

O'Reilly, C. A., and Chatman, J. A. (1996). Culture as social control: Corporations, cults, and commitment. *Research in Organizational Behavior*, 18, 157.

Orlando City Soccer. (2013). Orlando City to become USL affiliate of Major League Soccer's Sporting Kansas City. www.orlando citysoccer.com/news/?article_id=1176.

Ormsby, A. (2012). London 2012 opening ceremony draws 900 million viewers. www.gma network.com/news/story/268733/economy/business/olympics-london-2012-opening-ceremony-draws-900-million-viewers.

Ozanian, M. (2012). The Forbes fab 40: The world's most valuable sports brands. www.forbes.com/sites/mikeozanian/2012/10/17/the-forbes-fab-40-the-worlds-most-valuable-sports-brands-4.

Painter-Morland, M. (2008). Systemic leadership and the emergence of ethical responsiveness. *Journal of Business Ethics*, 82(2), 509-524. doi: 10.1007/s10551-008-9900-3

Painter-Morland, M. (2009). Leadership in complex adaptive systems. *Rotman Magazine*, Fall, 99-102.

Parks, J. B., Quarterman, J., and Thibault, L. (Eds.). (2007). *Contemporary sport management* (3rd ed.). Champaign, IL: Human Kinetics.

Pawlak, G. (1984). Organizational culture in functioning of sport associations. Sports et sociétés contemporaines. *International Committee for the Sociology of Sport: Eighth Symposium*. Paris: Institut National du Sport et de l'Education Physique. Société Francaise de Sociologie du Sport. 1984, pp. 565-574.

Peachey, J. W., and Burton, L. J. (2012). Transactional or transformational leaders in intercollegiate athletics? Examining the influence of leader gender and subordinate gender on evaluation of leaders during organizational culture change. *International Journal of Sport Management*, 13(2), 115-143.

Pearson, C. M., and Clair, J. A. (1998). Reframing crisis management. *Academy of Management Review*, 23(1), 59-76. doi: 10.5465/AMR.1998.192960

Pedersen, P. M., and Whisenant, W. A. (2005). Successful when given the opportunity: Investigating gender representation and success rates of interscholastic athletic directors. *Physical Educator*, 62(4), 178-186.

Petrides, K. V. (2011). Ability and trait emotional intelligence. In T. Chamorro-Premuzic, S. von Stumm, and A. Furnham (Eds.), *The Wiley-Blackwell handbook of individual differences.* Boston: Blackwell.

Petrides, K. V., and Furnham, A. (2001). Trait emotional intelligence: Psychometric investigation with reference to established trait taxonomies. *European Journal of Personality,* 15(6), 425-448. doi: 10.1002/per.416

Pittinsky, T. L. (2010). A two-dimensional model of intergroup leadership: The case of national diversity. *American Psychologist,* 65(3), 194-200. doi: 10.1037/a0017329

Planning in sport. (2004). Australian Sports Commission. Retrieved June 22, 2012 from www.ausport.gov.au/__data/assets/pdf_file/0020/115535/2._Effective_Planning_in Sport.pdf.

Plummer, D. C. (2006). Sportophobia: Why do some men avoid sport? *Journal of Sport and Social Issues,* 30, 122-137.

Podolny, J. M., Khurana, R., and Besharov, M. L. (2010). Revisiting the meaning of leadership. In N. Nohria and R. Khurana (Ed.), *Handbook of leadership theory and practice.* Boston: Harvard Business School.

Porter, M. E. (1980). *Competitive strategies: Techniques for analyzing industries and competitors.* New York: Free Press.

Pratt, S. R., and Eitzen, D. S. (1989). Contrasting leadership styles and organizational effectiveness: The case of athletic teams. *Social Science Quarterly,* 70(2), 311-322.

Proxmire, D. C. (2008). Coaching diversity: The Rooney rule, its application and ideas for expansion. www.acslaw.org/files/Proxmire%20Issue%20Brief.pdf.

Pruijn, G. H. J., and Boucher, R. L. (1995). The relationship of transactional and transformational leadership to the organizational effectiveness of Dutch National Sport Organizations. *European Journal for Sport Management,* 2(1), 72-87.

Quarterman, J. (1998). An assessment of the perception of management and leadership skills by intercollegiate athletics conference commissioners. *Journal of Sport Management,* 12(2), 146-164.

Quarterman, J., Allen, L., and Becker, A. (2005). Managerial roles of intercollegiate athletic directors of the NAIA: The Mintzberg model. *International Journal of Sport Management,* 6(2), 165.

Quinn, R. E., and Rohrbaugh, J. (1981). A competing values approach to organizational effectiveness. Public Productivity Review, 122-131.

Quinn, R. E., and Spreitzer, G. M. (1991). The psychometrics of the competing values culture instrument and an analysis of the impact of organizational culture on quality of life. *Research in Organizational Change and Development,* 5, 115-142.

Ramos, R. (2011). Division I leaders call for sweeping changes to college athletics. www.ncaa.org/wps/wcm/connect/public/NCAA/Resources/Latest+News/2011/August/Division+I+leaders+call+for+sweeping+changes+to+college+athletics.

Rath, T., and Conchie, B. (2008). *Strengths-based leadership.* New York: Gallup Press.

Rath, T., and Conchie, B. (2009). What followers want from leaders. Retrieved May 28, 2011 from http://businessjournal.gallup.com/content/113542/what-followers-want-from-leaders.aspx.

Reed, G. E. (2006). Leadership and systems thinking. *Defense AT&L,* 35(3), 10-13.

Repanich, J. (2010). Can cameras and software replace referees? Retrieved July 12, 2011 from www.popularmechanics.com/outdoors/sports/technology/cameras-fouls-and-referees.

Richard, P. J., Devinney, T. M., Yip, G. S., and Johnson, G. (2009). Measuring organizational performance: Towards methodological best practice. *Journal of Management,* 35(3), 718-804.

Ridley, T. J. (2011). Crisis leadership is better than crisis management. http://ezinearticles.com/?Crisis-Leadership-Is-Better-Than-Crisis-Management&id=5932587.

Rieke, M., Hammermeister, J., and Chase, M. (2008). Servant leadership in sport: A new paradigm for effective coach behavior. *International Journal of Sports Science & Coaching,* 3(2), 227-239.

Riemer, H. A., and Chelladurai, P. (1995). Leadership and satisfaction in athletics. *Journal of Sport & Exercise Psychology*, 17(3), 276-293.

Robbins, D. K., and Pearce, J. A. II. (1992). Turnaround: Retrenchment and recovery. *Strategic Management Journal*, 13(4), 287-309.

Robbins, S. P. (1996). *Organizational behavior: Concepts, controversies, applications* (7th ed.). Upper Saddle River, NJ: Prentice Hall.

Robbins, S. P. (1998). *Organizational behavior: Concepts, controversies, applications* (8th ed.). Upper Saddle River, NJ: Prentice Hall.

Robbins, S. P., and Judge, T. A. (2008). *Essentials of organizational behavior* (9th ed.). Upper Saddle River, NJ: Pearson Prentice Hall.

Robertson, R. (1992). *Globalization: Social theory and global culture*. Thousand Oaks, CA: Sage.

Rodriguez, M., and Romanello, M. L. (2008). Promoting multiculturalism in athletic training education. *Athletic Therapy Today*, 13(3), 40-43.

Rosenthall, K. (2012). Encouraging signs for MLB diversity. Retrieved September 10, 2012 from http://msn.foxsports.com/mlb/story/draft-mlb-african-american-diversity-byron-buxton-addison-russell-060512.

Rosete, D., and Ciarrochi, J. (2005). Emotional intelligence and its relationship to workplace performance outcomes of leadership effectiveness. *Leadership and Organization Development Journal*, 26(5), 388-399. doi: 10.1108/01437730510607871

Rost, J. C. (1993). Leadership development in the new millennium. *Journal of Leadership Studies*, 1(1), 91-110.

Runde, C. E., and Flanagan, T. A. (2007). *Becoming a conflict competent leader: How you and your organization can manage conflict effectively*. San Francisco: Jossey-Bass.

Sage, G. H. (2011). *Globalizing sport: How organizations, corporations, media, and politics are changing sport*. Boulder, CO: Paradigm.

Sakakeeny, B. (2010). The 15 best traditions in sport. Retrieved October 22, 2011from http://bleacherreport.com/articles/430099-the-best-traditions-in-all-of-sports.

Salovey, P., and Mayer, J. D. (1990). Emotional intelligence. *Imagination, Cognition, and Personality*, 9, 185-211.

Sarros, J. C., Cooper, B. K., and Santora, J. C. (2008). Building a climate for innovation through transformational leadership and organizational culture. *Journal of Leadership and Organizational Studies*, 15(2), 145-158.

Sarros, J. C., Gray, J., and Densten, I. L. (2002). Leadership and its impact on organizational culture. *International Journal of Business Studies*, 10(2), 1-26.

Sartore, M. L., and Cunningham, G. B. (2007). Explaining the under-representation of women in leadership positions of sport organizations: A symbolic interactionist perspective. *Quest*, 59(2), 244-265.

Sartore, M. L., and Cunningham, G. B. (2010). The lesbian stigma in the sport context: Implications for women of every sexual orientation. *Quest*, 61, 289-305.

Schein, E. H. (1992). *Organizational culture and leadership* (2nd ed.). San Francisco: Jossey-Bass.

Schein, E. H. (2004). *Organizational culture and leadership* (3rd ed.). San Francisco: Jossey-Bass.

Schneider, B., Gunnarson, S. K., and Niles-Jolly, K. (1994). Creating the climate and culture of success. *Organizational Dynamics*, 23(1), 17-29.

Schoemaker, P. J. (2012). 6 habits of true strategic thinkers. www.inc.com/paul-schoemaker/6-habits-of-strategic-thinkers.html.

Schoenberg, A. (2005). Do crisis plans matter? A new perspective on leading during a crisis. *Public Relations Quarterly*, 50(1), 2-6.

Schoenfeld, B. (2010). The turnaround artist. *Entrepreneur* magazine. Retrieved June 27, 2011 from www.entrepreneur.com/magazine/entrepreneur/2010/august/207494.html.

Schroeder, P. J. (2010). A model for assessing organizational culture in intercollegiate athletic departments. *Journal of Issues in Intercollegiate Athletics*, 3, 98-118.

Scott, D. K. (1997). Managing organizational culture in intercollegiate athletic organizations. *Quest*, 49(4), 403-415.

Scott, D. K. (1999). A multiframe perspective of leadership and organizational climate in intercollegiate athletics. *Journal of Sport Management,* 13(4), 298-316.

Scott, D.K. (2008). Leadership for Modern Sport Organizations. In Appenzeller, H. and Lewis, G. *Successful Sport Management (3ⁿᵈ Ed).* Durham, NC: Carolina Academic Press. 7-22.

Seeger, M., Sellnow, T., and Ulmer, R. (2003). *Communication and organizational crisis.* Westport, CT: Praeger.

Senge, P. M. (1990). *The fifth discipline: The art and practice of the learning organization.* New York: Doubleday Currency.

Senge, P. M. (2006). *The fifth discipline: The art and practice of the learning organization* (revised ed.). New York: Crown.

Sexual orientation discrimination: Your rights. (2012). Retrieved March 12, 2012 from www.nolo.com/legal-encyclopedia/sexual-orientation-discrimination-rights-29541.html.

Shah, A. (2010). Global financial crisis. Retrieved January 12, 2011 from www.globalissues.org/article/768/global-financial-crisis.

Sharp, L., Moorman, A., and Claussen, C. (2010). *Sport law: A managerial approach* (2nd ed.). Scottsdale, AZ: Holcomb Hathaway.

Shoop, R. J., and Scott, S. M. (2000). *Leadership lessons from Bill Snyder.* Manhattan, KS: AG Press.

Siang, S. (2012). Women, leadership, and sports: Looking back on London 2012. http://management.fortune.cnn.com/2012/09/26/women-leadership-and-sports-looking-back-on-london-2012.

Simon, H. A. (1986). The behavioral foundations of economic theory. *Journal of Business,* 59(4), 209-224.

Slack, F. J., Orife, J. N., and Anderson, F. P. (2010). Effects of commitment to corporate vision on employee satisfaction with their organization: An empirical study in the United States. *International Journal of Management,* 27(3), 421-436.

Slack, T., and Hinings, B. (1992). Understanding change in national sport organizations: An integration of theoretical perspectives. *Journal of Sport Management,* 6(2), 114-132.

Slack, T., and Parent, M. M. (2006). *Understanding sport organizations: The application of organization theory* (2nd ed.). Champaign, IL: Human Kinetics.

Smart, B. (2007). Not playing around: Global capitalism, modern sport and consumer culture. In R. Giulianotti and R. Robertson (Eds.), *Globalization and sport.* Oxford, UK: Blackwell.

Smart, D. L., and Wolfe, R. A. (2003). The contribution of leadership and human resources to organizational success: An empirical assessment of performance in major league baseball. *European Sport Management Quarterly,* 3(3), 165-188.

Smerek, R. E., and Denison, D. R. (2007). Social capital in organizations: Understanding the link to firm performance. *Academy of Management Annual Meeting Proceeding,* 1-6.

Smith, A. C. T. (2004). Complexity theory and change management in sport organizations. *Emergence: Complexity and Organization,* 6(1/2), 70-79.

Smith, C. (2012). Deion Sanders is funding free charter schools in Dallas, Fort Worth. http://sports.yahoo.com/blogs/highschool-prep-rally/deion-sanders-funding-free-charter-schools-dallas-fort-194956525.html.

Snowden, D. J., and Boone, M. E. (2007). A leader's framework for decision making. *Harvard Business Review,* 85(11), 68-76.

Snyder, C. J. (1990). The effects of leader behavior and organizational climate on intercollegiate coaches' job satisfaction. *Journal of Sport Management,* 4(1), 59-70.

Song, M., Im, S., Bij, H. V. D., and Song, L. Z. (2011). Does strategic planning enhance or impede innovation and firm performance? *Journal of Product Innovation Management,* 28(4), 503-520. doi: 10.1111/j.1540-5885.2011.00822.x

Sosik, J. J., and Megerian, L. E. (1999). Understanding leader emotional intelligence and performance. *Group and Organization Management*, 24(3), 367-390.

Soucie, D. (1994). Effective managerial leadership in sport organizations. *Journal of Sport Management*, 8(1), 1-13.

Southall, R. (2001). A study of organizational culture of Mountain West Conference intercollegiate athletic departments. *Dissertation Abstracts International*, 61, 4700.

Southall, R. M., Wells, D. E., and Nagel, M. S. (2005). Organizational culture perceptions of intercollegiate athletic department members. *Applied Research in Coaching & Athletics Annual*, 20, 65-93.

SportAccord. (2010). Factsheet: Sport Accord recognition. Retrieved June 22, 2012 from www.sportaccord.com/multimedia/docs/2010/12/Factsheet_SportAccord_Recognition.pdf.

Sports by Brooks (2011, February 8). UCLA Fan Sites Killed Defensive Coordinator Hire [Web log post]. Retrieved from www.sportsbybrooks.com/ucla-fan-sites-kill-asst-football-coach-hire-29478.

Sports Leadership Institute. (2013). Retrieved May 12, 2013, from www.evanta.com/sports.

Stein, R. (2011). Genetic testing for sports genes courts controversy. Retrieved August 1, 2011 from http://articles.washingtonpost.com/2011-05-18/national/35233442_1_genetic-clues-lainie-friedman-ross-tests.

Stenson, J. B. (2011). Professionalism & workplace savvy. Retrieved April 23, 2011, from www.parentleadership.com/worksavvy.html.

Stevens, J. A., and Slack, T. (1998). Integrating social action and structural constraints: Towards a more holistic explanation of organizational change. *International Review for the Sociology of Sport*, 33(2), 143-154.

Stevenson, B. (2010). Beyond the classroom: Using Title IX to measure the return to high school sports. *Review of Economics and Statistics*, 92(2), 284-301.

Stogdill, R. (1963). *Manual for the leader behavior description questionnaire–form XII*. Columbus, OH: Bureau of Business Research, Ohio State University.

Stogdill, R. M. (1948). Personal factors associated with leadership: A survey of the literature. *Journal of Psychology, 25*, 35–71.

Stogdill, R. M. (1974). *Handbook of leadership: A survey of theory and research*. New York: Free Press.

Sullivan, P. (2011). Final Cubs roster will be group decision. http://articles.chicagotribune.com/2011-03-08/sports/ct-spt-0309-cubs-spring-training-chic20110308_1_mike-quade-wrong-guy-tough-decisions.

Sullivan, P. J., and Kent, A. (2003). Coaching efficacy as a predictor of leadership style in intercollegiate athletics. *Journal of Applied Sport Psychology*, 15(1), 1-11.

Sullivan, P., Paquette, K. J., Holt, N. L., and Bloom, G. A. (2012). The relation of coaching context and coach education to coaching efficacy and perceived leadership behaviors in youth sport. *Sport Psychologist*, 26(1), 122-134.

Swart, K. (2005). Strategic planning–implications for the bidding of sport events in South Africa. *Journal of Sport and Tourism*, 10(1), 37-46.

Terzieff, J. (2012). Labor, rights issues surround major sports events. Retrieved August 28, 2012 originally from www.future500.org/blog/labor-rights-issues-surround-major-sports-events; article available at www.unm.edu/~dscott/TerzieffArticle.pdf.

Thibault, L. (2009). Globalization of sport: An inconvenient truth. *Journal of Sport Management*, 23(1), 1-20.

Thibault, L., and Slack, T. (1993). A framework for the analysis of strategy in nonprofit sport organizations. *Journal of Sport Management*, 7(1), 25-43.

Thibault, L., Slack, T., and Hinings, B. (1994). Strategic planning for nonprofit sport organizations: Empirical verification of a framework. *Journal of Sport Management*, 8(3), 218-233.

Thomas, K. (2011). College teams, relying on deception, undermine gender equity. www.nytimes.com/2011/04/26/sports/26titleix.html.

Thorn, I. M. (2012). Leadership in international organizations: Global leadership competencies. *Psychologist-Manager Journal*, 15, 158-163.

Thornton, P. K. (2010). *Sports law*. Burlington, MA: Jones & Bartlett.

Tichy, N., and Bennis, W. (2010). Wise judgment: It takes character and courage. *Leadership Excellence*, May, 2.

Tichy, N. M., and DeVanna, M. A. (1986). The transformational leader. *Training and Development Journal*, 40(7), 26.

Tong, J. (2009). Planning for the 2008 Olympics (V): Press conferences on economic and financial management. *Chinese Law & Government*, 42(3), 3-7.

Toohey, K., and Veal, A. J. (2007). The Olympic games: A social science perspective. Oxfordshire, UK: CABI.

twittercounter.com. (2011). SHAQ twitter statistics. Retrieved August 6, 2011 from http://twittercounter.com/The_Real_Shaq.

Uhl-Bien, M., Marion, R., and McKelvey, B. (2007). Complexity leadership theory: Shifting leadership from the industrial age to the knowledge era. *Leadership Quarterly*, 18(4), 298-318. doi: 10.1016/j.leaqua.2007.04.002.

Ulrich, D., Zenger, J., and Smallwood, N. (1999). *Results based leadership*. Boston: Harvard Business Press.

Upton, P. (2012). It's not just about the results. www.espncricinfo.com/magazine/content/story/583853.html.

Vancouver 2010 Olympic Winter Games (2010). Global television and online media overview. Retrieved July 18, 2012 from www.olympic.org/Documents/IOC_Marketing/Broadcasting/Vancouver2010OlympicWinterGames-BroadcastCoverageAudienceOverview.pdf.

Van Hilvoorde, I., and Landeweerd, L. (2010). Enhancing disabilities: Transhumanism under the veil of inclusion? *Disability & Rehabilitation*, 32(26), 2222-2227.

Van Rooy, D. L., Whitman, D. S., and Visweswaran, C. (2010). Emotional intelligence: Additional questions still unanswered. *Industrial & Organizational Psychology*, 3(2), 149-153. doi: 10.1111/j.1754-9434.2010.01216.x

Vardi, N. (2009). The greatest sports-business turnaround ever. www.forbes.com/2009/05/18/chicago-blackhawks-hockey-business-sports-nhl.html.

Visionary leadership: A talk with Jay Conger. (2001). *Leadership in Action*, 21(2), 19-22.

Vroom, V. H. (2003). Educating managers for decision making and leadership. *Management Decision*, 41(10), 968-978. doi: 10.1108/00251740310509490

Vroom, V. H., and Jago, A. G. (1988). *The new leadership: Managing participation in organizations*. Englewood Cliffs, NJ: Prentice Hall.

Vroom, V. H., and Jago, A. G. (2007). The role of the situation in leadership. *American Psychologist*, 62(1), 17-24. doi: 10.1037/0003-066x.62.1.17

Vroom, V. H., and Yetton, P. W. (1973). *Leadership and decision-making*. Pittsburgh: University of Pittsburgh Press.

Waldman, D. A., Bass, B. M., and Yammarino, F. J. (1990). Adding to contingent-reward behavior. *Group & Organization Studies*, 15(4), 381-394.

Wallace, M., and Weese, W. J. (1995). Leadership, organizational culture, and job satisfaction in Canadian YMCA organizations. *Journal of Sport Management*, 9(2), 182-193.

Walumbwa, F. O., Avolio, B. J., Gardner, W. L., Wernsing, T. S., and Peterson, S. J. (2008). Authentic leadership: Development and validation of a theory-based measure. *Journal of Management*, 34(1), 89-126.

Waterhouse, L. (2006). Inadequate evidence for multiple intelligences, Mozart effect, and emotional intelligence theories. *Educational Psychologist*, 41(4), 247-255. doi: 10.1207/s15326985ep4104_5

Watkins, M. D., and Bazerman, M. H. (2003). Predictable surprises: The disasters you should have seen coming. *Harvard Business Review*, 81(3), 72-80.

Weber, M. (1968). *Economy and society*. New York: Dedminister.

Weese, J. W., and Beard, S. (2012). Rethinking the teaching of leadership in sport management. *Sport Management Education Journal*, 6(1), 1-7.

Weese, W. J. (1995). Leadership and organizational culture: An investigation of Big Ten and Mid-American Conference campus recreation administrations. *Journal of Sport Management*, 9(2), 119-134.

Weese, W. J. (1996). Do leadership and organizational culture really matter? *Journal of Sport Management*, 10(2), 197-206.

Weese, W. J., MacLean, J., and Corlett, J. (1993). Coaches as leaders and culture builders. *Applied Research in Coaching & Athletics Annual*, 93-108.

Whisenant, W., Miller, J., and Pedersen, P. M. (2005). Systematic barriers for athletic administration: An analysis of job descriptions for interscholastic athletic directors. *Sex Roles*, 53, 911-918.

Whitelaw, K. (2010). Defining diversity: Beyond race and gender. Retrieved June 18, 2012 from www.npr.org/templates/story/story.php?storyId=122327104.

Wiersma, M.F. & Bantel, K.A. (1992). Top management team demography and corporate strategic change. *Academy of Management Journal*, 35, 91-121.

Wolfred, T. (2008). Building leaderful organizations: Succession planning for non-profits. *Executive Transition Monograph Series*, 6. Retrieved May 14, 2011 from www.aecf.org/~/media/Pubs/Other/B/Building-LeaderfulOrganizationsSuccessionPlann/Building%20Leaderful%20Organizations.pdf.

Wong, G. W. (2009). *The comprehensive guide to careers in sports*. Sudbury, MA: Jones & Bartlett.

Wooten, L. P., and James, E. H. (2008). Linking crisis management and leadership competencies: The role of human resource development. *Advances in Developing Human Resources*, 10(3), 352-379.

World of sport. (2013). Most widely played sports. Retrieved August 1, 2013 from www.topendsports.com/world/lists/popular-sport/federations.htm.

Xian-feng, A. (2009). Inter-cultural communicative competence in sports field in multicultural context. *Journal of Wuhan Institute of Physical Education*, 43(1), 28-34.

Yammarino, F. J., Dansereau, F., and Kennedy, C. J. (2001). A multiple-level multidimensional approach to leadership: Viewing leadership through an elephant's eye. *Organizational Dynamics*, 29(3), 149.

Yukl, G. (2002). *Leadership in organizations*. Upper Saddle River, NJ: Prentice Hall.

Yukl, G. (2009). *Leadership in organizations* (7th ed.). Upper Saddle River, NJ: Prentice Hall.

Yukl, G., and Lepsinger, R. (2004). *Flexible leadership: Creating value by balancing multiple challenges and choices*. Hoboken, NJ: Pfeiffer.

Yusof, A. (1998). The relationship between transformational leadership behaviors of athletic directors and coaches' job satisfaction. *Physical Educator*, 55(4), 170-175.

Zaccaro, S. J., Kemp, C., and Bader, P. (2004). Leader traits and attributes. In J. Antonakis, A. T. Cianciolo, and R. J. Sternberg (Eds.), *The nature of leadership* (pp. 101-124). Thousand Oaks, CA: Sage.

Zajac, E. J., and Kraatz, M. S. (1993). A diametric forces model of strategic change: Assessing the antecedents and consequences of restructuring in the higher education industry. *Strategic Management Journal*, 14, 83-102.

Zakus, D. H., and Skinner, J. (2008). Modelling organizational change in the International Olympic Committee. *European Sport Management Quarterly*, 8(4), 421-442.

Zeigler, E. (2007). An encounter with management in physical activity education and sport. Retrieved May 25, 2011 from www.nassm.com/files/Zeigler-Encounter.pdf.

Zemke, R. (1985). The Honeywell studies: How managers learn to manage. *Training*, 22(8), 46-51.

Zhang, J. (1994). Modification and revision of the leadership scale for sport. Eugene, Ore.; United States: Microform Publications, Int'l Institute for Sport and Human Performance, Univ. of Oregon.

Index

Note: Page numbers followed by an italicized *f* or *t* refer to the figure or table on that page, respectively.

About the Author

David Scott, EdD, is associate dean for research and information management in the college of education at the University of New Mexico. He received his bachelor of science in physical education from Texas A&M University, his master of science in physical education from Midwestern State University, and his doctor of education in physical education with specialization in sport administration from the University of Northern Colorado. Scott began his career as a teacher and coach of multiple sports in public schools and eventually coached intercollegiate football at the NAIA and NCAA Division II level. His university teaching has included undergraduate and

graduate courses in exercise science; sport leadership; organizational theory for sport; administration of sport personnel; public relations in health, physical education, and recreation; principles of coaching; and management concepts for sport and fitness. He has also advised numerous doctoral dissertations, graduate students in sport administration, athletes, and undergraduate physical education majors.

Scott's research emphasis is leadership and organizational behavior in sport organizations, with a secondary interest in predictive data mining for sport management. He also has an interest in coaching and athletic administration education and conducts workshops dealing with various aspects of leadership and management training for coaches and athletic administrators. He has published research and conceptual articles in several refereed journals, including *Journal of Sport Management*, *Quest*, *International Journal of Sport Management*, *International Journal of Sport Management & Marketing*, and *Journal of Contemporary Athletics*. He has also published several book chapters and has presented at multiple state, national, and international conferences. Scott is a member of the North American Society for Sport Management and the American Alliance for Health, Physical Education, Recreation and Dance.

In his free time, Scott enjoys trail running with his Alaskan malamutes, racquetball, tennis, hiking, and trout fishing.